Blackstone's Statutes on
ENGLISH LEGAL SYSTEM

Blackstone's Statutes on
ENGLISH LEGAL SYSTEM

Edited by

David A. Howarth LLB, Barrister
Principal Lecturer in Law, Newcastle upon Tyne Polytechnic

and

Stephen R. Wilson BA
Senior Lecturer in Law, Newcastle upon Tyne Polytechnic

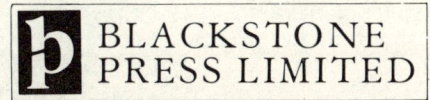

First published in Great Britain 1989 by Blackstone Press Limited, 9–15 Aldine Street, London W12 8AW. Telephone: 01-740 1173

© David A. Howarth and Stephen R. Wilson, 1989

ISBN: 1 85431 038 0

British Library Cataloguing in Publication Data
A CIP catalogue record for this book is available from the British Library

Typeset by Kerrypress Ltd, Luton, Beds
Printed by Redwood Burn Limited, Trowbridge, Wiltshire

All rights reserved. No part of this book may be reproduced or transmitted in any form or by any means, electronic or mechanical, including photocopying, recording, or any information storage or retrieval system without prior permission from the publisher.

CONTENTS

Editor's Preface vii

PART 1   STATUTES OF THE UK PARLIAMENT 1

Justices of the Peace Act 1361 1
Judicial Committee Act 1833 1
Judicial Committee Act 1844 2
Summary Jurisdiction Act 1857 3
Appellate Jurisdiction Act 1876 3
Judicial Committee Act 1881 5
Appellate Jurisdiction Act 1887 5
Criminal Evidence Act 1898 6
Parliament Act 1911 7
Administration of Justice (Appeals) Act 1934 9
Children and Young Persons Act 1933 9
Statutory Instruments Act 1946 15
Consolidation of Enactments (Procedure) Act 1949 17
Lands Tribunal Act 1949 19
Arbitration Act 1950 21
Administration of Justice Act 1960 25
Criminal Procedure (Insanity) Act 1964 29
Law Commissions Act 1965 31
Parliamentary Commissioner Act 1967 32
Criminal Justice Act 1967 39
Administration of Justice Act 1968 44
Criminal Appeal Act 1968 45
Children and Young Persons Act 1969 60
Administration of Justice Act 1969 62
Courts Act 1971 64
Tribunals and Inquiries Act 1971 66
Criminal Justice Act 1972 71
European Communities Act 1972 71
Powers of Criminal Courts Act 1973 74
Juries Act 1974 95
Solicitors Act 1974 101
Restrictive Practices Court Act 1976 112
Bail Act 1976 114
Interpretation Act 1978 125
Employment Protection (Consolidation) Act 1978 132
Arbitration Act 1979 139
Justices of the Peace Act 1979 142
Magistrates' Court Act 1980 151
Contempt of Court Act 1981 188
Supreme Court Act 1981 194
Criminal Justice Act 1982 231
County Courts Act 1984 238
Matrimonial and Family Proceedings Act 1984 257

Police and Criminal Evidence Act 1984 259
Prosecution of Offences Act 1985 259
Administration of Justice Act 1985 269
Insolvency Act 1986.. 271
European Communities (Amendment) Act 1986 271
Criminal Justice Act 1987 272
Coroners Act 1988 274
Criminal Justice Act 1988 278
Legal Aid Act 1988 283

PART 2   OTHER MATERIALS 299

Statutory Instruments Regulations 1947 (SI 1948/1) 299
The County Courts Jurisdiction Order 1981 (SI 1981 No 1123) 301
The County County Courts Appeals Order 1981 (SI 1981 No 1749)............ 302
The Court of Appeal (Civil Division) Order 1982 (SI 1982 No 543).......... 302
Magistrates' Courts (Advance Information) Rules 1985 (SI 1985 No 601) 303
Practice Statement [1966] 1 WLR 1234 304
Practice Direction (Crime: Majority Verdicts) [1967] 1 WLR 1198 305
Practice Note [1970] 1 WLR 916... 306
Practice Direction (Divorce Towns: Defended Cases) [1971] 1 WLR 1762....... 306
Practice Note (Court of Appeal: New Procedure) [1982] 1 WLR 1312 307
Practice Direction (Crown Court Business: Classification) [1987] 1 WLR 1671 ... 313
Practice Direction (County Court: Transfers Outside London) [1988] 1 WLR 987 317
Practice Direction (Court of Appeal: Presentation of Argument) [1989] 1 WLR
    281 318
Treaty of Rome, 1957 323
EC Council Decision, 1988 [1988] OJ L 319/1 330

Index 333

EDITORS' PREFACE

Anyone who writes or compiles materials for students of the English Legal System is faced at the present time with trying to meet the requirements of a wide variety of course titles, structures and content in the different teaching institutions. There seems however to be a core which is common to most courses, consisting of the structure of legal institutions and an introduction to legal method.

In making our selection of materials we have incorporated this core and built around it some material which is increasingly part of first year courses which come under the generic name, 'English Legal System', whatever their actual title. This material reflects the connection with those aspects of public law which relate to the making of law in all its forms and the important connections which now exist with European Community Law. Inevitably some material has had to be excluded, largely for reasons of space, but we have attempted to provide as comprehensive a range of material as possible bearing in mind our objectives.

These objectives are twofold. First, to provide students with the substance of the subject in a form which reveals many of the complexities in legislation generally and the interlocking structures of English Legal Institutions in particular. Second, it is intended that the statutes and other materials in the book will be a convenient vehicle to aid the development of interpretative skills, which are so much emphasised in today's student curriculum. In our own teaching we have found that statutes relating to the legal system demonstrate both that it is possible to have clearly drafted statutes which need no special interpretative skills, beyond those of the accurate and attentive reader, and also that some of our statutes are extremely complex and that elucidation of their meaning requires the special skills which lawyers call the construction and interpretation of statutes.

During the preparation of this book we have tried to comply with our own precepts laid down in many exhortations to our students; namely, the need for the law which they quote and rely on to be accurate and up to date. This exercise has brought home to us once again the difficulties created for the statute user by the English legislative process.

Inevitably, due to pressure of space, we have had to omit materials, such being marked by a row of asterisks. Repealed provisions are indicated by a row of dots and amendments are enclosed in square brackets.

The law is stated as applies to England and Wales and the texts printed here are as in force on 15 May 1989, subject to the following exceptions:

(a) Section 7(1) of the Criminal Appeal Act 1968 in the form in which it appears on page 47 is not in force. At this time the only ground on which the Court of Appeal may order a retrial is where an appeal is allowed on the basis of fresh evidence presented to the court under section 23 of the 1968 Act and it is in the interests of justice to do so;

(b) Sections 4 and 5(1)–(7) of the Children and Young Persons Act 1969 are not in force;

(c) Subsections (3)(b), (6)(b) and (10) of section 6 of the Powers of the Criminal Courts Act 1973 are not in force; and

(d) Insertions concerning the Housing Act 1988 in sections 66 and 77 of the County Courts Act 1984 are not in force.

Finally we would like to thank the Incorporated Council of Law Reporting for England and Wales for allowing us to include several extracts from the Weekly Law Reports. Thanks is also due to our publishers for their speed, efficiency and cheerfulness in dealing with our many queries. Any errors, of course, remain ours alone.

D.A. Howarth
S.R. Wilson

STATUTES OF THE UK PARLIAMENT
JUSTICES OF THE PEACE ACT 1361
(34 Edw 3 c 1)

Who shall be justices of the peace–Their jurisdiction over offenders; rioters; barrators; and vagabonds–Commissions of general inquiries to end–Fines to be reasonable

First, that in every county of England shall be assigned for the keeping of the peace, one lord, and with him three or four of the most worthy of the county, with some learned in the law, and they shall have power to restrain the offenders, rioters, and all other barrators and to pursue, arrest, take, and chastise them according their trespass or offence; and to cause them to be imprisoned and duly punished according to the law and customs of the realm, and according to that which to them shall seem best to do by their discretions and good advisement; . . . and to take and arrest all those that they may find by indictment, or by suspicion, and to put them in prison; and to take of all them that be [not] of good fame, where they shall be found, sufficient surety and mainprise of their good behaviour towards the King and his people, and the other duly to punish; to the intent that the people be not by such rioters or rebels troubled nor endamaged, nor the peace blemished, nor merchants nor other passing by the highways of the realm disturbed, nor [put in the peril which may happen] of such offenders . . .

JUDICIAL COMMITTEE ACT 1833
(1833, c. 41)

An Act for the better Administration of Justice in His Majesty's Privy Council.

[14th August 1833]

1. **Certain Persons to form a Committee, to be styled "The Judicial Committee of the Privy Council."**
The President for the time being of His Majesty's Privy Council . . . and such of the members of His Majesty's Privy Council as shall from time to time hold any of the offices following, that is to say, the office of lord keeper or first lord commissioner of the great seal of Great Britain . . . and also all persons, members of His Majesty's Privy Council who shall have been President thereof . . . or shall have held any of the other offices hereinbefore mentioned, shall form a committee of His Majesty's said Privy Council, and shall be styled "The Judicial Committee of the Privy Council": Provided nevertheless, that it shall be lawful for His Majesty from time to time, as and when he shall think fit, by his sign manual, to appoint any two other persons, being privy councillors, to be members of the said Committee.

2. *****

3. **All appeals from Sentence of any Judge, &c. to be referred by His Majesty to the Committee, to report theron.**
All appeals or complaints in the nature of appeals whatever, which either by virtue of this Act, or of any law, statute, or custom, may be brought before His Majesty or His Majesty in Council from or in respect of the determination, sentence, rule, or order of any court, judge, or judicial officer, and all such appeals as are now pending and unheard, shall from and after the passing of this Act be referred by His Majesty to the said Judicial Committee of his Privy Council, and such appeals, causes, and matters shall be heard by the said Judicial Committee, and a report or recommendation thereon shall be made to His Majesty in Council for his decision thereon as heretofore, in the same manner and form as has been heretofore the custom with respect to matters referred by His Majesty to the whole of his Privy Council or a committee thereof (the nature of such report or recommendation being always stated in open court).

4. His Majesty may refer any other Matters to Committee
It shall be lawful for His Majesty to refer to the said Judicial Committee for hearing or consideration any such other matters whatsoever as His Majesty shall think fit; and such Committee shall thereupon hear or consider the same, and shall advise His Majesty thereon in manner aforesaid.

5. No Matter to be heard unless in Presence of Four Members of the Committee.
. . . no report or recommendation shall be made to His Majesty unless a majority of the members of such Judicial Committee present at the hearing shall concur in such report or recommendation: Provided always, that nothing herein contained shall prevent His Majesty, if he shall think fit, from summoning any other of the members of his said Privy Council to attend the meetings of the said Committee.

6. In case the King directs the Attendance of any Judge, a Member of the Committee, the other Judges of the Court to which he belongs to make Arrangements with regard to Business of the Court.
In case His Majesty shall be pleased, by directions under his sign manual, to require the attendance at the said Committee for the purposes of this Act of any member or members of the said Privy Council who shall be a judge or judges of the Court of King's Bench or of the Court of Common Pleas, or of the Court of Exchequer, such arrangements for dispensing with the attendance of such judge or judges upon his or their ordinary duties during the time of such attendance at the Privy Council as aforesaid shall be made by the judges of the court or courts to which such judge or judges shall belong respectively in regard to the business of the court, and by the judges of the said three courts, or by any eight or more of such judges, including the chiefs of the several courts, in regard to all other duties, as may be necessary and consistent with the public service.

JUDICIAL COMMITTEE ACT 1844
(1844, c. 69)

An Act for amending an Act passed in the Fourth Year of the Reign of His late Majesty, intituled "An Act for the better Administration of Justice in His Majesty's Privy Council"; and to extend its Jurisdiction and Powers.

[6th August 1844]

1. Her Majesty by Order in Council, may provide for the admission of an appeal from any colony, although there shall not be a Court of Error or of Appeal in such colony; and may revoke such Orders.
It shall be competent to Her Majesty, by any order or orders to be from time to time for that purpose made with the advice of her Privy Council, to provide for the admission of any appeal or appeals to Her Majesty in Council from any judgments, sentences, decrees, or orders of any court of justice within any British colony or possession abroad, although such court shall not be a court of errors or a court of appeal within such colony or possession; and it shall also be competent to Her Majesty, by any such order or orders as aforesaid, to make all such provisions as to Her Majesty in Council shall seem meet for the instituting and prosecuting any such appeals, and for carrying into effect any such decisions or sentences as Her Majesty in Council shall pronounce thereon: Provided always, that it shall be competent to Her Majesty in Council to revoke, alter, and amend any such order or orders as aforesaid, as to Her Majesty in Council shall seem meet: Provided also, that any such order as aforesaid may be either general and extending to all appeals to be brought from any such court of justice as aforesaid, or special and extending only to an appeal to be brought in any particular case: Provided

also, that nothing herein contained shall be construed to extend to take away or diminish any power now by law vested in Her Majesty for regulating appeals to Her Majesty in Council from the judgments, sentences, decrees, or orders of any courts of justice within any of Her Majesty's colonies or possessions abroad.

SUMMARY JURISDICTION ACT 1857
(1857, c. 43)

An Act to improve the Administration of the Law so far as respects summary Proceedings before Justices of the Peace. [17th August 1857]

1.—5. . . .

6. Superior Court to determine the questions on the case.
the Court to which a case is transmitted under [the Magistrates' Court Act 1980] shall hear and determine the question or questions of law arising thereon, and shall thereupon reverse, affirm, or amend the determination in respect of which the case has been stated, or remit the matter to the justice or justices, with the opinion of the Court thereon, or may make such other order in relation to the matter and make such orders as to costs, as to the Court may seem fit; and [except as provided by the Administration of Justice Act 1960] all such orders shall be final and conclusive on all parties: Provided always, that no justice or justices of the peace, who shall state and deliver a case in pursuance of [the Magistrates' Courts Act 1980], shall be liable to any costs in respect or by reason of such appeal against his or their determination.

7. Case may be sent back for amendment.
The Court for the opinion of which a case is stated shall have power, if they think fit, to cause the case to be sent back for amendment; and thereupon the same shall be amended accordingly, and judgment shall be delivered after it shall have been amended.

8., 9. . . .

10. Certiorari not to be required for proceedings under this Act.
No writ of certiorari or other writ shall be required for the removal of any conviction, order, or other determination in relation to which a case is stated under [the Magistrates' Courts Act 1980], or otherwise for obtaining the judgment or determination of the Superior Court on such case under [the Magistrates' Courts Act 1980].

11. . . .

12. "Justices" to include a stipendiary magistrate.
The words "justice or justices" in this Act shall include a magistrate of the police courts of the Metropolis and any stipendiary magistrate.

APPELLATE JURISDICTION ACT 1876
(39 & 40 Vict c. 59)

An Act for amending the Law in respect of the Appellate Jurisdiction of the House of Lords; and for other purposes. [11th August 1876]

2. . . .

Appeal

3. Cases in which appeal lies to House of Lords.
Subject as in this Act mentioned an appeal shall lie to the House of Lords from any order or judgment of any of the courts following; that is to say,
  (1) Of Her Majesty's Court of Appeal in England; and

(2) Of any Court in Scotland from which error or an appeal at or immediately before the commencement of this Act lay to the House of Lords by common law or by statute; and

(3) ...

4. Form of appeal to House of Lords.

Every appeal shall be brought by way of petition to the House of Lords, praying that the matter of the order or judgment appealed against may be reviewed before Her Majesty the Queen in her Court of Parliament, in order that the said Court may determine what of right, and according to the law and custom of this realm, ought to be done in the subject-matter of such appeal.

5. Attendance of certain number of Lords of Appeal required at hearing and determination of appeals.

An appeal shall not be heard and determined by the House of Lords unless there are present at such hearing and determination not less than three of the following persons, in this Act designated Lords of Appeal; that is to say,

(1) The Lord Chancellor of Great Britain for the time being; and

(2) The Lords of Appeal in Ordinary to be appointed as in this Act mentioned; and

(3) Such Peers of Parliament as are for the time being holding or have held any of the offices in this Act described as high judicial offices.

6. Appointment of Lords of Appeal in Ordinary by Her Majesty.

For the purpose of aiding the House of Lords in the hearing and determination of appeals, Her Majesty may ... by letters patent appoint ... qualified persons to be Lords of Appeal in Ordinary ...

A person shall not be qualified to be appointed by Her Majesty a Lord of Appeal in Ordinary unless he has been at or before the time of his appointment the holder for a period of not less than two years of some one or more of the offices in this Act described as high judicial offices, or has been at or before such time as aforesaid, for not less than fifteen years, a practising barrister in England or Ireland, or a practising advocate in Scotland.

Every Lord of Appeal in Ordinary shall hold his office during good behaviour, ... but he may be removed from such office on the address of both Houses of Parliament.

Every Lord of Appeal in Ordinary, unless he is otherwise entitled to sit as a member of the House of Lords, shall by virtue and according to the date of his appointment be entitled during his life to rank as a Baron by such style as Her Majesty may be pleased to appoint, and shall ... be entitled to a writ of summons to attend, and to sit and vote in the House of Lords; his dignity as a Lord of Parliament shall not descend to his heirs.

On any Lord of Appeal in Ordinary vacating his office, by death resignation or otherwise, Her Majesty may fill up the vacancy by the appointment of another qualified person.

A Lord of Appeal in Ordinary shall, if a Privy Councillor, be a member of the Judicial Committee of the Privy Council, and, subject to the due performance by a Lord of Appeal in Ordinary of his duties as to the hearing and determining of appeals in the House of Lords, it shall be his duty, being a Privy Councillor, to sit and act as a member of the Judicial Committee of the Privy Council.

Supplemental Provisions

7. ...

8., 9. *****

Appellate Jurisdiction Act 1876

10. ...

11. *****

12. **Certain cases excluded from appeal.**
Except in so far as may be authorised by orders of the House of Lords an appeal shall not lie to the House of Lords from any court in Scotland . . . in any case, which according to the law or practice hitherto in use, could not have been reviewed by that House, either in error or on appeal.

13. ...

Amendment of Acts

14.—22. ...

Repeal and Definitions

24. ...

25. **Definitions:**
In this Act, if not inconsistent with the context, the following expressions have the meaning herein-after respectively assigned to them; that is to say,
"High judicial office" means any of the following offices: that is to say,
The office of Lord Chancellor of Great Britain . . ., or of Judge of one of Her Majesty's superior courts of Great Britain and Ireland:
"Superior courts of Great Britain and Ireland" means and includes,—
As to England, Her Majesty's High Court of Justice and Her Majesty's Court of Appeal, . . .; and
As to Ireland, the superior courts of law and equity at [Belfast]; and
As to Scotland, the Court of Session: . . .

JUDICIAL COMMITTEE ACT 1881
(1881, c. 3)

An Act to further improve the Administration of Justice in the Judicial Committee of the Privy Council. [17th February 1881]

1. **Lords Justices of Appeal to be members of Judicial Committee.**
Every person holding or who has held in England the office of a Lord Justice of Appeal shall, if a member of Her Majesty's Privy Council in England, be a member of the Judicial Committee of the Privy Council.

APPELLATE JURISDICTION ACT 1887
(50 & 51 Vict c. 70)

An Act to amend the Appellate Jurisdiction Act 1876. [16th September 1887]

1. *****

2. ...

3. **Amendment of 3 & 4 Will. 4. c. 41.**
The Judicial Committee of the Privy Council as formed under the provisions of the first section of the Judicial Committee Act 1833 shall include such members of Her Majesty's Privy Council as are for the time being holding or have held any of the offices in the Appellate Jurisdiction Act 1876 and this Act, described as high judicial offices.

4. ...

5. Amendment of 39 & 40 Vict. c. 59, s. 25.
The expression "high judicial office" as defined in the twenty-fifth section of the Appellate Jurisdiction Act 1876 shall be deemed to include the office of a Lord of Appeal in Ordinary and the office of a member of the Judicial Committee of the Privy Council.

CRIMINAL EVIDENCE ACT 1898
(1898, c. 36)

An Act to amend the Law of Evidence. [12th August 1898]

1. Competency of witnesses in criminal cases.
Every person charged with an offence, and the wife or husband, as the cae may be, of the person so charged, shall be a competent witness for the defence at every stage of the proceedings, whether the person so charged is charged solely or jointly with any other person. Provided as follows:—

(a) A person so charged shall not be called as a witness in pursuance of this Act except upon his own application:

(b) The failure of any person charged with an offence, or of the wife or husband, as the case may be, of the person so charged, to give evidence shall not be made the subject of any comment by the prosecution:

(c) The wife or husband of the person charged shall not, save as in this Act mentioned, be called as a witness in pursuance of this Act except upon the application of the person so charged:

(d) Nothing in this Act shall make a husband compellable to disclose any communication made to him by his wife during the marriage, or a wife compellable to disclose any communication made to her by her husband during the marriage:

(e) A person charged and being a witness in pursuance of this Act may be asked any question in cross-examination notwithstanding that it would tend to criminate him as to the offence charged:

(f) A person charged and called as a witness in pursuance of this Act shall not be asked, and if asked shall not be required to answer, any question tending to show that he has committed or been convicted of or been charged with any offence other than that wherewith he is then charged, or is of bad character, unless—

(i) the proof that he has committed or been convicted of such other offence is admissible evidence to show that he is guilty of the offence wherewith he is then charged; or

(ii) he has personally or by his advocate asked questions of the witnesses for the prosecution with a view to establish his own good character, or has given evidence of his good character, or the nature or conduct of the defence is such as to involve imputations on the character of the prosecutor or the witnesses for the prosecution; or

(iii) he has given evidence against any other person charged with the same offence:

(g) Every person called as a witness in pursuance of this Act shall, unless otherwise ordered by the court, give his evidence from the witness box or other place from which the other witnesses give their evidence:

(h) Nothing in this Act shall affect the provisions of section [twelve] of the [Criminal Justice Act 1925], or any right of the person charged to make a statement without being sworn.

2. Evidence of person charged.
Where the only witness to the facts of the case called by the defence is the person

charged, he shall be called as a witness immediately after the close of the evidence for the prosecution.

3. **Right of reply.**
[In cases where the right of reply depends upon the question whether evidence has been called for the defence,] the fact that the person charged has been called as a witness shall not of itself confer on the prosecution the right of reply.

4. **Calling of wife or husband in certain cases.**
(1) The wife or husband of a person charged with an offence under any enactment mentioned in the schedule to this Act may be called as a witness either for the prosecution or defence and without the consent of the person charged.

(2) Nothing in this Act shall affect a case where the wife or husband of a person charged with an offence may at common law be called as a witness without the consent of that person.

5. ...

6. **Provisions as to previous Acts.**
(1) This Act shall apply to all criminal proceedings [including proceedings in courts-martial] [under the Army Act 1955 and the Air Force Act 1955, and proceedings in courts-martial and disciplinary courts under the Naval Discipline Act 1957] [and in Standing Civilian Courts established under the Armed Forces Act 1976], notwithstanding any enactment in force at the commencement of this Act, except that nothing in this Act shall affect the Evidence Act 1877.

(2) ...

PARLIAMENT ACT 1911
(1 & 2 Geo. 5, c. 13)

An Act to make provision with respect to the powers of the House of Lords in relation of the House of Commons, and to limit the duration of Parliament

Preamble
Whereas it is expedient that provision should be made for regulating the relations between the two Houses of Parliament:
And whereas it is intended to substitute for the House of Lords as it at present exists a Second Chamber constituted on a popular instead of hereditary basis, but such substitution cannot be immediately brought into operation:
And whereas provision will require hereafter to be made by Parliament in a measure effecting such substitution for limiting and defining the powers of the new Second Chamber, but it is expedient to make such provision as in this Act appears for restricting the the existing powers of the House of Lords:

1. **Powers of House of Lords as to Money Bills**
(1) If a Money Bill, having been passed by the House of Commons, and sent up to the House of Lords at least one month before the end of the session, is not passed by the House of Lords without amendment within one month after it is so sent up to that House, the Bill shall, unless the House of Commons direct to the contrary, be presented to His Majesty and become an Act of Parliament on the Royal Assent being signified, notwithstanding that the House of Lords have not consented to the Bill.

(2) A Money Bill means a Public Bill which in the opinion of the Speaker of the House of Commons contains only provisions dealing with all or any of the following subjects, namely, the imposition, repeal, remission, alteration, or regulation of taxation; the imposition for the payment of debt or other financial purposes of charges on the

Consolidated Fund, [the National Loans Fund] or on money provided by Parliament, or the variation or repeal of any such charges; supply; the appropriation, receipt, custody, issue or audit of accounts of public money; the raising or guarantee of any loan or the repayment thereof; or subordinate matters incidental to those subjects or any of them. In this subsection the expressions "taxation", "public money", and "loan" respectively do not include any taxation, money, or loan raised by local authorities or bodies for local purposes.

(3) There shall be endorsed on every Money Bill when it is sent up to the House of Lords and when it is presented to His Majesty for assent the certificate of the Speaker of the House of Commons signed by him that it is a Money Bill. Before giving his certificate, the Speaker shall consult, if practicable, two members to be appointed from the Chairmen's Panel at the beginning of each Session by the Committee of Selection.

2. Restriction of the Powers of the House of Lords as to Bills other than Money Bills

(1) If any Public Bill (other than a Money Bill or a Bill containing any provision to extend the maximum duration of Parliament beyond five years) is passed by the House of Commons [in two successive sessions] (whether of the same Parliament or not), and, having been sent up to the House of Lords at least one month before the end of the session, is rejected by the House of Lords in each of those session, that Bill shall, on its rejection [for the second time] by the House of Lords, unless the House of Commons direct to the contrary, be presented to His Majesty and become an Act of Parliament on Royal Assent being signified thereto, notwithstanding that the House of Lords have not consented to the Bill: Provided that this provision shall not take effect unless [one year has elapsed] between the date of the second reading in the first of those sessions of the Bill in the House of Commons and the date on which it passes the House of Commons [in the second of those sessions].

(2) When a Bill is presented to His Majesty for assent in pursuance of the provisions of this section, there shall be endorsed on the Bill the certificate of the Speaker of the House of Commons signed by him that the provisions of this section have been duly complied with.

(3) A bill shall be deemed to be rejected by the House of Lords if it is not passed by the House of Lords either without amendment or with such amendments only as may be agreed to by both Houses.

(4) A Bill shall be deemed to be the same Bill as a former Bill sent up to the House of Lords in the preceding session if, when it is sent up to the House of Lords, it is identical with the former Bill or contains only such alterations as are certified by the Speaker of the House of Commons to be necessary owing to the time which has elapsed since the date of the former Bill, or to represent any amendments which have been made by the House of Lords in the former Bill in the preceding session, and any amendments which are certified by the Speaker to have been made by the House of Lords [in the second session] and agreed to by the House of Commons shall be inserted in the Bill as presented for Royal Assent in pursuance of this section:

Provided that the House of Commons may, if they think fit, on the passage of such a Bill through the House [in the second session], suggest any further amendments without inserting the amendments in the Bill, and any such suggested amendments shall be considered by the House of Lords, and, if agreed to by that House, shall be treated as amendments made by the House of Lords and agreed to by the House of Commons; but the exercise of this power by the House of Commons shall not affect the operation of this section in the event of the Bill being rejected by the House of Lords.

3. Certificate of Speaker

Any certificate of the Speaker of the House of Commons given under this Act shall be conclusive for all purposes, and shall not be questioned in any court of law.

4. Enacting words

(1) In every Bill presented to His Majesty under the preceding provisions of this Act, the words of enactment shall be as follows, that is to say:—

"Be it enacted by the King's most Excellent Majesty, by and with the advice and consent of the Commons in this present Parliament assembled, in accordance with the provisions of [the Parliament Acts 1911 and 1949], and by authority of the same, as follows."

(2) Any alteration of a Bill necessary to give effect to this section shall not be deemed to be an amendment of the Bill.

5. Provisional Order Bills excluded

In this Act the expression "Public Bill" does not include any Bill for confirming a Provisional Order.

6. Saving for existing rights and privileges of the House of Commons

Nothing in this Act shall diminish or qualify the existing rights and privileges of the House of Commons.

7. Duration of Parliament

Five years shall be substituted for seven years as the time fixed for the maximum duration of Parliament under the Septennial Act, 1715.

ADMINISTRATION OF JUSTICE (APPEALS) ACT 1934
(24 & 25 Geo. 5, c. 40)

An Act to provide that no appeal shall lie from the Court of Appeal to the House of Lords except with the leave of that Court or the House of Lords, to make further provision as respects appeals from county courts, and for purposes connected with the matters aforesaid. [25th July 1934]

1. Restriction on appeals from Court of Appeal to House of Lords.

(1) No appeal shall lie to the House of Lords from any order or judgment made or given by the Court of Appeal after the first day of October nineteen hundred and thirty-four, except with the leave of that Court or of the House of Lords.

(2) The House of Lords may by order provide for the hearing and determination by a Committee of that House of petitions for leave to appeal from the Court of Appeal:

Provided that section five of the Appellate Jurisdiction Act 1876 shall apply to the hearing and determination of any such petition by a Committee of the House as it applies to the hearing and determination of an appeal by the House.

(3) Nothing in this section shall affect any restriction existing, apart from this section, on the bringing of appeals from the Court of Appeal to the House of Lords.

CHILDREN AND YOUNG PERSONS ACT 1933
(23 & 24 Geo. 5, c. 12)

*****

Principles to be observed by all Courts in dealing with Children and Young Persons

44. General considerations.

(1) Every court in dealing with a child or young person who is brought before it, either as . . . an offender or otherwise, shall have regard to the welfare of the child or young person and shall in a proper case take steps for removing him from undesirable surroundings, and for securing that proper provision is made for his education and training.

(2) . . .

Juvenile Courts

45. Constitution of juvenile courts.

Courts of summary jurisdiction constituted in accordance with the provisions of the Second Schedule of this Act and sitting for the purpose of hearing any charge against a child or young person or for the purpose of exercising any other jurisdiction conferred on juvenile courts by or under this or any other Act, shall be known as juvenile courts and in whatever place sitting shall be deemed to be petty sessional courts.

46. Assignment of certain matters to juvenile courts.

(1) Subject as hereinafter provided, no charge against a child or young person, and no application whereof the hearing is by rules made under this section assigned to juvenile courts, shall be heard by a court of summary jurisdiction which is not a juvenile court:
Provided that—

    (a)   a charge made jointly against a child or young person and a person who has attained the age of seventeen years shall be heard by a court of summary jurisdiction other than a juvenile court; and

    (b)   where a child or young person is charged with an offence, the charge may be heard by a court of summary jurisdiction which is not a juvenile court if a person who has attained the age of seventeen years is charged at the same time with aiding, abetting, causing, procuring, allowing or permitting that offence; and

    (c)   where, in the course of any proceedings before any court of summary jurisdiction other than a juvenile court, it appears that the person to whom the proceedings relate is a child or young person, nothing in this subsection shall be construed as preventing the court, if it thinks fit so to do, from proceedings with the hearing and determination of those proceedings.

[(1A) If a notification that the accused desires to plead guilty without appearing before the court is received by the clerk of a court in pursuance of [section 12 of the Magistrates' Courts Act 1980] and the court has no reason to believe that the accused is a child or young person, then, if he is a child or young person he shall be deemed to have attained the age of seventeen for the purposes of subsection (1) of this section in its application to the proceedings in question.]

(2) No direction, whether contained in this or any other Act, that a charge shall be brought before a juvenile court shall be construed as restricting the powers of any justice or justices to entertain an application for bail or for a remand, and to hear such evidence as may be necessary for that purpose.

(3) . . .

47. Procedure in juvenile courts.

(1) Juvenile courts shall sit as often as may be necessary for the purpose of exercising any jurisdiction conferred on them by or under this or any other Act.

(2) A juvenile court shall [not sit in a room in which sittings of a court other than a juvenile court are held if a sitting of that other court has been or will be held there within an hour before or after the sitting of the juvenile court]; and no person shall be present at any sitting of a juvenile court except—

    (a)   members and officers of the court;

    (b)   parties to the case before the court, their solicitors and counsel, and witnesses and other persons directly concerned in that case;

    (c)   bona fide representatives of newspapers or news agencies;

    (d)   such other persons as the court may specially authorise to be present:

(3) . . .

Children and Young Persons Act 1933

48. Miscellaneous provisions as to powers of juvenile courts.

(1) A juvenile court sitting for the purpose of hearing a charge against, . . ., a person who is believed to be a child or young person may, if it thinks fit to do so, proceed with the hearing and determination of the charge . . . notwithstanding that it is discovered that the person in question is not a child or young person.

(2) The attainment of the age of seventeen years by . . . a person in whose case an order for conditional discharge has been made, shall not deprive a juvenile court of jurisdiction to enforce his attendance and deal with him in respect of . . . the commission of a further offence . . .

(3) When a juvenile court has remanded a child or young person for information to be obtained with respect to him, any juvenile court acting for the same petty sessional division or place—

    (a) may in his absence extend the period for which he is remanded, so, however, that he appears before a court or a justice of the peace at least once in every twenty-one days;

    (b) when the required information has been obtained, may deal with him finally;

. . .

(4) . . . a juvenile court may sit on any day for the purpose of hearing and determining a charge against a child or young person in respect of an indictable offence.

(5) A juvenile court sitting in [the inner London area] shall have all the powers of a metropolitan police magistrate; and for the purposes of any enactment by virtue of which any powers are exercisable—

    (a) by a court of summary jurisdiction acting for the same petty sessional division or place as a juvenile court by which some previous act has been done; or

    (b) by a juvenile court acting for the same petty sessional division or place as a court of summary jurisdiction by which some previous act has been done,

[the inner London area] shall be deemed to be the place for which all metropolitan police magistrates sitting in that area and all juvenile courts sitting in that area act.

(6) . . .

49. Restrictions on newspaper reports of proceedings in juvenile courts.

(1) Subject as hereinafter provided, no newspaper report of any proceedings in a juvenile court shall reveal the name, address or school, or include any particulars calculated to lead to the identification, of any child or young person concerned in those proceedings, either as being the person against or in respect of whom the proceedings are taken or as being a witness therein, nor shall any picture be published in any newspaper as being or including a picture of any child or young person so concerned in any such proceedings as aforesaid:

Provided that the court or the Secretary of State may in any case, if satisfied that it is [appropriate to do so for the purpose of avoiding injustice to a child or young person], by order dispense with the requirements of this section [in relation to him] to such extent as may be specified in the order.

(2) Any person who publishes any matter in contravention of this section shall on summary conviction be liable in respect of each offence to a fine not exceeding [£500].

Juvenile Offenders

50. Age of criminal responsibility.

It shall be conclusively presumed that no child under the age of [ten] years can be guilty of any offence.

51., 52. . . .

53. Punishment of certain grave crimes.

[(1) A person convicted of an offence who appears to the court to have been under the age of eighteen years at the time the offence was committed shall not, if he is convicted of murder, be sentenced to imprisonment for life, nor shall sentence of death be pronounced on or recorded against any such person; but in lieu thereof the court shall (notwithstanding anything in this or in any other Act) sentence him to be detained during Her Majesty's pleasure, and if so sentenced he shall be liable to be detained in such place under such conditions as the Secretary of State may direct.]

(2) Where a child or young person is convicted on indictment of [any offence punishable in the case of an adult with imprisonment for fourteen years or more, not being an offence the sentence for which is fixed by law], and the court is of opinion that none of the other methods in which the case may legally be dealt with is suitable, the court may sentence the offender to be detained for such period [not exceeding the maximum term of imprisonment with which the offence is punishable in the case of an adult] as may be specified in the sentence; and where such a sentence has been passed the child or young person shall, during that period . . . be liable to be detained in such place and on such conditions as the Secretary of State may direct.

(3) A person detained pursuant to the directions of the Secretary of State under this section shall, while so detained, be deemed to be in legal custody.

(4) . . .

54. . . .

55. Power to order parent to pay fine, &c., instead of child or young person.

(1) Where a [child or] young person is [found guilty of] any offence for the commission of which [a fine or costs may be imposed or a compensation order may be made under [section 35 of the Powers of Criminal Courts Act 1973]] if the court is of opinion that the case would be best met by [the imposition of a fine or costs or the making of such an order] whether with or without any other punishment, the court may [in any case, and shall if the offender is a child] order that [the fine, compensation or costs awarded] be paid by the parent or guardian of the [child or] young person instead of by the [child or] young person, unless the court is satisfied that the parent or guardian cannot be found or that he has not conduced to the commission of the offence by neglecting to exercise due care [or control] of the [child or] young person.

(2) . . .

(3) An order under this section may be made against a parent or guardian who, having been required to attend, has failed to do so, but, save as aforesaid, no such order shall be made without giving the parent or guardian an opportunity of being heard.

(4) . . .

(5) A parent or guardian may appeal against an order under this section—
    (a)   if made by a court of summary jurisdiction, to [the Crown Court]; and
    (b)   [if made by the Crown Court, to the Criminal Division of the Court of Appeal in accordance with Part I of the Criminal Appeal Act 1968], as if the parent or guardian against whom the order was made had been convicted on indictment, and the order were a sentence passed on his conviction.

[SCHEDULE 2]
CONSTITUTION OF JUVENILE COURTS
PART I
OUTSIDE METROPOLITAN AREA

Juvenile court panels

1. The following provisions of this Part of this Schedule shall have effect as respects

any area outside the metropolitan stipendiary court area and the City of London.

2. A justice shall not be qualified to sit as a member of a juvenile court unless he is a member of a juvenile court panel, that it to say, a panel of justices specially qualified to deal with juvenile cases.

3. Subject to the following provisions of this Part of this Schedule, a juvenile court panel shall be formed for every petty sessions area.

Combined juvenile court panels

4. A magistrates' courts committee may make recommendations to the Secretary of State—

    (a)   for the formation of a combined juvenile court panel for two or more petty sessions areas, or

    (b)   for the dissolution of any such combined juvenile court panel,

if the committee's area comprises at least one of the petty sessions areas concerned.

5. It shall be the duty of the magistrates' courts committee for any area, if directed to do so by the Secretary of State, to review the functioning of juvenile courts in their area and on completion of the review to submit to the Secretary of State either a report making such recommendations as are mentioned in paragraph 4 of this Schedule or a report giving reasons for making no such recommendations.

6. Subject to the provisions of this Schedule—

    (a)   where a magistrates' courts committee make such recommendations to the Secretary of State, he may make an order giving effect to them subject to any modifications he thinks fit; and

    (b)   where a magistrates' courts committee fail to comply within six months with a direction of the Secretary of State under the preceding paragraph, or the Secretary of State is dissatisfied with the report submitted in pursuance of such a direction, he may make such order as he thinks fit for the purposes mentioned in paragraph 4 of this Schedule.

Effect of order establishing combined panel

7. Where a combined juvenile court panel is formed for any petty sessions areas any justice who is a member of the panel may exercise in relation to each of the areas any jurisdiction exercisable by him as a member of a juvenile court.

Restrictions on formation of combined panels

8. No order under this Schedule shall provide for the formation of a combined juvenile court panel for an area which includes—

    (a)   a county or part of a county and the whole or part of another county;

. . .

    (b)   . . .

9. An order under this Schedule providing for the formation of a combined juvenile court panel for an area which comprises a borough having a separate magistrates' courts committee shall not be made except with the consent of every magistrates' courts committee the whole or part of whose area is included in the area for which the combined panel is formed.

Consultations and notices

10. A magistrates' courts committee, before submitting recommendations for an order under this Schedule, shall consult and, when submitting any such recommendations, shall give notice to—

    (a)   the justices acting for any petty sessions area concerned which is within the committee's area (except where the committee's area is a borough); and

(b) any other magistrates' courts committee the whole or part of whose area is concerned;
and shall also consult the said justices before commenting on any recommendations on which they are consulted under this paragraph by another magistrates' courts committee.

11. Where the Secretary of State proposes to make an order under this Schedule in a case where either no recommendations have been made to him or the proposed order departs from the recommendations made ot him, he shall send a copy of the proposed order to the magistrates' courts committee for any area the whole or part of which is concerned and to the justices acting for any petty sessions area concerned.

12. Where notice of recommendations or a copy of a proposed order is required to be sent under the preceding paragraphs to any justices or committee, the Secretary of State shall, before making an order, consider any representations made to him by the justices or committee, or by any juvenile court panel concerned, within one month from the time the notice was given or the copy of the proposed order was sent.

PART II
METROPOLITAN AREA

13. The following provisions of this Part of this Schedule shall have effect as respects [the inner London area] and the City of London (in this Part of this Schedule referred to as the metropolitan area).

14. Juvenile courts shall be constituted for the whole of the metropolitan area but shall sit for such divisions and in such places as the Secretary of State may by order specify, without prejudice, however, to their jurisdiction with respect to the whole area.

15. Subject to the following provisions of this Schedule—
    (a) each juvenile court shall consist of a chairman and two other members and shall have both a man and a woman among its members;
    (b) the chairman shall be a person nominated by [the Lord Chancellor] to act as chairman of juvenile courts for the metropolitan area and shall be either a metropolitan stipendiary magistrate or [a lay justice for the inner London area] selected, in such manner as may be provided by an order of [the Lord Chancellor], from a panel of such justices from time to time nominated by him; and
    (c) the other members shall be justices so selected from that panel.

16. If at any time, by reason of illness or other emergency, no person nominated under paragraph 15(b) of this Schedule is available to act as chairman of a juvenile court, any metropolitan stipendiary magistrate or, with the consent of [the Lord Chancellor] any justice of the peace selected as aforesaid from the said panel, may act temporarily as chairman.

17. Where it appears to the chairman that a juvenile court cannot, without adjournment, be fully constituted, and that an adjournment would not be in the interests of justice, the chairman may sit with one other member (whether a man or a woman) or, if a metropolitan stipendiary magistrate, may sit alone.

18. [The Lord Chancellor], in nominating any persons under this Part of this Schedule shall have regard to the previous experience of the persons available and their special qualifications for dealing with juvenile cases; and every such nomination shall be for a specified period and shall be revocable by [the Lord Chancellor].

19. The enactments relating to the provision of land and buildings required for the purposes of metropolitan magistrates' courts shall extend and be deemed always to have extended to the provision of land and buildings required for the purposes of juvenile courts constituted for the metropolitan area.

STATUTORY INSTRUMENTS ACT 1946
(9 & 10 Geo. 6, c. 36)

An Act to repeal the Rules Publication Act 1893, and to make further provison as to the instruments by which statutory powers to make orders, rules, regulations and other subordinate legislation are exercised [26th March 1946]

1. **Definition of "Statutory Instrument"**

(1) Where by this Act or any Act passed after the commencement of this Act power to make, confirm or approve orders, rules, regulations or other subordinate legislation is conferred on His Majesty in Council or on any Minister of the Crown then, if the power is expressed—

(a) in the case of a power conferred on His Majesty, to be exercisable by Order in Council;

(b) in the case of a power conferred on a Minister of the Crown, to be exercisable by statutory instrument,

any document by which that power is exercised shall be known as a "statutory instrument" and the provisions of this Act shall apply thereto accordingly.

(2) Where by any Act passed before the commencement of this Act power to make statutory rules within the meaning of the Rules Publication Act, 1893, was conferred on any rule-making authority within the meaning of that Act, any document by which that power is exercised after the commencement of this Act shall, save as is otherwise provided by regulations made under this Act, be known as a "statutory instrument" and the provisions of this Act shall apply thereto accordingly.

2. **Numbering, printing, publication and citation**

(1) Immediately after the making of any statutory instrument, it shall be sent to the King's printer of Acts of Parliament and numbered in accordance with regulations made under this Act, and except in such cases as may be provided by any Act passed after the commencement of this Act or prescribed by regulations made under this Act, copies thereof shall as soon as possible be printed and sold by the King's printer of Acts of Parliament.

(2) Any statutory instrument may, without prejudice to any other mode of citation, be cited by the number given to it in accordance with the provisions of this section, and the calendar year.

3. **Supplementary provisions as to publication**

(1) Regulations made for the purposes of this Act shall make provision for the publication by His Majesty's Stationery Office of lists showing the date upon which every statutory instrument printed and sold by the King's printer of Acts of Parliament was first issued by that office; and in any legal proceedings a copy of any list so published purporting to bear the imprint of the King's printer shall be received in evidence as a true copy, and an entry therein shall be conclusive evidence of the date on which any statutory instrument was first issued by His Majesty's Stationery Office.

(2) In any proceedings against any person for an offence consisting of a contravention of any such statutory instrument, it shall be a defence to prove that the instrument had not been issued by His Majesty's Stationery Office at the date of the alleged contravention unless it is proved that at that date reasonable steps had been taken for the purpose of bringing the purport of the instrument to the notice of the public, or of persons likely to be affected by it, or of the person charged.

(3) Save as therein otherwise expressly provided, nothing in this section shall affect any enactment or rule of law relating to the time at which any statutory instrument comes into operation.

4. **Statutory Instruments which are required to be laid before Parliament**

(1) Where by this Act or any Act passed after the commencement of this Act any

statutory instrument is required to be laid before Parliament after being made, a copy of the instrument shall be laid before each House of Parliament and, subject as hereinafter provided, shall be so laid before the instrument comes into operation:
Provided that if is essential that any such instrument should come into operation before copies thereof can be so laid as aforesaid, the instrument may be made so as to come into operation before it has been so laid; and where any statutory instrument comes into operation before it is laid before Parliament, notification shall forthwith be sent to the Lord Chancellor and to the Speaker of the House of Commons drawing attention to the fact that copies of the instrument have yet to be laid before Parliament and explaining why such copies were not so laid before the instrument came into operation.

(2) Every copy of any such statutory instrument sold by the King's printer of Acts of Parliament shall bear on the face thereof—

    (a)   a statement showing the date on which the statutory instrument came or will come into operation; and

    (b)   either a statement showing the date on which copies thereof were laid before Parliament or a statement that such copies are to be laid before Parliament.

(3) Where any Act passed before the date of the commencement of this Act contains provisions requiring that any Order in Council or other document made in exercise of any power conferred by that or any other Act be laid before Parliament after being made, any statutory instrument made in exercise of that power shall by virtue of this Act be laid before Parliament and the foregoing provisions of this section shall apply thereto accordingly in substitution for any such provisions as aforesaid contained in the Act passed before the said date.

5. Statutory Instruments which are subject to annulment by resolution of either House of Parliament

(1) Where by this Act or any Act passed after the commencement of this Act, it is provided that any statutory instrument shall be subject to annulment in pursuance of resolution of either House of Parliament, the instrument shall be laid before Parliament after being made and the provisions of the last foregoing section shall apply thereto accordingly, and if either House within the period of forty days beginning with the day on which a copy thereof is laid before it, resolves that an Address be presented to His Majesty praying that the instrument be annulled, no further proceedings shall be taken thereunder after the date of the resolution, and His Majesty may by Order in Council revoke the instrument, so, however, that any such resolution and revocation shall be without prejudice to the validity of anything previously done under the instrument or to the making of a new statutory instrument.

(2) Where any Act passed before the date of the commencement of this Act contains provisions requiring that any Order in Council or other document made in exercise of any power conferred by that or any other Act shall be laid before Parliament after being made and shall cease to be in force or may be annulled, as the case may be, if within a specified period either House presents an address to His Majesty or passes a resolution to that effect, then, subject to the provisions of any Order in Council made under this Act, any statutory instrument made in exercise of the said power shall by virtue of this Act be subject to annulment in pursuance of a resolution of either House of Parliament and the provisions of the last foregoing subsection shall apply thereto accordingly in substitution for any such provisions as aforesaid contained in the Act passed before the said date.

6. Statutory Instruments of which drafts are to be laid before Parliament

(1) Where by this Act or any Act passed after the commencement of this Act it is provided that a draft of any statutory instrument shall be laid before Parliament, but the Act does not prohibit the making of the instrument without the approval of Parliament, then, in the case of an Order in Council the draft shall not be submitted

to His Majesty in Council, and in any other case the statutory instrument shall not be made, until after the expiration of a period of forty days beginning with the day on which a copy of the draft is laid before each House of Parliament, or if such copies are laid on different days, with the later of the two days, and if within that period either House resolves that the draft be not submitted to His Majesty or that the statutory instrument be not made, as the case may be, no further proceedings shall be taken thereon, but without prejudice to the laying before Parliament of a new draft.

(2) Where any Act passed before the date of the commencement of this Act contains provisions requiring that a draft of any Order of the Council or other document to be made in exercise of any power conferred by that or any other Act shall be laid before Parliament before being submitted to His Majesty, or before being made, as the case may be, and that it shall not be so submitted or made if within a specified period either House presents an address to His Majesty or passes a resolution to that effect, then, subject to the provisions of any Order in Council made under this Act, a draft of any statutory instrument made in exercise of the said power shall by virtue of this Act be laid before Parliament and the provisions of the last foregoing subsection shall apply thereto accordingly in substitution for any such provision as aforesaid contained in the Act passed before the said date.

7. **Supplementary provisions as to ss 4, 5 and 6**

(1) In reckoning for the purposes of either of the last two foregoing sections any period of forty days, no account shall be taken of any time during which Parliament is dissolved or prorogued or during which both Houses are adjourned for more than four days.

(2) In relation to any instrument required by any Act, whether passed before or after the commencement of this Act, to be laid before the House of Commons only, the provisions of the last three foregoing sections shall have effect as if references to that House were therein substituted for references to Parliament and for references to either House and each House thereof.

(3) The provisions of sections four and five of this Act shall not apply to any statutory instrument being an order which is subject to special Parliamentary procedure, or to any other instrument which is required to be laid before Parliament, or before the House of Commons, for any period before it comes into operation.

8.—13. *****

CONSOLIDATION OF ENACTMENTS (PROCEDURE) ACT 1949
(12, 13 & 14 Geo. 6, c. 33)

An Act to facilitate the preparation of Bills for the purpose of consolidating the enactments relating to any subject [31 May 1949]

1. **Procedure for making corrections and minor improvements**

(1) If at any time it appears to the Lord Chancellor to be expedient that a Bill should be prepared for the purpose of consolidating the enactments relating to any subject, but that, in order to facilitate the consolidation of those enactments, corrections and minor improvements ought to be made in such enactments, he may cause to be laid before Parliament a memorandum proposing such corrections and minor improvements therein as he thinks to be expedient.

(2) Before any such memorandum is laid before Parliament there shall be published in the Gazette a notice specifying the place where copies of the memorandum may be obtained, and the address to which, and the time within which, representations in writing with respect thereto be made.

(3) If, at or after the time when any such memorandum is laid before Parliament,

a Bill to consolidate the enactments to which the memorandum relates with such corrections and minor improvements as may be authorised under this Act is presented to either House of Parliament, and the bill and the memorandum are referred to a joint committee of both Houses, any representations made with respect to the memorandum in accordance with the provisions of the notice published in the Gazette shall also be referred to the joint committee; and that committee, after considering any such representations, shall, before reporting the Bill, inform the Lord Chancellor and the Speaker of the House of Commons what corrections and minor improvements in the said enactments the committee are prepared to approve:

Provided that the committee shall not consider any such memorandum until at least one month after it has been laid before Parliament.

(4) If the joint committee approve the proposals contained in the memorandum, with or without alterations, and the Lord Chancellor and the Speaker inform the committee that they concur in such approval the committee, after making in the Bill such amendments, if any, as may be necessary to give effect to any alterations made in the proposals, may, in reporting the Bill, report that the Bill, or the Bill as amended by the committee, as the case may be, re-enacts the existing law with such corrections and minor improvements only as have been approved by the committee with the concurrence of the Lord Chancellor and of the Speaker in accordance with the Provisions of this Act.

(5) The joint committee shall not approve any corrections and minor improvements, and neither the Lord Chancellor nor the Speaker shall concur in approving any corrections and minor improvements under this Act unless they are, or he is, satisfied that the corrections and minor improvements do not effect any changes in the existing law of such importance that they ought, in their or his opinion, to be separately enacted by Parliament.

(6) If the corrections and minor improvements approved by the joint committee with the concurrence of the Lord Chancellor and of the Speaker differ in any respect from those proposed in the memorandum laid before Pariament under subsection (1) of this section, the corrections and minor improvements so approved shall be appended to the report of the joint committee.

(7) When a Bill has been reported by the joint committee with such a report as is mentioned in subsection (4) of this section, then, for the purposes of any further proceedings in Parliament relating to the Bill, but not for any other purpose, the corrections and minor improvements approved by the joint committee with the concurrence of the Lord Chancellor and of the Speaker shall be deemed to have become law in like manner as if they had been made by an Act.

2. Interpretation

In this Act the following expressions have the meanings hereby respectively assigned to them, that is to say—

"corrections and minor improvements" means amendments of which the effect is confined to resolving ambiguities, removing doubts, bringing obsolete provisions into conformity with modern practice, or removing unnecessary provisions or anomalies which are not of substantial importance, and amendments designed to facilitate improvement in the form or manner in which the law is stated, and includes any transitional provisions which may be necessary in consequence of such amendments:

"the Gazette" means the London Gazette and, in relation to a memorandum preparatory to a Bill intended to extend to Scotland or Northern Ireland, includes the Edinburgh Gazette or Belfast Gazette, as the case may be, so, however, that, in relation to a memorandum preparatory to a Bill intended to extend only to Scotland, the said expression means the Edinburgh Gazette.

LANDS TRIBUNAL ACT 1949
(1949, c. 42)

An Act to establish new tribunals to determine in place of official arbitrators and others certain questions relating to compensation for the compulsory acquisition of land and other matters, to amend the Acquisition of Land (Assessment of Compensation) Act 1919, with respect to the failure to deliver a notice of claim, and for purposes connected therewith. [14th July 1949]

1. Establishment and jurisdiction of Lands Tribunal.

(1) There shall be set up, to exercise the jurisdiction hereafter mentioned in this Act, the following tribunals, namely—

    (a)   a tribunal for Scotland, to be called "the Lands Tribunal for Scotland"; and

    (b)   a tribunal for the remainder of the United Kingdom, to be called "the Lands Tribunal".

(2) Except in so far as the context otherwise requires, references in this Act to the Lands Tribunal shall be taken, in relation to Scotland, as references to the Lands Tribunal for Scotland.

(3) There shall be referred to and determined by the Lands Tribunal—

    (a)   any question which is by any Act (including a local or private Act) directed, in whatever terms, to be determined by a person or one or more persons selected from either of the following panels, that is to say,—

        (i)   the panel of official arbitrators appointed under the Acquisition of Land Act; and

        (ii)   the panel of referees appointed under Part I of the Finance (1909-10) Act 1910;

or which is so directed to be determined in the absence of agreement to the contrary;

    (b)   any other question of disputed compensation under the Lands Clauses Act, where the claim is for the injurious affection of any land . . .

    (c)   any question arising . . . as to the apportionment mentioned in section one hundred and sixteen of the Lands Clauses Consolidation Act 1845, of any rent charge or other matter to which that section applies;

    (d)   any dispute arising in relation to the determination of the development values of interests in land by the Central Land Board or other authority prescribed under section sixty of the Town and County Planning Act 1947;

    (e)   any question on which, but for this provision, an appeal or reference to the county court would or might be made by virtue of section . . ., sixty-two or eighty-seven of the Local Government Act 1948.

(4) The Lands Tribunal shall also exercise—

    (a)   the jurisdiction conferred on the Authority under section eighty-four of the Law of Property Act 1925 (which relates to the discharge and modification of restrictive covenants); and

    (b)   any other jurisdiction conferred by any Act (including a local or private Act), or instrument made under any such Act, on a person or one or more persons selected as mentioned in paragraph (a) of the last foregoing subsection . . .

(5) The Lands Tribunal may also act as arbitrator under a reference by consent, and any agreement entered into before the commencement of this Act which provides for referring any matter to arbitration by a person or one or more persons selected as aforesaid shall, subject to any subsequent agreement, have effect as if it provided for referring the matter to arbitration by the Lands Tribunal.

(6) Where [any person] is or may be liable for any compensation falling to be determined under section fifty-eight or one hundred and six of the Lands Clauses

Consolidation Act 1845 (which sections relate to the procedure in default of a claimant), the surveyor referred to in those sections, . . . shall be selected as hereinafter mentioned from the members of the Lands Tribunal.

(7), (8) . . .

2. Members, officers and expenses of Lands Tribunal.

(1) The Lands Tribunal shall consist of a President and such number of other members as the Lord Chancellor may determine, to be appointed by the Lord Chancellor.

(2) The President shall be either a person who has held judicial office under the Crown (whether in the United Kingdom or not) or a barrister-at-law of at least seven years' standing, and of the other members of the Lands Tribunal such number as the Lord Chancellor may determine shall be barristers-at-law or solicitors of the like standing and the others shall be persons who have had experience in the valuation of land appointed after consultation with the president of the Royal Institution of Chartered Surveyors.

(3) In the case of the temporary absence or inability to act of the President, the Lord Chancellor may appoint another member of the Lands Tribunal to act as deputy for the President, and a member so appointed shall, when so acting, have all the functions of the President.

(4) If a member of the Lands Tribunal becomes, in the opinion of the Lord Chancellor, unfit to continue in office or incapable of performing his duties, the Lord Chancellor shall forthwith declare his office to be vacant and shall notify the fact in such manner as he thinks fit, and thereupon the office shall become vacant.

(5) Subject to the last foregoing subsection, the appointment of a member of the Lands Tribunal shall be for such term as may be determined by the Lord Chancellor, with the approval of the Treasury, before his appointment, and shall be subject to such conditions as may be so determined, and a person who ceases to hold office as a member of the Lands Tribunal shall be eligible for re-appointment thereto.

(6) There may be paid to the members of the Lands Tribunal such remuneration, and such travelling and subsistence allowances, and to persons who have been members thereof such superannuation allowances, as the Lord Chancellor may, with the approval of the Treasury, determine.

(7) The Lord Chancellor may appoint such officers and servants of the Lands Tribunal as he may, with the approval of the Treasury as to numbers and remuneration, determine.

(8) The remuneration and allowances of members and superannuation allowances of past members of the Lands Tribunal, the remuneration of the officers and servants appointed by the Lord Chancellor, and such other expenses of the Lands Tribunal as the Treasury may determine, shall be defrayed out of moneys provided by Parliament.

3., 4. ★★★★★

5. . . .

6., 7. ★★★★★

8. Interpretation.

(1) In this Act—

"the Acquisition of Land Act" means the Acquisition of Land (Assessment of Compensation) Act 1919;

"arbitrator", in relation to Scotland, means arbiter;

"barrister-at-law" means a member of the bar whether of England or Northern Ireland or both.

(2) Except in so far as the context otherwise requires, any reference in this Act to an enactment shall be construed as referring to that enactment as amended, extended or applied by any other enactment.

(3) Any power under this Act to make rules shall be exercisable by statutory instrument, . . .

ARBITRATION ACT 1950
(14 Geo. 6, c. 27)

An Act to consolidate the Arbitration Acts 1889 to 1934 [28th July 1950]

PART I
GENERAL PROVISIONS AS TO ARBITRATION
Effect of Arbitration Agreements, etc.

1. Authority of arbitrators and umpires to be irrevocable
The authority of an arbitrator or umpire appointed by or by virtue of an arbitration agreement shall, unless a contrary intention is expressed in the agreement, be irrevocable except by leave of the High Court or a judge thereof.

2., 3. *****

4. Staying court proceedings where there is submission to arbitration
(1) If any party to an arbitration agreement, or any person claiming through or under him, commences any legal proceedings in any court against any other party to the agreement, or any person claiming through or under him, in respect of any matter agreed to be referred, any party to those legal proceedings may at any time after appearance, and before delivering any pleadings or taking any other steps in the proceedings, apply to that court to stay the proceedings, and that court or a judge thereof, if satisfied that there is no sufficient reason why the matter should not be referred in accordance with the agreement, and that the applicant was, at the time when the proceedings were commenced, and still remains, ready and willing to do all things necessary to the proper conduct of the arbitration, may make an order staying the proceedings.
(2) . . .

5. *****

Arbitrators and Umpires

6. When reference is to a single arbitrator
Unless a contrary intention is expressed therein, every arbitration agreement shall, if no other mode of reference is provided, be deemed to include a provision that the reference shall be to a single arbitrator.

7. Power of parties in certain cases to supply vacancy
Where an arbitration agreement provides that the reference shall be to two arbitrators, one to be appointed by each party, then, unless a contrary intention is expressed therein—
    (a) if either of the appointed arbitrators refuses to act, or is incapable of acting, or dies, the party who appointed him may appoint a new arbitrator in his place;
    (b) if, on such a reference, one party fails to appoint an arbitrator, either orginally, or by way of substitution as aforesaid, for seven clear days after the other party, having appointed his arbitrator, has served the party making default with notice to make the appointment, the party who has appointed an arbitrator may appoint that arbitrator to act as sole arbitrator in the reference and his award shall be binding on both parties as if he had been appointed by consent:
Provided that the High Court or a judge thereof may set aside any appointment made in pursuance of this section.

8. Umpires

(1) Unless a contrary intention is expressed therein, every arbitration agreement shall, where the reference is to two arbitrators, be deemed to include a provision that the two arbitrators [may appoint an umpire at any time] after they are themselves appointed [and shall do so forthwith if they cannot agree.]

(2) Unless a contrary intention is expressed therein, every arbitration agreement shall, where such a provision is applicable to the reference, be deemd to include a provision that if the arbitrators have delivered to any party to the arbitration agreement, or to the umpire, a notice in writing stating that they cannot agree, the umpire may forthwith enter on the reference in lieu of the arbitrators.

(3) At any time after the appointment of an umpire, however appointed, the High Court may, on the application of any party to the reference and notwithstanding anything to the contrary in the arbitration agreement, order that the umpire shall enter upon the reference in lieu of the arbitrators and as if he were a sole arbitrator [and shall do so forthwith if they cannot agree.]

9. [Majority Award of Three Arbitrators

Unless the contrary intention is expressed in the arbitration agreement, in any case where there is a reference to three arbitrators, the award of any two of the arbitrators shall be binding.]

10. Power of court in certain cases to appoint an arbitrator or umpire

In any of the following cases—

(a) where an arbitration agreement provides that the reference shall be to a single arbitrator, and all the parties do not, after differences have arisen, concur in the appointment of an arbitrator;

(b) if an appointed arbitrator refuses to act, or is incapable of acting or dies, and the arbitration agreement does not show that it was intended that the vacancy should not be supplied and the parties do not supply the vacancy;

(c) where the parties or two arbitrators are required or are at liberty to appoint an umpire or third arbitrator and do not appoint him;

(d) where an appointed umpire or third arbitrator refuses to act, or is incapable of acting, or dies, and the arbitration agreement does not show that it was intended that the vacancy should not be supplied, and the parties or arbitrators do not supply the vacancy;

any party may serve the other parties or the arbitrators, as the case may be, with a written notice to appoint or, as the case may be, concur in appointing, an arbitrator, umpire or third arbitrator, and if the appointment is not made within seven clear days after the service of the notice, the High Court or a judge thereof may, on application by the party who gave the notice, appoint an arbitrator, umpire or third arbitrator who shall have the like powers to act in the reference and make an award as if had been appointed by consent of all parties.

[(2) In any case where—

(a) an arbitration agreement provides for the appointment of an arbitrator or umpire by a person who is neither one of the parties nor an existing arbitrator (whether the provision applies directly or in default of agreement by the parties or otherwise), and

(b) that person refuses to make the appointment or does not make it within the time specified in the agreement or, if no time is so specified, within a reasonable time,

any party to the agreement may serve the person in question with a written notice to appoint an arbitrator or umpire and, if the appointment is not made within seven clear days after the service of the notice, the High Court or a judge thereof may, on the application of the party who gave the notice, appoint an arbitrator or umpire who shall have the like powers to act in the reference and make an award as if he had been appointed in accordance with the terms of the agreement].

[(3) In any case where—

(a) an arbitration agreement provides that the reference shall be to three arbitrators, one to be appointed by each party and the third to be appointed by the two appointed by the parties or in some other manner specified in the agreement; and

(b) one of the parties ("the party in default") refuses to appoint an arbitrator or does not do so within the time specified in the agreement or, if no time is specified, within a reasonable time,

the other party to the agreement, having appointed his arbitrator, may serve the party in default with a written notice to appoint an arbitrator and, if the appointment is not made within seven clear days after the service of the notice, the High Court or a judge thereof may, on the application of the party who gave the notice, appoint an arbitrator on behalf of the party in default who shall have the like powers to act in the reference and make an award (and, if the case so requires, the like duty in relation to the appointment of a third arbitrator) as if he had been appointed in accordance with the terms of the agreement.

(4) Except in a case where the arbitration agreement shows that it was intended that the vacancy should not be supplied, paragraph (b) of each of subsections (2) and (3) shall be construed as extending to any such refusal or failure by a person as is there mentioned arising in connection with the replacement of an arbitrator who was appointed by that person (or, in default of being so appointed, was under that subsection) but who refuses to act, or is incapable of acting or has died.]

Conduct of Proceedings, Witnesses, etc.

12. Conduct of proceedings, witnesses, etc.

(1) Unless a contrary intention is expressed therein, every arbitration agreement shall, where such a provision is applicable to the reference, be deemed to contain a provision that the parties to the reference, and all persons claiming through them respectively, shall, subject to any legal objection, submit to be examined by the arbitrator or umpire, on oath or affirmation, in relation to the matters in dispute, and shall, subject as aforesaid, produce before the arbitrator or umpire all documents within their possession or power respectively which may be required or called for, and do all other things which during the proceedings on the reference the arbitrator or umpire may require.

(2) Unless a contrary intention is expressed therein, every arbitration agreement shall, where such a provision is applicable to the reference, be deemed to contain a provision that the witnesses on the reference shall, if the arbitrator or umpire thinks fit, be examined on oath or affirmation.

(3) An arbitrator or umpire shall, unless a contrary intention is expressed in the arbitration agreement, have power to administer oaths to, or take the affirmations of, the parties to and witnesses on a reference under the agreement.

(4) Any party to a reference under an arbitration agreement may sue out a writ of subpoena ad testificandum or a writ of subpoena duces tecum, but no person shall be compelled under any such writ to produce any document which he could not be compelled to produce on the trial of an action, and the High Court or a judge thereof may order that a writ of subpoena ad testificandum or of subpoena duces tecum shall issue to compel the attendance before an arbitrator or umpire of a witness wherever he may be within the United Kingdom.

(5) The High Court or a judge thereof may also order that a writ of habeas corpus ad testificandum shall issue to bring up a prisoner for examination before an arbitrator or umpire.

(6) The High Court shall have, for the purpose of and in relation to a reference, the same power of making orders in respect of—
- (a)   security for costs;
- (b)   discovery of documents and interrogatories;
- (c)   the giving of evidence by affidavit;
- (d)   examination on oath of any witness before an officer of the High Court or any other person, and the issue of a commission or request for the examination of a witness out of the jurisdiction;
- (e)   the preservation, interim custody or sale of any goods which are the subject matter of the reference;
- (f)   securing the amount in dispute in the reference;
- (g)   the detention, preservation or inspection of any property or thing which is the subject of the reference or as to which any question may arise therein, and authorising for any of the purposes aforesaid any persons to enter upon or into any land or building in the possession of any party to the reference, or authorising any samples to be taken or any observation to be made or experiment to be tried which may be necessary or expedient for the purpose of obtaining full information or evidence; and
- (h)   interim injunctions or the appointment of a receiver;

as it has for the purpose of and in relation to an action or matter in the High Court: Provided that nothing in this subsection shall be taken to prejudice any power which may be vested in an arbitrator or umpire of making orders with respect to any of the matters aforesaid.

13.–20.   *****

Special Cases, Remission and Setting aside of Awards, etc.

21.   . . .

22. Power to remit award

(1) In all cases of reference to arbitration the High Court or a judge thereof may from time to time remit the matters referred, or any of them, to the reconsideration of the arbitrator or umpire.

(2) Where an award is remitted, the arbitrator or umpire shall, unless the order otherwise directs, make his award within three months after the date of the order.

23. Removal of arbitrator and setting aside of award

(1) Where an arbitrator or umpire has misconducted himself or the proceedings, the High Court may remove him.

(2) Where an arbitrator or umpire has misconducted himself or the proceedings, or an arbitration or award has been improperly procured the High Court may set the award aside.

(3) Where an application is made to set aside an award, the High Court may order that any money made payable by the award shall be brought into court or otherwise secured pending the determination of the application.

24.   *****

25. Power of court where arbitrator is removed or authority of arbitrator is revoked

(1) Where an arbitrator (not being a sole arbitrator), or two or more arbitrators (not being all the arbitrators) or an umpire who has not entered on the reference is or are removed by the High Court [or the Court of Appeal], the High Court [or the Court of Appeal as the case may be], may, on the application of any party to the arbitration agreement, appoint a person or persons to act as arbitrator or arbitrators or umpire in the place of the person or persons so removed.

(2) Where the authority of an arbitrator or arbitrators or umpire is revoked by leave of the High Court [or the Court of Appeal], or a sole arbitrator or all the arbitrators or an umpire who has entered on the reference is or are removed by the High Court [or the Court of Appeal], the High Court [or the Court of Appeal as the case may be,] may, on the application of any party to the arbitration agreement, either—

   (a)   appoint a person to act as sole arbitrator in place of the person or persons removed; or

   (b)   order that the arbitration agreement shall cease to have effect with respect to the dispute referred.

(3) A person appointed under this section by the High Court [or the Court of Appeal] as an arbitrator or umpire shall have the like power to act in the reference and to make an award as if he had been appointed in accordance with the terms of the arbitration agreement.

(4) Where it is provided (whether by means of a provision in the arbitration agreement or otherwise) that an award under an arbitration agreement shall be a condition precedent to the bringing of an action with respect to any matter to which the agreement applies, the High Court [or the Court of Appeal], if it orders (whether under this section or under any other enactment) that the agreement shall cease to have effect as regards any particular dispute, may further order that the provision making an award a condition precedent to the bringing of an action shall also cease to have effect as regards that dispute.

Enforcement of Award

26. Enforcement of award

(1) An award on an arbitration agreement may, by leave of the High Court or a judge thereof, be enforced in the same manner as a judgment or order to the same effect, and where leave is so given, judgment may be entered in terms of the award.

[(2) If—

   (a)   the amount sought to be recovered does not exceed the [county court limit] and

   (b)   a county court so orders,

it shall be recoverable (by execution issued from the county or otherwise) as if payable under an order of that court and shall not be enforceable under subsection (1) above.

(3) An application to the High Court under this section shall preclude an application to a county court and an application to a county court under this section shall preclude an application to the High Court.]

[(4) In subsection (2)(a) above, the "county court limit" means the amount which for the time being is the county court limit for the purposes of section 16 of the County Courts Act 1984 (money recoverable by statute).]

27.—31. *****

32. Meaning of "arbitration agreement"

In this Part of this Act, unless the context otherwise requires, the expression "arbitration agreement" means a written agreement to submit present or future differences to arbitration, whether an arbitrator is named therein or not.

ADMINISTRATION OF JUSTICE ACT 1960
(1960, c. 65)

An Act to make further provision for appeals to the House of Lords in criminal cases; to amend the law relating to contempt of court, habeas corpus and certiorari; and for purposes connected with the matters aforesaid

[27 October 1960]

Appeal to House of Lords in Criminal Cases

1. Right of appeal

(1) Subject to the provisions of this section, an appeal shall lie to the House of Lords, at the instance of the defendant or the prosecutor,—

(a) from any decision of a Divisonal Court of the Queen's Bench Division in a criminal cause or matter;

(b) ...

(2) No appeal shall lie under this section except with the leave of the court below or of the House of Lords; and such leave shall not be granted unless it is certified by the court below that a point of law of general public importance is involved in the decision and it appears to that court or to the House of Lords, as the case may be, that the point is one which ought to be considered by that House.

(3) Section five of the Appellate Jurisdiction Act 1876 (which regulates the composition of the House of Lords for the hearing and determination of appeals) shall apply to the hearing and determination of an appeal or application for leave to appeal under this section as it applies to the hearing and determination of an appeal under that Act; and any order of that House which provides for the hearing of such applications by a committee constituted in accordance with the said section five may direct that the decision of that committee shall be taken on behalf of the House.

(4) For the purpose of disposing of an appeal under this section the House of Lords may exercise any powers of the court below or may remit the case to that court.

(5) In this Act, unless the context otherwise requires, "leave to appeal" means leave to appeal to the House of Lords under this section.

2. Application for leave to appeal

(1) Subject to the provisions of this section, an application to the court below for leave to appeal shall be made within the period of fourteen days beginning with the date of the decision of that court; and an application to the House of Lords for such leave shall be made within the period of fourteen days beginning with the date on which the application is refused by the court below.

(2) ...

(3) Except in a case involving sentence of death, the House of Lords or the court below may, upon application made at any time by the defendant, extend the time within which an application may be made by him to that House or that court under subseciton (1) of this section.

3. Special provisions as to capital cases

(1) Any application for leave to appeal in a case involving sentence of death, and any appeal for which leave is granted on such an application, shall be heard and determined with as much expedition as practicable.

(2) ...

4. Admission of appellant to bail

(1) ...

(2) The power of the High Court under any enactment or rule of law to grant bail in connection with proceedings pending before a Divisional Court shall include power to grant bail to [an appellant under section 1 of this Act, or a person applying for leave to appeal thereunder, pending the appeal]; and in relation to [the time and place of appearance appointed and] any recognizance to be entered into [by any surety] under section thirty-seven of the Criminal Justice Act 1948 as applied to this subsection, any reference in that section to the judgment of the High Court shall be construed as a reference to the judgment of the House of Lords or, if the case is remitted by that House to the court below, to the judgment of that court on the case as so remitted.

(3) Where application is made to a Divisional Court for leave to appeal, that court

may give such directions as it thinks fit for discharging or enlarging any recognizances entered into by . . . any surety, under any enactment or otherwise, with reference to the proceedings of that court.

5. Power to order detention or admission to bail of defendant

(1) Where the defendant in any proceedings from which an appeal lies under section one of this Act would, but for the decision of the court below, be liable to be detained, and immediately after the decision the prosecutor is granted, or gives notice that he intends to apply for, leave to appeal, the court may make an order providing for the detention of the defendant, or directing that he shall not be released except on bail [(which may be granted by the court as under section 4 above)], so long as any appeal under section one of this Act is pending.

(2) . . .

(3) An order under subsection (1) of this section shall (unless the appeal has previously been disposed of) cease to have effect at the expiration of the period for which the defendant would have been liable to be detained but for the decision of the court below.

(4) Any order made under the said subsection (1) for the detention of a defendant who, but for the decision of the court below, would be liable to be detained in pursuance of an order or direction under [Part III of the Mental Health Act 1983 (other than under section 35, 36 or 38)], shall be an order authorising his continued detention in pursuance of the order or direction under [the said Part III], and the provisions of the said Act with respect to persons so liable (including provisions as to the renewal of authority for detention and the removal or discharge of patients) shall apply accordingly.

[(4A) Where an order is made under the said subsection (1) in the case of a defendant who, but for the decision of the court below, would be liable to be detained in pursuance of an interim hospital order under [section 38 of the Mental Health Act 1983], the order may, if the court thinks fit, be one authorising his continued detention in a hospital or mental nursing home and in that event—

(a)   subsection (3) of this section shall not apply to the order;

(b)   [Part III of the said Act of 1983] shall apply as if he had been ordered under this section to be detained in custody so long as any appeal under section 1 of this Act is pending and were detained in pursuance of a transfer direction together with a restriction direction; and

(c)   if the defendant is detained by virtue of this subsection and the appeal by the prosecutor succeeds, subsection (2) of [the said section 38] (power of court to make hospital order in the absence of an offender who is subject to an interim hospital order) shall apply as if the defendant were still subject to an interim hospital order.]

(5) Where the court below has power to make an order under subsection (1) of this section, and either no such order is made or the defendant is released or discharged by virtue of [subsection (3), (4) or (4A)] of this section before the appeal is disposed of, the defendant shall not be liable to be again detained as the result of the decision of the House of Lords on the appeal.

6. Computation of sentence where bail granted

(1) Where a person subject to a sentence is [granted] bail pending an appeal under section one of this Act, the time during which he is [released on bail] shall be disregarded in computing the term of his sentence.

(2) . . .

(3) Subject to the foregoing provisions of this section, any sentence passed on an appeal under section one of this Act in substitution for another sentence shall, unless the House of Lords or the court below otherwise directs, begin to run from the time when that other sentence would have begun to run.

7., 8.   . . . [Repealed by Criminal Appeal Act 1968 & Criminal Appeal (Northern Ireland) Act 1968]

9.   *****

10.   . . .[Repealed by Courts-Martial (Appeals) Act 1968]

11.   . . . [Repealed by Contempt of Court Act 1981]

12.   *****

13.   Appeal in cases of contempt of court

(1) Subject to the provisions of this section, an appeal shall lie under this section from any order or decision of a court in the exercise of jurisdiction to punish for contempt of court (including criminal contempt); and in relation to any such order or decision the provisions of this section shall have effect in substitution for any other enactment relating to appeals in civil or criminal proceedings.

(2) An appeal under this section shall lie in any case at the instance of the defendant and, in the case of an application for committal or attachment, at the instance of the applicant; and the appeal shall lie—

(a)   from an order or decision of any inferior court not referred to in the next following paragraph, to a Divisional Court of the High Court;

(b)   from an order or decision of a county court or any other inferior court from which appeals generally lie to the Court of Appeal, and from an order or decision . . ., of a single judge of the High Court, or of any court having the powers of the High Court or of a judge of that court, to the Court of Appeal;

[(bb) from an order or decision of the Crown Court to the Court of Appeal]

(c)   from an order or decision of a Divisional Court or the Court of Appeal (including a decision of either of those courts on an appeal under this section), and from an order or decision of the Court of Criminal Appeal or the Courts-Martial Appeal Court, to the House of Lords.

(3) The court to which an appeal is brought under this section may reverse or vary the order or decision of the court below, and make such other order as may be just; and without prejudice to the inherent powers of any court referred to in subsection (2) of this section, provision may be made by rules of court for authorising the release on bail of an appellant under this section.

(4) Subsections (2) to (4) of section one and section two of this Act shall apply to an appeal to the House of Lords under this section as they apply to an appeal to that House under the said section one, except that so much of the said subsection (2) as restricts the grant of leave to appeal shall apply only where the decision of the court below is a decision on appeal to that court under this section.

(5) In this section "court" includes any tribunal or person having power to punish for contempt; and references in this section to an order or decision of a court in the exercise of jurisdiction to punish for contempt of court include references—

(a)   to an order or decision of the High Court, [the Crown Court] or a county court under any enactment enabling that court to deal with an offence as if it were contempt of court;

(b)   to an order or decision of a county court, or of any court having the powers of a county court, under [section 14, 92 or 118 of the County Courts Act 1984];

(c)   to an order or decision of a magistrates' court under [subsection (3) of section 63 of the Magistrates' Courts Act 1980],

but do not include references to orders under section five of the Debtors Act 1869, or under any provision of [the Magistrates' Courts Act 1980] or the County Courts Act [1984], except those referred to in paragraphs (b) and (c) of this subsection and except sections [sections 38 and 142] of the last mentioned Act so far as those sections confer jurisdiction in respect of contempt of court.

(6) This section does not apply to a conviction or sentence in respect of which an appeal lies under [Part I of the Criminal Appeal Act 1968, or to a decision of the criminal division of the Court of Appeal under that Part of that Act; . . .] . . .

Supplementary

17. Interpretation

(1) In this Act any reference to the defendant shall be construed—

    (a) in relation to proceedings for an offence, and in relation to an application for an order of mandamus, prohibition or certiorari in connection with such proceedings, as a reference to the person who was or would have been the defendant in those proceedings;

    (b) in relation to any proceedings or order for or in respect of contempt of court, as a reference to the person against whom the proceedings were brought or the order was made;

    (c) in relation to a criminal application for habeas corpus, as a reference to the person by or in respect of whom that application was made,

and any reference to the prosecutor shall be construed accordingly.

(2) *****

(3) In this Act any reference to the court below shall, in relation to any function of a Divisional Court, be construed as a reference to the Divisional Court or to a judge according as the function is by virtue of rules or court exercisable by the Divisional Court or a judge.

(4) An appeal under section one of this Act shall be treated for the purposes of this Act pending until any application for leave to appeal is disposed of and, if leave to appeal is granted, until the appeal if disposed of; and for the purposes of this Act an application for leave to appeal shall be treated as disposed of at the expiration of the time within which it may be made, if it is not made within that time.

(5) . . .

(6) Any reference in this Act to any other enactment is a reference thereto as amended by or under any other enactment, including this Act.

CRIMINAL PROCEDURE (INSANITY) ACT 1964
(1964, c.84)

An Act to amend the form of the special verdict required by section 2 of the Trial of Lunatics Act 1883 and the procedure for determining whether an accused person is under a disability such as to constitute a bar to his being tried; to provide for an appeal against such a special verdict or a finding that the accused is under such a disability; to confer on the court of trial and the Court of Criminal Appeal further powers to making orders for admission to hospital; to empower the prosecution to put forward evidence of insanity or diminished responsibility; and for purposes connected with the matters aforesaid.

[31st July 1964]

1. Acquittal on grounds of insanity. 1883 c. 38.

The special verdict required by section 2 of the Trial of Lunatics Act 1883 (hereinafter referred to as a "special verdict") shall be that the accused is not guilty by reason of insanity; these words amend section 2 of the Trial of Lunatics Act 1883.

2.,3. . . .[Repealed by Criminal Appeal Act 1968]

4. Unfitness to plead.

(1) Where on the trial of a person the question arises (at the instance of the defence

or otherwise) whether the accused is under disability, that is to say under any disability such that apart from this Act it would constitute a bar to his being tried, the following provisions shall have effect.

(2) The court, if having regard to the nature of the supposed disability the court are of opinion that it is expedient so to do and in the interests of the accused, may postpone consideration of the said question (hereinafter referred to as "the question of fitness to be tried") until any time up to the opening of the case for the defence, and if before the question of fitness to be tried falls to be determined the jury return a verdict of acquittal on the count or each of the counts on which the accused is being tried that question shall not be determined.

(3) Subject to the foregoing subsection, the question of fitness to be tried shall be determined as soon as it arises.

(4) The question of fitness to be tried shall be determined by a jury; and—

    (a) where it falls to be determined on the arraignment of the accused, then if the trial proceeds the accused shall be tried by a jury other than that which determined that question;

    (b) where it falls to be determined at any later time it shall be determined by a separate jury or by the jury by whom the accused is being tried, as the court may direct.

(5) Where in accordance with subsection (2) or (3) of this section it is determined that the accused is under disability, the trial shall not proceed or further proceed.

(6), (7). . . [Repealed by Criminal Appeal Act 1968 and Mental Health Act 1983.]

5. Orders for admission to hospital.

(1) Where—
    (a) a special verdict is returned, or
    (b) . . .
    (c) a finding is recorded that the accused is under disability,
    (d) . . .
the court shall make an order that the accused be admitted to such hospital as may be specified by the Secretary of State.

(2) . . .

(3) The provisions in that behalf of Schedule 1 to this Act shall have effect in relation to orders for admission to hospital made under this section.

(4) Subject to the provisions of the said Schedule, if while a person is detained in pursuance of an order under paragraph (c) of subsection (1) of this section the Secretary of State, after consultation with the responsible medical officer, is satisfied that the said person can properly be tried, the Secretary of State may remit that person to prison, or to a remand centre provided under section 43 of the Prison Act 1952, for trial . . .; and on his arrival at the prison or remand centre the order under subsection (1)(c) shall cease to have effect.
In relation to persons ordered under section 2 of the Criminal Lunatics Act 1800 to be kept in custody this subsection and paragraph 2(2) of Schedule 1 to this Act shall apply as if the order were an order under subsection (1)(c) of this section.

(5) . . .

6. Evidence by prosecution of insanity of diminished responsibility.

Where on a trial for murder the accused contends—

    (a) that at the time of the alleged offence he was insane so as not to be responsible according to law for his actions; or

    (b) that at that time he was suffering from such abnormality of mind as is specified in subsection (1) of section 2 of the Homicide Act 1957 (diminished responsibility), the court shall allow the prosecution to adduce or elicit evidence tending to prove the other of those contentions, and may give directions as to the stage of the proceedings at which the prosecution may adduce such evidence.

7. ...

8.
    (1) In this Act—
        "special verdict" has the meaning assigned by section 1 of this Act,
        "under disability" has the meaning assigned by section 4 of this Act,
        "verdict of acquittal" does not include a special verdict, and any reference to acquittal shall be construed accordingly,
and other expressions used in this Act and in the [Mental Health Act 1983] have the same meanings in this Act as [in Part III of that Act]; and references to that Act in [sections 137 to 139] thereof shall include references to Schedule 1 to this Act.
    (4) This Act, except as respects courts-martial and matters arising out of proceedings in courts-martial, shall extend to England and Wales only.
    (5) ...

LAW COMMISSIONS ACT 1965
(1965, c. 22)

An Act to provide for the constitution of Commissions for the reform of the Law

[15 June 1965]

1. The Law Commission
    (1) For the purpose of promoting the reform of the law there shall be constituted in accordance with this section a body of Commissioners, to be known as the Law Commission, consisting [(except during any temporary vacancy)] of a Chairman and four other Commissioners appointed by the Lord Chancellor.
    (2) The persons appointed to be Commissioners shall be persons appearing to the Lord Chancellor to be suitably qualified by the holding of judicial office or by experience as a barrister or solicitor or as a teacher of law in a university.
    (3) A person appointed to be Commissioner shall be appointed for such term (not exceeding five years) and subject to such conditions as may be determined by the Lord Chancellor at the time of his appointment; but a Commissioner may at any time resign his office and a person who ceases to be a Commissioner shall be eligible for reappointment.
    (4) A person who holds judicial office may be appointed as a Commissioner without relinquishing that office, but shall not (unless otherwise provided by the terms of his appointment) be required to perform his duties as the holder of that office while he remains a member of the Commission.
    (5) In this section "the law" does not include the law of Scotland or any law of Northern Ireland which the Parliament of Northern Ireland has power to amend.

2. [Establishes the Scottish Law Commission]

3. Functions of the Commissions
    (1) It shall be the duty of each of the Commissions to take and keep under review all the law with which they are respectively concerned with a view to its systematic development and reform, including in particular the codification of such law, the elimination of anomalies, the repeal of obsolete and unnecessary enactments, the reduction of the number of separate enactments and generally the simplification and modernisation of the law, and for that purpose—
        (a)   to receive and consider any proposals for the reform of the law which may be made or referred to them;

(b) to prepare and submit to the Minister from time to time programmes for the examination of different branches of the law with a view to reform, including recommendations as to the agency (whether the Commission or another body) by which any such examination should be carried out;

(c) to undertake, pursuant to any such recommendations approved by the Minister, the examination of particular branches of the law and the formulation, by means of draft Bills or otherwise, of proposals for reform therein;

(d) to prepare from time to time at the request of the Minister comprehensive programmes of consolidation and statute law revision, and to undertake the preparation of draft Bills pursuant to any such programme approved by the Minister;

(e) to provide advice and information to government departments and other authorities or bodies concerned at the instance of the Government with proposals for the reform or amendment of any branch of the law;

(f) to obtain such information as to the legal systems of other countries as appears to the Commissioners likely to facilitate the performance of any of their functions.

(2) The Minister shall lay before Parliament any programmes prepared by the Commission and approved by him and any proposals for reform formulated by the Commission pursuant to such programmes.

(3) Each of the Commissions shall make an annual report to the Minister on their proceedings, and the Minister shall lay the report before Parliament with such comments (if any) as he thinks fit.

(4) In the exercise of their functions under this Act the Commissions shall act in consultation with each other.

4. Remuneraton and pensions of Commissioners.

(1) There shall be paid to the Commissioners of the Law Commission and the Scottish Law Commission, other than a Commissioner who holds high judicial office, such salaries or remuneration as may be determined, with the approval of the Treasury, by the Lord Chancellor or the Secretary of State, as the case may be.

(4) The salaries or remuneration of the Commissioners, and any sums payable to or in respect of the Commissioners under subsection (2) of this section, shall be paid out of moneys provided by Parliament.

5. ★★★★★

6. Supplemental

(1) . . .

(2) In this Act "high judicial office" has the same meaning as in the Appellate Jurisdiction Act 1876 as amended by the Appellate Jurisdiction Act 1887; and "the Minister" means, in relation to the Law Commission the Lord Chancellor and in relation to the Scottish Law Commission . . . and the Lord Advocate.

PARLIAMENTARY COMMISSIONER ACT 1967
(1967, c. 13)

An Act to make provision for the appointment and functions of a Parliamentary Commissioner for the investigation of administrative action taken on behalf of the Crown, and for purposes connected therewith. [22nd March 1967]

The Parliamentary Commissioner for Administration

1. Appointment and tenure of office.

(1) For the purpose of conducting investigations in accordance with the following

provisions of this Act there shall be appointed a Commissioner, to be known as the Parliamentary Commissioner for Administration.

(2) Her Majesty may by Letters Patent from time to time appoint a person to be the Commissioner, and any person so appointed shall (subject to subsections (3) and (3A) of this section) hold office during good behaviour.

(3) A person appointed to be the Commissioner may be relieved of office by Her Majesty at his own request, or may be removed from office by Her Majesty in consequence of Addresses from both Houses of Parliament, and shall in any case vacate office on completing the year of service in which he attains the age of sixty-five years.

[(3A) Her Majesty may declare the office of Commissioner to have been vacated if satisfied that the person appointed to be the Commissioner is incapable for medical reasons—
- (a) of performing the duties of his office; and
- (b) of requesting to be relieved of it.]

(4) . . .
(5) . . .

2. *****

3. Administrative provisions.

(1) The Commissioner may appoint such officers as he may determine with the approval of the Treasury as to numbers and conditions of service.

(2) Any function of the Commissioner under this Act may be performed by any officer of the Commissioner authorised for that purpose by the Commissioner.

(3) The expenses of the Commissioner under this Act, to such amount as may be sanctioned by the Treasury, shall be defrayed out of moneys provided by Parliament.

3A. *****

4. Departments etc subject to investigation

(1) Subject to the provisions of this section and to the notes contained in Schedule 2 to this Act, this Act applies to the government departments corporations and unincorporated bodies listed in that Schedule; and references in this Act to an authority to which this Act applies are references to any such corporation or body.

(2) Her Majesty may by Order in Council amend Schedule 2 to this Act by the alteration of any entry or note, the removal of any entry or note or the insertion of any additional entry or note.

(3) An Order in Council may only insert an entry if—
- (a) it relates—
    - (i) to a government department; or
    - (ii) to a corporation or body whose functions are exercised on behalf of the Crown; or
- (b) it relates to a corporation or body—
    - (i) which is established by virtue of Her Majesty's prerogative or by an Act of Parliament or an Order in Council or order made under an Act of Parliament or which is established in any other way by a Minister of the Crown in his capacity as a Minister or by a government department;
    - (ii) at least half of whose revenues derive directly from money provided by Parliament, a levy authorised by an enactment, a fee or charge of any other description so authorised or more than one of those sources; and
    - (iii) which is wholly or partly constituted by appointment made by Her Majesty or a Minister of the Crown or government department.

(4) No entry shall be made in respect of a corporation or body whose sole activity is, or whose main activities are, included among the activities specified in subsection (5) below.

(5) The activities mentioned in subsection (4) above are—
    (a)   the provision of education, or the provision of training otherwise than under the Industrial Training Act 1982;
    (b)   the development of curricula, the conduct of examinations or the validation of educational courses;
    (c)   the control of entry to any profession or the regulation of the conduct of members of any profession;
    (d)   the investigation of complaints by members of the public regarding the actions of any person or body, or the supervision or review or such investigations or of steps taken following them.
(6) No entry shall be made in respect of a corporation or body operating in an exclusively or predominantly commercial manner or a corporation carrying on under national ownership an industry or undertaking or part of an industry or undertaking.
(7) Any statutory instrument made by virtue of this section shall be subject to annulment in pursuance of a resolution of either House of Parliament.
(8) In this Act—
    (a)   any reference to a government department to which this Act applies includes a reference to any of the Ministers or officers of such a department; and
    (b)   any reference to an authority to which this Act applies includes a reference to any members or officers of such an authority.

5. Matters subject to investigation

(1) Subject to the provisions of this section, the Commissioner may investigate any action taken by or on behalf of a government department or other authority to which this Act applies, being action taken in the exercise of administrative functions of that department or authority, in any case where—
    (a)   a written complaint is duly made to a member of the House of Commons by a member of the public who claims to have sustained injustice in consequence of maladministration in connection with the action so taken; and
    (b)   the complaint is referred to the Commissioner, with the consent of the person who made it, by a member of that House with a request to conduct an investigation thereon.
(2) Except as hereinafter provided, the Commissioner shall not conduct an investigation under this Act in respect of any of the following matters, that is to say—
    (a)   any action in respect of which the person aggrieved has or had a right of appeal, reference or review to or before a tribunal constituted by or under any enactment or by virtue of Her Majesty's prerogative;
    (b)   any action in respect of which the person aggrieved has or had a remedy by way of proceedings in any court of law:
Provided that the Commissioner may conduct an investigation notwithstanding that the person aggrieved has or had such a right or remedy if satisfied that in the particular circumstances it is not reasonable to expect him to resort or have resorted to it.
(3) Without prejudice to subsection (2) of this section, the Commissioner shall not conduct an investigation under this Act in respect of any such action or matter as is described in Schedule 3 to this Act.
(4) Her Majesty may by Order in Council amend the said Schedule 3 so as to exclude from the provisions of that Schedule such actions or matters as may be described in the Order; and any statutory instrument made by virtue of this subsection shall be subject to annulment in pursuance of a resolution of either House of Parliament.
(5) In determining whether to initiate, continue or discontinue an investigation under this Act, the Commissioner shall, subject to the foregoing provisions of this section, act in accordance with his own discretion; and any question whether a complaint is duly made under this Act shall be determined by the Commissioner.

6. Provisions relating to complaints.

(1) A complaint under this Act may be made by any individual, or by any body of persons whether incorporated or not, not being—

    (a)   a local authority or other authority or body constituted for purposes of the public service or of local government or for the purposes of carrying on under national ownership any industry or undertaking or part of an industry or undertaking;

    (b)   any other authority or body whose members are appointed by Her Majesty or any Minister of the Crown or government department, or whose revenues consist wholly or mainly of moneys provided by Parliament.

(2) Where the person by whom a complaint might have been made under the foregoing provisions of this Act has died or is for any reason unable to act for himself, the complaint may be made by his personal representative or by a member of his family or other individual suitable to represent him; but except as aforesaid a complaint shall not be entertained under this Act unless made by the person aggrieved himself.

(3) A complaint shall not be entertained under this Act unless it is made to a member of the House of Commons not later than twelve months from the day on which the person aggrieved first had notice of the matters alleged in the complaint; but the Commissioner may conduct an investigation pursuant to a complaint not made within that period if he considers that there are special circumstances which make it proper to do so.

(4) [Except as provided in sub-section (5) below] A complaint shall not be entertained under this Act unless the person aggrieved is resident in the United Kingdom (or, if he is dead, was so resident at the time of his death) or the complaint relates to action taken in relation to him while he was present in the United Kingdom or on an installation in a designated area within the meaning of the Continental Shelf Act 1964 or on a ship registered in the United Kingdom or an aircraft so registered, or in relation to rights or obligations which accrued or arose in the United Kingdom or on such an installation, ship or aircraft.

[(5) A complaint may be entertained under this Act in circumstances not falling within subsection (4) above where—

    (a)   the complaint relates to action taken in any country or territory outside the United Kingdom by an officer (not being an honorary consular officer) in the exercise of a consular function on behalf of the Government of the United Kingdom; and

    (b)   the person aggrieved is a citizen of the United Kingdom and Colonies who, under section 2 of the Immigration Act 1971, has the right of abode in the United Kingdom.]

7. Procedure in respect of investigations.

(1) Where any Commissioner proposes to conduct an investigation pursuant to a complaint under this Act, he shall afford to the principal officer of the department or authority concerned, and to any other person who is alleged in the complaint to have taken or authorised the action complained of, an opportunity to comment on any allegations contained in the complaint.

(2) Every such investigation shall be conducted in private, but except as aforesaid the procedure for conducting an investigation shall be such as the Commissioner considers appropriate in the circumstances of the case; and without prejudice to the generality of the foregoing provision the Commissioner may obtain information from such persons and in such manner, and make such inquiries, as he thinks fit, and may determine whether any person may be represented, by counsel or solicitor or otherwise, in the investigation.

(3) The Commissioner may, if he thinks fit, pay to the person by whom the complaint was made and to any other person who attends or furnishes information for the purposes of an investigation under this Act—

(a) sums in respect of expenses properly incurred by them;
(b) allowances by way of compensation for the loss of their time,
in accordance with such scales and subject to such conditions as may be determined by the Treasury.

(4) The conduct of an investigation under this Act shall not affect any action taken by the department or authority concerned, or any power or duty of that department or authority to take further action with respect to any matters subject to the investigation; but where the person aggrieved has been removed from the United Kingdom under any Order in force under the Aliens Restriction Acts 1914 and 1919 or under the Commonwealth Immigrants Act 1962, he shall, if the Commissioner so directs, be permitted to re-enter and remain in the United Kingdom, subject to such conditions as the Secretary of State may direct, for the purposes of the investigation.

8. Evidence

(1) For the purposes of an investigation under this Act the Commissioner may require any Minister, officer or member of the department or authority concerned or any other person who in his opinion is able to furnish information or produce documents relevant to the investigation to furnish any such information or produce any such document.

(2) For the purposes of any such investigation the Commissioner shall have the same powers as the Court in respect of the attendance and examination of witnesses (including the administration of oaths or affirmations and the examination of witnesses abroad) and in respect of the production of documents.

(3) No obligation to maintain secrecy or other restriction upon the disclosure of information obtained by or furnished to persons in Her Majesty's service, whether imposed by any enactment or by any rule of law, shall apply to the disclosure of information for the purposes of an investigation under this Act; and the Crown shall not be entitled in relation to any such investigation to any such privilege in respect of the production of documents or the giving of evidence as is allowed by law in legal proceedings.

(4) No person shall be required or authorised by virtue of this Act to furnish any information or answer any question relating to proceedings of the Cabinet or of any committee of the Cabinet or to produce so much of any document as relates to such proceedings; and for the purposes of this subsection a certificate issued by the Secretary of the Cabinet with the approval of the Prime Minister and certifying that any information, question, document or part of a document so relates shall be conclusive.

(5) Subject to subsection (3) of this section, no person shall be compelled for the purposes of an investigation under this Act to give any evidence or produce any document which he could not be compelled to give or produce in [civil] proceedings before the Court.

9. Obstruction and contempt.

(1) If any person without lawful excuse obstructs the Commissioner or any officer of any Commissioner in the performance of his functions under this Act, or is guilty of any which, if that investigation were a proceeding in the Court, would constitute contempt of court, the Commissioner may certify the offence to the Court.

(2) Where an offence is certified under this section, the Court may inquire into the matter and, after hearing any witnesses who may be produced against or on behalf of the person charged with the offence, and after hearing any statement that may be offered in defence, deal with him in any manner in which the Court could deal with him if he had committed the like offence in relation to the Court.

(3) Nothing in this section shall be construed as applying to the taking of any such action as is mentioned in subsection (4) of section 7 of this Act.

Parliamentary Commissioner Act 1967

10. Reports by Commissioner

(1) In any case where the Commissioner conducts an investigation under this Act or decides not to conduct such an investigation, he shall send to the member of the House of Commons by whom the request for investigation was made (or if he is no longer a member of that House, to such member or that House as the Commissioner thinks appropriate) a report of the results of the investigation or, as the case may be, a statement of his reasons for not conducting an investigation.

(2) In any case where the Commissioner conducts an investigation under this Act, he shall also send a report of the results of the investigation to the principal officer of the department or authority concerned and to any other person who is alleged in the relevant complaint to have taken or authorised the action complained of.

(3) If, after conducting an investigation under this Act, it appears to the Commissioner that injustice has been caused to the person aggrieved in consequence of maladministration and that the injustice has not been, or will not be, remedied, he may, if he thinks fit, lay before each House of Parliament a special report upon the case.

(4) The Commissioner shall annually lay before each House of Parliament a general report on the performance of his functions under this Act and may from time to time lay before each House of Parliament such other reports with respect to those functions as he thinks fit.

(5) For the purposes of the law of defamation, any such publication as is hereinafter mentioned shall be absolutely privileged, that is to say—

    (a) the publication of any matter by the Commissioner in making a report to either House of Parliament for the purposes of this Act;

    (b) the publication of any matter by a member of the House of Commons in communicating with the Commissioner or his officers for those purposes or by the Commissioner or his officers in communicating with such a member for those purposes;

    (c) the publication by such a member to the person by whom a complaint was made under this Act of a report or statement sent to the member in respect of this complaint in pursuance of subsection (1) of this section;

    (d) the publication by the Commissioner to such a person as is mentioned in subsection (2) of this section of a report sent to that person in pursuance of that subsection.

11. Provision for secrecy of information.

(1) It is hereby declared that the Commissioner and his officers hold office under Her Majesty within the meaning of the Official Secrets Act 1911.

(2) Information obtained by the Commissioner or his officers in the course of or for the purposes of an investigation under this Act shall not be disclosed except—

    (a) for the purposes of the investigation and of any report to be made thereon under this Act;

    (b) for the purposes of any proceedings for an offence [under the Official Secrets Acts 1911 to 1989] alleged to have been committed in respect of information obtained by the Commissioner or any of his officers by virtue of this Act or for an offence of perjury alleged to have been committed in the course of an investigation under this Act or for the purposes of an inquiry with a view to the taking of such proceedings; or

    (c) for the purposes of any proceedings under section 9 of this Act;

    (2A) *****

and the Commissioner and his officers shall not be called upon to give evidence in any proceedings (other than such proceedings as aforesaid) of matters coming to his or their knowledge in the course of an investigation under this Act.

(3) A Minister of the Crown may give notice in writing to the Commissioner, with respect to any document or information specified in the notice, or any class of documents

or information so specified, that in the opinion of the Minister the disclosure of that document or information, or of documents or information of that class, would be prejudicial to the safety of the State or otherwise contrary to the public interest; and where such a notice is given nothing in this Act shall be construed as authorising or requiring the Commissioner or any officer of the Commissioner to communicate to any person or for any purpose any document or information specified in the notice, or any document or information of a class so specified.

(4) The references in this section to a Minister of the Crown include references to the Commissioners of Customs and Excise and the Commissioners of Inland Revenue.

11A. *****

Supplemental

12. Interpretation

(1) In this Act the following expressions have the meanings hereby respectively assigned to them, that is to say—

"action" includes failure to act, and other expressions connoting action shall be construed accordingly;

"the Commissioner" means the Parliamentary Commissioner for Administration;

"the Court" means, in relation to England and Wales the High Court, in relation to Scotland the Court of Session, and in relation to Northern Ireland the High Court of Northern Ireland;

"enactment" includes an enactment of the Parliament of Northern Ireland, and any instrument made by virtue of an enactment;

"officer" includes employee;

"person aggrieved" means the person who claims or is alleged to have sustained such injustice as is mentioned in section 5(1)(a) of this Act;

"tribunal" includes the person constituting a tribunal consisting of one person.

(2) *****

(3) It is hereby declared that nothing in this Act authorises or requires the Commissioner to question the merits of a decision taken without maladministration by a government department or other authority in the exercise of a discretion vested in that department or authority.

13., 14. *****

Schedule 2

Note—Schedule 2 lists all the main government departments and many public bodies deriving their authority from government departments.

Section 5

SCHEDULE 3
Matters Not Subject to Investigation

1. Action taken in matters certified by a Secretary of State or other Minister of the Crown to affect relations or dealings between the Government of the United Kingdom and any other Government or any international organisation of States or Governments.

2. Action taken, in any country or territory outside the United Kingdom, by or on behalf of any officer representing or acting under the authority of Her Majesty in respect of the United Kingdom, or any other officer of the Government of the United Kingdom, (other than action which is taken by an officer (not being an honorary consular officer) in the exercise of a consular function on behalf of the Government of the United Kingdom).

3. Action taken in connection with the administration of the government of any country or territory outside the United Kingdom which forms part of Her Majesty's dominions or in which Her Majesty has jurisdiction.

4. Action taken by the Secretary of State under the Extradition Act 1870 or the Fugitive Offenders Act 1881.

5. Action taken by or with the authority of the Secretary of State for the purposes of investigating crime or of protecting the security of the State, including action so taken with respect to passports.

6. The commencement or conduct of civil or criminal proceedings before any court of law in the United Kingdom, of proceedings at any place under the Naval Discipline Act 1957, the Army Act 1955 or the Air Force Act 1955, or of proceedings before any international court or tribunal.

7. Any exercise of the prerogative of mercy or of the power of a Secretary of State to make a reference in respect of any person to the Court of Appeal, the High Court of Justiciary or the Courts-Martial Appeal Court.

8. Action taken on behalf of the Minister of Health or the Secretary of State by a Regional Hospital Board, Board of Governors of a Teaching Hospital, Hospital Management Committee or Board of Management, or by the Public Health Laboratory Service Board.

9. Action taken in matters relating to contractual or other commercial transactions, whether within the United Kingdom or elsewhere, being transactions of a government department or authority to which this Act applies or of any such authority or body as is mentioned in paragraph (a) or (b) of subsection (1) of section 6 of this Act and not being transactions for or relating to—

    (a) the acquisition of land compulsorily or in circumstances in which it could be acquired compulsorily.

    (b) the disposal as surplus of land acquired compulsorily or in such circumstances as aforesaid.

10. Action taken in respect of appointments or removals, pay, discipline, superannuation or other personnel matters, in relation to—

    (a) service in any of the armed forces of the Crown, including reserve and auxiliary and cadet forces;

    (b) service in any office or employment under the Crown or under any authority listed in Schedule 2 to this Act; or

    (c) service in any office or employment, or under any contract for services, in respect of which power to take action, or to determine or approve the action to be taken, in such matters is vested in Her Majesty, any Minister of the Crown or any such authority as aforesaid.

11. The grant of honours, awards or privileges within the gift of the Crown, including the grant of Royal Charters.

CRIMINAL JUSTICE ACT 1967
(1967, c. 80)

An Act to amend the law relating to the proceedings of criminal courts, including the law relating to evidence, and to the qualification of jurors, in such proceedings and to appeals in criminal cases; to reform existing methods and provide new methods of dealing with offenders; to make further provision for the treatment of offenders, the management of prisons and other institutions and the arrest of offenders unlawfully at large; to make further provisions with respect to legal aid and advice in criminal proceedings; to amend the law relating to firearms and ammunition; to alter the penalties which may be imposed for certain offences; and for connected purposes [27 July 1967]

Part I
Criminal Procedure, etc

1.–6. **[Repealed by Magistrates' Courts Act 1980]**

7. Signature of depositions

An examining justice who signs a certificate authenticating one or more depositions or statements tendered under [section 102 of the Magistrates' Courts Act 1980] shall be treated for the purposes of section 13(3)(c) of the Criminal Justice Act 1925 (requirement that depositions read at the trial must have been signed by an examining justice) as signing that deposition or statement or each of those depositions and statements.

Miscellaneous provisions as to evidence, procedure and trial

8. Proof of criminal intent

A court or jury, in determining whether a person has committed an offence,—

    (a) shall not be bound in law to infer that he intended or foresaw a result of his actions by reason only of its being a natural and probable consequence of those actions; but

    (b) shall decide whether he did intend or foresee that result by reference to all the evidence, drawing such inferences from the evidence as appear proper in the circumstances.

9. Proof by written statement

(1) In any criminal proceedings, other than committal proceedings, a written statement by any person shall, if such of the conditions mentioned in the next following subsection as are applicable are satisfied, be admissible as evidence to the like extent as oral evidence to the like effect by that person.

(2) The said conditions are—

    (a) the statement purports to be signed by the person who made it;

    (b) the statement contains a declaration by that person to the effect that it is true to the best of his knowledge and belief and that he made the statement knowing that, if it were tendered in evidence, he would be liable to prosecution if he wilfully stated in it anything which he knew to be false or did not believe to be true;

    (c) before the hearing at which the statement is tendered in evidence, a copy of the statement is served, by or on behalf of the party proposing to tender it, on each of the other parties to the proceedings; and

    (d) none of the other parties or their solicitors, within seven days from the service of the copy of the statement, serves a notice on the party so proposing objecting to the statement being tendered in evidence under this section:

Provided that the conditions mentioned in paragraphs (c) and (d) of this subsection shall not apply if the parties agree before or during the hearing that the statement shall be so tendered.

(3) The following provisions shall also have effect in relation to any written statement tendered in evidence under this section, that is to say—

    (a) if the statement is made by a person under the age of twenty-one, it shall give his age;

    (b) if it is made by a person who cannot read it, it shall be read to him before he signs it and shall be accompanied by a declaration by the person who so read the statement to the effect that it was so read; and

    (c) if it refers to any other document as an exhibit, the copy served on any other party to the proceedings under paragraph (c) of the last foregoing subsection shall be accompanied by a copy of that document or by such information as may be necessary in order to enable the party on whom it is served to inspect that document or a copy thereof.

(4) Notwithstanding that a written statement made by any person may be admissible as evidence by virtue of this section—

    (a)   the party by whom or on whose behalf a copy of the statement was served may call that person to give evidence; and

    (b)   the court may, of its own motion or on the application of any party to the proceedings, require that person to attend before the court and give evidence.

(5) An application under paragraph (b) of the last foregoing subsection to a court other than a magistrates' court may be made before the hearing and on any such application the powers of the court shall be exercisable [by a puisne judge of the High Court, a Circuit judge or Recorder sitting alone.]

(6) So much of any statement as is admitted in evidence by virtue of this section shall, unless the court otherwise directs, be read aloud at the hearing and where the court so directs an account shall be given orally of so much of any statement as is not read aloud.

(7) Any document or object referred to as an exhibit and identified in a written statement tendered in evidence under this section shall be treated as if it had been produced as an exhibit and identified in court by the maker of the statement.

(8) A document required by this section to be served on any person may be served—

    (a)   by delivering it to him or to his solicitor; or

    (b)   by addressing it to him and leaving it at his usual or last known place of abode or place of business or by addressing it to his solicitor and leaving it at his office; or

    (c)   by sending it in a registered letter or by the recorded delivery service addressed to him at his usual or last known place of abode or place of business or addressed to his solicitor at his office; or

    (d)   in the case of a body corporate, by delivering it to the secretary or clerk of the body at its registered or principal office or sending it in a registered letter or by the recorded delivery service addressed to the secretary or clerk of that body at that office.

10. Proof by formal admission

(1) Subject to the provisions of this section, any fact of which oral evidence may be given in any criminal proceedings may be admitted for the purpose of those proceedings by or on behalf of the prosecutor or defendant, and the admission by any party of any such fact under this section shall as against that party be conclusive evidence in those proceedings of the fact admitted.

(2) An admission under this section—

    (a)   may be made before or at the proceedings;

    (b)   if made otherwise than in court, shall be in writing;

    (c)   if made in writing by an individual, shall purport to be signed by the person making it and, if so made by a body corporate, shall purport to be signed by a director or manager, or the secretary or clerk, or some other similar officer of the body corporate;

    (d)   if made on behalf of a defendant who is an individual, shall be made by his counsel or solicitor;

    (e)   if made at any stage before the trial by a defendant who is an individual, must be approved by his counsel or solicitor (whether at the time it was made or subsequently) before or at the proceedings in question.

(3) An admission under this section for the purpose of proceedings relating to any matter shall be treated as an admission for the purpose of any subsequent criminal proceedings relating to that matter (including any appeal or retrial).

(4) An admission under this section may with the leave of the court be withdrawn

in the proceedings for the purpose of which it is made or any subsequent criminal proceedings relating to the same matter.

11. Notice of alibi

(1) On a trial on indictment the defendant shall not without the leave of the court adduce evidence in support of an alibi unless, before the end of the prescribed period, he gives notice of particulars of the alibi.

(2) Without prejudice to the foregoing subsection, on any such trial the defendant shall not without the leave of the court call any other person to give such evidence unless—

    (a) the notice under that subseciton includes the name and address of the witness or, if the name or address is not known to the defendant at the time he gives the notice, any information in his possession which might be of material assitance in finding the witness;

    (b) if the name or the address is not included in that notice, the court is satisfied that the defendant, before giving the notice, took and thereafter continued to take all reasonable steps to secure that the name or address would be ascertained;

    (c) if the name or the address is not included in that notice, but the defendant subsequently discovers the name or address or receives other information which might be of material assistance in finding the witness, he forthwith gives notice of the name, address or other information, as the case may be; and

    (d) if the defendant is notified by or on behalf of the prosecutor that the witness has not been traced by the name or at the address given, he forthwith gives notice of any such information which is then in his possession or, on subsequently receiving any such information, forthwith gives notice of it.

(3) The court shall not refuse leave under this section if it appears to the court that the defendant was not informed in accordance with rules under [section 144 of the Magistrates' Courts Act 1980] (rules of procedure for magistrates' courts) of the requirements of this section.

(4) Any evidence tendered to disprove an alibi may, subject to any directions by the court as to the time it is to be given, be given before or after evidence is given in support of the alibi.

(5) Any notice purporting to be given under this section on behalf of the defendant by his solicitor shall, unless the contrary is proved, be deemed to be given with the authority of the defendant.

(6) A notice under subsection (1) of this section shall either be given in court during, or at the end of, the proceedings before the examining justices or be given in writing to the solicitor for the prosecutor, and a notice under paragraph (c) or (d) of subsection (2) of this section shall be given in writing to that solicitor.

(7) A notice required by this section to be given to the solicitor for the prosecutor may be given by delivering it to him, or by leaving it at his office, or by sending it in a registered letter or by the recorded delivery service addressed to him at his office.

(8) In this section—

"evidence in support of an alibi" means evidence tending to show that by reason of the presence of the defendant at a particular place or in a particular area at a particular time he was not, or was unlikely to have been, at the place where the offence is alleged to have been committed at the time of its alleged commission.

"the prescribed period" means the period of seven days from the end of the proceedings before the examining justices [or where a notice of transfer has been given under section 4 of the Criminal Justice Act 1987, of the giving of that notice].

(9) In computing the said period a Sunday, Christmas Day, Good Friday, a day

Criminal Justice Act 1967

which is a bank holiday under the Bank Holidays Act 1871 in England and Wales or a day appointed for public thanksgiving or mourning shall be disregarded.

12. *****

13.–16. ...

17. Entry of verdict of not guilty by order of a judge
Where a defendant arraigned on an indictment or inquisition pleads not guilty and the prosecutor proposes to offer no evidence against him, the court before which the defendant is arraigned may, if it thinks fit, order that a verdict of not guilty shall be recorded without the defendant being given in charge to a jury, and the verdict shall have the same effect as if the defendant had been tried and acquitted on the verdict of a jury.

18.–19. ...

20. *****

21. ...

22. Extension of power of High Court to grant, or vary conditions of, bail
(1) Where [a magistrates' court] withholds bail in criminal proceedings or imposes conditions in granting bail in criminal proceedings, the High Court may grant bail or vary the conditions.

(2) Where the High Court grants a person bail under this section it may direct him to appear at a time and place which the [magistrates' courts] could have directed and the recognizance of any surety shall be conditioned accordingly.]

(3) Subsection . . ., (4) and (6) of section 37 of the Criminal Justice Act 1948 (ancillary provisions as to persons [granted] bail by the High Court under that section and the currency of sentence in the case of persons so admitted) shall apply in relation to the powers conferred by this section and persons [granted] bail in pursuance of those powers as it applies in relation to the powers conferred by that section and persons admitted to bail in pursuance of those powers, except that the said subsection (6) shall not apply in relation to a person [granted] bail pending an appeal from a magistrates' court to [the Crown Court].

(4) In this section ["bail in criminal proceedings" and "vary" have the same meanings as they have in the Bail Act 1976].

(5) The powers conferred on the High Court by this section shall be in substitution for the powers so conferred by paragraphs (a), (b) and (c) of section 37(1) of the Criminal Justice Act 1948, but except as aforesaid this section shall not prejudice any powers of the High Court to admit or direct the admission of persons to bail.

PART II
POWERS OF COURTS TO DEAL WITH OFFENDERS
Miscellaneous

56. Committal for sentence for offences tried summarily
[(1) Where a magistrates' court ("the committing court") commits a person in custody or on bail to the Crown Court under any enactment to which this section applies to be sentenced or otherwise dealt with in respect of an offence ("the relevant offence"), the committing court—

  (a) if the relevant offence is an indictable offence, may also commit him, in custody or on bail as the case may require, to the Crown Court to be dealt with in respect of any other offence whatsoever in respect of which the committing court has power to deal with him (being an offence of which he has been convicted by that or any other court); or

(b)   if the relevant offence is a summary offence, may commit him, as aforesaid, to the Crown Court to be dealt with in respect of—
(i)   any other offence of which the committing court has convicted him, being either an offence punishable with imprisonment or an offence in respect of which the committing court has a power or duty to order him to be disqualified under [section 93 of the Road Traffic Act 1972, or section 19 of the Transport Act 1981 or sections 34 to 36 of the Road Traffic Offenders Act 1988] (disqualification for certain motoring offences); or
(ii)   any suspended sentence in respect of which the committing court has under section 24(1) of the Powers of Criminal Courts Act 1973 power to deal with him.]
(2) The enactments to which this section applies are the Vagrancy Act 1824 (incorrigible rogues), [[sections 37 and 38 of the Magistrates' Courts Act 1980] (committal for sentence) and section 62(6) of this Act [section 8(6) of the Powers of Criminal Courts Act 1973 (probationer convicted of subsequent offence) and section 24(2) of that Act and paragraph 2(2)(a) of Schedule 9 to the Criminal Law Act 1977 (committal to be dealt with in respect of a wholly or party suspended sentence).]
(3) The power of a magistrates' court under section 8(4) of the Criminal Justice Act 1948 to commit to a [Crown Court] a person subject to a probation order or an order for conditional discharge who has been convicted of an offence by the magistrates' court shall be exercisable notwithstanding that the magistrates' court has not dealt with him in respect of that offence; . . .
(4) . . .
(5) Where under subsection (1) of this section a magistrates' court commits a person to be dealt with by a [Crown Court] in respect of an offence, the latter court may after inquiring into the circumstances of the case deal with him in any way in which the magistrates' court might have dealt with him, and, without prejudice to the foregoing provision, where under that subsection or any enactment to which this section applies a magistrates' court so commits a person, any duty or power which, apart from this subsection, would fall to be discharged or exercised by the magistrates' court shall not be discharged or exercised by that court but shall instead be discharged or may instead be exercised by the [Crown Court].
(6) Any duty imposed or power conferred by virtue of the last foregoing subsection on a [Crown Court], in a case where an offender has been committed to the court under [section 37 of the Magistrates' Courts Act 1980], shall be discharged or may be exercised by the court notwithstanding that it sentences him to borstal training and in that or any other case shall be discharged or may be exercised notwithstanding anything in any other enactment and, in particular, in [sections 34 to 36 and 44 of the Road Traffic Offenders Act 1988] [or section 19 of the Transport Act 1981].
(7)–(12) . . .
(13) In this section—
"disqualified" means disqualified for holding or obtaining a licence under Part II of the Road Traffic Act 1960 [or Part III of the Road Traffic Act 1972, or section 19 of the Transport Act 1981 or Part III of the Road Traffic Act 1988];
. . .

ADMINISTRATION OF JUSTICE ACT 1968
(1968, c. 5)

An Act to make provision with respect to the maximum numbers of Lords of Appeal in Ordinary and certain other judges   [15th February 1968]

1. Maximum numbers of Lords of Appeal in Ordinary and certain other judges.
(1) The maximum number—

Criminal Appeal Act 1968

    (a)   of Lords of Appeal in Ordinary shall be eleven;
    (b)   in England and Wales—
        (i)   of ordinary judges of the Court of Appeal shall be [twenty-eight];
        (ii)   of puisne judges of the High Court shall be [eighty-five];
        (iii)   ...
    (c)   in Scotland, of judges of the Court of Session shall be [twenty-two];
    (d)   in Northern Ireland, of puisne judges of the High Court shall be [five].

CRIMINAL APPEAL ACT 1968
(1968, c. 19)

An Act to consolidate certain enactments relating to appeals in criminal cases to the criminal division of the Court of Appeal, and thence to the House of Lords.

[8th May 1968]

PART I
APPEAL TO COURT OF APPEAL IN CRIMINAL CASES
Appeal against conviction on indictment

1. Right of appeal.
[Subject to subsection (3) below] a person convicted of an offence on indictment may appeal to the Court of Appeal against his conviction.
    (2) The appeal may be—
        (a)   on any ground which involves a question of law alone; and
        (b)   with the leave of the Court of Appeal, on any ground which involves a question of fact alone, or a question of mixed law and fact, or on any other ground which appears to the Court of Appeal to be a sufficient ground of appeal;
but if the judge of the court of trial grants a certificate that the case is fit for appeal on a ground which involves a question of fact, or a question of mixed law and fact, an appeal lies under this section without the leave of the Court of Appeal.
    [(3) Where a person is convicted before the Crown Court of a scheduled offence it shall not be open to him to appeal to the Court of Appeal against the conviction on the ground that the decision of the court which committed him for trial as to the value involved was mistaken.
    (4) In subsection (3) above "scheduled offence" and "the value involved" have the same meanings as they have in section 22 of the Magistrates' Courts Act 1980 (certain offences against property to be tried summarily if value of property or damage is small).]

2. Grounds for allowing appeal under s. 1.
    (1) Except as provided by this Act, the Court of Appeal shall allow an appeal against conviction if they think—
        (a)   that the [conviction] should be set aside on the ground that under all the circumstances of the case it is unsafe or unsatisfactory; or
        (b)   that the judgment of the court of trial should be set aside on the ground of a wrong decision of any question of law; or
        (c)   that there was a material irregularity in the course of the trial,
and in any other case shall dismiss the appeal;
Provided that the Court may, notwithstanding that they are of opinion that the point raised in the appeal might be decided in favour of the appellant, dismiss the appeal if they consider that no miscarriage of justice has actually occurred.
    (2) In the case of an appeal against conviction the Court shall, if they allow the appeal, quash the conviction.
    (3) An order of the Court of Appeal quashing a conviction shall, except when under

section 7 below the appellant is ordered to be retried, operate as a direction to the court of trial to enter, instead of the record of conviction, a judgment and verdict of acquittal.

3. Power to substitute conviction of alternative offence.

(1) This section applies on an appeal against conviction, where the appellant has been convicted of an offence and the jury could on the indictment have found him guilty of some other offence, and on the finding of the jury it appears to the Court of Appeal that the jury must have been satisfied of facts which proved him guilty of the other offence.

(2) The Court may, instead of allowing or dismissing the appeal, substitute for the verdict found by the jury a verdict of guilty of the other offence, and pass such sentence in substitution for the sentence passed at the trial as may be authorised by law for the other offence, not being a sentence of greater severity.

4. Sentence when appeal allowed on part of an indictment.

(1) This section applies where, on an appeal against conviction on an indictment containing two or more counts, the Court of Appeal allow the appeal in respect of part of the indictment.

(2) Except as provided by subsection (3) below, the Court may in respect of any count on which the appellant remains convicted pass such sentence, in substitution for any sentence passed thereon at the trial, as they think proper and is authorised by law for the offence of which he remains convicted on that count.

(3) The Court shall not under this section pass any sentence such that the appellant's sentence on the indictment as a whole will, in consequence of the appeal, be of greater severity than the sentence (taken as a whole) which was passed at the trial for all offences of which he was convicted on the indictment.

5. Disposal of appeal against conviction on special verdict.

(1) This section applies on an appeal against conviction by a person in whose case the jury have found a special verdict.

(2) If the Court of Appeal consider that a wrong conclusion has been arrived at by the court of trial on the effect of the jury's verdict they may, instead of allowing the appeal, order such conclusion to be recorded as appears to them to be in law required by the verdict, and pass such sentence in substitution for the sentence passed at the trial as may be authorised by law.

6. Substitution of finding of insanity or unfitness to plead.

(1) Where, on an appeal against conviction, the Court of Appeal are of opinion—

    (a) that the proper verdict would have been one of not guilty by reason of insanity; or

    (b) that the case is not one where there should have been a verdict of acquittal, but that there should have been a finding that the accused was under disability,
the Court shall make an order that the appellant be admitted to such hospital as may be specified by the Secretary of State.

(2) Schedule 1 to this Act applies with respect to the consequences and effect of an order made by the Court of Appeal under this section.

(3) On making an order under this section in the case of any person, the Court of Appeal may give such directions as they think fit for his conveyance to a place of safety and his detention there pending his admission to hospital within the relevant period specified by Schedule 1 to this Act.

(4) In [section 47 of the Mental Health Act 1983] (which relates to the removal to hospital of persons serving sentences of imprisonment and is applied by [subsection (5)] of the section to persons in other forms of detention) references to a person serving

a sentence of imprisonment shall be construed as not including references to a person subject to an order of the Court of Appeal under this section.

Retrial

7. Power to order retrial.

(1) Where the Court of Appeal allow an appeal against conviction . . . and it appears to the Court that the interests of justice so require, they may order the appellant to be retried.

(2) A person shall not under this section be ordered to be retried for any offence other than—

    (a) the offence of which he was convicted at the original trial and in respect of which his appeal is allowed as mentioned in subsection (1) above;

    (b) an offence of which he could have been convicted at the original trial on an indictment for the first-mentioned offence; or

    (c) an offence charged in an alternative count of the indictment in respect of which the jury were discharged from giving a verdict in consequence of convicting him of the first-mentioned offence.

8. Supplementary provisions as to retrial.

(1) A person who is to be retried for an offence in pursuance of an order under section 7 of this Act shall be tried on a fresh indictment preferred by direction of the Court of Appeal, . . . [but after the end of two months from the date of the order for his retrial he may not be arraigned on an indictment preferred in pursuance of such a direction unless the Court of Appeal give leave.]

[(1A) Where a person has been ordered to be retried but may not be arraigned without leave, he may apply to the Court of Appeal to set aside the order for retrial and to direct the court of trial to enter a judgment and verdict of acquittal of the offence for which he was ordered to be retried.

(1B) On an application under subsection (1) or (1A) above the Court of Appeal shall have power—

    (a) to grant leave to arraign; or

    (b) to direct the entry of a judgment and verdict of acquittal,

but shall not give leave to arraign unless they are satisfied—

    (i) that the prosecution has acted with all due expedition; and

    (ii) that there is a good and sufficient cause for a retrial in spite of the lapse of time since the order under section 7 of this Act was made.]

(2) The Court of Appeal may, on ordering a retrial, make such orders as appear to them to be necessary or expedient—

    (a) for the custody or [release on bail] of the person ordered to be retried pending his retrial; or

    (b) for the retention pending the retrial of any property or money forfeited, restored or paid by virtue of the original conviction or any order made on that conviction.

(3) If the person ordered to be retried was, immediately before the determination of his appeal, liable to be detained in pursuance of an order or direction under Part V of the Mental Health Act 1959, [or under Part III of the Mental Health Act 1983 (other than under section 35, 36 or 38 of that Act)],—

    (a) that order or direction shall continue in force pending the retrial as if the appeal had not been allowed; and

    (b) any order made by the Court of Appeal under this seciton for his custody or [release on] bail shall have effect subject to the said order or direction.

(3A) If the person ordered to be retried was, immediately before the determination of his appeal, liable to be detained in pursuance of a remand under [section 36 of the Mental Health Act 1983] or an interim hospital order under [section 38 of that Act], the Court of Appeal may, if they think fit, order that he shall continue to be detained in a hospital or mental nursing home, and in that event [Part III of that Act] shall apply as if he had been ordered under this section to be kept in custody pending his retrial and were detained in pursuance of a transfer direction together with a restriction direction.]

(4) Schedule 2 to this Act has effect with respect to the procedure in the case of a person ordered to be retried, the sentence which may be passed if the retrial results in his conviction and the order for costs which may be made if he is acquitted.

Appeal against sentence

9. Appeal against sentence following conviction on indictment.
(1) A person who has been convicted of an offence on indictment may appeal to the Court of Appeal against any sentence (not being a sentence fixed by law) passed on him for the offence, whether passed on his conviction or in subsequent proceedings.

[(2) A person who on conviction on indictment has also been convicted of a summary offence under section 41 of the Criminal Justice Act 1988 (power of Crown Court to deal with summary offence where person committed for either way offence) may appeal to the Court of Appeal against any sentence passed on him for the summary offence (whether on his conviction or in subsequent proceedings) under subsection (7) of that section.]

10. Appeal against sentence in other cases dealt with at assizes or quarter sessions.
(1) This section has effect for providing rights of appeal against sentence when a person is dealt with by [the Crown Court] (otherwise than on appeal from a magistrates' court) for an offence of which he was not convicted on indictment.

(2) The proceedings from which an appeal against sentence lies under this section are those where an offender convicted of an offence by a magistrates' court—

    (a) is committed by the court to be dealt with for his offence [before the Crown Court]; or

    (b) having been made the subject of a probation order [a community service order] or an order for conditional discharge [or an attendance centre order] or given a [wholly or partly] suspended sentence, appears or is brought before [the Crown Court] to be further dealt with for his offence.

(3) An offender dealt with for an offence [before the Crown Court] in a proceedings to which subsection (2) of this section applies may appeal to the Court of Appeal against sentence in any of the following cases:—

    (a) where either for that offence alone or for that offence and other offences for which sentence is passed in the same proceedings, he is sentenced to imprisonment [or to youth custody under section 6 of the Criminal Justice Act 1982] for a term of six months or more; or

    (b) where the sentence is one which the court convicting him had not power to pass; or

    (c) where the court in dealing with him for the offence makes in respect of him—

        (i) a recommendation for deportation; or

        (ii) an order disqualifying him for holding or obtaining a licence to drive a motor vehicle under Part II of the Road Traffic Act 1960; or

        (iii) an order under [section 23 of the Powers of Criminal Courts Act 1973] (orders as to existing suspended sentence when person subject to the sentence is again convicted).

[or

(d) where the court makes in respect of him an order under section 12 of the Criminal Justice Act 1961 (return to borstal institution on re-conviction).]

(4) For purposes of subsection (3)(a) of this section [and section 11 of this Act], any two or more sentences are to be treated as passed in the same proceeding if—

(a) they are passed on the same day; or

(b) they are passed on different days but the court in passing any one of them states that it is treating that one together with the other or others as substantially one sentence;

and consecutive terms of imprisonment and terms which are wholly or partly concurrent are to be treated as a single term.

[(5) If by virtue of an order made under section 14 of the Criminal Justice Act 1982, the term of 4 months specified in section 4 of that Act is increased to a term of 6 months or more, subsection (3)(a) above shall have effect, for so long as the term so specified is 6 months or more, as if after the word "more" there were inserted the words "or an order for his detention in a detention centre for a term of 6 months or more has been made under section 4 of the Criminal Justice Act 1982.]

11. Supplementary provisions as to appeal against sentence

(1) [Subject to subsection (1A) below, an] appeal against sentence, whether under section 9 or under section 10 of this Act, lies only with the leave of the Court of Appeal.

[(1A) If the judge who passed the sentence grants a certificate that the case is fit for appeal under section 9 or 10 of this Act, an appeal lies under this section without the leave of the Court of Appeal.]

(2) Where [the Crown Court], in dealing with an offender either on his conviction on indictment or in a proceeding to which section 10(2) of this Act applies, has passed on him two or more sentences in the same proceeding (which expression has the same meaning in this subsection as it has for the purposes of section 10), being sentences against which an appeal lies under section 9[1] or section 10, an appeal or application for leave to appeal against any one of those sentences shall be treated as an appeal or application in respect of both or all of them.

[(2A) Where following conviction on indictment a person has been convicted under section 41 of the Criminal Justice Act 1988 of a summary offence an appeal or application for leave to appeal against any sentence for the offence triable either way shall be treated also as an appeal or application in respect of any sentence for the summary offence and an appeal or application for leave to appeal against any sentence for the summary offence shall be treated also as an appeal or application in respect of the offence triable either way.

(2B) If the appellant or applicant was convicted on indictment of two or more offences triable either way, the references to the offence triable either way in subsection (2A) above are to be construed, in relation to any summary offence of which he was convicted under section 41 of the Criminal Justice Act 1988 following the conviction on indictment, as references to the offence triable either way specified in the notice relating to that summary offence which was given under subsection (2) of that section.]

(3) On an appeal against sentence the Court of Appeal, if they consider that the appellant should be sentenced differently for an offence for which he was dealt with by the court below may—

(a) quash any sentence or order which is the subject of the appeal; and

(b) in place of it pass such sentence or make such order as they think appropriate for the case and as the court below had power to pass or make when dealing with him for the offence;

but the Court shall so exercise their powers under this subsection that, taking the case as a whole, the appellant is not more severely dealt with on appeal than he was dealt with by the court below.

(4) The power of the Court of Appeal under subsection (3) of this section to pass a sentence which the court below had power to pass for an offence shall, notwithstanding that the court below made no order under section 23(1) of the Powers of Criminal Courts Act 1973 or section 47(4) of the Criminal Law Act 1977 in respect of a suspended or partly suspended sentence previously passed on the appellant for another offence, include power to deal with him in respect of that sentence where the court below made no order in respect of it.'.

[(5) The fact that an appeal is pending against an interim hospital order under the [Mental Health Act 1983] shall not affect the power of the court below to renew or terminate the order or to deal with the appellant on its termination; and where the Court of Appeal quash such an order but do not pass any sentence or make any other order in its place the Court may direct the appellant to be kept in custody or released on bail pending his being dealt with by the court below.

(6) Where the Court of Appeal make an interim hospital order by virtue of subsection (3) of this section—

(a) the power of renewing or terminating it and of dealing with the appellant on its termination shall be exercisable by the court below and not by the Court of Appeal; and

(b) the court below shall be treated for the purposes of [section 38(7) of the said Act of 1983] (absconding offenders) as the court that made the order.]

Appeal in cases of insanity

12. Appeal against verdict of not guilty by reason of insanity.
A person in whose case there is returned a verdict of not guilty by reason of insanity may appeal to the Court of Appeal against the verdict—

(a) on any ground of appeal which involves a question of law alone; and

(b) with the leave of the Court of Appeal, on any ground which involves a question of fact alone, or a question of mixed law and fact, or on any other ground which appears to the Court of Appeal to be a sufficient ground of appeal;

but if the judge of the court of trial grants a certificate that the case is fit for appeal on a ground which involves a question of fact, or a question of mixed law and fact, an appeal lies under this section without the leave of the Court of Appeal.

13. Disposal of appeal under s. 12

(1) Subject to the provisions of this section, the Court of Appeal shall allow an appeal under section 12 of this Act if they are of opinion—

(a) that the verdict should be set aside on the ground that under all the circumstances of the case it is unsafe or unsatisfactory; or

(b) that the order of the court giving effect to the verdict should be set aside on the ground of a wrong decision of any question of law; or

(c) that there was a material irregularity in the course of the trial,

and in any other case shall dismiss the appeal.

(2) The Court of Appeal may dismiss an appeal under section 12 of this Act, if of opinion that, notwithstanding that the point raised in the appeal might be decided in favour of the appellant, no miscarriage of justice has actually occurred.

(3) Where apart from this subsection—

(a) an appeal under section 12 of this Act would fall to be allowed; and

(b) none of the grounds for allowing it relates to the question of the insanity of the accused,

the Court of Appeal may dismiss the appeal if they are of the opinion that, but for the insanity of the accused, the proper verdict would have been that he was guilty of an offence other than the offence charged.

(4) Where an appeal under section 12 of this Act is allowed, the following provisions apply:—

(a) if the ground, or one of the grounds, for allowing the appeal is that the finding of the jury as to the insanity of the accused ought not to stand and the Court of Appeal are of opinion that the proper verdict would have been that he was guilty of an offence (whether the offence charged or any other offence of which the jury could have found him guilty), the Court—

(i) shall substitute for the verdict of not guilty by reason of insanity a verdict of guilty of that offence; and

(ii) shall, subject to subsection (5) below, have the like powers of punishing or otherwise dealing with the appellant, and other powers, as the court of trial would have had if the jury had come to the substituted verdict; and

(b) in any other case, the Court of Appeal shall substitute for the verdict of the jury a verdict of acquittal.

(5) The Court of Appeal shall not by virtue of subsection (4)(a) above sentence any person to death; but where under that paragraph they substitute a verdict of guilty of an offence for which apart from this subsection they would be required to sentence the appellant to death, their sentence shall (whatever the circumstances) be one of imprisonment for life.

(6) An order of the Court of Appeal allowing an appeal in accordance with this section shall operate as a direction to the court of trial to amend the record to conform with the order.

14. Hospital order on disposal of appeal

(1) Where, on an appeal under section 12 of this Act, the Court of Appeal are of opinion that the case is not one where there should have been a verdict of acquittal but that there should have been a finding that the accused was under disability, the Court shall make an order that the appellant be admitted to such hospital as may be specified by the Secretary of State.

(2) Where in accordance with section 13(4)(b) of this Act the Court of Appeal substitute a verdict of acquittal, and they are of opinion—

(a) that the appellant is suffering from mental disorder of a nature or degree which warrants his [detention in a hospital for assessment (or for assessment followed by medical treatment)] for at least a limited period; and

(b) that he ought to be so detained in the interests of his own health or safety or with a view to the protection of other persons,

the Court shall make an order that the appellant be [admitted for assessment] to such hospital as may be specified by the Secretary of State.

(3) Schedule 1 to this Act applies with respect to the consequences and effect of an order made by the Court of Appeal under this section.

(4) On making an order under this section in the case of any person, the Court of Appeal may give such directions as they think fit for his conveyance to a place of safety and his detention there pending his admission to hospital within the relevant period specified in Schedule 1 to this Act.

(5) In [Section 47 of the Mental Health Act 1983] (which relates to the removal to hospital of persons serving sentences of imprisonment and is applied by [subsection (5)] of the section also to persons in other forms of detention) references to a person serving a sentence of imprisonment shall be construed as not including references to a person subject to an order of the Court of Appeal under subsection (1) of this section.

Unfitness to stand trial

15. Right of appeal against finding of disability

(1) Where there has been a determination under section 4 of the Criminal Procedure (Insanity) Act 1964 of the question of a person's fitness to be tried, and the jury has returned a finding that he is under disability, the person may appeal to the Court of Appeal against the finding.

(2) An appeal under this section may be—
    (a) on any ground of appeal which involves a question of law alone; and
    (b) with the leave of the Court of Appeal, on any ground which involves a question of fact alone, or a question of mixed law and fact, or on any other ground which appears to the Court of Appeal to be a sufficient ground of appeal;
but if the judge of the court of trial grants a certificate that the case is fit for appeal on a ground which involves a question of fact, or a question of mixed law and fact, an appeal lies under this section without the leave of the Court of Appeal.

16. Disposal of appeal under s. 15

(1) The Court of Appeal shall allow an appeal under section 15 of this Act if they are of opinion—
    (a) that the finding of the jury should be set aside on the ground that under all the circumstances of the case it is unsafe or unsatisfactory; or
    (b) that the order of the court giving effect to the finding should be set aside on the ground of a wrong decision of any question of law; or
    (c) that there was a material irregularity in the course of the determination of the question of fitness to be tried;
and in any other case (except one to which subsection (2) below applies) shall dismiss the appeal; but they may dismiss the appeal if of opinion that, notwithstanding that the point raised in the appeal might be decided in favour of the appellant, no miscarriage of justice has actually occurred.

(2) An appeal under section 15 of this Act may, in a case where the question of fitness to be tried was determined later than on arraignment, be allowed by the Court of Appeal (notwithstanding that the finding was properly come to) if the Court are of opinion that the case is one in which the accused should have been acquitted before the question of fitness to be tried was considered; and, if an appeal is allowed under this subsection, the Court of Appeal shall, in addition to quashing the finding, direct a verdict of acquittal to be recorded (but not a verdict of not guilty by reason of insanity).

(3) Subject to subsection (2) above, where an appeal under section 15 of this Act is allowed, the appellant may be tried accordingly for the offence with which he was charged, and the Court of Appeal may make such orders as appear to them to be necessary or expedient pending any such trial for his custody, [release on] bail or continued detention under the Mental Health Act 1983]; and Schedule 3 to this Act has effect for applying provisions in [Part III] of that Act to persons in whose case an order is made by the Court of Appeal under this subsection.

Review by Court of Appeal of cases tried on indictment

17. Reference by Home Secretary

(1) Where a person has been convicted on indictment, or been tried on indictment and found not guilty by reason of insanity, or been found by a jury to be under disability, the Secretary of State may, if he thinks fit, at any time either—
    (a) refer the whole case to the Court of Appeal and the case shall then be treated for all purposes as an appeal to the Court by that person; or
    (b) if he desires the assistance of the Court on any point arising in the case, refer that point to the Court for their opinion thereon, and the Court shall consider

the point so referred and furnish the Secretary of State with their opinion thereon accordingly.

(2) A reference by the Secretary of State under this section may be made by him either on an application by the person referred to in subsection (1), or without any such application.

Procedure from notice of appeal to hearing

18. Initiating procedure.

(1) A person who wishes to appeal under this Part of this Act to the Court of Appeal, or to obtain the leave of that court to appeal, shall give notice of appeal or, as the case may be, notice of application for leave to appeal, in such manner as may be directed by rules of court.

(2) Notice of appeal, or of application for leave to appeal, shall be given within twenty-eight days from the date of the conviction, verdict or finding appealed against, or in the case of appeal against sentence, from the date on which sentence was passed or, in the case of an order made or treated as made on conviction, from the date of the making of the order.

(3) The time for giving notice under this section may be extended, either before or after it expires, by the Court of Appeal.

[18A. Appeals in case of contempt of court

(1) A person who wishes to appeal under section 13 of the Administration of Justice Act 1960 from any order or decision of the Crown Court in the exercise of jurisdiction to punish for contempt of court shall give notice of appeal in such manner as may be directed by rules of court.

(2) Notice of appeal shall be given within twenty-eight days from the date of the order or decision appealed against.

(3) The time for giving notice under this section may be extended, either before or after its expiry, by the Court of Appeal.]

19. Bail

[(1) The Court of Appeal may, if they think fit,—
 (a) grant an appellant bail pending the determination of his appeal; or
 (b) revoke bail granted to an appellant by the Crown Court under paragraph (f) of section 81(1) of the Supreme Court Act 1981 [or paragraph (a) above]; or
 (c) vary the conditions of bail granted to an appellant in the exercise of the power conferred by [either of those paragraphs.]

(2) The powers conferred by subsection (1) above may be exercised—
 (a) on the application of an appellant; or
 (b) if it appears to the registrar of criminal appeals of the Court of Appeal (hereafter referred to as "the registrar") that any of them ought to be exercised, on a reference to the court by him.]

20. Disposal of groundless appeal

If it appears to the registrar of criminal appeals of the Court of Appeal that a notice of an appeal purporting to be on a ground of appeal which involves a question of law alone does not show any substantial ground of appeal, he may refer the appeal to the Court for summary determination; and where the case is so referred the Court may, if they consider that the appeal is frivolous or vexatious, and can be determined without adjourning it for a full hearing, dismiss the appeal summarily, without calling on any one to attend the hearing or to appear for the Crown thereon.

21. Preparation of case for hearing.

(1) The registrar shall—

    (a) take all necessary steps for obtaining a hearing of any appeal or application of which notice is given to him and which is not referred and dismissed summarily under the foregoing section; and

    (b) obtain and lay before the Court of Appeal in proper form all documents, exhibits and other things which appear necessary for the proper determination of the appeal or application.

(2) Rules of court may enable an appellant to obtain from the registrar any documents or things, including copies or reproductions of documents, required for his appeal and may authorise the registrar to make charges for them in accordance with scales and rates fixed from time to time by the Treasury.

The hearing

22. Right of appellant to be present.

(1) Except as provided by this section, an appellant shall be entitled to be present, if he wishes it, on the hearing of his appeal, although he may be in custody.

(2) A person in custody shall not be entitled to be present—

    (a) where his appeal is on some ground involving a question of law alone; or

    (b) on an application by him for leave to appeal; or

    (c) on any proceedings preliminary or incidental to an appeal; or

    (d) where he is in custody in consequence of a verdict of not guilty by reason of insanity or of a finding of disability,

unless the Court of Appeal give him leave to be present.

(3) The power of the Court of Appeal to pass sentence on a person may be exercised although he is for any reason not present.

23. Evidence

(1) For purposes of this Part of this Act the Court of Appeal may, if they think it necessary or expedient in the interests of justice—

    (a) order the production of any document, exhibit or other thing connnected with the proceedings, the production of which appears to them necessary for the determination of the case;

    (b) order any witness who would have been a compellable witness in the proceedings from which the appeal lies to attend for examination and be examined before the Court, whether or not he was called in those proceedings; and

    (c) subject to subsection (3) below, receive the evidence, if tendered, of any witness.

(2) Without prejudice to subsection (1) above, where evidence is tendered to the Court of Appeal thereunder the Court shall, unless they are satisfied that the evidence, if received, would not afford any ground for allowing the appeal, exercise their power of receiving it if—

    (a) it appears to them that the evidence is likely to be credible and would have been admissible in the proceedings from which the appeal lies on an issue which is the subject of the appeal; and

    (b) they are satisfied that it was not adduced in those proceedings but there is a reasonable explanation for the failure to adduce it.

(3) Subsection (1)(c) above applies to any witness (including the appellant) who is competent but not compellable, and applies also to the appellant's husband or wife where the appellant makes an application for that purpose and the evidence of the

husband or wife could not have been given in the proceedings from which the appeal lies except on such an application.

(4) For purposes of this Part of this Act, the Court of Appeal may, if they think necessary or expedient in the interests of justice, order the examination of any witness whose attendance might be required under subsection (1)(b) above to be conducted, in manner provided by rules of court, before any judge or officer of the Court or other person appointed by the Court for the purpose, and allow the admission of any depositions so taken as evidence before the Court.

24.–28. . . .

Other matters depending on result of appeal

29. Effect of appeal on sentence.

(1) The time during which an appellant is in custody pending the determination of his appeal shall, subject to any direction which the Court of Appeal may give to the contrary, be reckoned as part of the term of any sentence to which he is for the time being subject.

(2) Where the Court of Appeal give a contrary direction under subsection (1) above, they shall state their reasons for doing so; and they shall not give any such direction where—
- (a) leave to appeal has been granted; or
- (b) a certificate has been given by the judge of the court of trial [under—
  - (i) section 1 or 11(1A) of this Act; or
  - (ii) section 81(1B) of the Supreme Court Act 1981;] or
- (c) the case has been referred to them by the Secretary of State under section 17 of this Act.

(3) When an appellant is [granted] bail under section 19 of this Act, the time during which he is [released on bail] shall be disregarded in computing the term of any sentence to which he is for the time being subject.

(4) The term of any sentence passed by the Court of Appeal under section 3, 4, 5, 11 or 13(4) of this Act shall, unless the Court otherwise directs, begin to run from the time when it would have begun to run if passed in the proceedings from which the appeal lies.

[30. Restitution of property

(1) The operation of an order for the restitution of property to a person made by the Crown Court shall, unless the Court direct to the contrary in any case in which, in their opinion, the title to the property is not in dispute, be suspended until (disregarding any power of a court to grant leave to appeal out of time) there is no further possibility of an appeal on which the order could be varied or set aside, and provision may be made by rules of court for the custody of any property in the meantime.

(2) The Court of Appeal may by order annul or vary any order made by the court of trial for the restitution of property to any person, although the conviction is not quashed; and the order, if annulled, shall not take effect and, if varied, shall take effect as so varied.

(3) Where the House of Lords restores a conviction, it may make any order for the restitution of property which the court of trial could have made.]

Supplementary

31. Powers of Court under Part I which are exercisable by single judge.

[(1) There may be exercised by a single judge in the same manner as by the Court of Appeal and subject to the same provisions—

    (a)   the powers of the Court of Appeal under this Part of this Act specified in subsection (2) below;

    (b)   the power to give directions under section 4(4) of the Sexual Offences (Amendment) Act 1976; and

    (c)   the powers to make orders for the payment of costs under sections 16 to 18 of the Prosecution of Offences Act 1985 in proceedings under this Part of this Act.

(2) The powers mentioned in subsection (1)(a) above.]

    (a)   to give leave to appeal;

    (b)   to extend the time within which notice of appeal or of application for leave to appeal may be given;

    (c)   to allow an appellant to be present at any proceedings;

    (d)   to order a witness to attend for examination;

    [(e)   to grant bail to an appellant];

    (f)   to make order under section 8(2) of this Act and discharge or vary such orders;

    (g)   . . .

    (h)   to give directions under section 29(1) of this Act.

[(2A) The power of the Court of Appeal to suspend a person's disqualification under [section 40(2) of the Road Traffic Offenders Act 1988] may be exercised by a single judge in the same manner as it may be exercised by the Court.]

[(2B) The power of the Court of Appeal to grant leave to appeal under section 159 of the Criminal Justice Act 1988 may be exercised by a single judge in the same manner as it may be exercised by the Court.]

(3) If the single judge refuses an application on the part of an appellant to exercise in his favour any of the powers above specified, the appellant shall be entitled to have the application determined by the Court of Appeal.

32. Transcripts

(1) Rules of court may provide—

    (a)   for the making of a record (whether by means of shorthand notes, by mechanical means or otherwise) of any proceedings in respect of which an appeal lies (with or without leave) to the Court of Appeal; and

    (b)   for the making and verification of a transcript of any such record and for supplying the transcript (on payment of such charge, if any, as may be fixed for the time being by the Treasury) to the registrar for the use of the Court of Appeal or any judge exercising the powers of a judge of the Court, and to such other persons and in such circumstances as may be prescribed by the rules.

(2) Without prejudice to subsection (1) above, the Secretary of State may, if he thinks fit, in any case direct that a transcript shall be made of any such record made in pursuance of the rules and be supplied to him.

(3) The cost—

    (a)   of making any such record in pursuance of the rules; and

    (b)   of making and supplying in pursuance of this section any transcript ordered to be supplied to the registrar or the Secretary of State,

shall be defrayed, in accordance with scales of payment fixed for the time being by the Treasury, out of moneys provided by Parliament; and the cost of providing and installing at a court any equipment required for the purpose of making such a record or transcript shall also be defrayed out of moneys so provided.

PART II
APPEAL TO HOUSE OF LORDS FROM COURT OF APPEAL
(CRIMINAL DIVISION)
The appeal

33. Right of appeal to House of Lords.
(1) An appeal lies to the House of Lords, at the instance of the defendant or the prosecutor, from any decision of the Court of Appeal on an appeal to that court under Part I of this Act [or section 9 (preparatory hearings) of the Criminal Justice Act 1987.]

(2) The appeal lies only with the leave of the Court of Appeal or the House of Lords; and leave shall not be granted unless it is certified by the Court of Appeal that a point of law of general public importance is involved in the decision and it appears to the Court of Appeal or the House of Lords (as the case may be) that the point is one which ought to be considered by that House.

[(3) Except as provided by this Part of this Act and section 13 of the Administration of Justice Act 1960 (appeal in cases of contempt of court), no appeal shall lie from any decision of the criminal division of the Court of Appeal.]

34. Application for leave to appeal.
(1) An application to the Court of Appeal for leave to appeal to the House of Lords shall be made within the period of fourteen days beginning with the date of the decision of the Court; and an application to the House of Lords for leave shall be made within the period of fourteen days beginning with the date on which the application for leave is refused by the Court of Appeal.

(2) The House of Lords or the Court of Appeal may, upon application made at any time by the defendant, extend the time within which an application may be made by him to that House of the Court under subsection (1) above.

(3) An appeal to the House of Lords shall be treated as pending until any application for leave to appeal is disposed of and, if leave to appeal is granted, until the appeal is disposed of; and for purposes of this Part of this Act an application for leave to appeal shall be treated as disposed of at the expiration of the time within which it may be made, if it is not made within that time.

35. Hearing and disposal of appeal.
(1) An appeal under this Part of this Act shall not be heard and determined by the House of Lords unless there are present at least three of the persons designated Lords of Appeal by section 5 of the Appellate Jurisdiction Act 1876.

(2) Any order of the House of Lords which provides for the hearing of applications for leave to appeal by a committee constituted in accordance with section 5 of the said Act of 1876 may direct that the decision of that committee shall be taken on behalf of the House.

(3) For the purpose of disposing of an appeal, the House of Lords may exercise any powers of the Court of Appeal or may remit the case to the Court.

Matters preliminary to hearing

36., 37. *****
Note—Sections 36 and 37 give the House of Lords powers corresponding to those of the Court of Appeal with respect to the granting of bail and the detention of the defendant whilst an appeal is outstanding.

38. Presence of defendant at hearing.
A defendant who [has been convicted of an offence and,] is detained pending an appeal

to the House of Lords shall not be entitled to be present on the hearing of the appeal or of any proceedings preliminary or incidental thereto, except where an order of the House of Lords authorises him to be present, or where the House or the Court of Appeal, as the case may be, give him leave to be present.

39.-41. . . .

Supplementary

42. Restitution of property

(1) Where the operation of an order for the restitution of property made on conviction on indictment is suspended until the determination of an appeal under Part I of this Act to the Court of Appeal, then, if the conviction is not quashed on that appeal, the operation of the order shall continue to be suspended—

    (a) in any case, until the expiration of the time within which an application for leave to appeal to the House of Lords may be made (disregarding any extension of time which may be granted under section 34 of this Act);

    (b) if any such application is made within that time, so long as the appeal to the House of Lords is pending.

(2) Where the operation of any such order is suspended under this section,—

    (a) the order shall not take effect if the conviction is quashed on appeal to the House of Lords;

    (b) such steps shall be taken for the safe custody of the property in question during the period during which the operation of the order is suspended as may be prescribed by rules of court.

(3) Where by reason of the quashing by the Court of Appeal of a person's conviction any such order does not take effect, and on an appeal to the House of Lords the conviction is restored by that House, the House may make any order for the restitution of property which could be made on his conviction by the court which convicted him.

(4) . . .

43. Effect of appeal on sentence

(1) Where a person subject to a sentence is [granted] bail under section 36 or 37 of this Act, the time during which he is [released on bail] shall be disregarded in computing the term of his sentence.

(2) Subject to the foregoing subsection, any sentence passed on an appeal to the House of Lords in substitution for another sentence shall, unless that House or the Court of Appeal otherwise direct, begin to run from the time when the other sentence would have begun to run.

44. Powers of Court of Appeal under Part II which are exercisable by single judge.

[(1) There may be exercised by a single judge—

    (a) the powers of the Court of Appeal under this Part of this Act—

        (i) to extend the time for making an application for leave to appeal;

        (ii) to make an order for or in relation to bail; and

        (iii) to give leave for a person to be present at the hearing of any proceedings preliminary or incidental to an appeal; and

    (b) their powers to make orders for the payment of costs under sections 16 and 17 of the Prosecution of Offences Act 1985 in proceedings under this Part of this Act.',] but where the judge refuses an application to exercise any of the said powers the applicant shall be entitled to have the application determined by the Court of Appeal.

[(2) The power of the Court of Appeal to suspend a person's disqualification under [section 40(3) of the Road Traffic Offenders Act 1988] may be exercised by a single judge, but where the judge refuses an application to exercise that power the applicant shall be entitled to have the application determined by the Court of Appeal.]

PART III
MISCELLANEOUS GENERAL

45. *****

46., 47 ...

48. Appeal in capital cases.
Schedule 4 to this Act shall have effect so as to modify and supplement certain provisions in Parts I and II of this Act in relation to cases involving sentence of death.

49. Saving for prerogative of mercy.
Nothing in this Act is to be taken as affecting Her Majesty's prerogative of mercy.

50. Meaning of "sentence".
(1) In this Act, "sentence", in relation to an offence includes any order made by a court when dealing with an offender (including a hospital order under [Part III of the Mental Health Act 1983 with or without a restriction order, and an interim hospital order under that Part] and also includes a recommendation for deportation.

[(1A) Section 13 of the Powers of Criminal Courts Act 1973 (under which a conviction of an offence for which a probabtion order or an order for conditional or absolute discharge is made is deemed not to be a conviction except for certain purposes) shall not prevent an appeal under this Act, whether against conviction or otherwise.]

(2) Any power of the criminal division of the Court of Appeal to pass a sentence includes a power to make a recommendation for deportation in cases where the court from which the appeal lies had power to make such a recommendation.

51. Interpretation.
(1) In this Act, except where the context otherwise requires—

"appeal", where used in Part I or II of this Act, means appeal under that Part, and "appellant" has a corresponding meaning and in Part I includes a person who has given notice of application for leave to appeal;

"the court of trial", in relation to an appeal, means the court from which the appeal lies;

"the defendant", in Part II of this Act, means, in relation to an appeal, the person who was the appellant before the criminal division of the Court of Appeal, and references to the prosecutor shall be construed accordingly;

["the judge of the court of trial" means, where the Crown Court comprises justices of the peace, the judge presiding;]

"under disability" has the meaning assigned to it by section 4 of the Criminal Procedure (Insanity) Act 1964 (unfitness to plead); and

(2) Any expression used in this Act which is defined in [section 145(1) of the Mental Health Act 1983] has the same meaning in this Act as in that Act.

(3) Part I of this Act applies in relation to proceedings on a coroner's inquisition, and to matters arising out of such proceedings, as it applies in relation to proceedings on indictment and matters arising out of them.

52. ...

53.–55. *****

CHILDREN AND YOUNG PERSONS ACT 1969
(1969, c. 54)

An act to amend the law relating to children and young persons; and for purposes connected therewith. [22 October 1969]

Consequential changes in criminal proceedings etc.

4. Prohibition of criminal proceedings for offences by children.
A person shall not be charged with an offence, except homicide, be reason of anything done or omitted while he was a child.

5. Restrictions on criminal proceedings for offences by young persons.
(1) A person other than a qualified informant shall not lay an information in respect of an offence if the alleged offender is a young person.

(2) A qualified informant shall not lay an information in respect of an offence if the alleged offender is a young person unless the informant is of opinion that the case is of a description prescribed in pursuance of subsection (4) of this section and that it would not be adequate for the case to be dealt with by a parent, teacher or other person or by means of a caution from a constable or through an exercise of the powers of a local authority or other body not involving court proceedings or by means of proceedings under section 1 of this Act.

(3) A qualified informant shall not come to a decision in pursuance of the preceding subsection to lay an information unless—

    (a) he has told the appropriate local authority that the laying of the information is being considered and has asked for any observations which the authority may wish to make on the case to the informant; and

    (b) the authority either have notified the informant that they do not wish to make such observations or have not made any during the period or extended period indicated by the informant as that which in the circumstances he considers reasonable for the purpose or the informant has considered the observations made by the authority during that period;

but the informant shall be entitled to disregard the foregoing provisions of this subsection in any case in which it appears to him that the requirements of the preceding subsection are satisfied and will continue to be satisfied notwithstanding any observations which might be made in pursuance of this subsection.

(4) The Secretary of State may make regulations specifying, by reference to such considerations as he thinks fit, the descriptions of cases in which a qualified informant may lay an information in respect of an offence if the alleged offender is a young person; but no regulations shall be made under this subsection unless a draft of the regulations has been approved by a resolution of each House of Parliament.

(5) An information laid by a qualified informant in a case where the informant has reason to believe that the alleged offender is a young person shall be in writing and shall—

    (a) state the alleged offender's age to the best of the informant's knowledge; and

    (b) contain a certificate signed by the informant stating that the requirements of subsecitions (2) and (3) of this section are satisfied with respect to the case or that the case is one in which the requirements of the said subsection (2) are satisfied and the informant is entitled to disregard the requirements of the said subsection (3).

(6) If at the time when justices begin to inquire into a case, either as examining

justices or on the trial of an information, they have reason to believe that the alleged offender is a young person and either—

    (a)   it appears to them that the person who laid the information in question was not a qualified informant when he laid it; or

    (b)   the information is not in writing or does not contain such a certificate as is mentioned in subsection (5)(b) of this section,

it shall be their duty to quash the information, without prejudice to the laying of a further information in respect of the matter in question; but no proceedings shall be invalidated by reason of a contravention of any provision of this section and no action shall lie, by reason only of such a contravention, in respect of proceedings in respect of which such a contravention has occurred.

(7) Nothing in the preceding provisions of this section applies to an information laid with the consent of the Attorney General or laid by or on behalf or with the consent of the Director of Public Prosecutions.

(8) It shall be the duty of a person who decides to lay an information in respect of an offence in a case where he has reasons to believe that the alleged offender is a young person to give notice of the decision to the appropriate local authority unless he is himself that authority.

(9) In this section—

"the appropriate local authority", in relation to a young person, means the local authority for the area in which it appears to the informant in question that the young person resides or, if the young person appears to the informant not to reside in the area of a local authority, the local authority in whose area it is alleged that the relevant offence or one of the relevant offences was committed; and

"qualified informant" means a servant of the Crown, a police officer and a member of designated police force acting in his capacity as such a servant, officer or member, a local authority, the Greater London Council, the council of a [district] and any body designated as a public body for the purpose of this section;

and in this subsection "designated" means designated by an order made by the Secretary of State; but nothing in this section shall be construed as preventing any council or other body from acting by an agent for the purposes of this section.

6. . . .

7. Alterations in treatment of young offenders etc.

(1)–(4) . . .

(5) An order sending a person to an approved school shall not be made after such day as the Secretary of State may by order specify for the purposes of this subsection.

(6) . . .

(7) Subject [to subsection (7A) of this section and] to the enactments requiring cases to be remitted to juvenile courts and to section 53(1) of the Act of 1933 (which provides for detention for certain crimes), where a child is found guilty of homicide or a young person is found guilty of any offence by or before any court, that court or the court to which his case if remitted shall have power—

    (a)   if the offence is punishable in the case of an adult with imprisonment, to make a care order (other than an interim order) in respect of him; or

    (b)   to make a supervision order in respect of him; or

    (c)   with the consent of his parent or guardian, to order the parent or guardian to enter into a recognisance to take proper care of him and exercise proper control over him,

and, if it makes such an order as is mentioned in this subsection while another such order made by any court is in force in respect of the child or young person, shall also have power to discharge the earlier order; and subsection (13) of section 2 of this Act shall apply to an order under paragraph (c) of this subsection as it applies to such an order as is mentioned in that subsection.

ADMINISTRATION OF JUSTICE ACT 1969
(1969, c. 58)

1.—11. ...

PART II
APPEAL FROM HIGH COURT TO HOUSE OF LORDS

12. Grant of certificate by trial judge

(1) Where on the application of any of the parties to any proceedings to which this section applies the judge is satisfied:

    (a) that the relevant conditions are fulfilled in relation to his decision in those proceedings, and

    (b) that a sufficient case for an appeal to the House of Lords under this Part of this Act has been made out to justify an application for leave to bring such an appeal, and

    (c) that all the parties to the proceedings consent to the grant of a certificate under this section.

the judge, subject to the following provisions of this Part of this Act, may grant a certificate to that effect.

(2) This section applies to any civil proceedings in the High Court which are either—

    (a) proceedings before a single judge of the High Court . . ., or

    (b) ...

    (c) proceedings before a Divisional Court.

(3) Subject to any Order in Council made under the following provisions of this section, for the purposes of this section the relevant conditions, in relation to a decision of the judge in any proceedings, are that a point of law of general public importance is involved in that decision and that that point of law either—

    (a) relates wholly or mainly to the construction of an enactment or of a statutory instrument, and has been fully argued in the proceedings and fully considered in the judgment of the judge in the proceedings, or

    (b) is one in respect of which the judge is bound by a decision of the Court of Appeal or of the House of Lords in previous proceedings, and was fully considered in the judgments given by the Court of Appeal or the House of Lords (as the case may be) in those previous proceedings.

(4) Any application for a certificate under this section shall be made to the judge immediately after he gives judgment in the proceedings:

Provided that the judge may in any particular case entertain any such application made at any later time before the end of the period of fourteen days beginning with the date on which that judgment is given or such other period as may be prescribed by rules of court.

(5) No appeal shall lie against the grant or refusal of a certificate under this section.

(6) Her Majesty may by Order in Council amend subsection (3) of this section by altering, deleting, or substituting one or more new paragraphs for, either or both of paragraphs (a) and (b) of that subsection, or by adding one or more further paragraphs.

(7) Any Order in Council made under this section shall be subject to annulment in pursuance of a resolution of either House of Parliament.

(8) In this Part of this Act "civil proceedings" means any proceedings other than proceedings in a criminal cause or matter, and "the judge", in relation to any proceedings to which this section applies, means the judge . . . referred to in paragraph (a) . . .

Administration of Justice Act 1969

of subsection (2) of this section, or the Divisional Court referred to in paragraph (c) of that subsection, as the case may be.

13. Leave to appeal to House of Lords

(1) Where in any proceedings the judge grants a certificate under section 12 of this Act, then, at any time within one month from the date on which that certificate is granted or such extended time as in any particular case the House of Lords may allow, any of the parties to the proceedings may make an application to the House of Lords under this section.

(2) Subject to the following provisions of this section, if on such an application it appears to the House of Lords to be expedient to do so, the House may grant leave for an appeal to be brought directly to the House; and where leave is granted under this section—

    (a) no appeal from the decision of the judge to which the certificate relates shall lie to the Court of Appeal, but

    (b) an appeal shall lie from that decision to the House of Lords.

(3) Applications under this section shall be determined without a hearing.

(4) Any order of the House of Lords which provides for applications under this section to be determined by a committee of the House—

    (a) shall direct that the committee shall consist of or include not less than three of the persons designated as Lords of Appeal in accordance with section 5 of the Appellate Jurisdiction Act 1876, and

    (b) may direct that the decision of the committee on any such application shall be taken on behalf of the House.

(5) Without prejudice to subsection (2) of this section, no appeal shall lie to the Court of Appeal from a decision of the judge in respect of which a certificate is granted under section 12 of this Act until—

    (a) the time within which an application can be made under this section has expired, and

    (b) where such an application is made, that application has been determined in accordance with the preceding provisions of this section.

14. Appeal where leave granted

In relation to any appeal which lies to the House of Lords by virtue of subsection (2) of section 13 of this Act—

    (a) section 4 of the Appellate Jurisdiction Act 1876 (which provides for the bringing of appeals to the House of Lords by way of petition),

    (b) section 5 of that Act (which regulates the composition of the House for the hearing and determination of appeals), and

    (c) except in so far as those orders otherwise provide, any orders of the House of Lords made with respect to the matters specified in section 11 of that Act (which relates to the procedure on appeals),

shall have effect as they have effect in relation to appeals under that Act.

15. Cases excluded from s. 12

(1) No certificate shall be granted under section 12 of this Act in respect of a decision of the judge in any proceedings where by virtue of any enactment, apart from the provisions of this Part of this Act, no appeal would lie from that decision to the Court of Appeal, with or without the leave of the judge or of the Court of Appeal.

(2) No certificate shall be granted under section 12 of this Act in respect of a decision of the judge where—

    (a) . . .

    (b) by virtue of any enactment, apart from the provisions of this Part of this Act, no appeal would (with or without the leave of the Court of Appeal or of the

House of Lords) lie from any decision of the Court of Appeal on an appeal from the decision of the judge.

(3) Where by virtue of any enactment, apart from the provisions of this Part of this Act, no appeal would lie to the Court of Appeal from the decision of the judge except with the leave of the judge or of the Court of Appeal, no certificate shall be granted under section 12 of this Act in respect of that decision unless it appears to the judge that apart from the provisions of this Part of this Act it would be a proper case for granting such leave.

(4) No certificate shall be granted under section 12 of this Act where the decision of the judge, or any order made by him in pursuance of that decision, is made in the exercise of jurisdiction to punish for contempt of court.

COURTS ACT 1971
(1971, c. 23)

An act to make further provision as respects the Supreme Court and county courts, judges and juries, to establish a Crown Court as part of the Supreme Court to try indictments and exercise certain other jurisdiction, to abolish courts of assize and certain other courts and to deal with their jurisdiction and other consequential matters, and to amend in other respects the law about courts and court proceedings. [12 May 1971]

1.—15. ... [Repealed by the Supreme Court Act 1981].

PART III
JUDGES

16. Appointment of Circuit Judges

(1) Her Majesty may from time to time appoint as Circuit judges, to serve in the Crown Court and county courts and to carry out such other judicial functions as may be conferred on them under this or any other enactment, such qualified persons as may be recommended to Her by the Lord Chancellor.

(2) The maximum number of Circuit judges shall be such as may be determined from time to time by the Lord Chancellor with the concurrence of the Minister for the Civil Service.

(3) No person shall be qualified to be appointed a Circuit judge unless he is a barrister of at least ten years' standing or a Recorder who has held that office for at least [three] years.

(4) Before recommending any person to Her Majesty for appointment as a Circuit judge, the Lord Chancellor shall take steps to satisfy himself that that person's health is satisfactory.

(5) The provisions of Part I of Schedule 2 to this Act shall have effect with respect to the appointment as Circuit judges of the holders of certain judicial offices, and the supplementary provisions in Part II of that Schedule shall have effect.

17. Retirement, removal and disqualifications of Circuit judges

(1) Subject to subsections (2) to (4) below, a Circuit judge shall vacate his office at the end of the completed year of service in which he attains the age of seventy-two.

(2) Where the Lord Chancellor considers it desirable in the public interest to retain a Circuit judge in office after the time at which he would otherwise retire in accordance with subsection (1) above, he may from time to time authorise the continuance in office of that judge until such date, not being later than the date on which the judge attains the age of seventy-five, as he thinks fit.

(3) For the purposes of subsection (1) above a person who becomes a Circuit judge by virtue of any provision of paragraph 1 of Schedule 2 to this Act shall be treated

as completing a year of service on the anniversary of his appointment to the office by virtue of which he becomes a Circuit judge.

(4) The Lord Chancellor may, if he thinks fit, remove a Circuit judge from office on the ground of incapacity or misbehaviour.

(5) . . .

(6) So long as he holds office as such, no Circuit judge shall practice as a barrister, or act for any remuneration to himself as arbitrator or referee, or be directly or indirectly concerned as a conveyancer, notary public or solicitor.

18., 19. *****

20. (1)—(4) **Repealed by County Courts Act 1984**

21. Appointment of Recorders

(1) Her Majesty may from time to time appoint qualified persons, to be known as Recorders, to act as part-time judges of the Crown Court and to carry out such other judicial functions as may be conferred on them under this or any other enactment.

(2) Every appointment of a person to be a Recorder shall be of a person recommended to Her Majesty by the Lord Chancellor, and no person shall be qualified to be appointed a Recorder unless he is a barrister or solicitor of at least ten years' standing.

(3) The appointment of a person as a Recorder shall specify the term for which he is appointed and the frequency and duration of the occasions during that term on which he will be required to be available to undertake the duties of a Recorder.

(4) Subject to subsection (5) below the Lord Chancellor may, with the agreement of the Recorder concerned, from time to time extend for such period as he thinks appropriate the term for which a Recorder is appointed.

(5) Neither the initial term for which a Recorder is appointed nor any extension of that term under subsection (4) above shall be such as to continue his appointment as a Recorder after the end of the completed year of service in which he attains the age of seventy-two.

(6) The Lord Chancellor may if he thinks fit terminate the appointment of a Recorder on the ground of incapacity or misbehaviour or of a failure to comply with any requirement specified under subsection (3) above in the terms of his appointment.

(7) There shall be paid to Recorders out of money provided by Parliament such remuneration and allowances as the Lord Chancellor may, with the approval of the Minister for the Civil Service, determine.

22. *****

[24. Deputy Circuit judges and assistant Recorders

(1) If it appears to the Lord Chancellor it is expedient as a temporary measure to make an appointment under this section in order to facilitate the disposal of business in the Crown Court or a county court or official referees' business in the High Court, he may—

    (a) appoint to be a deputy Circuit judge, during such period or on such occasions as he thinks fit, any person who has held office as a judge of the Court of Appeal or of the High Court or as a Circuit judge; or

    (b) appoint to be an assistant Recorder, during such period or on such occasions as he thinks fit, any barrister or solicitor of at least ten years' standing.

(2) Except as provided by subsection (3) below, during the period or on the occasions for which a deputy Circuit judge or assistant Recorder is appointed under this section he shall be treated for all purposes as, and accordingly may perform any of the functions of, a Circuit judge or a Recorder, as the case may be.

(3) A deputy Circuit judge appointed under this section shall not be treated as a Circuit judge for the purpose of any provision made by or under any enactment

and relating to the appointment, retirement, removal or disqualification of Circuit judges, the tenure of office and oaths to be taken by such judges, or the remuneration, allowances or pensions of such judges; and section 21 of this Act shall not apply to an assistant Recorder appointed under this section.

(4) Notwithstanding the expiry of any period for which a person is appointed under this section a deputy Circuit judge or an assistant Recorder, he may attend at the Crown Court or a county court or, [in the case of a deputy Circuit judge, as regards] official referees' business, at the High Court for the purpose of continuing to deal with, giving judgment in, or dealing with any ancillary matter relating to, any case which may have been begun before him when sitting as a deputy Circuit judge or an assistant Recorder, and for that purpose and for the purpose of any proceedings subsequent thereon he shall be treated as a Circuit judge or a Recorder, as the case may be.

(5) There shall be paid out of money provided by Parliament to deputy Circuit judges and assistant Recorders appointed under this section such remuneration and allowances as the Lord Chancellor may, with the approval of the Minister for the Civil Service, determine.]

TRIBUNALS AND INQUIRIES ACT 1971
(1971, c. 62)

An Act to consolidate the Tribunals and Inquiries Acts 1958 and 1966 as amended
[27 July 1971]

The Council on Tribunals and its functions

1. Council on Tribunals

(1) There shall continue to be a council entitled the Council on Tribunals (being the council constituted by the Tribunals and Inquiries Act 1958)—

(a) to keep under review the constitution and working of the tribunals specified in Schedule 1 to this Act (being the tribunals constituted under or for the purposes of the statutory provisions specified in that Schedule) and, from time to time, to report on their constitution and working;

(b) to consider and report on such particular matters as may be referred to the Council under this Act with respect to tribunals other than the ordinary courts of law, whether or not specified in Schedule 1 to this Act, or any such tribunal;

(c) to consider and report on such matters as may be referred as aforesaid, or as the Council may determine to be of special importance, with respect to administrative procedures involving, or which may involve, the holding by or on behalf of a Minister of a statutory inquiry, or any such procedure.

(2) Nothing in this seciton shall authorise or require the Council to deal with any matter with respect to which the Parliament of Northern Ireland has power to make laws.

2. Composition of the Council and the Scottish Committee

(1) Subject to subsection (3) of this section the Council on Tribunals (in this Act referred to as "the Council") shall consist of not more than fifteen nor less than ten members appointed by the Lord Chancellor and the Secretary of State, and one of the members shall be so appointed to be chairman of the Council.

(2) . . . [relates to the Scottish Committee]

(3) In addition to the persons appointed or designated as aforesaid, the Parliamentary Commissioner for Administration shall, by virtue of his office, be a member of the Council and of the Scottish Committee.

(4) In appointing members of the Council regard shall be had to the need for representation of the interests of persons in Wales.

3. Tenure of office, remuneration and expenses

(1) Persons appointed under section 2 of this Act shall hold and vacate office under the terms of the instruments under which they are appointed, but may resign office by notice in writing to the Minister or Ministers by whom they were appointed; and any such person who ceases to hold office shall be eligible for re-appointment.

(2) There shall be paid to the chairman of the Council and the chairman of the Scottish Committee such salaries, and to the other members of the Council and of the Scottish Committee such fees (if any) as may be determined by the Treasury.

(3) The salaries and fees payable under subsection (2) of this section, together with such expenses of the Council and of the Scottish Committee (including subsistence allowances for and travelling expenses of their members) as may be approved by the Treasury shall be defrayed out of moneys provided by Parliament.

4. *****

5. Recommendations of Council as to appointment of members of tribunals

(1) Without prejudice to the generality of section 1(1)(a) of this Act, the Council may make to the appropriate Minister general recommendations as to the making of appointments to membership of any such tribunals as are specified in Schedule 1 to this Act or of panels constituted for the purposes of any such tribunals; and (without prejudice, however, to any statutory provisions having effect with respect to such appointments) the appropriate Minister shall have regard to recommendations under this section.

(2) In this section "the appropriate Minister" means, in relation to appointments of any description, the Minister making the appointments or, if they are not made by a Minister, the Minister in charge of the government department concerned with the tribunals in question.

(3) The following provisions shall have effect as respects any such tribunal as is specified in Part II of Schedule 1 to this Act—

    (a)   the Council shall not make any such recommendations as aforesaid until they have referred the matter of the recommendations for consideration, and report to the Council, by the Scottish Committee and have considered the report of that Committee;

    (b)   without prejudice to the generality of section 4(5) of this Act, the Scottish Committee may of its own motion propose any such general recommendations as aforesaid as expedient to be made by the Council to the appropriate Minister;

    (c)   if the Council, in making recommendations under this section on any matter which they have referred to the Scottish Committee or on which that Committee has made proposals, do not adopt the report or proposals of that Committee without modification, or if the Council do not make recommendations on matters on which the Scottish Committee has made proposals to the Council, the Scottish Committee may submit its report or proposals to the Secretary of State.

6. *****

Composition and procedure of tribunals and inquiries

7. Chairmen etc of certain tribunals: provisions as to appointment

(1) The chairman, or any person appointed to act as chairman, of any of the tribunals to which this subsection applies shall (without prejudice to any statutory provisions as to qualifications) be selected by the appropriate authority from a panel of persons appointed by the Lord Chancellor.

(2) Members of panels constituted under this section shall hold and vacate office

under the terms of the instruments under which they are appointed, but may resign office by notice in writing to the Lord Chancellor; and any such member who ceases to hold office shall be eligible for re-appointment.

(3) Subsection (1) of this section applies to any such tribunal as is specified in paragraph . . .19(a), (b) or (e) [. . . [or 30A (a) or (c)]] of Schedule 1 to this Act, . . .

(4) The person or persons constituting any such tribunal as is specified in paragraph 16 of Schedule 1 to this Act shall be appointed by the Lord Chancellor, and where such a tribunal consists of more than one person the Lord Chancellor shall designate which of them is to be the chairman.

(5) In this section "the appropriate authority" means the Minister who apart from this Act would be empowered to appoint or select the chairman, person to act as chairman, members or member of the tribunal in question.

(6) A panel may be constituted under this section for the purposes either of a single tribunal or of two or more tribunals, whether or not of the same description.

(7) *(Applies to Scotland only.)*

(8) *(Applies to Northern Ireland only.)*

8. Concurrence required for removal of members of certain tribunals

(1) Subject to subsection (2) of this section, no power of a Minister other than the Lord Chancellor to terminate a person's membership of any such tribunal as is specified in Schedule 1 to this Act, or of a panel constituted for the purposes of any such tribunal, shall be exercisable except with the consent of—

(a) the Lord Chancellor, the Lord President of the Court of Session and the Lord Chief Justice of Northern Ireland, if the tribunal sits in all parts of the United Kingdom;

(b) the Lord Chancellor and the Lord President of the Court of Session, if the tribunal sits in all parts of Great Britain;

(c) the Lord Chancellor and the Lord Chief Justice of Northern Ireland, if the tribunal sits both in England and Wales and in Northern Ireland;

(d) the Lord Chancellor, if the tribunal does not sit outside England and Wales;

(e) the Lord President of the Court of Session, if the tribunal sits only in Scotland;

(f) the Lord Chief Justice of Northern Ireland, if the tribunal sits only in Northern Ireland.

(2) This section does not apply to any such tribunal as is specified in paragraph [2A] [5A], [5B], [6A], [6B], [10A], 17(a), 22, 25(a), 29(b), 30, 35 . . . or 41(a) of Schedule 1 to this Act.

(3) For the purposes of this section in its application to any such tribunal as is specified in paragraph 8(a) of Schedule 1 to this Act, an adjudicator who has sat only in England or Wales or who has sat only in Scotland or who has sat only in Northern Ireland shall be deemed to constitute a tribunal which does not sit outside England and Wales or which sits only in Scotland or which sits only in Northern Ireland, as the case may be.

9. . . .

10. Procedural rules for tribunals

(1) No power of a Minister, the Lord President of the Court of Session [the Commissioners of Inland Revenue, the Commissioners of Customs and Excise or the Foreign Compensation Commission] to make, approve, confirm or concur in procedural rules for any such tribunal as is specified in Schedule 1 to this Act shall be exercisable except after consultation with the Council.

(2) The Council, in the exercise of their functions under this section as respects

any such tribunal as is specified in Part II of Schedule 1 to this Act, shall consult with the Scottish Committee.

(3) In this section "procedural rules" includes any statutory provision relating to the procedure of the tribunal in question.

11. Procedure in connection with statutory inquiries
*****

12. Reasons to be given for decisions of tribunals and Ministers
(1) Subject to the provisions of this section, where—
 (a) any such tribunal as is specified in Schedule 1 to this Act gives any decision; or
 (b) any Minister notifies any decision taken by him after the holding by him or on his behalf of a statutory inquiry, or taken by him in a case in which a person concerned could (whether by objecting or otherwise) have required the holding as aforesaid of a statutory inquiry,
it shall be the duty of the tribunal or Minister to furnish a statement, either written or oral, of the reasons for the decision if requested, on or before the giving or notification of the decision, to state the reasons.

(2) The said statement may be refused, or the specification of the reasons restricted, on grounds of national security, and the tribunal or Minister may refuse to furnish the statement to a person not primarily concerned with the decision if of opinion that to furnish it would be contrary to the interests of any person primarily concerned.

(3) Subsection (1) of this section shall not apply to any decision taken by a Minister after the holding by him or on his behalf of any inquiry or hearing which is a statutory inquiry by virtue only of an order made under section 19(2) of this Act unless the order contains a direction that this section is to apply in relation to any inquiry or hearing to which the order applies.

(4) Subsection (1) of this section shall not apply to decisions in respect of which any statutory provision has effect, apart from this section, as to the giving of reasons, or to decisions of a Minister in connection with the preparation, making, approval, confirmation, or concurrence in regulations, rules, or byelaws, or orders or schemes of a legislative and not executive character.

(5) Any statement of the reasons for such a decision as is mentioned in paragraph (a) or (b) of subsection (1) of this section, whether given in pursuance of that subsection or of any other statutory provisions, shall be taken to form part of the decision and accordingly to be incorporated in the record.

(6) If, after consultation with the Council, it appears to the Lord Chancellor and the Secretary of State that it is expedient that decisions of any particular tribunal or any description of such decisions, or any description of decisions of a Minister should be excluded from the operation of subsection (1) of this section on the ground that the subject-matter of such decisions, or the circumstances in which they are made, make the giving of reasons unnecessary or impracticable, the Lord Chancellor and the Secretary of State may by order direct that subsection (1) of this section shall not apply to such decisions.

Judicial control of tribunals etc

13. Appeals from certain tribunals
(1) If any party to proceedings before any such tribunal as is specified in paragraph 2(b), 4, [6(a)], [6B], 10, [10A], 17(b), 18(a), 21, 26, 28 . . .(b) or 32 of Schedule 1 to this Act [or to proceedings before a Registered Homes Tribunal] is dissatisfied in point of law with a decision of the tribunal he may, according as rules of court may provide, either appeal therefrom to the High Court or require the tribunal to state and sign a case for the opinion of the High Court.

[(1A) Subsection (1) of this section shall not apply in relation to proceedings before industrial tribunals which arise under or by virtue of any of the enactments mentioned in section 136(1) of the Employment Protection (Consolidation) Act 1978.]

(2) Rules of court made with respect to all or any of the said tribunals may provide for authorising or requiring a tribunal, in the course of proceedings before it, to state, in the form of a special case for the decision of the High Court, any question of law arising in the proceedings; and a decision of the High Court on a case stated by virtue of this subsection shall be deemed to be a judgment of the Court within the meaning of section [16 of the Supreme Court Act 1981] (jurisdiction of Court of Appeal to hear and determine appeals from judgments of the High Court).

(3) In relation to proceedings in the High Court or the Court of Appeal brought by virtue of this section the power to make rules of court shall include power to make rules prescribing the powers of the High Court or the Court of Appeal with respect to—

    (a)   the giving of any decision which might have been given by the tribunal;

    (b)   the remitting of the matter with the opinion or direction of the court for rehearing and determination by the tribunal

    (c)   the giving of directions to the tribunal;

and different provisions may be made for different tribunals.

(4) . . . no appeal to the Court of Appeal shall be brought by virtue of this section except with the leave of the High Court or the Court of Appeal.

(5) . . .

[(5A) Subsection (1) of this section shall apply to a decision of the Secretary of State on an appeal under section 41 of the Consumer Credit Act 1974 from a determination of the Director General of Fair Trading as it applies to a decision of any of the tribunals mentioned in that subsection, but with the substitution for the reference to a party to proceedings of a reference to any person who had a right to appeal to the Secretary of State (whether or not he has exercised that right); and accordingly references in subsections (1) and (3) of this section to a tribunal shall be construed, in relation to such an appeal, as references to the Secretary of State.]

(6)—(10)   *****

14. Extension of supervisory powers of superior courts

(1) As respects England and Wales or Northern Ireland, any provision in an Act passed before 1st August 1958 that any order or determination shall not be called into question in any court, or any provision in such an Act which by similar words excludes any of the powers of the High Court, shall not have effect so as to prevent the removal of the proceedings into the High Court by order of certiorari or to prejudice the powers of the High Court to make orders of mandamus:

Provided that this subsection, so far as it relates to the High Court in Northern Ireland, shall not affect any provision in its application to a matter with respect to which the Parliament of Northern Ireland has power to make laws.

(2) *(Applies to Scotland only.)*

(3) Nothing in this section shall . . . apply to any order or determination of a court of law or where an Act makes special provision for application to the High Court or the Court of Session within a time limited by the Act.

15.—20.   *****

CRIMINAL JUSTICE ACT 1972
(1972, c. 46)

36. Reference to Court of Appeal of point of law following acquittal on indictment

(1) Where a person tried on indictment has been acquitted (whether in respect of the whole or part of the indictment) the Attorney General may, if he desires the opinion of the Court of Appeal on a point of law which has arisen in the case, refer that point to the court, and the court shall, in accordance with this section, consider the point and give their opinion on it.

(2) For the purpose of their consideration of a point referred to them under this section the Court of Appeal shall hear argument—

(a) by, or by counsel on behalf of, the Attorney General; and
(b) if the acquitted person desires to present any argument to the court, by counsel on his behalf or, with the leave of the court, by the acquitted person himself.

(3) Where the Court of Appeal have given their opinion on a point referred to them under this section, the court may, or their own motion or in pursuance of an application in that behalf, refer the point to the House of Lords if it appears to the court that the point ought to be considered by that House.

(4) If a point is referred to the House of Lords under subsection (3) of this section, the House shall consider the point and give their opinion on it accordingly; and section 35(1) of the Criminal Appeal Act 1968 (composition of House for appeals) shall apply also in relation to any proceedings of the House under this section.

(5) Where, on a point being referred to the Court of Appeal under this section or further referred to the House of Lords, the acquitted person appears by counsel for the purpose of presenting any argument to the court or the House, he shall be entitled to his costs, that is to say to the payment out of central funds of such sums as are reasonably sufficient to compensate him for expenses properly incurred by him for the purpose of being represented on the reference or further reference; and any amount recoverable under this subsection shall be ascertained, as soon as practicable, by the registrar of criminal appeals or, as the case may be, such officer as may be prescribed by order of the House of Lords.

[(5A) Section 20(1) of the Prosecution of Offences Act 1985 (regulations as to scales and rates of payment of costs payable out of central funds) shall apply in relation to this section as it applies in relation to Part II of that Act.]

(6) Subject to rules of court made under section 1(5) if the Criminal Appeal Act 1966 (power by rules to distribute business of Court of Appeal between its civil and criminal divisions), the jurisdiction of the Court of Appeal under this section shall be exercised by the criminal division of the court; and references in this section to the Court of Appeal shall be construed accordingly as references to that division of the court.

(7) A reference under this section shall not affect the trial in relation to which the reference is made or any acquittal in that trial.

EUROPEAN COMMUNITIES ACT 1972
(1972, c. 68)

An Act to make provision in connection with the enlargement of the European Communities to include the United Kingdom, together with (for certain purposes) the Channel Islands, the Isle of Man and Gibraltar [17 October 1972]

PART I
GENERAL PROVISIONS

1. Short title and interpretation

(1) This Act may be cited as the European Communities Act 1972.

(2) In this Act . . .

"the Communities" means the European Economic Community, the European Coal and Steel Community and the European Atomic Energy Community;

"the Treaties" or "the Community Treaties" means, subject to subsection (3) below, the pre-accession treaties, that is to say, those described in Part I of Schedule I to this Act, taken with—

***** [full list omitted]

and any expression defined in Schedule I to this Act has the meaning there given to it.

(3) If Her Majesty by Order in Council declares that a treaty specified in the Order is to be regarded as one of the Community Treaties as herein defined, the Order shall be conclusive that it is to be so regarded; but a treaty entered into by United Kingdom after the 22nd January 1972, other than a pre-accession treaty to which the United Kingdom accedes on terms settled on or before that date, shall not be so regarded unless it is so specified, nor be so specified unless a draft of the Order in Council has been approved by resolution of each House of Parliament.

(4) For purposes of subsections (2) and (3) above, "treaty" includes any international agreement, and any protocol or annex to a treaty or international agreement.

2. General implementation of Treaties

(1) All such rights, powers, liabilities, obligations and restrictions from time to time created or arising by or under the Treaties, and all such remedies and procedures from time to time provided for by or under the Treaties, as in accordance with the Treaties are without further enactment to be given legal effect or used in the United Kingdom shall be recognised and available in law, and be enforced, allowed and followed accordingly; and the expression "enforceable Community right" and similar expressions shall be read as referring to one to which this subsection applies.

(2) Subject to Schedule 2 to this Act, at any time after its passing Her Majesty may by Order in Council, and any designated Minister or department may by regulations, make provision—

(a) for the purpose of implementing any Community obligation of the United Kingdom, or enabling any such obligation to be implemented, or of enabling any rights enjoyed or to be enjoyed by the United Kingdom under or by virtue of the Treaties to be exercised; or

(b) for the purpose of dealing with matters arising out of or related to any such obligation or rights or the coming into force, or the operation from time to time, of subsection (1) above;

and in the exercise of any statutory power or duty, including any power to give directions or to legislate by means or orders, rules, regulations or other subordinate instrument, the person entrusted with the power or duty may have regard to the objects of the Communities and to any such obligation or rights as aforesaid.

In this subsection "designated Minister or Department" means such Minister of the Crown or government department as may from time to time be designated by Order in Council in relation to any matter or for any purpose, but subject to such restrictions or conditions (if any) as may be specified by the Order in Council.

(3) There shall be charged on and issued out of the Consolidated Fund or, if so determined by the Treasury, the National Loans Fund the amounts required to meet any Community obligation to make payments to any of the Communities or member States, or any Community obligation in respect of contributions to the captial or reserves

of the European Investment Bank or in respect of loans to the Bank, or to redeem any notes or obligations issued or created in respect of any such Community obligation; and, except as otherwise provided by or under any enactment,—

    (a)   any other expenses incurred under or by virtue of the Treaties or this Act by any Minister of the Crown or government department may be paid out of moneys provided by Parliament; and

    (b)   any sums received under or by virtue of the Treaties or this Act by any Minister of the Crown or government department, save for such sums as may be required for disbursements permitted by any other enactment, shall be paid into the Consolidated Fund or, if so determined by the Treasury, the National Loans Fund.

(4) The provision that may be made under subsection (2) above includes, subject to Schedule 2 to this Act, any such provision (of any such extent) as might be made by Act of Parliament, and any enactment passed or to be passed, other than one contained in this Part of this Act, shall be construed and have effect subject to the foregoing provisions of this section; but, except as may be provided by any Act passed after this Act, Schedule 2 shall have effect in connection with the powers conferred by this and the following sections of this Act to make Orders in Council and regulations.

(5), (6)   *****

3. Decisions on, and proof of, Treaties and Community instruments, etc.

(1) For the purposes of all legal proceedings any question as to the meaning or effect of any of the Treaties, or as to the validity, meaning or effect of any Community instrument, shall be treated as a question of law (and, if not referred to the European Court, be for determination as such in accordance with the principles laid down by and any relevant [decision of the European Court or any court attached thereto)].

(2) Judicial notice shall be taken of the Treaties, of the Official Journal of the Communities and of any decision of, or expression of opinion by, the European Court [or any court attached thereto] on any such question as aforesaid; and the Official Journal shall be admissible as evidence of any instrument or other act thereby communicated of any of the Communities or of any Community institution.

(3), (4), (5)   *****

*****

SCHEDULE 2

Section 2

PROVISIONS AS TO SUBORDINATE LEGISLATION

1.—(1) The powers conferred by section 2(2) of this Act to make provision for the purposes mentioned in section 2(2)(a) and (b) shall not include power—

    (a)   to make any provision imposing or increasing taxation; or

    (b)   to make any provision taking effect from a date earlier than that of the making of the instrument containing the provision; or

    (c)   to confer any power to legislate by means of orders, rules regulations or other subordinate instrument, other than rules of procedure for any court or tribunal; or

    (d)   to create any new criminal offence punishable with imprisonment for more than two years or punishable on summary conviction with imprisonment for more than three months or with a fine of more than [level 5 on the standard scale] (if not calculated on a daily basis) or with a fine of more than [£100 a day].

(2) Sub-paragraph (1)(c) above shall not be taken to preclude the modification of a power to legislate conferred otherwise than under section 2(2), or the extension of any such power to purposes of the like nature as those for which it was conferred;

and a power to give directions as to matters of administration is not to be regarded as a power to legislate within the meaning of sub-paragraph (1)(c).

2.—(1) Subject to paragraph 3 below, where a provision contained in any section of this Act confers power to make regulations (otherwise than by modification or extension of an existing power), the power shall be exercisable by statutory instrument.

(2) Any statutory instrument containing an Order in Council or regulations made in the exercise of a power so conferred, if made without a draft having been approved by resolution of each House of Parliament, shall be subject to annulment in pursuance of a resolution of either House.

POWERS OF CRIMINAL COURTS ACT 1973
(1973, c. 62)

An Act to consolidate certain enactments relating to the powers of courts to deal with offenders and defaulters, to the treatment of offenders and to arrangements for persons on bail.

[25 October 1973]

PART I
POWERS OF COURTS TO DEAL WITH OFFENDERS

Preliminary

1. Deferment of sentence

(1) Subject to the provisions of this section, the Crown Court or a magistrates' court may defer passing sentence on an offender for the purpose of enabling the court [or any other court to which it falls to deal with him to have regard, in dealing with him], to his conduct after conviction (including, where appropriate, the making by him of reparation for his offence) or to any change in his circumstances.

(2) Any deferment under this section shall be until such date as may be specified by the court, not being more than six months after the date [on which the deferment is announced by the court]; and [subject to subsection (8A) below] where the passing of sentence has been deferred under this section it shall not be further deferred thereunder.

(3) The power conferred by this section shall be exercisable only if the offender consents and the court is satisfied, having regard to the nature of the offence and the character and circumstances of the offender, that it would be in the interests of justice to exercise the power.

(4) A court which under this section has deferred passing sentence on an offender may [deal with] him before the expiration of the period of deferment if during that period he is convicted in Great Britain of any offence.

[(4A) If an offender on whom a court has under this section deferred passing sentence in respect of one or more offences is during the period of deferment convicted in England or Wales of any offence ('the subsequent offence'), then, without prejudice to subsection (4) above, the court which (whether during that period or not) passes sentence on him for the subsequent offence may also, if this has not already been done, pass sentence on him for the first-mentioned offence or offences: Provided that—

(a) the power conferred by this subsection shall not be exercised by a magistrates' court if the court which deferred passing sentence was the Crown Court; and

(b) the Crown Court, in exercising that power in a case in which the court which deferred passing sentence was a magistrates' court, shall not pass any sentence which could not have been passed by a magistrates' court in exercising it.]

(5) Where a court which under this section has deferred passing sentence on an offender proposes to [deal with] him, whether on the date originally specified by the court or by virtue of subsection (4) above before that date, [or where the offender

does not appear on the date specified, the court] may issue a summons requiring him to appear before the court, or may issue a warrant for his arrest.

[(6) It is hereby declared that in deferring the passing of sentence under this section a magistrates' court is to be regarded as exercising the power of adjourning the trial which is conferred by [section 10(1) of the Magistrates' Courts Act 1980] and that accordingly [sections 11(1) and 13(1), (2) and (5) of that Act] (non-appearance of the accused) [apply] (without prejudice to subsection (5) above) if the offender does not appear on the date specified in pursuance of subsection (2) above.

(6A) Notwithstanding any enactment, a court which under this section defers passing sentence on an offender shall not on the same occasion remand him.]

(7) Nothing in this section shall affect the power of the Crown Court to bind over an offender to come up for judgment when called upon or the power of any court to defer passing sentence for any purpose for which it may lawfully do so apart from this section.

[(8) The power of a court under this section to deal with an offender in a case where the passing of sentence has been deferred thereunder—

    (a) includes power to deal with him in any way in which the court which deferred passing sentence could have dealt with him; and

    (b) without prejudice to the generality of the foregoing, in the case of a magistrates' court, includes the power conferred by section 37 or 38 of the Magistrates' Courts Act 1980 to commit him to the Crown Court for sentence.

(8A) Where, in a case where the passing of sentence of an offender in respect of one or more offences has been deferred under this section, a magistrates' court deals with him by committing him to the Crown Court under section 37 or 38 of the Act of 1980, the power of the Crown Court to deal with him includes the same power to defer passing sentence on him as if he had just been convicted of the offence or offences on indictment before the court.]

Probation and discharge

2. Probation

(1) Where a court by or before which a person of or over seventeen years of age is convicted of an offence (not being an offence the sentence for which is fixed by law) is of opinion that having regard to the circumstances, including the nature of the offence and the character of the offender, it is expedient to do so, the court may, instead of sentencing him, make a probation order, that is to say, an order requiring him to be under the supervision of a probation officer for a period to be specified in the order of [not less than six months] nor more than three years.

For the purposes of this subsection the age of a person shall be deemed to be that which it appears to the court to be after considering any available evidence.

(2) A probation order shall name the petty sessions area in which the offender resides or will reside; and the offender shall (subject to the provisions of Schedule 1 to this Act relating to probationers who change their residence) be required to be under the supervision of a probation officer appointed for or assigned to that area.

In this Act "supervising court" means, in relation to a probation order, a magistrates' court acting for the petty sessions area for the time being named in the order.

(3) Subject to the provisions of subsection (4) below and sections 3 and [4A and 4B] of this Act a probation order may in addition require the offender to comply during the whole or any part of the probation period with such requirements as the court, having regard to the circumstances of the case, considers necessary for securing the good conduct of the offender or for preventing a repetition by him of the same offence or the commission of other offences.

(4) Without prejudice to the power of the court under section 35 of this Act to make a compensation order, the payment of sums by way of damages for injury or

compensation for loss shall not be included among the requirements of a probation order.

(5) Without prejudice to the generality of subsection (3) above, a probation order may include requirements relating to the residence of the offender, but—

    (a) before making an order containing any such requirements, the court shall consider the home surroundings of the offender; and

    [(b) where the order requires the offender to reside in an approved probation hostel or any other institution, the period for which he is so required to reside shall be specified in the order.]

(6) Before making a probation order, the court shall explain to the offender in ordinary language the effect of the order (including any additional requirements proposed to be inserted therein . . .) and that if he fails to comply with it or commits another offence he will be liable to be sentenced for the original offence; and the court shall not make the order unless he expresses his willingness to comply with its requirements.

(7) The court by which a probation order is made shall forthwith give copies of the order to a probation officer assigned to the court, and he shall give a copy to the offender, to the probation officer responsible for the supervision of the offender and to the person in charge of any institution in which the probationer is required by the order to reside; and the court shall, except where it is itself the supervising court, send to the clerk to the justices for the petty sessions area named in the order a copy of the order, together with such documents and information relating to the case as it considers likely to be of assistance to the supervising court.

(8) . . .

[(9) The Secretary of State may by order direct that subsection (1) above shall be amended by substituting, for the minimum or maximum period specified in that subsection as originally enacted or as previously amended under this subsection, such period as may be specified in the order.

(10) An order under subsection (9) above may make in paragraph 3(2)(a) of Schedule 1 to this Act any amendment which the Secrtetary of State thinks necessary in consequence of any substitution made by the order.]

3.—5. *****

6. Breach of requirement of probation order

(1) If at any time during the probation period it appears on information to a justice of the peace on whom jurisdiction is conferred by subsection (2) below that the probationer has failed to comply with any of the requirements of the order, the justice may issue a summons requiring the probationer to appear at the place and time specified therein, or may, if the information is in writing and on oath, issue a warrant for his arrest.

(2) *****

(3) If it is proved to the satisfaction of the magistrates' court before which a probationer appears or is brought under this section that the probationer has failed to comply with any of the requirements of the probation order, then, subject to the following provisions of this subsection, that court may deal with him in respect of the failure in any one of the following ways, that is to say:

    (a) it may impose on him a fine not exceeding [£400];

    (b) subject to subsection (10) below, it may make a community service order in respect of him;

    (c) in a case to which section [17 of the Criminal Justice Act 1982] applies, it may make an order under that section requiring him to attend at an attendance centre; or

    (d) where the probation order was made by a magistrates' court, it may deal with him for the offence in respect of which the probation order was made, in any manner in which it could deal with him if it had just convicted him of that offence.

(4) Where the probation order was made by the Crown Court, and a magistrates' court has power to deal with the probationer under subsection (3)(a), (b) or (c) above in respect of a failure to comply with any of the requirements of the order, the magistrates' court may instead commit him to custody or release him on bail until he can be brought or appear before the Crown Court.

(5) *****

(6) Where by virtue of subsection (4) above the probationer is brought or appears before the Crown Court, and it is proved to the satisfaction of the court that he has failed to comply with any of the requirements of the probation order, the court may deal with him in respect of the failure in any one of the following ways, that is to say:—

    (a)   it may impose on him a fine not exceeding [£400];

    (b)   subject to subsection (10) below, it may make a community service order in respect of him; or

    (c)   it may deal with him for the offence in respect of which the probation order was made in any manner in which it could deal with him if he had just been convicted before the Crown Court of that offence.

(7)—(10) *****

7. Absolute and conditional discharge

(1) Where a court by or before which a person is convicted of an offence (not being an offence the sentence for which is fixed by law) is of opinion, having regard to the circumstances including the nature of the offence and the character of the offender, that it is inexpedient to inflict punishment and that a probation order is not appropriate, the court may make an order discharging him absolutely, or, if the court thinks fit, discharging him subject to the condition that he commits no offence during such period, not exceeding three years from the date of the order, as may be specified therein.

(2) An order discharging a person subject to such a condition is in this Act referred to as "an order for conditional discharge", and the period specified in any such order (subject to section 8(1) of this Act) as "the period of conditional discharge".

(3) Before making an order for conditional discharge the court shall explain to the offender in ordinary language that if he commits another offence during the period of conditional discharge he will be liable to be sentenced for the original offence.

(4) Where, under the following provisions of this Part of this Act, a person conditionally discharged under this section is sentenced for the offence in respect of which the order for conditional discharge was made, that order shall cease to have effect.

[(5) The Secretary of State may by order direct that subsection (1) above shall be amended by substituting, for the maximum period specified in that subsection as originally enacted or as previously amended under this subsection, such period as may be specified in the order.]

8. Commission of further offence by probationer or person conditionally discharged

(1) If it appears to the Crown Court, where that court has jurisdiction in accordance with subsection (2) below, or to a justice of the peace having jurisdiction in accordance with that subsection, that a person in whose case a probation order or an order for conditional discharge has been convicted by a court in any part of Great Britain of an offence committed during the relevant period, and has been dealt with in respect of that offence, that court or justice may, subject to subsection (3) below, issue a summons requiring that person to appear at the place and time specified therein or a warrant for his arrest.

In this section "the relevant period" means, in relation to a probation order, the probation period, and in relation to an order for conditional discharge, the period of conditional discharge.

(2) Jurisdiction for the purposes of subsection (1) above may be exercised—

    (a) if the probation order or order for conditional discharge was made by the Crown Court, by that court;

    (b) if the order was made by a magistrates' court, by a justice acting for the petty sessions area for which that court acts;

    (c) in the case of a probation order, by whatever court it was made, by a justice acting for the petty sessions area for which the supervising court acts.

(3)—(6) *****

(7) Where it is proved to the satisfaction of the court by which a probation order or an order for conditional discharge was made, or to the satisfaction of that court or the supervising court in the case of a probation order made by a magistrates' court, that the person in whose case the order was made has been convicted of an offence committed during the relevant period, the court may deal with him, for the offence for which the order was made, in any manner in which it could deal with him if he had just been convicted by or before that court of that offence.

(8) If a person in whose case a probation order or an order for conditional discharge has been made by a magistrates' court is convicted before the Crown Court of an offence committed during the relevant period, or is dealt with by the Crown Court for any such offence in respect of which he was committed for sentence to the Crown Court, the Crown Court may deal with him, for the offence for which the order was made, in any manner in which the magistrates' court could deal with him if it had just convicted him of that offence.

(9) *****

9., 10. *****

11. Substitution of conditional discharge for probation

(1) Where on an application made by the probationer or the probation officer it appears to the court having power to discharge a probation order that the order is no longer appropriate in the case of the probationer, the court may make, in substitution for the probation order, an order discharging him in respect of the original offence, subject to the condition that he commits no offence between the making of the order under this section and the expiration of the probation period.

[(1A) No application may be made under subsection (1) above while an appeal against the probation order is pending.]

(2) A person in respect of whom an order is made under this section shall so long as the condition mentioned in subsection (1) above continues in force be treated in all respects and in particular for the purposes of section 8 of this Act as if the original order made in his case had been an order for conditional discharge made by the court which made the original order and as if the period of conditional discharge were the same as the probation period.

(3) Where an application under this section is made by the probation officer, it may be heard in the absence of the probationer if the officer produces to the court a statement by him that he understands the effect of an order under this section and consents to the application being made.

(4) On the making of an order under this section the appropriate officer of the court shall forthwith give copies of the order to the probation officer, who shall give a copy to the person in respect of whom the order is made and to the person in charge of any institution in which that person was required by the probation order to reside.

12., 13. *****

Community service orders

14. Community service orders in respect of convicted persons

(1) Where a person of or over sixteen years of age is convicted of an offence punishable with imprisonment, the court by or before which he is convicted may, instead of dealing with him in any other way (but subject to subsection (2) below) make an order (in this Act referred to as "a community service order") requiring him to perform unpaid work in accordance with the subsequent provisions of this Act . . .

The reference in this subsection to an offence punishable with imprisonment shall be construed without regard to any prohibition or restriction imposed by or under any enactment on the imprisonment of young offenders.

[(1A) The number of hours which a person may be required to work under a community service order shall be specified in the order and shall be in the aggregate—
  (a) no less than 40; and
  (b) not more—
      (i) in the case of an offender aged sixteen, than 120; and
      (ii) in other cases, than 240.]

[(2) A court shall not make a community service order in respect of any offender unless the offender consents and after considering a report by a probation officer or by a social worker of a local authority social services department about the offender and his circumstances and, if the court thinks it necessary, hearing a probation officer or a social worker of a local authority social services department, the court is satisfied that the offender is a suitable person to perform work under such an order.]

[(2A) Subject to sections 17A and 17B below,—
  (a) a court shall not make a community service order in respect of any offender who is of or over seventeen years of age unless the court is satisfied that provision for him to perform work under such an order can be made under the arrangements for persons to perform work under such orders which exist in the petty sessions area in which he resides or will reside; and
  (b) a court shall not make a community service order in respect of an offender who is under seventeen years of age unless—
      (i) it has been notified by the Secretary of State that arrangements exist for persons of the offender's age who reside in the petty sessions area in which the offender resides or will reside to perform work under such orders; and
      (ii) it is satisfied that provision can be made under the arrangements for him to do so.

(3) Where a court makes community service orders in respect of two or more offences of which the offender has been convicted by or before the court, the court may direct that the hours of work specified in any of those orders shall be concurrent with or additional to those specified in any other of those orders, but so that the total number of hours which are not concurrent shall not exceed the maximum [specified in paragraph (b)(i) or(ii) of subsection (1A) above.]

(4) A community service order shall specify the petty sessions area in which the offender resides or will reside; and the functions conferred by the subsequent provisions of this Act on the relevant officer shall be discharged by a probation officer appointed for or assigned to the area for the time being specified in the order (whether under this subsection or by virtue of section 17(5) of this Act), or by a person appointed for the purposes of those provisions by the [probation committee] for that area.

(5) Before making a community service order the court shall explain to the offender in ordinary language—
  (a) the purpose and effect of the order (and in particular the requirements of the order as specified in section 15 of this Act);

(b) the consequences which may follow under section 16 if he fails to comply with any of those requirements; and

(c) that the court has under section 17 the power to review the order on the application either of the offender or of a probation officer.

(6) The court by which a community service order is made shall forthwith give copies of the order to a probation officer assigned to the court and he shall give a copy to the offender and to the relevant officer; and the court shall, except where it is itself a magistrates' court acting for the petty sessions area specified in the order, send to the clerk to the justices for the petty sessions area specified in the order a copy of the order, together with such documents and information relating to the case as it considers likely to be of assistance to a court acting for that area in exercising its functions in relation to the order.

(7) *****

(8) Nothing in subsection (1) above shall be construed as preventing a court which makes a community service order in respect of any offence from making an order for costs against, or imposing any disqualification on, the offender or from making in respect of the offence an order under section 35, 39, 43 or 44 of this Act, or under section 29 of the Theft Act 1968.

15. *****

16. Breach of requirements of community service order

(1) If at any time while a community service order is in force in respect of an offender it appears on information to a justice of the peace acting for the petty sessions area for the time being specified in the order that the offender has failed to comply with any of the requirements of section 15 of this Act (including any failure satisfactorily to perform the work which he has been instructed to do), the justice may issue a summons requiring the offender to appear at the place and time specified therein, or may, if the information is in writing and on oath, issue a warrant for his arrest.

(2) Any summons or warrant issued under this section shall direct the offender to appear or be brought before a magistrates' court acting for the petty sessions area for the time being specified in the community service order.

(3) If it is proved to the satisfaction of the magistrates' court before which an offender appears or is brought under this section that he has failed without reasonable excuse to comply with any of the requirements of section 15 the court may, without prejudice to the continuance of the order, impose on him a fine not exceeding [£400] or may—

(a) if the community service order was made by a magistrates' court, revoke the order and deal with the offender, for the offence in respect of which the order was made, in any manner in which he could have been dealt with for that offence by the court which made the order if the order had not been made;

(b) if the order was made by the Crown Court, commit him to custody or release him on bail until he can be brought or appear before the Crown Court.

(4) A magistrates' court which deals with an offender's case under subsection (3)(b) above shall send to the Crown Court a certificate signed by a justice of the peace certifying that the offender has failed to comply with the requirements of section 15 in the respect specified in the certificate, together with such other particulars of the case as may be desirable; and a certificate purporting to be so signed shall be admissible as evidence of the failure before the Crown Court.

(5) Where by virtue of subsection (3)(b) above the offender is brought or appears before the Crown Court and it is proved to the satisfaction of the court that he has failed to comply with any of the requirements of section 15, that court may either—

(a) without prejudice to the continuance of the order, impose on him a fine not exceeding [£400]; or

(b) revoke the order and deal with him, for the offence in respect of which the order was made, in any manner in which he could have been dealt with for that offence by the court which made the order if the order had not been made.

(6) A person sentenced under subsection (3)(a) above for an offence may appeal to the Crown Court against the sentence.

(7) In proceedings before the Crown Court under this section any question whether the offender has failed to comply with the requirements of section 15 shall be determined by the court and not by the verdict of a jury.

(8) A fine imposed under this section shall be deemed for the purposes of any enactment to be a sum adjudged to be paid by a conviction.

17., 17A., B and C *****

Imprisonment, Borstal training and detention:
general provisions

18. General power of Crown Court
(1) Where a person is convicted on indictment of an offence against any enactment and is for that offence liable to be sentenced to imprisonment, but the sentence is not by any enactment either limited to a specified term or expressed to extend to imprisonment for life, the person so convicted shall be liable to imprisonment for not more than two years.

(2) . . .

19. . . .

20. Restriction on imposing sentences of imprisonment on persons who have not previously served prison sentences
(1) No court shall pass a sentence of imprisonment on a person of or over twenty-one years of age on whom such a sentence has not previously been passed by a court in any part of the United Kingdom unless the court is of opinion that no other method of dealing with him is appropriate; and for the purpose of determining whether any other method of dealing with any such person is appropriate the court shall obtain and consider information before the court which is relevant to his character and his physical and mental condition.

(2) Where a magistrates' court passes a sentence of imprisonment on any such person as is mentioned in subsection (1) above, the court shall state the reason for its opinion that no other method of dealing with him is appropriate, and cause that reason to be specified in the warrant of commitment and to be entered in the register.

(3) For the purposes of this section—
(a) a previous sentence of imprisonment which has been suspended and which has not taken effect under section 23 of this Act or under section 19 of the Treatment of Offenders Act (Northern Ireland) 1968 shall be disregarded; and
(b) "sentence of imprisonment" does not include a committal or attachment for contempt of court.

(4) Subsection (1) above does not affect the power of a court to pass sentence on any person for an offence the sentence for which is fixed by law.

[(5) For the purposes of this section the age of a person shall be deemed to be that which it appears to the court to be after considering the available evidence.]

[20A. Social inquiry report for purposes of s. 20
(1) Subject to subsection (2) below, the court shall in every case obtain a social inquiry report for the purpose of determining under section 20(1) above whether there is any appropriate method of dealing with an offender other than imprisonment.

(2) Subsection (1) above does not apply if, in the circumstances of the case, the court is of the opinion that it is unnecessary to obtain a social inquiry report.

(3) Where a magistrates' court passes a sentence of imprisonment on a person of or over 21 years of age on whom such a sentence has not previously been passed by a court in any part of the United Kingdom without obtaining a social inquiry report, it shall state in open court the reason for its opinion that it was unnecessary to obtain such a report.

(4) A magistrates' court shall cause a reason stated under subsection (3) above to be specified in the warrant of commitment and to be entered in the register.

(5) No sentence shall be invalidated by the failure of a court to comply with subsection (1) above, but any other court on appeal from that court shall obtain a social inquiry report if none was obtained by the court below, unless it is of the opinion that in the circumstances of the case it is unnecessary to do so.]

(6) In determining whether it should deal with the appellant otherwise than by passing a sentence of imprisonment on him the court hearing the appeal shall consider any social inquiry report obtained by it or by the court below.

(7) In this section "social inquiry report" means a report about a person and his circumstances made by a probation officer.

21. Restriction on imposing sentences of imprisonment, Borstal training or detention on persons not legally represented

(1) A magistrates' court on summary conviction or the Crown Court on committal for sentence or on conviction on indictment shall not pass a sentence of imprisonment . . . on a person who is not legally represented in that court and has not been previously sentenced to that punishment by a court in any part of the United Kingdom, unless either—

(a) he applied for legal aid and the application was refused on the ground that it did not appear his means were such that he required assistance; or

(b) having been informed of his right to apply for legal aid and had the opportunity to do so, he refused or failed to apply.

(2) For the purposes of this section a person is to be treated as legally represented in a court if, but only if, he has the assistance of counsel or a solicitor to represent him in the proceedings in that court at some time after he is found guilty and before he is sentenced, and in subsection (1)(a) and (b) above "legal aid" means legal aid for the purposes of proceedings in that court, whether the whole proceedings or the proceedings on or in relation to sentence; but in the case of a person committed to the Crown Court for sentence or trial, it is immaterial whether he applied for legal aid in the Crown Court to, or was informed of his right to apply by, that court or the court which committed him.

(3) For the purposes of this section—

(a) a previous sentence of imprisonment which has been suspended and which has not taken effect under section 23 of this Act or under section 19 of the Treatment of Offenders Act (Northern Ireland) 1968 shall be disregarded;

(b) "sentence of imprisonment" does not include a committal or attachment for contempt of court; and

(c) . . .

Suspended sentences of imprisonment

22. Suspended sentences of imprisonment

(1) Subject to subsection (2) below, a court which passes a sentence of imprisonment for a term of not more than two years for an offence may order that the sentence shall not take effect unless, during a period specified in the order, being not less than one year or more than two years from the date of the order, the offender commits in Great Britain another offence punishable with imprisonment and thereafter a court having power to do so orders under section 23 of this Act that the original sentence

shall take effect; and in this Part of this Act "operational period", in relation to a suspended sentence, means the period so specified.

(2) A court shall not deal with an offender by means of a suspended sentence unless the case appears to the court to be one in which a sentence of imprisonment would have been appropriate in the absence of any power to suspend such a sentence by an order under subsection (1) above.

(3) A court which passes a suspended sentence on any person for an offence shall not make a probation order in his case in respect of another offence of which he is convicted by or before the court or for which he is dealt with by the court.

(4) On passing a suspended sentence the court shall explain to the offender in ordinary language his liability under section 23 of this Act if during the operational period he commits an offence punishable with imprisonment.

(5) *****

(6) Subject to any provision to the contrary contained in the Criminal Justice Act 1967, this Act or any enactment passed or instrument made under any enactment after 31st December 1967—

    (a) a suspended sentence which has not taken effect under section 23 of this Act shall be treated as a sentence of imprisonment for the purposes of all enactments and instruments made under enactments except any enactment or instrument which provides for disqualification for or loss of office, or forfeiture of pensions, of persons sentenced to imprisonment; and

    (b) where a suspended sentence has taken effect under that section, the offender shall be treated for the purposes of the enactments and instruments excepted by paragraph (a) above as having been convicted on the ordinary date on which the period allowed for making an appeal against an order under that section expires or, if such an appeal is made, the date on which it is finally disposed of or abandoned or fails for non-prosecution.

23. Power of court on conviction of further offence to deal with suspended sentence

(1) Where an offender is convicted of an offence punishable with imprisonment committed during the operational period of a suspended sentence and either he is so convicted by or before a court having power under section 24 of this Act to deal with him in respect of the suspended sentence or he subsequently appears or is brought before such a court, then, unless the sentence has already taken effect, that court shall consider his case and deal with him by one of the following methods:—

    (a) the court may order that the suspended sentence shall take effect with the original term unaltered;

    (b) it may order that the sentence shall take effect with the substitution of a lesser term for the original term;

    (c) it may by order vary the original order under section 22(1) of this Act by substituting for the period specified therein a period expiring not later than two years from the date of the variation; or

    (d) it may make no order with respect to the suspended sentence;

and a court shall make an order under paragraph (a) of this subsection unless the court is of opinion that it would be unjust to do so in view of all the circusmtances . . . including the facts of the subsequent offence, and where it is of that opinion the court shall state its reasons.

(2) Where a court orders that a suspended sentence shall take effect, with or without any variation of the original term, the court may order that that sentence shall take effect immediately or that the term thereof shall commence on the expiration of another term of imprisonment passed on the offender by that or another court.

(3)—(5) . . .

(6) In proceedings for dealing with an offender in respect of a suspended sentence which take place before the Crown Court any question whether the offender has been convicted of an offence punishable with imprisonment committed during the operational period of the suspended sentence shall be determined by the court and not by the verdict of a jury.

(7) Where a court deals with an offender under this section in respect of a suspended sentence the appropriate officer of the court shall notify the appropriate officer of the court which passed the sentence of the method adopted.

(8) Where on consideration of the case of an offender a court makes no order with respect to a suspended sentence, the appropriate officer of the court shall record that fact.

(9) For the purposes of any enactment conferring rights of appeal in criminal cases any order made by a court with respect to a suspended sentence shall be treated as a sentence passed on the offender by that court for the offence for which the suspended sentence was passed.

24. Court by which suspended sentence may be dealt with

(1) An offender may be dealt with in respect of a suspended sentence by the Crown Court or, where the sentence was passed by a magistrates' court, by any magistrates' court before which he appears or is brought.

(2) Where an offender is convicted by a magistrates' court of an offence punishable with imprisonment and the court is satisfied that the offence was committed during the operational period of a suspended sentence passed by the Crown Court—

(a) the court may, if it thinks fit, commit him in custody or on bail to the Crown Court; and

(b) if it does not, shall give written notice of the conviction to the appropriate officer of the Crown Court.

(3) For the purposes of this section and of section 25 of this Act a suspended sentence passed on an offender on appeal shall be treated as having been passed by the court by which he was originally sentenced.

25. Procedure where court convicting of further offence does not deal with suspended sentence

(1) If it appears to the Crown Court, where that court has jurisdiction in accordance with subsection (2) below, or to a justice of the peace having jurisdiction in accordance with that subsection, that an offender has been convicted in Great Britain of an offence punishable with imprisonment committed during the operational period of a suspended sentence and that he has not been dealt with in respect of the suspended sentence, that court or justice may, subject to the following provisions of this section, issue a summons requiring the offender to appear at the place and time specified therein, or a warrant for his arrest.

(2) Jurisdiction for the purposes of subsection (1) above may be exercised—

(a) if the suspended sentence was passed by the Crown Court, by that court;

(b) if it was passed by a magistrates' court, by a justice acting for the area for which that court acted.

(3) Where an offender is convicted by a court in Scotland of an offence punishable with imprisonment and the court is informed that the offence was committed during the operational period of a suspended sentence passed in England or Wales, the court shall give written notice of the conviction to the appropriate officer of the court by which the suspended sentence was passed.

(4) Unless he is acting in consequence of a notice under subsection (3) above, a justice of the peace shall not issue a summons under this section except on information and shall not issue a warrant under this section except on information in writing and on oath.

(5) A summons or warrant issued under this section shall direct the offender to appear or to be brought before the court by which the suspended sentence was passed.

26. Suspended sentence supervision orders.

(1) Where a court passes on an offender a suspended sentence for a term of more than six months for a single offence, the court may make a suspended sentence supervision order (in this Act referred to as "a supervision order") placing the offender under the supervision of a supervising officer for a period specified in the order, being a period not exceeding the operational period of the suspended sentence.

(2) The Secretary of State may by order—

    (a) direct that subsection (1) above be amended by substituting, for the number of months specified in the subsection as originally enacted or as previously amended under this paragraph, such other number (not more than six) as the order may specify; or

    (b) make in that subsection the repeals necessary to enable a court to make a supervision order thereunder in the case of any suspended sentence, whatever the length of the term.

(3) A supervision order shall specify the petty sessions area in which the offender resides or will reside; and the supervising officer shall be a probation officer appointed for or assigned to the area for the time being specified in the order (whether under this subsection or by virtue of subsection (6) below).

(4) An offender in respect of whom a supervision order is in force shall keep in touch with the supervising officer in accordance with such instructions as he may from time to time be given by that officer and shall notify him of any change of address.

(5) The court by which a supervision order is made shall forthwith give copies of the order to a probation officer assigned to the court, and he shall give a copy to the offender and the supervising officer; and the court shall, except where it is itself a magistrates' court acting for the petty sessions area specified in the order, send to the clerk to the justices for the petty sessions area specified in the order a copy of the order, together with such documents and information relating to the case as it considers likely to be of assistance to a court acting for that area in exercising its functions in relation to the order.

(6) If a magistrates' court acting for the petty sessions area for the time being specified in a supervision order is satisfied that the offender proposes to change, or has changed, his residence from that petty sessions area to another petty sessions area, the court may, and on the application of the supervising officer shall, amend the order by substituting the other petty sessions area for the area specified in the order.

(7) Where a supervision order is amended by a court under subsection (6) above the court shall send to the clerk to the justices for the new area specified in the order a copy of the order, together with such documents and information relating to the case as it considers likely to be of assistance to a court acting for that area in exercising its functions in relation to the order.

(8) A supervision order shall cease to have effect if before the end of the period specified in it—

    (a) a court orders under section 23 of this Act that a suspended sentence passed in the proceedings in which the order was made shall have effect; or

    (b) the order is discharged or replaced under the subsequent provisions of this section.

(9) A supervision order may be discharged, on the application of the supervising officer or the offender—

    (a) if it was made by the Crown Court and includes a direction reserving the power of discharging it to that court, by the Crown Court;

(b) in any other case by a magistrates' court acting for the petty sessions area for the time being specified in the order.

(10) Where under section 23 of this Act a court deals with an offender in respect of a suspended sentence by varying the operational period of the sentence or by making no order with respect to the sentence, the court may make a supervision order in respect of the offender—

 (a) in place of any such order made when the suspended sentence was passed; or

 (b) if the court which passed the sentence could have made such an order but did not do so; or

 (c) if that court could not then have made such an order but would have had power to do so if subsection (1) above had then had effect as it has effect at the time when the offender is dealt with under section 23.

(11) On making a supervision order the court shall in ordinary language explain its effect to the offender.

27. Breach of requirement of suspended sentence supervision order

(1) If at any time while a supervision order is in force in respect of an offender it appears on information to a justice of the peace acting for the petty sessions area for the time being specified in the order that the offender has failed to comply with any of the requirements of section 26(4) of this Act, the justice may issue a summons requiring the offender to appear at the place and time specified therein, or may, if the information is in writing and on oath, issue a warrant for his arrest.

(2) Any summons or warrant issued under this section shall direct the offender to appear or be brought before a magistrates' court acting for the petty sessions area for the time being specified in the supervision order.

(3) If it is proved to the satisfaction of the court before which an offender appears or is brought under this section that he has failed without reasonable cause to comply with any of the requirements of section 26(4) the court may, without prejudice to the continuance of the order, impose on him a fine not exceeding [£400].

(4) A fine imposed under this section shall be deemed for the purposes of any enactment to be a sum adjudged to be paid by a conviction.

Powers relating to persistent offenders

28. Punishment of persistent offenders

(1) Where an offender is convicted on indictment of an offence punishable with imprisonment for a term of two years or more and the conditions specified in subsection (3) below are satisfied, then, if the court is satisfied, by reason of his previous conduct and of the likelihood of his committing further offences, that it is expedient to protect the public from him for a substantial time, the court may impose an extended term of imprisonment under this section.

(2) The extended term which may be imposed under this section for any offence may exceed the maximum term authorised for the offence apart from this section if the maximum so authorised is less than ten years, but shall not exceed ten years if the maximum so authorised is less than ten years or exceed five years if the maximum so authorised is less than five years.

(3) The conditions referred to in subsection (1) above are:—

 (a) the offence was committed before the expiration of three years from a previous conviction of an offence punishable on indictment with imprisonment for a term of two years or more or from his final release from prison after serving a sentence of imprisonment, corrective training or preventive detention passed on such a conviction; and

(b) the offender has been convicted on indictment on at least three previous occasions since he attained the age of twenty-one of offences punishable on indictment with imprisonment for a term of two years or more; and

(c) the total length of the sentences of imprisonment, corrective training or preventive detention to which he was sentenced on those occasions was not less than five years and—

(i) on at least one of those occasions a sentence of preventive detention was passed on him; or

(ii) on at least two of those occasions a sentence of imprisonment (other than a suspended sentence which has not taken effect) or of corrective training was so passed and of those sentences one was a sentence of imprisonment for a term of three years or more in respect of one offence or two were sentences of imprisonment each for a term of two years or more in respect of one offence.

(4) Where an extended term of imprisonment is imposed on an offender under this section, the court shall issue a certificate (hereafter in this Act referred to as "an extended sentence certificate") stating that the term was so imposed.

29. *****

Crown Court fines, etc.

30. General power of Crown Court to fine offender convicted on indictment

(1) Where a person is convicted on indictment of an offence other than an offence for which the sentence is fixed by law, the court, if not precluded from sentencing the offender by its exercise of some other power (such as the power to make a probation order), may impose a fine in lieu of or in addition to dealing with him in any other way in which the court has power to deal with him, subject however to any enactment . . . requiring the offender to be dealt with in a particular way.

(2) . . .

31. Powers, etc., of Crown Court in relation to fines and forfeited recognizances

(1) Subject to the provisions of this section, if the Crown Court imposes a fine on any person or forfeits his recognizance, the Court may make an order—

(a) allowing time for the payment of the amount of the fine or the amount due under the recognizance;

(b) directing payment of that amount by instalments of such amounts and on such dates respectively as may be specified in the order;

(c) in the case of a recognizance, discharging the recognizance or reducing the amount due thereunder.

[(2) Subject to the provisions of this section, if the Crown Court imposes a fine on any person or forfeits his recognizance, the court shall make an order fixing a term of imprisonment or of detention under section 9 of the Criminal Justice Act 1982 (detention of persons aged 17 to 20 for default) which he is to undergo if any sum which he is liable to pay is not duly paid or recovered.

(3) No person shall on the occasion when a fine is imposed on him or his recognizance is forfeited by the Crown Court be committed to prison or detained in pursuance of an order under subsection (2) above unless—

(a) in the case of an offence punishable with imprisonment, he appears to the court to have sufficient means to pay the sum forthwith;

(b) it appears to the court that he is unlikely to remain long enough at a place of abode in the United Kingdom to enable payment of the sum to be enforced by other methods; or

(c) on the occasion when the order is made the court sentences him to immediate imprisonment, custody for life, youth custody or detention in a detention centre for that or another offence, or sentences him as aforesaid for an offence in addition to forfeiting his recognizance, or he is already serving a sentence of custody for life or a term—

    (i)   of imprisonment;
    (ii)   of youth custody;
    (iii)   of detention in a detention centre; or
    (iv)   of detention under section 9 of the Criminal Justice Act 1982.

(3A) Subject to subsections (3B) and (3C) below, the periods set out in the second column of the following Table shall be the maximum periods of imprisonment or detention under subsection (2) above applicable respectively to the amounts set out opposite thereto.

TABLE

Amount	Period
[An amount not exceeding [£50]	5 days
An amount exceeding [£50] but not exceeding [£100]	7 days
An amount exceeding [£100] but not exceeding [£400]	14 days
An amount exceeding [£400] but not exceeding [£1,000]	30 days
An amount exceeding [£1,000] but not exceeding [£2,000]	45 days
An amount exceeding [£2,000] but not exceeding [£5,000]	3 months
An amount exceeding [£5,000] but not exceeding [£10,000]	6 months
An amount exceeding [£10,000] but not exceeding [£20,000]	12 months
An amount exceeding [£20,000] but not exceeding [£50,000]	18 months
An amount exceeding [£50,000] but not exceeding [£100,000]	2 years
An amount exceeding [£100,000] but not exceeding [£250,000]	3 years
An amount exceeding [£250,000] but not exceeding [£1 million]	5 years
An amount exceeding £1 million	10 years

(3B) Where the amount due at the time imprisonment or detention is imposed is so much of a fine or forfeited recognizance as remains due after part payment, then, subject to subsection (3C) below, the maximum period application to the amount shall be the period applicable to the whole sum reduced by such number of days as bears to the total number of days therein the same proportion as the part paid bears to the total sum.

(3C) In calculating the reduction required under subsection (3B) above any fraction of a day shall be left out of account and the maximum period shall not be reduced to less than five days.

(4) Where any person liable for the payment of a fine or a sum due under a recognizance to which this section applies is sentenced by the court to, or is serving or otherwise liable to serve, a term of imprisonment or youth custody or a term of detention under section 4 or 9 of the Criminal Justice Act 1982, the court may order that any term of imprisonment or detention fixed under subsection (2) above shall not begin to run until after the end of the first-mentioned term.]

(5) The power conferred by this section to discharge a recognizance or reduce the amount due thereunder shall be in addition to the powers conferred by any other Act relating to the discharge, cancellation, mitigation or reduction of recognizances or sums forfeited thereunder.

(6) Subject to subsection (7) below, the powers conferred by this section shall not be taken as restricted by any enactment about committal by a magistrates' court to the Crown Court which authorises the Crown Court to deal with an offender in any way in which the magistrates' court might have dealt with him.

[(7) Any term fixed under subsection (2) above as respects a fine imposed in pursuance of such an enactment, that is to say a fine which the magistrates' court could have imposed, shall not exceed the period applicable to that fine (if imposed by the magistrates' court) under section 149(1) of the Customs and Excise Management Act 1979.

(8) This section shall not apply to a fine imposed by the Crown Court on appeal against a decision of a magistrates' court, but subsections (2) to (3C) above shall apply in relation to a fine imposed or recognizance forfeited by the criminal division of the Court of Appeal, or by the House of Lords on appeal from that division, as they apply in relation to a fine imposed or recognizance forfeited by the Crown Court, and the references to the Crown Court in subsections (2) and (3) above shall be construed accordingly.]

32. Enforcement, etc., of fines imposed and recognizances forfeited by Crown Court

(1) Subject to the provisions of subsection (4) below, a fine imposed or a recognizance forfeited by the Crown Court after 31st December 1967 shall be treated for the purposes of collection, enforcement and remission of the fine or other sum as having been imposed or forfeited—

    (a)   by a magistrates' court specified in an order made by the Crown Court; or

    (b)   if no such order is made, by the magistrates' court by which the offender was committed to the Crown Court to be tried or dealt with;

and in the case of a fine as having been so imposed on conviction by the magistrates' court in question.

(2) The term of imprisonment [or detention under section 9 of the Criminal Justice Act 1982] specified in any warrant of commitment issued by a magistrates' court on a default in the payment of a fine imposed, or sum due under a recognizance forfeited, by the Crown Court as the term which the offender is liable to serve shall be the term fixed by the latter court under section 31(2) of this Act or, if that term has been reduced under [section 79(2) of the Magistrates' Courts Act 1980] (part payment) or [section 85(1) of the that Act] (remission) that term as so reduced, notwithstanding that the term exceeds the period applicable to the case under . . . [section 149(1) of the Customs and Excise Management Act 1979] (maximum periods of imprisonment in default of payment of fines, etc.).

(3) The preceding provisions of this section shall apply in relation to a fine imposed or recognizance forfeited by the criminal division of the Court of Appeal, or by the House of Lords on appeal from that division, as they apply in relation to a fine imposed or recognizance forfeited by the Crown Court, and references in those provisions to the Crown Court shall be construed accordingly.

(4) A magistrates' court shall not under [section 85(1) or 120 of the Magistrates' Courts Act 1980] as applied by subsection (1) above, remit the whole or any part of a fine imposed or a sum due under a recognizance forfeited by the Crown Court without the consent of that court, and [section 85(1)] shall have effect accordingly.

(5) A fine imposed or a recognizance forfeited by the criminal division of the Court of Appeal on appeal from the Crown Court or by the House of Lords on appeal from that division shall be treated for the purposes of collection, enforcement and remission of the fine or other sum as having been imposed or forfeited by the Crown Court.

(6) Any fine or other sum the payment of which is enforceable by a magistrates' court by virtue of this section shall be treated for the purposes of the [Justices of

the Peace Act 1979 and, in particular, section 61 thereof (application of fines and fees)] as having been imposed by a magistrates' court, or as being due under a recognizance forfeited by such a court.

33. ...

34. Power of Crown Court to allow time for payment, or payment by instalments, of costs and compensation
Where the Crown Court makes any such order as is mentioned in Part I of Schedule 9 to the Administration of Justice Act 1970 (orders against accused for the payment of costs or compensation), the court may—
    (a)   allow time for the payment of the sum due under the order;
    (b)   direct payment of that sum by instalments of such amounts and on such dates respectively as the court may specify.

[34A. Power of Crown Court to order search of persons before it
(1) Where—
    (a)   the Crown Court imposes a fine on a person or forfeits his recognizance;
    (b)   the Crown Court makes against a person any such order as is mentioned in paragraph 3, 4 or 9 of Schedule 9 to the Administration of Justice Act 1970 (orders for the payment of costs);
    (c)   the Crown Court makes against a person any such order as is mentioned in paragraph 12 of that Schedule (fines etc. payable by parents or guardians); or
    [(cc)   the Crown Court makes an order against a person under section 35 of this Act;]
    (d)   on the determination of an appeal brought by a person under section 83 of the Magistrates' Courts Act 1952 a sum is payable by him, whether by virtue of an order of the Crown Court or by virtue of a conviction or order of the magistrates' court against whose decision the appeal was brought,
then, if that person is before it, the Crown Court may order him to be searched.
(2) Any money found on a person in a search under this section may be applied, unless the court otherwise directs, towards payment of the fine or other sum payable by him; and the balance, if any, shall be returned to him.]

Compensation orders

[35. Compensation orders against convicted persons
(1) Subject to the provisions of this Part of this Act and to section 40 of the Magistrates' Courts Act 1980 (which imposes a monetary limit on the powers of a magistrates' court under this section), a court by or before which a person is convicted of an offence, instead of or in addition to dealing with him in any other way, may, on application or otherwise, make an order (in this Act referred to as "a compensation order") requiring him to pay compensation for any personal injury, loss or damage resulting from that offence or any other offence which is taken into consideration by the court in determining sentence [or to make payments for funeral expenses or bereavement in respect of a death resulting from any such offence, other than a death due to an accident arising out of the presence of a motor vehicle on a road; and a court shall give reasons, on passing sentence, if it does not make such an order in a case where this section empowers it to do so.]
(2) In the case of an offence under the Theft Act 1968, where the property in question is recovered, any damage to the property occurring while it was out of the owner's possession shall be treated for the purposes of subsection (1) above as having resulted from the offence, however and by whomsoever the damage was caused.
[(3) A compensation order may only be made in respect of injury, loss or damage

Powers of Criminal Courts Act 1973

(other than loss suffered by a person's dependants in consequence of his death) which was due to an accident arising out of the presence of a motor vehicle on a road, if—

    (a)   it is in respect of damage which is treated by subsection (2) above as resulting from an offence under the Theft Act 1968; or

    (b)   it is in respect of injury, loss or damage as respects which—

        (i)   the offender is uninsured in relation to the use of the vehicle; and

        (ii)   compensation is not payable under any arrangements to which the Secretary of State is a party;

and, where a compensation order is made in respect of injury, loss or damage due to such an accident, the amount to be paid may include an amount representing the whole or part of any loss of or reduction in preferential rates of insurance attributable to the accident.

(3A) A vehicle the use of which is exempted from insurance by section 144 of the Road Traffic Act 1972 is not uninsured for the purposes of subsection (3) above.

(3B) A compensation order in respect of funeral expenses may be made for the benefit of anyone who incurred the expenses.

(3C) A compensation order in respect of bereavement may only be made for the benefit of a person for whose benefit a claim for damages for bereavement could be made under section 1A of the Fatal Accidents Act 1976.

(3D) The amount of compensation in respect of bereavement shall not exceed the amount for the time being specified in section 1A(3) of the Fatal Accidents Act 1976.]

[(4) In determining whether to make a compensation order against any person, and in determining the amount to be paid by any person under such an order, it shall be the duty of the court—

    (a)   to have regard to his means so far as they appear or are known to the court; and

    (b)   in a case where it is proposed to make against him both a compensation order and a confiscation order under Part VI of the Criminal Justice Act 1988, also to have regard to its duty under section 72(7) of that Act (duty where the court considers that the offender's means are insufficient to satisfy both orders in full to order the payment out of sums recovered under the confiscation order of sums due under the compensation order).]

(5) . . .

[36. **Enforcement and appeals**

(1) A person in whose favour a compensation order is made shall not be entitled to receive the amount due to him until (disregarding any power of a court to grant leave to appeal out of time) there is no further possibility of an appeal on which the order could be varied or set aside.

(2) Rules under section 144 of the Magistrates' Courts Act 1980 may make provision regarding the way in which the magistrates' court for the time being having functions (by virtue of section 41(1) of the Administration of Justice Act 1970) in relation to the enforcement of a compensation order is to deal with money paid in satisfaction of the order where the entitlement of the person in whose favour it was made is suspended.

(3) The Court of Appeal may by order annul or vary any compensation order made by the court of trial, although the conviction is not quashed; and the order, if annulled, shall not take effect and, if varied, shall take effect as varied.

(4) Where the House of Lords restores a conviction, it may make any compensation order which the court of trial could have made.

(5) Where a compensation order has been made against any person in respect of an offence taken into consideration in determining his sentence—

    (a)   the order shall cease to have effect if he successfully appeals against his conviction of the offence or, if more than one, all the offences, of which he was convicted in the proceedings in which the order was made;

(b) he may appeal against the order as if it were part of the sentence imposed in respect of the offence or, if more than one, any of the offences, of which he was so convicted.

37. Review of compensation orders
At any time before the person against whom a compensation order has been made has paid into court the whole of the compensation which the order requires him to pay, but at a time when (disregarding any power of a court to grant leave to appeal out of time) there is no further possibility of an appeal on which the order could be varied or set aside, the magistrates' court for the time being having functions in relation to the enforcement of the order may, on the application of the person against whom it was made, discharge the order, or reduce the amount which remains to be paid, if it appears to the court—

(a) that the injury, loss or damage in respect of which the order was made has been held in civil proceedings to be less than it was taken to be for the purposes of the order; or

(b) in the case of an order in respect of the loss of any property, that the property has been recovered by the person in whose favour the order was made; or

(c) that the means of the person against whom the order was made are insufficient to satisfy in full both the order and a confiscation order under Part VI of the Criminal Justice Act 1988 made against him in the same proceedings; or

(d) that the person against who the order was made has suffered a substantial reduction in his means which was unexpected at the time when the compensation order was made, and that his means seem unlikely to increase for a considerable period;

but where the order was made by the Crown Court, a magistrates' court shall not exercise any power conferred by this section in a case where it is satisfied as mentioned in paragraph (c) or (d) above unless it has first obtained the consent of the Crown Court.

38. Effect of compensation order on subsequent award of damages in civil proceedings
(1) This section shall have effect where a compensation order has been made in favour of any person in respect of any injury, loss or damage and a claim by him in civil proceedings for damages in respect of the injury, loss or damage subsequently falls to be determined.

(2) The damages in the civil proceedings shall be assessed without regard to the order; but the plaintiff may only recover an amount equal to the aggregate of the following—

(a) any amount by which they exceed the compensation; and

(b) a sum equal to any portion of the compensation which he fails to recover, and may not enforce the judgment, so far as it relates to a sum such as is mentioned in paragraph (b) above, without the leave of the court.]

Miscellaneous powers

42. Power of Crown Court on committal for sentence
[(1)] Where an offender is committed by a magistrates' court for sentence under [section 38 of the Magistrates' Courts Act 1980] or section 62 of the Criminal Justice Act 1967, the Crown Court shall enquire into the circumstances of the case and shall have power to deal with the offender in any manner in which it could deal with him if he had just been convicted of the offence on indictment before the court.

[(2) Where an offender is committed by a magistrates' court for sentence under section 37 of the Magistrates' Courts Act 1980 (committal for sentence of offender aged 15 or 16 convicted of indictable offences), the Crown Court shall enquire into the circumstances of the case and shall have power—

(a) subject so section 7(8) of the Criminal Justice Act 1982 (term of youth custody for offenders aged 15 or 16 not to exceed twelve months), to sentence him to a term of youth custody not exceeding the maximum term of imprisonment for the offence on conviction on indictment; or

(b) to deal with him in any manner in which the magistrates' court might have dealt with him.]

43. Power to deprive offender of property used, or intended for use, for purposes of crime

[(1) Subject to the following provisions of this section, where a person is convicted of an offence and—

(a) the court by or before which he is convicted is satisfied that any property which has been lawfully seized from him or which was in his possession or under his control at the time when he was apprehended for the offence or when a summons in respect of it was issued—

(i) has been used for the purpose of committing, or facilitating the commission of, any offence; or

(ii) was intended by him to be used for that purpose;

or

(b) the offence, or an offence which the court has taken into consideration in determining his sentence, consists of unlawful possession of property which—

(i) has been lawfully seized from him; or

(ii) was in his possession or under his control at the time when he was apprehended for the offence of which he has been convicted or when a summons in respect of that offence was issued,

the court may make an order under this section in respect of that property, and may do so whether or not it also deals with the offender in respect of the offence in any other way and without regard to any restrictions on forfeiture in an enactment contained in an Act passed before the Criminal Justice Act 1988.

(1A) In considering whether to make such an order in respect of any property a court shall have regard—

(a) to the value of the property; and

(b) to the likely financial and other effects on the offender of the making of the order (taken together with any other order that the court contemplates making).

(2) Facilitating the commission of an offence shall be taken for the purposes of this section and section 44 of this Act to include the taking of any steps after it has been committed for the purpose of disposing of any property to which it relates or of avoiding apprehension or detection, and references in this or that section to an offence punishable with imprisonment shall be construed without regard to any prohibition or restriction imposed by or under any enactment on the imprisonment of young offenders.]

(3) An order under this section shall operate to deprive the offender of his rights, if any, in the property to which it relates, and the property shall (if not already in their possession) be taken into the possession of the police.

(4) The Police (Property) Act 1897 shall apply, with the following modifications, to property which is in the possession of the police by virtue of this section—

(a) no application shall be made under section 1(1) of that Act by any claimant of the property after the expiration of six months from the date on which the order in respect of the property was made under this section; and

(b) no such application shall succeed unless the claimant satisfies the court either that he had not consented to the offender having possession of the property, or, where an order is made under subsection (1)(a) above, that he did not know, and had no reason to suspect, that the property was likely to be used for the purpose mentioned in that paragraph'.

(5) In relation to property which is in the possession of the police by virtue of this section, the power to make regulations under section 2(1) of the Police (Property) Act 1897 (disposal of property in cases where the owner of the property has not been ascertained and no order of a competent court has been made with respect thereto) shall include power to make regulations for disposal in cases where no application by a claimant of the property has been made within the period specified in subsection (4)(a) above or no such application has succeeded.

[**43A. Application of proceeds of forfeited property**

(1) Where a court makes an order under section 43 above in a case where—

(a) the offender has been convicted of an offence which has resulted in a person suffering personal injury, loss or damage; or

(b) any such offence is taken into consideration by the court in determining sentence,

the court may also make an order that any proceeds which arise from the disposal of the property and which do not exceed a sum specified by the court shall be paid to that person.

(2) The court may only make an order under this section if it is satisfied that but for the inadequacy of the means of the offender it would have made a compensation order under which the offender would have been required to pay compensation of an amount not less than the specified amount.

(3) An order under this section has no effect—

(a) before the end of the period specified in section 43(4)(a) above; or

(b) if a successful application under section 1(1) of the Police (Property) Act 1897 has been made.]

44. *****

57. Interpretation

(1) In this Act, except so far as the context otherwise requires, the following expressions have the meanings hereby respectively assigned to them, that is to say—

"the appropriate officer of the court" means, in relation to a magistrates' court, the clerk of the court;

"approved bail hostel" means a bail hostel approved by the Secretary of State under section 49(1) of this Act;

"approved probation hostel" [means a probation hostel approved] by the Secretary of State under section 49(1) of this Act;

"bail hostel" means premises for the accommodation of persons remanded on bail;

"community service order" has the meaning assigned to it by section 14(1) of this Act;

"compensation order" has the meaning assigned to it by section 35(1) of this Act;

"court" does not include a court-martial;

"criminal bankruptcy order" means an order under section 39(1) of this Act;

"day training centre" means premises at which persons may be required to attend by a probation order containing a requirement under section 4 of this Act;

"extended sentence certificate" has the meaning assigned to it by section 29 of this Act;

"local authority" means, in relation to any probation and aftercare area, any authority out of whose funds the salary of the clerk to the justices for a petty sessions area contained in the probation and after-care area is paid;

"order for conditional discharge" has the meaning assigned to it by section 7 of this Act;

"period of conditional discharge" has the meaning assigned to it by section 7 of this Act;

"probationer" means a person for the time being under supervision by virtue of a probation order;

"probation hostel" means premises for the accommodation of persons who may be required to reside there by a probation order, . . .;

"probation order" has the meaning assigned to it by section 2 of this Act;

"probation period" means the period for which a probationer is place under supervision by a probation order;

"the register" means the register of proceedings before a magistrates' court required by rules made under section 144 of the Magistrates' Courts Act 1980 to be kept by the clerk of the court;

"sentence of imprisonment" does not include a committal in default of payment of any sum of money, or for want of sufficient distress to satisfy any sum of money, or for failure to do or abstain from doing anything required to be done or left undone;

"supervising court" has the meaning assigned to it by section 2(2) of this Act;

"supervision order" has the meaning assigned to it by section 26(1) of this Act;

"suspended sentence" means a sentence to which an order under section 22(1) of this Act relates.

(2) For the purposes of any reference in this Act, however, expressed, to the term of imprisonment or other detention to which a person has been sentenced or which, or part of which, he has served, consecutive terms and terms which are wholly or partly concurrent shall, unless the context otherwise requires, be treated as a single term.

(3) Without prejudice to sections 20(1) and 21(1) of this Act, any reference in this Act however expressed to a previous conviction or sentence shall be construed as a reference to a previous conviction by a court in any part of Great Britain and to a previous sentence passed by any such court.

(4) Without prejudice to the meaning of references in sections 14, 43 and 44 of this Act to any offence punishable with imprisonment, any such reference elsewhere in this Act shall be construed, in relation to any offender, without regard to any prohibition or restriction imposed by or under any enactment on the imprisonment of offenders of his age.

(5) For the purposes of this Act a compensation order, supervision order or community service order made on appeal from a decision of a magistrates' court or the Crown Court shall be treated as if it had been made by a magistrates' court or the Crown Court, as the case may be.

(6) Any reference to this Act to any other enactment is a reference thereto as amended, and includes a reference thereto as extended or applied, by or under any other enactment, including this Act.

JURIES ACT 1974
(1974, c. 23)

An Act to consolidate certain enactments relating to juries, jurors and jury service with corrections and improvements made under the Consolidation of Enactments (Procedure) Act 1949 [9 July 1974]

1. Qualification for jury service

Subject to the provisions of this Act, every person shall be qualified to serve as a juror in the Crown Court, the High Court and county courts and be liable accordingly to attend for jury service when summoned under this Act, if—

(a) he is for the time being registered as a parliamentary or local government elector and is not less than eighteen nor more than [seventy] years of age; and

(b) he has been ordinarily resident in the United Kingdom, the Channel Islands or the Isle of Man for any period of at least five years since attaining the age of thirteen, but not if he is for the time being ineligible or disqualified for jury service; and the persons who are ineligible, and those who are disqualified, are those respectively listed in Parts I and II of Schedule 1 to this Act.

2.—8.*****

9. Excusal for certain persons and discretionary excusal

(1) A person summoned under this Act shall be entitled, if he so wishes, to be excused from jury service if he is among the persons listed in Part III of Schedule 1 to this Act but, except as provided by that Part of that Schedule in the case of members of the forces . . ., a person shall not by this section be exempt from his obligation to attend if summoned unless he is excused from attending under subsection (2) below.

(2) If any person summoned under this Act shows to the satisfaction of the appropriate officer that there is good reason why he should be excused from attending in pursuance of the summons, the appropriate officer may excuse him from so attending and shall do so if the reason shown is that the person is entitled under subsection (1) above to excusal.

(3) Crown Court rules shall provide a right of appeal to the court (or one of the courts) before which the person is summoned to attend against any refusal of the appropriate officer to excuse him under subsection (2) above.

(4) Without prejudice to the preceding provisions of this section, the court (or any of the courts) before which a person is summoned to attend under this Act may excuse that person from so attending.

[9A. Discretionary deferral

(1) If any person summoned under this Act shows to the satisfaction of the appropriate officer that there is good reason why his attendance in pursuance of the summons should be deferred, the appropriate officer may defer his attendance, and, if he does so, he shall vary the days on which that person is summoned to attend and the summons shall have effect accordingly.

(2) If an application under subsection (1) above has been granted or refused, the powers conferred by that subsection may not be exercised subsequently in relation to the same summons.

(3) Crown Court Rules shall provide a right of appeal to the court (or one of the courts) before which the person is summoned to attend against any refusal of the appropriate officer to defer his attendance under subsection (1) above.

(4) Without prejudice to the preceding provisions of this section, the court (or any of the courts) before which a person is summoned to attend under this Act may defer his attendance.]

10. Discharge of summonses in case of doubt as to capacity to act effectively as a juror

Where it appears to the appropraite officer, in the case of a person attending in pursuance of a summons under this Act, that on account of physical disability or insufficient understanding of English there is doubt as to his capacity to act effectively as a juror, the person may be brought before the judge, who shall determine whether or not he should act as a juror and, if not, shall discharge the summons; and for this purpose "the judge" means any judge of the High Court or any Circuit judge or Recorder.

11. The ballot and swearing of jurors

(1) The jury to try an issue before a court shall be selected by ballot in open court from the panel, or part of the panel, of jurors summoned to attend at the time and place in question.

(2) The power of summoning jurors under section 6 of this Act may be exercised after balloting has begun, as well as earlier, and if exercised after balloting has begun the court may dispense with balloting for persons summoned under that section.

(3) No two or more members of a jury to try an issue in a court shall be sworn together.

(4) Subject to subsection (5) below, the jury selected by any one ballot shall try only one issue (but any juror shall be liable to be selected on more than one ballot).

(5) Subsection (4) above shall not prevent—
 (a) the trial of two or more issues by the same jury if the trial of the second or last issue begins within 24 hours from the time when the jury is constituted, or
 (b) in a criminal case, the trial of fitness to plead by the same jury as that by whom the accused is being tried, if that is so directed by the court under section 4(4)(b) of the Criminal Procedure (Insanity) Act 1964, or
 (c) in a criminal case beginning with a special plea, the trial of the accused on the general issue by the jury trying the special plea.

(6) In the cases within subsection (5)(a), (b) and (c) above the court may, on the trial of the second or any subsequent issue, instead of proceeding with the same jury in its entirety, order any juror to withdraw, if the court considers he could be justly challenged or excused, or if the parties to the proceedings consent, and the juror to replace him shall, subject to subsection (2) above, be selected by ballot in open court.

12. Challenge

(1) In proceedings for the trial of any person for an offence on indictment—
 (a) that person may challenge . . . all or any of the jurors for cause, and
 (b) any challenge for cause shall be tried by the judge before whom that person is to be tried.

(2) Any party to county court proceedings to be tried by a jury shall have the same right of challenge to all or any of the jurors as he would have in the High Court.

(3) A challenge to a juror in any court shall be made after his name has been drawn by ballot (unless the court, pursuant to section 11(2) of this Act, has dispensed with balloting for him) and before he is sworn.

(4) The fact that a person summoned to serve on a jury is not qualified to serve shall be a ground of challenge for cause; but subject to that, and to the foregoing provisions of this section, nothing in this Act affects the law relating to challenge of jurors.

 (5) *****

(6) Without prejudice to subsection (4) above, the right of challenge to the array, that is to say the right of challenge on the ground that the person responsible for summoning the jurors in question is biased or has acted improperly, shall continue to be unaffected by the fact that, since the coming into operation of section 31 of the Courts Act 1971 (which is replaced by this Act), the responsibility for summoning jurors for service in the Crown Court, the High Court and county courts has lain with the Lord Chancellor.

13. Separation

Upon the trial of any person for an offence on indictment the court may, if it thinks fit, at any time before the jury consider their verdict, permit them to separate.

14., 15. *****

16. Continuation of criminal trial on death or discharge of a juror

(1) Where in the course of a trial of any person for an offence on indictment any member of the jury dies or is discharged by the court whether as being through illness incapable of continuing to act or for any other reason, but the number of its members is not reduced below nine, the jury shall nevertheless (subject to subsections (2) and (3) below) be considered as remaining for all the purposes of that trial properly constituted, and the trial shall proceed and a verdict may be given accordingly.

(2) On a trial for any offence punishable with death subsection (1) above shall not apply on the death or discharge of any member of the jury unless assent to its then applying is given in writing by or on behalf of both the prosecution and the accused or each of the accused.

(3) Notwithstanding subsection (1) above, on the death or discharge of a member of the jury in the course of a trial of any person for an offence on indictment the court may discharge the jury in any case where the court sees fit to do so.

17. Majority verdicts

(1) Subject to subsections (3) and (4) below, the verdict of a jury in proceedings in the Crown Court or the High Court need not be unanimous if—

    (a) in a case where there are not less than eleven jurors, ten of them agree on the verdict; and

    (b) in a case where there are ten jurors, nine of them agree on the verdict.

(2) Subject to subsection (4) below, the verdict of a jury (that is to say a complete jury of eight) in proceedings in a county court need not be unanimous if seven of them agree on the verdict.

(3) The Crown Court shall not accept a verdict of guilty by virtue of subsection (1) above unless the foreman of the jury has stated in open court the number of jurors who respectively agreed to and dissented from the verdict.

(4) No court shall accept a verdict by virtue of subsection (1) or (2) above unless it appears to the court that the jury have had such period of time for deliberation as the court thinks reasonable having regard to the nature and complexity of the case; and the Crown Court shall in any event not accept such a verdict unless it appears to the court that the jury have had at least two hours for deliberation.

(5) This section is without prejudice to any practice in civil proceedings by which a court may accept a majority verdict with the consent of the parties, or by which the parties may agree to proceed in any case with an incomplete jury.

18. Judgments: stay or reversal

(1) No judgment after verdict in any trial by jury in any court shall be stayed or reversed by reason—

    (a) that the provisions of this Act about the summoning or impanelling of jurors, or the selection of jurors by ballot, have not been complied with, or

    (b) that a juror was not qualified in accordance with section 1 of this Act, or

    (c) that any juror was misnamed or misdescribed, or

    (d) that any juror was unfit to serve.

(2) Subsection (1)(a) above shall not apply to any irregularity if objection is taken at, or as soon as practicable after, the time it occurs, and the irregularity is not corrected.

(3) Nothing in subsection (1) above shall apply to any objection to a verdict on the ground of personation.

19., 20. *****

SCHEDULES

SCHEDULE 1

Section 1

INELIGIBILITY AND DISQUALIFICATION FOR AND EXCUSAL FROM JURY SERVICE

PART I
PERSONS INELIGIBLE

GROUP A

The Judiciary

Holders of high judicial office within the meaning of the Appellate Jurisdiction Act 1876.
Circuit judges and Recorders.
Masters of the Supreme Court.
Registrars and assistant registrars of any court.
Metropolitan and other stipendiary magistrates.
Justices of the peace.
The Chairman or President, the Vice-Chairman or Vice-President, and the registrar and assistant registrar of any Tribunal.
A person who has at any time been a person falling within any description specified above in this Group.

GROUP B

Others concerned with administration of justice

Barristers and solicitors, whether or not in actual practice as such.
Solicitors' articled clerks.
Barristers' clerks and their assistants.
Legal executives in the employment of solicitors.
The Director of Public Prosecutions and members of his staff.
Officers employed under the Lord Chancellor and concerned wholly or mainly with the day-to-day administration of the legal system or any part of it.
Officers and staff of any court, if their work is wholly or mainly concerned with the day-to-day administration of the court.
Coroners, deputy coroners and assistant coroners.
Justices' clerks and their assistants.
Clerks and other officers appointed under section 15 of the Administration of Justice Act 1964 (Inner London magistrates' courts administration).
Active Elder Brethren of the Corporation of Trinity House of Deptford Strond.
A shorthandwriter in any court.
Governors, chaplains, medical officers and other officers of penal establishments; members of boards of visitors for penal establishments.
("Penal establishment" for this purpose means any prison, remand centre, detention centre or [youth custody centre].)
The warden or a member of the staff of a probation home, probation hostel or bail hostel (within the meaning of the Powers of Criminal Courts Act 1973).
Probation officers and persons appointed to assist them.

Members of the Parole Board; members of local review committees established under the Criminal Justice Act 1967.

A member of any police force (including a person on central service under section 43 of the Police Act 1964); special constables; a member of any constabulary maintained under statute; a person employed in any capacity by virtue of which he has the powers and privileges of a constable.

Inspectors of Constabulary appointed by Her Majesty; assistant inspectors of constabulary appointed by the Secretary of State.

[Civilians employed for police purposes under section 10 of the Police Act 1964]; members of the metropolitan civil staffs within the meaning of section 15 of the Superannuation (Miscellaneous Provisions) Act 1967 (persons employed under the Commissioner of Police of the Metropolis, Inner London justices' clerks, etc.).

A person in charge of, or employed in, any forensic science laboratory.

A person who at any time within the last ten years has been a person falling within any description specified above in this Group.

GROUP C

The clergy, etc.

A man in holy orders; a regular minister of any religious denomination.

A vowed member of any religious order living in a monastery, convent or other religious community.

[GROUP D

Mentally disordered persons

A person who suffers or has suffered from mental illness, psychopathic disorder, mental handicap or severe mental handicap and on account of that condition either—
    (a)   is resident in a hospital or other similar institution; or
    (b)   regularly attends for treatment by a medical practitioner.
A person for the time being in guardianship under [section 7 of the Mental Health Act 1983].

A person who, under [Part VII of that Act], has been determined by a judge to be incapable, by reason of mental disorder, of managing and administering his property and affairs.

(In this Group—
    (a)   "mental handicap" means a state of arrested or incomplete development of mind (not amounting to severe mental handicap) which includes significant impairment of intelligence and social functioning;
    (b)   "severe mental handicap" means a state of arrested or incomplete development of mind which includes severe impairment of intelligence and social functioning;
    (c)   other expressions are to be construed in accordance with [the said Act of 1983].)]

PART II
PERSONS DISQUALIFIED

A person who has at any time been sentenced in the United Kingdom, the Channel Islands or the Isle of Man—
    (a)   to imprisonment for life [, custody for life or to a term of imprisonment or youth custody of five years or more]; or
    (b)   to be detained during Her Majesty's pleasure, during the pleasure of the Secretary of State or during the pleasure of the Government of Northern Ireland.

Juries Act 1974

[A person who at any time in the last ten years has, in the United Kingdom or the Channel Islands or the Isle of Man—
    (a)   served any part of a sentence of imprisonment, youth custody or detention; or
    (b)   been detained in a Borstal institution; or
    (c)   had passed on him or (as the case may be) made in respect of him a suspended sentence of imprisonment or order for detention; or
    (d)   had made in respect of him a community service order.
A person who at any time in the last five years has, in the United Kingdom or the Channel Islands or the Isle of Man, been placed on probation.]

PART III
PERSONS EXCUSABLE AS OF RIGHT

GENERAL

[Persons more than sixty-five years of age.]

Parliament

Peers and peeresses entitled to receive writs of summons to attend the House of Lords.
Members of the House of Commons.
Officers of the House of Lords.
Officers of the House of Commons

[*European Assembly*

Representatives to the Assembly of the European Communities,]

The Forces

Full-time serving members of —
any of Her Majesty's naval, military or air forces,
. . .
(A person excusable under this head shall be under no obligation to attend in pursuance of a summons for jury service if his commanding officer certifies to the officer issuing the summons that it would be prejudicial to the efficiency of the service if the person were required to be absent from duty.)

Medical and other similar professions

The following, if actually practising their profession and registered (including provisionally or temporarily registered), enrolled or certified under the enactments relating to that profession—
medical prctitioners,
dentists,
nurses,
midwives,
veterinary surgeons and veterinary practitioners,
pharmaceutical chemists.

SOLICITORS ACT 1974
(1974, c. 47)

An Act to consolidate the Solicitors Acts 1957 to 1974 and certain other enactments relating to solicitors   [31 July 1974]

PART I
RIGHT TO PRACTISE AS SOLICITOR

Qualifications and training

1. Qualifications for practising as solicitor
No person shall be qualified to act as a solicitor unless—
- (a) he has been admitted as a solicitor, and
- (b) his name is on the roll, and
- (c) he has in force a certificate issued by the Society in accordance with the provisions of this Part authorising him to practise as a solicitor (in this Act referred to as a "practising certificate").

4.—18. *****

Rights and privileges of solicitors

19. Rights of practising and rights of audience
(1) Subject to subsection (2), every person qualified in accordance with section 1 may practise as a solicitor—
- (a) in the Supreme Court;
- (b) in any county court;
- (c) in all courts and before all persons having jurisdiction in ecclesiastical matters; and
- (d) in all matters relating to applications to obtain notarial faculties,

and shall be entitled to all the rights and privileges, and may exercise and perform all the powers and duties, formerly appertaining to the office or profession of a proctor in the provincial, diocesan or other jurisdictions in England and Wales.

(2) Nothing in subsection (1) shall affect the provisions of section [94 of the Supreme Court Act 1981] [section 13 or 60 of the County Courts Act 1984] or any other enactment in force at the commencement of this Act which restricts the right of any solicitor to practise as such in any court.

(3) Nothing in subsection (1) or (2) shall prejudice or affect any right of practising or being heard in, before or by any court, tribunal or other body which immediately before the commencement of this Act was enjoyed by virtue of any enactment, rule, order or regulation or by custom or otherwise by persons qualified to act as solicitors.

Unqualified persons acting as solicitors

20. Unqualified person not to act as solicitor
(1) No unqualified person shall—
- (a) act as a solicitor, or as such issue any writ or process, or commence, prosecute or defend any action, suit or other proceeding, in his own name or in the name of any other person, in any court of civil or criminal jurisdiction; or
- (b) act as a solicitor in any cause or matter, civil or criminal, to be heard or determined before any justice or justices or any commissioners of Her Majesty's revenue.

(2) Any person who contravenes the provisions of subsection (1)—
- (a) shall be guilty of an offence and liable on conviction on indictment to imprisonment for not more than two years or to a fine or to both; and
- (b) shall be guilty of contempt of the court in which the action, suit, cause, matter or proceeding in relation to which he so acts is brought or taken and may be punished accordingly; and
- (c) in addition to any other penalty or forfeiture and any disability to which he may be subject, shall be liable to a penalty of £50 to be recovered, with the full costs of the action, by an action brought by the Society with the consent of the Attorney

Solicitors Act 1974

General in the High Court or in any county court, and to be applied to the use of Her Majesty.

21. Unqualified person not to pretend to be a solicitor
Any unqualified person who wilfully pretends to be, or takes or uses any name, title, addition or description implying that he is, qualified or recognised by law as qualified to act as a solicitor shall be guilty of an offence and liable on summary conviction to a fine not exceeding [the fourth level on the standard scale].

22. Unqualified person not to prepare certain instruments
(1) Subject to [subsections (2) and (2A)], any unqualified person who directly or indirectly—

    (a) draws or prepares any instrument of transfer or charge for the purposes of the Land Registration Act 1925, or makes any application or lodges any document for registration under that Act at the registry, or

    (b) draws or prepares any other instrument relating to real or personal estate, or any legal proceeding,

shall, unless he proves that the act was not done for or in expectation of any fee, gain or reward, be guilty of an offence and liable on summary conviction to a fine not exceeding [level 3 on the standard scale].

(2) Subsection (1) does not apply to—

    (a) a barrister or duly certificated notary public;

    (b) any public officer drawing or preparing instruments or applications in the course of his duty;

    (c) any person employed merely to engross any instrument, application or proceeding;

and paragraph (b) of that subsection does not apply to a duly certificate solicitor in Scotland.

[(2A) Subsection (1) also does not apply to any act done by a person at the direction and under the supervision of another person if—

    (a) that other person was at the time his employer, a partner of his employer or a fellow employee; and

    (b) the act could have been done by that other person for or in expectation of any fee, gain or reward without committing an offence under this section.]

(3) For the purposes of subsection (1)(b), "instrument" [includes a contract for the sale or other disposition of land (except a contract to grant such a lease as is referred to in section 54(2) of the Law of Property Act 1925 (short leases)), but] does not include—

    (a) a will or other testamentary instrument;

    (b) an agreement not under seal [other than a contract that is included by virtue of the preceding provisions of this subsection];

    (c) a letter or power of attorney; or

    (d) a transfer of stock containing no trust or limitation thereof.

[(4) A local weights and measures authority may institute proceedings for an offence under this section.]

[23. Unqualified person not to prepare papers for probate etc
(1) Subject to subsections (2) and (3), any unqualified person who, directly or indirectly, draws or prepares any papers on which to found or oppose—

    (a) a grant of probate, or

    (b) a grant of letters of administration,

shall, unless he proves that the act was not done for or in expectation of any fee, gain or reward, be guilty of an offence and liable on summary conviction to a fine not exceeding the first level on the standard scale.

(2) Subsection (1) does not apply to a barrister or duly certificated notary public.

(3) Subsection (1) also does not apply to any act done by a person at the direction and under the supervision of another person if—
    (a) that other person was at the time his employer, a partner of his employer or a fellow employee; and
    (b) the act could have been done by that other person for or in expectation of any fee, gain or reward without committing an offence under this section.]

24. *****

25. Costs where unqualified person acts as a solicitor

(1) No costs in respect of anything done by any unqualified person acting as a solicitor shall be recoverable by him, or by any other person, in any action, suit or matter.

(2) Nothing in subsection (1) shall prevent the recovery of money paid or to be paid by a solicitor on behalf of a client in respect of anything done by the solicitor while acting for the client without holding a practising certificate in force if that money would have been recoverable if he had held such a certificate when so acting.

26.—30. *****

PART II
PROFESSIONAL PRACTICE, CONDUCT AND DISCIPLINE OF SOLICITORS AND CLERKS

Practice rules

31. Rules as to professional practice, conduct and discipline

(1) Without prejudice to any other provision of this Part the Council may, if they think fit, make rules, with the concurrence of the Master of the Rolls, for regulating in respect of any matter the professional practice, conduct and discipline of solicitors.

(2) If any solicitor fails to comply with rules made under this section, any person may make a complaint in respect of that failure to the Tribunal.

Accounts etc.

32.—34. *****

Intervention in solicitor's practice, Compensation Fund and professional indemnity

35. Intervention in solicitor's practice

The powers conferred by Part II of Schedule 1 shall be exercisable in the circumstances specified in Part I of that Schedule.

36. Compensation fund

(1) The fund, known as the "Compensation Fund", shall be maintained and administered in accordance with the provisions of Schedule 2.

(2) Where the Council are satisfied—
    (a) that a person has suffered or is likely to suffer loss in consequence of dishonesty on the part of a solicitor, or of an employee of a solicitor, in connection with that solicitor's practice or purported practice or in connection with any trust of which that solicitor is or formerly was a trustee; or
    (b) that a person has suffered or is likely to suffer hardship in consequence of failure on the part of a solicitor to account for money which has come to his hands in connection with his practice or purported practice or in connection with any trust of which he is or formerly was a trustee; or
    (c) that a solicitor has suffered or is likely to suffer loss or hardship by reason

of his liability to any of his or his firm's clients in consequence of some act or default of any of his partners or employees in circumstances where but for the liability of that solicitor a grant might have been made out of the Compensation Fund to some other person;
the Society may make a grant out of the Compensation Fund for the purpose of relieving that loss or hardship.

(3)—(8) *****

37. Professional indemnity

(1) The Council, with the concurrence of the Master of the Rolls, may make rules (in this Act referred to as "indemnity rules") concerning indemnity against loss arising from claims in respect of any description of civil liability incurred—

    (a)   by a solicitor or former solicitor in connection with his practice or with any trust of which he is or formerly was a trustee;

    (b)   by an employee or former employee of a solicitor or former solicitor in connection with that solicitor's practice or with any trust of which that solicitor or the employee is or formerly was a trustee.

(2) For the purpose of providing such indemnity, indemnity rules—

    (a)   may authorise or require the Society to establish and maintain a fund or funds;

    (b)   may authorise or require the Society to take out and maintain insurance with authorised insurers;

    (c)   may require solicitors or any specified class of solicitors to take out and maintain insurance with authorised insurers.

(3)—(5) *****

38.—40. *****

Restrictions on employment of certain persons

41. Employment by solicitor of person struck off or suspended

(1) No solicitor shall, except in accordance with a written permission granted under this section, employ or remunerate in connection with his practice as a solicitor any person who to his knowledge is disqualified from practising as a solicitor by reason of the fact that—

    (a)   his name has been struck off the roll, or

    (b)   he is suspended from practising as a solicitor, or

    (c)   his practising certificate is suspended while he is an undischarged bankrupt.

(2) The Society may grant a permission under this section for such period and subject to such conditions as the Society thinks fit.

(3) A solicitor aggrieved by the refusal of the Society to grant a permission under subsection (2), or by any conditions attached by the Society to the grant of any such permission, may appeal to the Master of the Rolls who may—

    (a)   confirm the refusal or the conditions, as the case may be; or

    (b)   grant a permission under this section for such period and subject to such conditions as he thinks fit.

(4)—(5) *****

42. Failure to disclose fact of having been struck off or suspended

(1) Any person who, while he is disqualified from practising as a solicitor by reason of the fact that—

    (a)   his name has been struck off the roll, or

    (b)   he is suspended from practising as a solicitor, or

    (c)   his practising certificate is suspended while he is an undischarged bankrupt,

seeks or accepts employment by a solicitor in connection with that solicitor's practice without previously informing him that he is so disqualified shall be guilty of an offence and liable on summary conviction to a fine not exceeding [level 3 on the standard scale].

(2) *****

43. Control of employment of certain clerks

(1) Where a person who is or was a clerk to a solicitor but is not himself a solicitor—

(a) has been convicted of a criminal offence which discloses such dishonesty that in the opinion of the Society it would be undesirable for him to be employed by a solicitor in connection with his practice; or

(b) has, in the opinion of the Society, occasioned or been a party to, with or without the connivance of the solicitor to whom he is or was clerk, an act or default in relation to that solicitor's practice [which involved conduct on his part of such a nature that in the opinion of the society it would be undesirable for him to be employed by a solicitor in connection with his practice,]

an application may be made to the Tribunal with respect to that person by or on behalf of the Society.

(2) The Tribunal, on the hearing of any application under subsection (1), may make an order that as from such date as may be specified in the order no solicitor shall, except in accordance with permission in writing granted by the Society for such period and subject to such conditions as the Society may think fit to specify in the permission, employ or remunerate, in connection with his practice as a solicitor, the person with respect to whom the application is made.

(3)—(7) *****

44. Offences in connection with orders under section 43(2)

(1) Any person who, while there is in force in respect of him an order under section 43(2), seeks or accepts any employment by or remuneration from a solicitor in connection with that solicitor's practice without previously informing him of that order shall be guilty of an offence and liable on summary conviction to a fine not exceeding [level 3 on the standard scale].

(2) Where an order is made under section 43(2) in respect of any person and that order is one—

(a) against which no appeal has been made or which has been confirmed on appeal; and

(b) which has not been revoked under section 43(3),

then, if any solicitor knowingly acts in contravention of that order or of any conditions subject to which permission for the employment of that person has been granted under it, a complaint in respect of that contravention may be made to the Tribunal by or on behalf of the Society.

(3) Any document purporting to be an order under section 43(2) and to be duly signed in accordance with section 48(1) shall be received in evidence in any proceedings under this section and be deemed to be such an order without further proof unless the contrary is shown.

(4) Notwithstanding anything in [the Magistrates' Courts Act 1980], proceedings under subsection (1) may be commenced at any time before the expiration of six months from the first discovery of the offence by the prosecutor, but no such proceedings shall be commenced, except with the consent of the Director of Public Prosecutions, by any person other than the Society or a person acting on behalf of the Society.

[44A. Power of Council to impose sanctions for inadequate professional services

(1) Where it appears to the Council that the professional services provided by a solicitor in connection with any matter in which he or his firm had been instructed

by a client were in any respect not of the quality that could reasonably have been expected of him as a solicitor, then (subject to subsection (3)), the Council may, if they think fit, do one or more of the following things, namely—

(a) determine that the costs to which the solicitor shall be entitled in respect of those services shall be limited to such amount as may be specified in their determination and direct the solicitor to comply, or to secure compliance, with such one or more requirements falling within subsection (2) as appear to them to be necessary in order to give effect to their determination;

(b) direct the solicitor to secure the rectification, at the expense of the solicitor or his firm, of any such error, omission or other deficiency arising in connection with the said matter as they may specify;

(c) direct the solicitor to take, at the expense of the solicitor or his firm, such other action in the interests of the client as they may specify.

(2) The requirements referred to in subsection (1)(a) are—

(a) a requirement to refund the whole or part of any amount already paid by or on behalf of the client in respect of the solicitor's costs in respect of his services in connection with the said matter;

(b) a requirement to remit the whole or part of those costs;

(c) a requirement to waive, whether wholly or to any specified extent, the right to recover those costs.

(3) The Council shall not exercise any of their powers under subsection (1) unless they are satisfied that it would in all the circumstances be appropriate to do so; and in determining whether in any case it would be appropriate to exercise any of those powers the Council may have regard—

(a) to the existence of any remedy that could reasonably be expected to be available to the client in civil proceedings; and

(b) where proceedings seeking any such remedy have not been commenced by him, to whether it would be reasonable to expect him to commence such proceedings.

(4) Where the Council have given a direction under subsection (1)(a) in order to give effect to a determination by them under that provision as to the costs of a solicitor in respect of any services provided by him, then—

(a) for the purposes of any taxation of a bill covering those costs the amount charged by the bill in respect of those costs shall be deemed to be limited to the amount specified in the Council's determination; and

(b) where a bill covering those costs has not been taxed in accordance with paragraph (a), the client shall, for the purposes of the recovery of those costs (by whatever means) and notwithstanding any statutory provision or agreement, be deemed to be liable to pay in respect of those costs only the amount specified in the Council's determination.

(5) Where a bill covering those costs has been taxed in accordance with subsection (4)(a), the Council's direction under subsection (1)(a) shall, so far as relating to those costs, cease to have effect.

(6) If a solicitor fails to comply with a direction given by the Council under this section, any person may make a complaint in respect of that failure to the Tribunal; but no other proceedings whatever shall be brought in respect of it.

(7) On the hearing of a complaint under subsection (6) relating to a direction given by the Council the Tribunal may, if it thinks fit (whether or not it makes any order on the hearing under section 47(2)), direct that the Council's direction shall be treated, for the purpose of enforcement, as if it were contained in an order made by the High Court.

(8) The powers conferred on the Council by subsection (1)(a) shall be exercisable in relation to a person notwithstanding that his name has been removed from or struck off the roll, and references to a solicitor—

(a) in the provisions of this section so far as they relate to the exercise of those powers; and

(b) if a complaint is made to the Tribunal under subsection (6), in section 47(2), shall be construed accordingly.

(9) In subsection (1)6c) and (3)(a) "client", in relation to any matter in which a solicitor or his firm has been instructed, includes any person on whose behalf the person who gave the instructions was acting.]

44B. *****

Lay observers

45. Investigation by lay observers of Society's treatment of complaints

(1) The Lord Chancellor may, if he thinks fit, appoint one or more persons (in this section referred to as "lay observers") to examine any written allegation made by or on behalf of a member of the public concerning the Society's treatment of a complaint about a solicitor or an employee of a solicitor made to the Society by that member of the public or on his behalf.

(2) No solicitor or barrister shall be appointed a lay observer.

(3) A lay observer shall hold and vacate his office in accordance with the terms of his appointment, and shall, on ceasing to hold office, be eligible for reappointment.

(4) The Lord Chancellor may give general directions to lay observers about the scope and discharge of their functions, and shall publish any such directions.

(5) The Society shall consider any report or recommendation which it receives from a lay observer and shall notify him of any action which it has taken in consequence.

[(5A) Where it appears to a lay observer, in examining any such allegation as is mentioned in subsection (1)—

(a) that there arises out of the complaint in respect of which the allegation has been made both—

(i) a question as to the professional conduct of a solicitor, and

(ii) a question as to the quality of any professional services provided by him; and

(b) that it would be appropriate for the latter question to be considered by the Tribunal with a view to determining whether to exercise any of its powers under section 47A in relation to the solicitor,

the lay observer may make an application to the Tribunal with respect to the solicitor.]

(6) The Lord Chancellor may appoint staff for lay observers.

(7) Remuneration for lay observers and their staff and any other expenses of lay observers shall be paid out of money provided by Parliament.

(8) In determining the numbers, terms of employment and remuneration of lay observers and their staff and any amount payable by way of expenses under subsection (7), the Lord Chancellor shall act only with the approval of the Minister for the Civil Service.

(9) The Society shall furnish a lay observer with such information as he may from time to time reasonably require.

(10) The Lord Chancellor shall direct the submission to him of annual reports by lay observers on the discharge of the functions conferred on them by this section.

(11) The Lord Chancellor shall lay a copy of any report under subsection (10) before each House of Parliament.

Disciplinary proceedings before Solicitors
Disciplinary Tribunal

46. Solicitors Disciplinary Tribunal

(1) Applications and complaints made by virtue of any provision of this Act shall

Solicitors Act 1974

be made, except so far as other provision is made by this Act or by any regulations under it, to the tribunal known as the "Solicitors Disciplinary Tribunal".

(2) The Master of the Rolls shall appoint the members of the Tribunal.

(3) The Tribunal shall consist—
    (a) of practising solicitors of not less than ten years' standing (in this section referred to as "solicitor members"); and
    (b) of persons who are neither solicitors nor barristers (in this section referred to as "lay members").

(4) A member of the Tribunal shall hold and vacate his office in accordance with the terms of his appointment and shall, on ceasing to hold office, be eligible for re-appointment.

(5) *****

(6) Subject to subsections (7) and (8), the Tribunal shall be deemed to be properly constituted if—
    (a) at least three members are present; and
    (b) at least one lay member is present; and
    (c) the number of solicitor members present exceeds the number of lay members present.

(7) For the purpose of hearing and determining applications and complaints the Tribunal shall consist of not more than three members.

(8) A decision of the Tribunal on an application or complaint may be announced by a single member.

(9) Subject to subsections (6) to (8), the Tribunal, with the concurrence of the Master of the Rolls, may make rules—
    (a) empowering the Tribunal to elect a solicitor member to be its president; and
    (b) about the procedure and practice to be followed in relation to the making, hearing and determination of applications and complaints.

(10)—(12) *****

47. Jurisdiction and powers of Tribunal

(1) Any application—
    (a) to strike the name of a solicitor off the roll, or to require a solicitor to answer allegations contained in an affidavit, or
    (b) by a former solicitor whose name has been struck off the roll or to have his name restored to the roll,
shall be made to the Tribunal; but nothing in this subsection shall affect any jurisdiction over solicitors exercisable by the Master of the Rolls, or by any judge of the High Court, by virtue of section 50.

(2) Subject to subsection (3) and to section 54, on the hearing of any application or complaint made to the Tribunal under this Act, other than an application under section 43, the Tribunal shall have power to make such order as it may think fit, and any such order may in particular include provision for any of the following matters, that is to say—
    (a) the striking off the roll of the name of the solicitor to whom the application or complaint relates;
    (b) the suspension of that solicitor from practice;
    (c) the payment by that solicitor of a penalty not exceeding [£3000], which shall be forfeit to Her Majesty;
    (d) the restoration to the roll of the name of a former solicitor whose name has been struck off the roll and to whom the application relates;

(e)   the payment by any part of costs or a contribution towards costs of such amount as the Tribunal may consider reasonable.

(2A)—(2D)   *****

(3)   On proof of the commission of an offence with respect to which express provision is made by any section of this Act, the Tribunal shall, without prejudice to its power of making an order as to costs, impose the punishment, or one of the punishments, specified in that section.

(4), (5)   *****

[47A.   **Power of Tribunal to impose sanctions for inadequate professional services**

(1)   The powers conferred on the Tribunal by this section shall be exercisable on the hearing of—

    (a)   any application or complaint made to the Tribunal under this Act by or on behalf of the Society; or

    (b)   any application made to the Tribunal under section 45(5A) by a lay observer.

(2)   Where, on the hearing of any such application or complaint with respect to a solicitor, it appears to the Tribunal that the professional services provided by the solicitor in connection with any matter in which he or his firm had been instructed by a client were in any respect not of the quality that could reasonably have been expected of him as a solicitor, then (subject to subsection (4)), the Tribunal may, if it thinks fit, do one or more of the following things, namely—

    (a)   determine that the costs to which the solicitor shall be entitled in respect of those services shall be limited to such amount as may be specified in its determination and by order direct the solicitor to comply, or to secure compliance, with such one or more requirements falling within subsection (3) as appear to it to be necessary in order to give effect to its determination;

    (b)   by order direct the solicitor to secure the rectification, at the expense of the solicitor or his firm, of any such error, omission or other deficiency arising in connection with the said matter as it may specify;

    (c)   by order direct the solicitor to take, at the expense of the solicitor or his firm, such other action in the interests of the client as it may specify.

(3)   The requirements referred to in subsection (2)(a) are—

    (a)   a requirement to refund the whole or part of any amount already paid by or on behalf of the client in respect of the solicitor's costs in respect of his services in connection with the said matter;

    (b)   a requirement to remit the whole or part of those costs;

    (c)   a requirement to waive, whether wholly or to any specified extent, the right to recover those costs.

(4)   The Tribunal shall not exercise any of its powers under this section unless it is satisfied that it would in all the circumstances be appropriate to do so; and in determining whether in any case it would be appropriate to exercise any of those powers the Tribunal may have regard—

    (a)   to the existence of any remedy that could reasonably be expected to be available to the client in civil proceedings; and

    (b)   where proceedings seeking any such remedy have not been commenced by him, to whether it would be reasonable to expect him to commence such proceedings.

(5)   Where the Tribunal has given a direction under subsection (2)(a) in order to give effect to a determination by it under that provision as to the costs of a solicitor in respect of any services provided by him, then—

    (a)   for the purposes of any taxation of a bill covering those costs the amount charged by the bill in respect of those costs shall be deemed to be limited to the amount specified in the Tribunal's determination; and

(b) where a bill covering those costs has not been taxed in accordance with paragraph (a), the client shall, for the purposes of the recovery of those costs (by whatever means) and notwithstanding any statutory provision or agreement, be deemed to be liable to pay in respect of those costs only the amount specified in the Tribunal's determination.

(6) Where a bill covering those costs has been taxed in accordance with subsection (5)(a), the Tribunal's direction under subsection (2)(a) shall, so far as relating to those costs, cease to have effect.

(7) In subsections (2)(c) and (4)(a) "client", in relation to any matter in which a solicitor or his firm has been instructed, includes any person on whose behalf the person who gave the instructions was acting.]

48. *****

49. Appeals from Tribunal
(1) An appeal from the Tribunal shall lie—
    (a) in the case of an order on an application under section 43(3) or 47(1)(b) or the refusal of any such application, to the Master of the Rolls;
    (b) in any other case, to the High Court.

(2) Subject to subsection (3), an appeal shall lie at the instance of the applicant or complainant or of the person with respect to whom the application or complaint made.

(3) An appeal against an order under section 43(2) shall lie only at the instance of the person with respect to whom the application was made.

(4) The High Court and the Master of the Rolls shall have power to make such order on an appeal under this section as they may think fit.

(5) Subject to any rules of court, on an appeal against an order made by virtue of rules under section 46(10)(c) without hearing the applicant or complainant, the court—
    (a) shall not be obliged to hear the appellant, and
    (b) may remit the matter to the Tribunal instead of dismissing the appeal,

(6) Any decision of the Master of the Rolls on an appeal under this section and any decision of the High Court on an appeal against an order under section 43(2) shall be final.

(7) The Master of the Rolls may make regulations about appeals to him under this section.

Disciplinary proceedings before Supreme Court

50. Jursidiction of Supreme Court over solicitors
(1) Any person duly admitted as a solicitor shall be an officer of the Supreme Court.

(2) Subject to the provisions of this Act, the High Court, the Crown Court and the Court of Appeal respectively, or any division or judge of those courts, may exercise the same jurisdiction in respect of solicitors as any one of the superior courts of law or equity from which the Supreme Court was constituted might have exercised immediately before the passing of the Supreme Court of Judicature Act 1873 in respect of any solicitor, attorney or proctor admitted to practise there.

[(3) An appeal shall lie to the Court of Appeal from any order made against a solicitor by the High Court of the Crown Court in the exercise of its jurisdiction in respect of solicitors under sub-section (2).]

51.—80. *****

Miscellaneous

81. Administration of oaths and taking of affidavits

(1) Subject to the provisions of this section, every solicitor who holds a practising certificate which is in force shall have the powers conferred on a commissioner for oaths by the Commissioners for Oaths Acts 1889 and 1891 and section 24 of the Stamp Duties Management Act 1891; and any reference to such a commissioner in an enactment or instrument (including an enactment passed or instrument made after the commencement of this Act) shall include a reference to such a solicitor unless the context otherwise requires.

(2) A solicitor shall not exercise the powers conferred by this section in a proceeding in which he is solicitor to any of the parties, or in which he is interested.

(3) A solicitor before whom any oath or affidavit is taken or made shall state in the jurat or attestation at which place and on what date the oath or affidavit it taken or made.

(4) A document containing such a statement and purporting to be sealed or signed by a solicitor shall be admitted in evidence without proof of the seal or signature, and without proof that he is a solicitor or that he holds a practising certificate which is in force.

(5) Nothing in this section shall affect the power to appoint commissioners under the Commissioners for Oaths Act 1889.

81A. *****

RESTRICTIVE PRACTICES COURT ACT 1976
(1976, c. 33)

An Act to consolidate certain enactments relating to the Restrictive Practices Court

[22 July 1976]

1. The Court

(1) The Restrictive Practices Court ("the Court") established by the Restrictive Trade Practices Act 1956 shall continue in being by that name as a superior court of record.

(2) The Court shall consists of the following members—
    (a) five nominated judges; and
    (b) not more than ten appointed members.

(3) Of the nominated judges one, to be selected by the Lord Chancellor, shall be President of the Court.

(4) The Court shall have an official seal which shall be judicially noticed.

2. Judges of the Court

(1) The nominated judges of the court shall be—
    (a) three puisne judges of the High Court nominated by the Lord Chancellor;
    (b) one judge of the Court of Session nominated by the Lord President of that Court;
    (c) one judge of the Supreme Court of Northern Ireland nominated by the Lord Chief Justice of Northern Ireland.

(2) A judge of any court who is nominated under this section shall not be required to sit in any place outside the jurisdiction of that court, and shall be required to perform his duties as a judge of that court only when his attendance on the Restrictive Practices Court is not required.

(3) In the case of the temporary absence or inability to act of a nominated judge, the Lord Chancellor, the Lord President of the Court of Session, or the Lord Chief Justice of Northern Ireland (as the case may be) may nominate another judge of the

same court to act temporarily in his place, and a judge so nominated shall, when so acting, have all the functions of the judge in whose place he acts.

(4) No judge shall be nominated under this section except with his consent.

3. Non-judicial members

(1) The other members of the Court ("appointed members") may be appointed by Her Majesty on the recommendation of the Lord Chancellor, and any person recommended for appointment shall be a person appearing to the Lord Chancellor to be qualified by virtue of his knowledge of or experience in industry, commerce or public affairs.

(2) An appointed member shall hold office for such period (not less than three years) as may be determined at the time of his appointment, and shall be eligible for reappointment, but—

(a) he may at any time by notice in writing to the Lord Chancellor resign his office;

(b) the Lord Chancellor may, if he thinks fit, remove any appointed member for inability or misbehaviour, or on the ground of any employment or interest which appears to the Lord Chancellor incompatible with the functions of a member of the Court.

(3) In the case of the temporary absence or inability to act of an appointed member, the Lord Chancellor may appoint a temporary member, being a person appearing to him to be qualified as provided in subsection (1) above, to act in place of that member; and a temporary member shall, when so acting, have all the functions of an appointed member.

4., 5. *****

6. Administration

(1)—(3) *****

(4) Subject to its rules, the Court may sit at such times and in such place or places in any part of the United Kingdom as may be most convenient for the determination of proceedings before it.

(5) When sitting in public in London, the Court shall sit at the Royal Courts of Justice or at such other place as the Lord Chancellor may appoint.

(6) The Court may sit either as a single court or in two or more divisions concurrently and either in private or in public.

7. Hearing and judgment

(1) For the hearing of any proceedings the Court shall consist of a presiding judge and at least two other members, except that in the case of proceedings involving only issues of law the Court may instead consist of a single member being a judge.

(2) On the hearing of any proceedings, the opinion of the judge or judges sitting as members of the Court upon any question of law shall prevail; but subject to this the decision of the Court shall be taken by all the members sitting, or, in the event of a difference of opinion, by the votes of the majority of the members.

In the event of an equality of votes, the presiding judge shall be entitled to a second or casting vote.

(3) The judgment of the Court in any proceedings shall be delivered by the presiding judge.

8. Right of audience

(1) Every person who has the right of audience at the trial of an action in the High Court or in the Court of Session, or in proceedings preliminary to such a trial, shall have the like right at the hearing of any application to the Court, whether sitting

in England and Wales or in Scotland, or in proceedings preliminary to such a hearing, as the case may be.

(2) *****

9. Procedure

(1) The procedure in or in connection with any proceedings before the Court and, subject to the approval of the Treasury, the fees chargeable in respect of such proceedings, shall be such as may be determined by rules made by the Lord Chancellor.

Rules under this section shall be made by statutory instrument subject to annulment in pursuance of a resolution of either House of Parliament.

10. Appeal

(1) Subject to and in accordance with this section, an appeal lies from any decision or order of the Court—
    (a)   in the case of proceedings in England and Wales, to the Court of Appeal;
    (b), (c)   *****

(2) In proceedings under Part III of the Fair Trading Act 1973 (consumer protection) the appeal lies on a question of fact or on a question of law.

(3) In proceedings other than those referred to in subsection (2) above—
    (a)   the appeal lies on a question of law only and the Court's decision on a question of fact is final; and
    (b)   the appeal—
        (i)   to the Court of Appeal, or to the Court of Appeal in Northern Ireland, is by way of case stated: and
        (ii)   *****

11., 12   *****

BAIL ACT 1976
(1976, c. 63)

An Act to make provision in relation to bail in or in connection with criminal proceedings in England and Wales, to make it an offence to agree to indemnify sureties in criminal proceedings, to make provision for legal aid limited to questions of bail in certain cases and for legal aid for persons kept in custody for inquiries or reports, to extend the powers of coroners to grant bail and for connected purposes.   [15 November 1976]

Preliminary

1. Meaning of "bail in criminal proceedings"

(1) In this Act "bail in criminal proceedings" means—
    (a)   bail grantable in or in connection with proceedings for an offence to a person who is accused or convicted of the offence, or
    (b)   bail grantable in connection with an offence to a person who is under arrest for the offence or for whose arrest for the offence a warrant (endorsed for bail) is being issued.

(2) In this Act "bail" means bail grantable under the law (including common law) for the time being in force.

(3) Except as provided by section 13(3) of this Act, this section does not apply to bail in or in connection with proceedings outside England and Wales.

(4) This section does not apply to bail granted before the coming into force of this Act.

(5) This section applies—
    (a)   whether the offence was committed in England or Wales or elsewhere, and

(b) whether it is an offence under the law of England and Wales, or of any other country or territory.

(6) Bail in criminal proceedings shall be granted (and in particular shall be granted unconditionally or conditionally) in accordance with this Act.

2. Other definitions

(1) In this Act, unless the context otherwise requires, "conviction" includes—

(a) a finding of guilt,

(b) a finding that a person is not guilty by reason of insanity,

(c) a finding under [section 30(1) of the Magistrates' Courts Act 1980] (remand for medical examination) that the person in question did the act or made the omission charged, and

(d) a conviction of an offence for which an order is made placing the offender on probation or discharging him absolutely or conditionally,

and "convicted" shall be construed accordingly.

(2) In this Act, unless the context otherwise requires—

["bail hostel" and "probation hostel" have the same meanings as in the Powers of Criminal Courts Act 1973,]

"child" means a person under the age of fourteen,

"court" includes a judge of a court, [or a justice of the peace] and, in the case of a specified court, includes a judge or (as the case may be) justice having powers to act in connection with proceedings before that court,

"Courts-Martial Appeal rules" means rules made under section 49 of the Courts-Martial (Appeals) Act 1968,

"Crown Court rules" means rules made under section 15 of the Courts Act 1971,

"magistrates' courts rules" means rules made under section 15 of the Justices of the Peace Act 1949,

"offence" includes an alleged offence,

"proceedings against a fugitive offender" means proceedings under section 9 of the Extradition Act 1870, section 7 of the Fugitive Offenders Act 1967 or section 2(1) or 4(3) of the Backing of Warrants (Republic of Ireland) Act 1965.

"Supreme Court rules" means rules made under section 99 of the Supreme Court of Judicature (Consolidation) Act 1925,

"surrender to custody" means, in relation ito a person released on bail, surrendering himself into the custody of the court or of the constable (according to the requirements of the grant of bail) at the time and place for the time being appointed for him to do so,

"vary", in relation to bail, means imposing further conditions after bail is granted, or varying or rescinding conditions,

"young person" means a person who has attained the age of fourteen and is under the age of seventeen.

(3) Where an enactment (whenever passed) which relates to bail in criminal proceedings refers to the person bailed appearing before a court it is to be construed unless the context otherwise requires as referring to his surrendering himself into the custody of the court.

(4) Any reference in this Act to any other enactment is a reference thereto as amended, and includes a reference thereto as extended or applied, by or under any other enactment, including this Act.

Incidents of bail in criminal proceedings

3. General provisions

(1) A person granted bail in criminal proceedings shall be under a duty to surrender to custody, and that duty is enforceable in accordance with section 6 of this Act.

(2) No recognizance for his surrender to custody shall be taken from him.

(3) Except as provided by this section—
- (a) no security for his surrender to custody shall be taken from him,
- (b) he shall not be required to provide a surety or sureties for his surrender to custody, and
- (c) no other requirement shall be imposed on him as a condition of bail.

(4) He may be required, before release on bail, to provide a surety or sureties to secure his surrender to custody.

(5) If it appears that he is unlikely to remain in Great Britain until the time appointed for him to surrender to custody, he may be required, before release on bail, to give security for his surrender to custody.

The security may be given by him or on his behalf.

(6) He may be required (but only by a court) to comply, before release on bail or later, with such requirements as appear to the court to be necessary to secure that—
- (a) he surrenders to custody,
- (b) he does not commit an offence while on bail,
- (c) he does not interfere with witnesses or otherwise obstruct the course of justice whether in relation to himself or any other person,
- (d) he makes himself available for the purpose of enabling inquiries or a report to be made to assist the court in dealing with him for the offence.

[(6ZA) Where he is required under subsection (6) above to reside in a bail hostel or probation hostel, he may also be required to comply with the rules of the hostel.]

[(6A) In the case of a person accused of murder the court granting bail shall, unless it considers that satisfactory reports on his mental condition have already been obtained, impose as conditions of bail—
- (a) a requirement that the accused shall undergo examination by two medical practitioners for the purpose of enabling such reports to be prepared; and
- (b) a requirement that he shall for that purpose attend such an institution or place as the court directs and comply with any other directions which may be given to him for that purpose by either of those practitioners.

(6B) Of the medical practitioners referred to in subsection (6A) above at least one shall be a practitioner approved for the purposes of [section 12 of the Mental Health Act 1983.]]

(7) If a parent or guardian of a child or young person consents to be surety for the child or young person for the purposes of this subsection, the parent or guardian may be required to secure that the child or young person complies with any requirement imposed on him by virtue of subsection (6) above, but—
- (a) no requirement shall be imposed on the parent or the guardian of a young person by virtue of this subsection where it appears that the young person will attain the age of seventeen before the time to be appointed for him to surrender to custody; and
- (b) the parent or guardian shall not be required to secure compliance with any requirement to which his consent does not extend and shall not, in respect of those requirements to which his consent does extend, be bound in a sum greater than £50.

(8) Where a court has granted bail in criminal proceedings [that court or, where that court has committed a person on bail to the Crown Court for trial or to be sentenced or otherwise dealt with, that court or the Crown Court may] on application—
- (a) by or on behalf of the person to whom [bail was] granted, or
- (b) by the prosecutor or a constable,

vary the conditions of bail or impose conditions in respect of bail which [has been] granted unconditionally.

[(8A) Where a notice of transfer is given under section 4 of the Criminal Justice Act 1987, subsection (8) above shall have effect in relation to a person in relation to whose case the notice is given as if he had been committed on bail to the Crown Court for trial.]

(9) This section is subject to [subsection (2) of section 30 of the Magistrates' Courts Act 1980] (conditions of bail on remand for medical examination).

Bail for accused persons and others

4. General right to bail of accused persons and others

(1) A person to whom this section applies shall be granted bail except as provided in Schedule 1 to this Act.

(2) This section applies to a person who is accused of an offence when—

 (a) he appears or is brought before a magistrates' court or the Crown Court in the course of or in connection with proceedings for the offence, or

 (b) he applies to a court for bail in connection with the proceedings.

This subsection does not apply as respects proceedings on or after a person's conviction of the offence or proceedings against a fugitive offender for the offence.

(3) This section also applies to a person who, having been convicted of an offence, appears or is brought before a magistrates' court to be dealt with under section 6 or section 16 of the Powers of Criminal Courts Act 1973 (breach of requirement of probation or community service order).

(4) This section also applies to a person who has been convicted of an offence and whose case is adjourned by the court for the purpose of enabling inquiries or a report to be made to assist the court in dealing with him for the offence.

(5) Schedule 1 to this Act also has effect as respects conditions of bail for a person to whom this section applies.

(6) In Schedule 1 to this Act "the defendant" means a person to whom this section applies and any reference to a defendant whose case is adjourned for inquiries or a report is a reference to a person to whom this section applies by virtue of subsection (4) above.

(7) This section is subject to [section 41 of the Magistrates' Courts Act 1980] (restriction of bail by magistrates' court in cases of treason).

Supplementary

5. Supplementary provisions about decisions on bail

(1) Subject to subsection (2) below, where—

 (a) a court or constable grants bail in criminal proceedings, or

 (b) a court withholds bail in criminal proceedings from a person to whom section 4 of this act applies, or

 (c) a court, officer of a court or constable appoints a time or place or a court or officer of a court appoints a different time or place for a person granted bail in criminal proceedings to surrender to custody, or

 (d) a court varies any conditions of bail or imposes conditions in respect of bail in criminal proceedings,

that court, officer or constable shall make a record of the decision in the prescribed manner and containing the prescribed particulars and, if requested to do so by the person in relation to whom the decision was taken, shall cause him to be given a copy of the record of the decision as soon as practicable after the record is made.

(2) Where bail in criminal proceedings is granted by endorsing a warrant of arrest for bail the constable who releases on bail the person arrested shall make the record required by subsection (1) above instead of the judge or justice who issued the warrant.

(3) Where a magistrates' court or the Crown Court—

 (a) witholds bail in criminal proceedings, or

 (b) imposes conditions in granting bail in criminal proceedings, or

(c) varies any conditions of bail or imposes conditions in respect of bail in criminal proceedings,
and does so in relation to a person to whom section 4 of this Act applies, then the court shall, with a view to enabling him to consider making an application in the matter to another court, give reasons for withholding bail or for imposing or varying the conditions.

(4) A court which is by virtue of subsection (3) above required to give reasons for its decision shall include a note of those reasons in the record of its decision and shall (except in a case where, by virtue of subsection (5) below, this need not be done) give a copy of that note to the person in relation to whom the decision was taken.

(5) The Crown Court need not give a copy of the note of the reasons for its decision to the person in relation to whom the decision was taken where that person is represented by counsel or a solicitor unless his counsel or solicitor requests the court to do so.

(6) Where a magistrates' court withholds bail in criminal proceedings from a person who is not represented by counsel or a solicitor, the court shall—

(a) if it is committing him for trial to the Crown Court, [or if it issues a certificate under subsection (6A) below] inform him that he may apply to the High Court or to the Crown Court to be granted bail;

(b) in any other case, inform him that he may apply to the High Court for that purpose.

[(6A) Where in criminal proceedings—

(a) a magistrates' court remands a person in custody under any of the following provisions of the Magistrates' Courts Act 1980—

(i) section 5 (adjournment of inquiry into offence);

(ii) section 10 (adjournment of trial);

(iii) section 18 (initial procedure on information against adult for offence triable either way); or

(iv) section 30 (remand for medical examination),

after hearing full argument on an application for bail from him; and

(b) either—

(i) it has not previously heard such argument on an application for bail from him in those proceedings; or

(ii) it has previously heard full argument from him on such an application but it is satisfied that there has been a change in his circumstances or that new considerations have been placed before it,

it shall be the duty of the court to issue a certificate in the prescribed form that they heard full argument on his application for bail before they refused the application.

(6B) Where the court issues a certificate under subsection (6A) above in a case to which paragraph (b)(ii) of that subsection applies, it shall state in the certificate the nature of the change of circumstances or the new considerations which caused it to hear a further fully argued bail application.

(6C) Where a court issues a certificate under subsection (6A) above it shall cause the person to whom it refuses bail to be given a copy of the certificate.]

(7) Where a person has given security in pursuance of section 3(5) above and a court is satisfied that he failed to surrender to custody then, unless it appears that he had reasonable cause for his failure, the court may order the forfeiture of the security.

(8) If a court orders the forfeiture of a security under subsection (7) above, the court may declare that the forfeiture extends to such amount less than the full value of the security as it thinks fit to order.

[(8A) An order under subsection (7) above shall, unless previously revoked, have effect at the end of twenty-one days beginning with the day on which it is made.

(8B) A court which has ordered the forfeiture of a security under subsection (7) above may, if satisfied on an application made by or on behalf of the person who

Bail Act 1976

gave it that he did after all have reasonable cause for his failure to surrender to custody, by order remit the forfeiture or declare that it extends to such amount less than the full value of the security as it thinks fit to order.

(8C) An application under subsection (8B) above may be made before or after the order for forfeiture has taken effect, but shall not be entertained unless the court is satisfied that the prosecution was given reasonable notice of the applicant's intention to make it.]

(9) A security which has been ordered to be forfeited by a court under subsection (7) above shall, to the extent of the forfeiture—

    (a) if it consists of money, be accounted for and paid in the same manner as a fine imposed by that court would be;

    (b) if it does not consist of money, be enforced by such magistrates' court as may be specified in the order.

[(9A) Where an order is made under subsection (8B) above after the order for forfeiture of the security in question has taken effect, any money which would have fallen to be repaid or paid over to the person who gave the security if the order under subsection (8B) had been made bfore the order for forfeiture took effect shall be repaid or paid over to him.]

(10) In this section "prescribed" means, in relation to the decision of a court or an officer of a court, prescribed by Supreme Court rules, Courts-Martial Appeal rules, Crown Court rules or magistrates' courts rules, as the case requires or, in relatioon to a decision of a constable, prescribed by direction of the Secretary of State.

6. Offence of absconding by person released on bail

(1) If a person who has been released on bail in criminal proceedings fails without reasonable cause to surrender to custody he shall be guilty of an offence.

(2) If a person who—

    (a) has been released on bail in criminal proceedings, and

    (b) having reasonable cause therefor, has failed to surrender to custody,

fails to surrender to custody at the appointed place as soon after the appointed time as is reasonably practicable he shall be guilty of an offence.

(3) It shall be for the accused to prove that he had reasonable cause for his failure to surrender to custody.

(4) A failure to give to a person granted bail in criminal proceedings a copy of the record of the decision shall not constitute a reasonable cause for that person's failure to surrender to custody.

(5) An offence under subsection (1) or (2) above shall be punishable either on summary conviction or as if it were a criminal contempt of court.

(6) Where a magistrates' court convicts a person of an offence under subsection (1) or (2) above the court may, if it thinks—

    (a) that the circumstances of the offence are such that greater punishment should be inflicted for that offence than the court has power to inflict, or

    (b) in a case where it commits that person for trial to the Crown Court for another offence, that it would be appropriate for him to be dealt with for the offence under subsection (1) or (2) above by the court before which he is tried for the other offence,

commit him in custody or on bail to the Crown Court for sentence.

(7) A person who is convicted summarily of an offence under subsection (1) or (2) above and is not committed to the Crown Court for sentence shall be liable to imprisonment for a term not exceeding 3 months or to a fine not exceeding [level 5 on the standard scale] or to both and a person who is so committed for sentence or is dealt with as for such a contempt shall be liable to imprisonment for a term not exceeding 12 months or to a fine or to both.

(8) In any proceedings for an offence under subsection (1) or (2) above a document purporting to be a copy of the part of the prescribed record which relates to the time and place appointed for the person specified in the record to surrender to custody and to be duly certified to be a true copy of that part of the record shall be evidence of the time and place appointed for that person to surrender to custody.

(9) For the purposes of subsection (8) above—

(a) "the prescribed record" means the record of the decision of the court, officer or constable made in pursuance of section 5(1) of this Act;

(b) the copy of the prescribed record is duly certified if it is certified by the appropriate officer of the court or, as the case may be, by the constable who took the decision or a constable designated for the purpose by the officer in charge of the police station from which the person to whom the record relates was released;

(c) "the appropriate officer" of the court is—

(i) in the case of a magistrates' court, the justices' clerk or such other officer as may be authorised by him to act for the purpose;

(ii) in the case of the Crown Court, such officer as may be designated for the purpose in accordance with arrangements made by the Lord Chancellor;

(iii) in the case of the High Court, such officer as may be designated for the purpose in accordance with arrangements made by the Lord Chancellor;

(iv) in the case of the Court of Appeal, the registrar of criminal appeals or such other officer as may be authorised by him to act for the purpose;

(v) in the case of the Courts-Martial Appeal Court, the registrar or such other officer as may be authorised by him to act for the purpose.

7. Liability to arrest for absconding or breaking conditions of bail

(1) If a person who has been released on bail in criminal proceedings and is under a duty to surrender into the custody of a court fails to surrender to custody at the time appointed for him to do so the court may issue a warrant for his arrest.

(2) If a person who has been released on bail in criminal proceedings absents himself from the court at any time after he has surrendered into the custody of the court and before the court is ready to begin or to resume the hearing of the proceedings, the court may issue a warrant for his arrest; but no warrant shall be issued under this subsection where that person is absent in accordance with leave given to him by or on behalf of the court.

(3) A person who has been released on bail in criminal proceedings and is under a duty to surrender into the custody of a court may be arrested without warrant by a constable—

(a) if the constable has reasonable grounds for believing that that person is not likely to surrender to custody;

(b) if the constable has reasonable grounds for believing that that person is likely to break any of the conditions of his bail or has reasonable grounds for suspecting that that person has broken any of those conditions; or

(c) in a case where that person was released on bail with one or more surety or sureties, if a surety notifies a constable in writing that that person is unlikely to surrender to custody and that for that reason the surety wishes to be relieved of his obligations as a surety.

(4) a person arrested in pursuance of subsection (3) above—

(a) shall, except where he was arrested within 24 hours of the time appointed for him to surrender to custody, be brought as soon as practicable and in any event within 24 hours after his arrest before a justice of the peace for the petty sessions area in which he was arrested; and

(b) in the said expected case shall be brought before the court at which he was to have surrendered to custody.

[In reckoning for the purposes of this subsection any period of 24 hours, no account shall be taken of Christmas Day, Good Friday or any Sunday.]

(5) A justice of the peace before whom a person is brought under subsection (4) above may, subject to subsection (6) below, if of the opinion that that person—
  (a)   is not likely to surrender to custody, or
  (b)   has broken or is likely to break any condition of his bail,
remand him in custody or commit him to custody, as the case may require, or alternatively, grant him bail subject to the same or to different conditions, but if not of that opinion shall grant him bail subject to the same conditions (if any) as were originally imposed.

(6) Where the person so brought before the justice is a child or young person and the justice does not grant him bail, subsection (5) above shall have effect subject to the provisions of section 23 of the Children and Young Persons Act 1969 (remands to the care of local authorities).

8. Bail with sureties

(1) This section applies where a person is granted bail in criminal proceedings on condition that he provides one or more surety or sureties for the purpose of securing that he surrenders to custody.

(2) In considering the suitability for that purpose of a proposed surety, regard may be had (amongst other things) to—
  (a)   the surety's financial resources;
  (b)   his character and any previous convictions of his; and
  (c)   his proximity (whether in point if kinship, place of residence or otherwise) to the person for whom he is to be surety.

(3) Where a court grants a person bail in criminal proceedings on such a condition but is unable to release him because no surety or no suitable surety is available, the court shall fix the amount in which the surety is to be bound and subsections (4) and (5) below, or in a case where the proposed surety resides in Scotland subsection (6) below, shall apply for the purpose of enabling the recognizance of the surety to be entered into subsequently.

(4) Where this subsection applies the recognizance of the surety may be entered into before such of the following persons or descriptions of persons as the court may by order specify or, if it makes no such order, before any of the following persons, that is to say—
  (a)   where the decision is taken by a magistrates' court, before a justice of the peace, a justices' clerk or a police officer who either is of the rank of inspector or above or is in charge of a police station or, if magistrates' courts rules so provide, by a person of such other description as is specified in the rules;
  (b)   where the decision is taken by the Crown Court, before any of the persons specified in paragraph (a) above or, if Crown Court rules so provide, by a person of such other description as is specified in the rules;
  (c)   where the decision is taken by the High Court or the Court of Appeal, before any of the persons specified in paragraph (a) above or, if Supreme Court rules so provide, by a person of such other description as is specified in the rules;
  (d)   where the decision is taken by the Courts-Martial Appeal Court, before any of the persons specified in paragraph (a) above or, if Courts-Martial Appeal rules so provide, by a person of such other description as is specified in the rules;
and Supreme Court rules, Crown Court rules, Courts-Martial Appeal rules or magistrates' courts rules may also prescribe the manner in which a recognizance which is to be entered into before such a person is to be entered into and the persons by whom and the manner in which the recognizance may be enforced.

(5) Where a surety seeks to enter into his recognizance before any person in

accordance with subsection (4) above but that person declines to take his recognizance because he is not satisfied of the surety's suitability, the surety may apply to—

    (a)   the court which fixed the amount of the recognizance in which the surety was to be bound, or

    (b)   a magistrates' court for the petty sessions area in which he resides,

for that court to take his recognizance and that court shall, if satisfied of his suitability, take his recognizance.

(6) Where this subsection applies, the court, if satisfied of the suitability of the proposed surety, may direct that arrangements by made for the recognizance of the surety to be entered into in Scotland before any constable, within the meaning of the Police (Scotland) Act 1967, having charge at any police office or station in like manner as the recognizance would be entered into in England or Wales.

(7) Where, in pursuance of subsection (4) or (6) above, a recognizance is entered into otherwise than before the court that fixed the amount of the recognizance, the same consequences shall follow as if it had been entered into before that court.

Miscellaneous

9. Offence of agreeing to indemnify sureties in criminal proceedings

(1) If a person agrees with another to indemnify that other against any liability which that other may incur as a surety to secure the surrender to custody of a person accused or convicted of or under arrest for an offence, he and that other person shall be guilty of an offence.

(2) An offence under subsection (1) above is committed whether the agreement is made before or after the person to be indemnified becomes a surety and whether or not he becomes a surety and whether the agreement contemplates compensation in money or in money's worth.

(3) Where a magistrates' court convicts a person of an offence under subsection (1) above the court may, if it thinks—

    (a)   that the circumstances of the offence are such that greater punishment should be inflicted for that offence than the court has power to inflict, or

    (b)   in a case where it commits that person for trial to the Crown Court for another offence, that it would be appropriate for him to be dealt with for the offence under subsection (1) above by the court before which he is tried for the other offence.

commit him in custody or on bail to the Crown Court for sentence.

(4) A person guilty of an offence under subsection (1) above shall be liable—

    (a)   on summary conviction, to imprisonment for a term not exceeding 3 months or to a fine not exceeding [the prescribed sum] or to both; or

    (b)   on conviction on indictment or if sentence by the Crown Court on committal for sentence under subsection (3) above, to imprisonment for a term not exceeding 12 months or to a fine or to both.

(5) No proceedings for an offence under subsection (1) above shall be instituted except by or with the consent of the Director of Public Prosecutions.

10., 11. . . .

12., 13. *****

SCHEDULES

SCHEDULE 1
PERSONS ENTITLED TO BAIL: SUPPLEMENTARY PROVISIONS

PART I
DEFENDANTS ACCUSED OR CONVICTED OF IMPRISONABLE OFFENCES

Defendants to whom Part I applies

1. Where the offence or one of the offences of which the defendant is accused or convicted in the proceedings is punishable with imprisonment the following provisions of this Part of this Schedule apply.

Exceptions to right to bail

2. The defendant need not be granted bail if the court is satisfied that there are substantial grounds for believing that the defendant, if released on bail (whether subject to conditions or not) would—
   (a) fail to surrender to custody, or
   (b) commit an offence while on bail, or
   (c) interfere with witnesses or otherwise obstruct the course of justice, whether in relation to himself or any other person.

3. The defendant need not be granted bail if the court is satisfied that the defendant should be kept in custody for his own protection or, if he is a child or young person, for his own welfare.

4. The defendant need not be granted bail if he is in custody in pursuance of the sentence of a court or of any authority acting under any of the Services Acts.

5. The defendant need not be granted bail where the court is satisfied that it has not been practicable to obtain sufficient information for the purpose of taking the decisions required by this Part of this Schedule for want of time since the institution of the proceedings against him.

6. The defendant need not be granted bail if, having been released on bail in or in connection with the proceedings for the offence, he has been arrested in pursuance of section 7 of this Act.

Exception applicable only to defendant whose case is adjourned for inquiries or a report

7. Where his case is adjourned for inquiries or a report, the defendant need not be granted bail if it appears to the court that it would be impracticable to complete the inquiries or make the report without keeping the defendant in custody.

Restriction of conditions of bail

8.—(1) Subject to sub-paragraph (3) below, where the defendant is granted bail, no conditions shall be imposed under subsections (4) to (7) of section 3 of this Act unless it appears to the court that it is necessary to do so for the purpose of preventing the occurrence of any of the events mentioned in paragraph 2 of this Part of this Schedule or, in the case of a condition under subsection (6)(d) of that section, that it is necessary to impose it to enable inquiries or a report to be made into the defendant's physical or mental condition [or, where the condition is that the defendant reside in a bail hostel or probation hostel, that it is necessary to impose it to assess his suitability for being dealt with for the offence in a way which would involve a period of residence in a probation hostel.]

(2) Sub-paragraph (1) above also applies on any application to the court to vary the conditions of bail or to impose conditions in respect of bail which has been granted unconditionally.

(3) The restriction imposed by sub-paragraph (1) above shall not [apply to the conditions required to be imposed under section 3 (6A) of this Act or] operate to override the direction in [section 30(2) of the Magistrates' Courts Act 1980] to a magistrates'

court to impose conditions of bail under section 3(6)(d) of this Act of the description specified in the [said section 30(2) in the circumstances so specified.]

Decisions under paragraph 2

9. In taking the decisions required by paragraph 2 of this Part of this Schedule, the court shall have regard to such of the following considerations as appear to it to be relevant, that is to say—

    (a)   the nature and seriousness of the offence or default (and the probable method of dealing with the defendant for it),

    (b)   the character, antecedents, associations and community ties of the defendant,

    (c)   the defendant's record as respects the fulfilment of his obligations under previous grants of bail in criminal proceedings,

    (d)   except in the case of a defendant whose case is adjourned for inquiries or a report, the strength of the evidence of his having committed the offence or having defaulted,

as well as to any others which appear to be relevant.

[9A (1) If—

    (a)   the defendant is charged with an offence to which this paragraph applies; and

    (b)   representations are made as to an of the matters mentioned in paragraph 2 of this Part of this Schedule; and

    (c)   the court decides to grant him bail,

the court shall state the reasons for its decision and shall cause those reasons to be included in the record of the proceedings.

(2) The offences to which this paragraph applies are—

    (a)   murder;

    (b)   manslaughter;

    (c)   rape;

    (d)   attempted murder; and

    (e)   attempted rape.]

[Cases under section 128A of Magistrates' Courts Act 1980

9B. Where the court is considering exercising the power conferred by section 128A of the Magistrates' Courts Act 1980 (power to remand in custody for more than 8 clear days), it shall have regard to the total length of time which the accused would spend in custody if it were to exercise the power.]

PART II
DEFENDANTS ACCUSED OR CONVICTED OF NON-IMPRISONABLE OFFENCES

Defendants to whom Part II applies

1. Where the offence or every offence of which the defendant is accused or convicted in the proceedings is one which is not punishable with imprisonment the following provisions of this Part of this Schedule apply.

Exceptions to right to bail

2. The defendant need not be granted bail if—

    (a)   it appears to the court that, having been previously granted bail in criminal proceedings, he has failed to surrender to custody in accordance with his obligations under the grant of bail; and

    (b)   the court believes, in view of that failure, that the defendant, if released on bail (whether subject to conditions or not) would fail to surrender to custody.

3. The defendant need not be granted bail if the court is satisfied that the defendant should be kept in custody for his own protection or, if he is a child or young person, for his own welfare.

4. The defendant need not be granted bail if he is in custody in pursuance of the sentence of a court or of any authority acting under any of the Services Acts.

5. The defendant need not be granted bail if, having been released on bail in or in connection with the proceedings for the offence, he has been arrested in pursuance of section 7 of this Act.

[PART IIA
DECISIONS WHERE BAIL REFUSED ON PREVIOUS HEARING

1. If the court decides not to grant the defendant bail, it is the court's duty to consider, at each subsequent hearing while the defendant is a person to whom section 4 above applies and remains in custody, whether he ought to be granted bail.

2. At the first hearing after that at which the court decided not to grant the defendant bail he may support an application for bail with any argument as to fact or law that he desires (whether or not he has advanced that argument previously).

3. At subsequent hearings the court need not hear arguments as to fact or law which it has heard previously.]

INTERPRETATION ACT 1978
(1978, c. 30)

An Act to consolidate the Interpretation Act 1889 and certain other enactments relating to the construction and operation of Acts of Parliament and other instruments, with amendments to give effect to recommendations of the Law Commission and the Scottish Law Commission [20 July 1978]

General provisions as to enactment and operation

1. Words of enactment
Every section of an Act takes effect as a substantive enactment without introductory words.

2. Amendment or repeal in same Session
Any Act may be amended or repealed in the Session of Parliament in which it is passed.

3. Judical notice
Every Act is a public Act to be judicially noticed as such, unless the contrary is expressly provided by the Act.

4. Time of commencement
An Act or provision of an Act comes into force—
 (a) where provision is made for it to come into force on a particular day, at the beginning of that day;
 (b) where no provision is made for its coming into force, at the beginning of the day on which the Act receives the Royal Assent.

Interpretation and construction

5. Definitions
In any Act, unless the contrary intention appears, words and expressions listed in Schedule 1 to this Act are to be construed according to that Schedule.

6. Gender and number
In any Act, unless the contrary intention appears,—
    (a)   words importing the masculine gender include the feminine;
    (b)   words importing the feminine gender include the masculine;
    (c)   words in the singular include the plural and words in the plural include the singular.

7. References to service by post
Where an Act authorises or requires any document to be served by post (whether the expression "serve" or the expression "give" or "send" or any other expression is used) then, unless the contrary intention appears, the service is deemed to be effected by properly addressing, pre-paying and posting a letter containing the document and, unless the contrary is proved, to have been effected at the time at which the letter would be delivered in the ordinary course of post.

8. References to distance
In the measurement of any distance for the purposes of an Act, that distance shall, unless the contrary intention appears, be measured in a straight line on a horizontal plane.

9. References to time of day
Subject to section 3 of the Summer Time Act 1972 (construction of references to points of time during the period of summer time), whenever an expression of time occurs in an Act, the time referred to shall, unless it is otherwise specifically stated, be held to be Greenwich mean time.

10. References to the Sovereign
In any Act a reference to the Sovereign reigning at the time of the passing of the Act is to be construed, unless the contrary intention appears, as a reference to the Sovereign for the time being.

11. Construction of subordinate legislation
Where an Act confers power to make subordinate legislation, expressions used in that legislation have, unless the contrary intention appears, the meaning which they bear in the Act.

Statutory powers and duties

12. Continuity of powers and duties
(1) Where an Act confers a power or imposes a duty it is implied, unless the contrary intention appears, that the power may be exercised, or the duty is to be performed, from time to time as occasion requires.

(2) Where an Act confers a power or imposes a duty on the holder of an office as such, it is implied, unless the contrary intention appears, that the power may be exercised, or the duty is to be performed, by the holder for the time being of the office.

13. Anticipatory exercise of powers
Where an Act which (or any provision of which) does not come into force immediately on its passing confers power to make subordinate legislation, or to make appointments, give notices, prescribe forms or do any other thing for the purposes of the Act, then, unless the contrary intention appears, the power may be exercised, and any instrument made thereunder may be made so as to come into force, at any time after the passing of the Act so far as may be necessary or expedient for the purpose—
    (a)   of bringing the Act or any provision of the Act into force; or
    (b)   of giving full effect to the Act or any such provision at or after the time when it comes into force.

Interpretation Act 1978

14. Implied power to amend
Where an Act confers power to make—
      (a)   rules, regulations or byelaws; or
      (a)   Orders in Council, orders or other subordinate legislation to be made by statutory instrument,
it implies, unless the contrary intention appears, a power, exercisable in the same manner and subject to the same conditions or limitations, to revoke, amend or re-enact any instrument made under the power.

Repealing enactments

15. Repeal of repeal
Where an Act repeals a repealing enactment, the repeal does not revive any enactment previously repealed unless words are added reviving it.

16. General savings
(1) Without prejudice to section 15, where an Act repeals an enactment, the repeal does not, unless the contrary intention appears,—
      (a)   revive anything not in force or existing at the time at which the repeal takes effect;
      (b)   affect the previous operation of the enactment repealed or anything duly done or suffered under that enactment;
      (c)   affect any right, privilege, obligation or liability acquired, accrued or incurred under that enactment;
      (d)   affect any penalty, forfeiture or punishment incurred in respect of any offence committed against that enactment;
      (e)   affect any investigation, legal proceeding or remedy in respect of any such right, privilege, obligation, liability, penalty, forfeiture or punishment;
and any such investigation, legal proceeding or remedy may be instituted, continued or enforced, and any such penalty, forfeiture or punishment may be imposed, as if the repealing Act had not been passed.

(2) This section applies to the expiry of a temporary enactment as if it were repealed by an Act.

17. Repeal and re-enactment
(1) Where an Act repeals a previous enactment and substitutes provisions for the enactment repealed, the repealed enactment remains in force until the substituted provisions comes into force.

(2) Where an Act repeals and re-enacts, with or without modification, a previous enactment then, unless the contrary intention appears,—
      (a)   any reference in any other enactment to the enactment so repealed shall be construed as a reference to the provision re-enacted;
      (b)   in so far as any subordinate legislation made or other thing done under the enactment so repealed, or having effect as if so made or done, could have been made or done under the provision re-enacted, it shall have effect as if made or done under that provision.

Miscellaneous

18. Duplicated offences
Where an act or omission constitutes an offence under two or more Acts, or both under an Act and at common law, the offender shall, unless the contrary intention appears, be liable to be prosecuted and punished under either or any of those Acts or at common law, but shall not be liable to be punished more than once for the same offence.

19. Citation of other Acts

(1) Where an Act cites another Act by year, statute, session or chapter, or a section or other portion of another Act by number or letter, the reference shall, unless the contrary intention appears, be read as referring—

    (a)   in the case of Acts included in any revised edition of the statutes printed by authority, to that edition;

    (b)   in the case of Acts not so included but included in the edition prepared under the direction of the Record Commission, to that edition;

    (c)   in any other case, to the Acts printed by the Queen's Printer, or under the superintendence or authority of Her Majesty's Stationery Office.

(2) An Act may continue to be cited by the short title authorised by any enactment notwithstanding the repeal of that enactment.

20. References to other enactments

(1) Where an Act describes or cites a portion of an enactment by referring to words, sections or other parts from or to which (or from and to which) the portion extends, the portion described or cited includes the words, sections or other parts referred to unless the contrary intention appears.

(2) Where an Act refers to an enactment, the reference, unless the contrary intention appears, is a reference to that enactment as amended.

Supplementary

21. Interpretation etc.

(1) In this Act "Act" includes a local and personal or private Act; and "subordinate legislation" means Orders in Council, orders, rules, regulations, schemes, warrants, byelaws and other instruments made or to be made under any Act.

(2) This Act binds the Crown.

22., 23. *****

Section 5

SCHEDULE 1
WORDS AND EXPRESSIONS DEFINED

Note: The years or dates which follow certain entries in this Schedule are relevant for the purposes of paragraph 4 of Schedule 2 (application to existing enactments).

Definitions

"Associated state" means a territory maintaining a status of association with the United Kingdom in accordance with the West Indies Act 1967. [16th February 1967]

"Bank of England" means, as the context requires, the Governor and Company of the Bank of England or the bank of the Governor and Company of the Bank of England.

"Bank of Ireland" means, as the context requires, the Governor and Company of the Bank of Ireland or the bank of the Governor and Company of the Bank of Ireland.

"British Islands" means the United Kingdom, the Channel Islands and the Isle of Man. [1889]

"British possession" means any part of Her Majesty's dominions outside the United Kingdom; and where parts of such dominions are under both a central and a local legislature, all part under the central legislature are deemed, for the purpose of this definition, to be one British possession. [1889]

"Building regulations", in relation to England and Wales, [has the meaning given by section 122 of the Building Act 1984].

"Central funds", in an enactment providing in relation to England and Wales for the payment of costs out of central funds, means money provided by Parliament.

"Charity Commissioners" means the Charity Commissioners for England and Wales referred to in section 1 to the Charities Act 1960.

"Church Commissioners" means the Commissioners constituted by the Church Commissioners Measure 1947.

"Colonial legislature", and "legislature" in relation to a British possession, mean the authority, other than the Parliament of the United Kingdom or Her Majesty in Council, competent to make laws for the possession. [1889]

"Colony" means any part of Her Majesty's dominions outside the British Islands except—

(a) countries having fully responsible status within the Commonwealth;

(b) territories for whose external relations a country other than the United Kingdom is responsible;

(c) associated states;

and where parts of such dominions are under both a central and a local legislature, all parts under the central legislature are deemed for the purposes of this definition to be one colony. [1889]

"Commencement", in relation to an Act or enactment, means the time when the Act or enactment comes into force.

"Committed for trial" means—

(a) in relation to England and Wales, committed in custody or on bail by a magistrates' court pursuant to [section 6 of the Magistrates' Courts Act 1980], or by any judge or other authority having power to do so, with a view to trial before a judge and jury; [1889]

(b) (*relates to Northern Ireland.*)

"The Communities", "the Treaties" or "the Community Treaties" and other expressions defined by section 1 of and Schedule 1 to the European Communities Act 1972 have the meanings prescribed by that Act.

"Comptroller and Auditor General" means the Comptroller-General of the receipt and issue of Her Majesty's Exchequer and Auditor-General of Public Accounts appointed in pursuance of the Exchequer and Audit Departments Act 1866.

"Consular officer" has the meaning assigned by Article 1 of the Vienna Convention set out in Schedule 1 to the Consular Relations Act 1968

["The Corporation Tax Acts" means — the enactments relating to the taxation of income and chargeable gains of companies and of companies distributions (including provisions relating to income tax];

"County court" means—

(a) in relation to England and Wales, a court held for a district under [the County Courts Act 1984]; [1846]

(b) (*relates to Northern Ireland.*)

"Court of Appeal" means—

(a) in relation to England and Wales, Her Majesty's Court of Appeal in England;

(b) (*relates to Northern Ireland.*)

*****

"Crown Court" means—

(a) in relation to England and Wales, the Crown Court constituted by section 4 of the Courts Act 1971;

(b) (*relates to Northern Ireland.*)

"Crown Estate Commissioners" means the Commissioners refered to in section 1 of the Crown Estate Act 1961.

"England" means, subject to any alteration of boundaries under Part IV of the Local Government Act 1972, the area consisting of the counties established by section 1 of that Act, Greater London and the Isle of Scilly. [1st April 1974]

"Financial year" means, in relation to matters relating to the Consolidated Fund, the National Loans Fund, or moneys provided by Parliament, or to the Exchequer or to central taxes or finance, the twelve months ending with 31st March. [1889]

"Governor-General" includes any person who for the time being has the powers of the Governor-General, and "Governor", in relation to any British possession, includes the officer for the time being administering the government of that possession. [1889]

"High Court" means—
    (a)   in relation to England and Wales, Her Majesty's High Court of Justice in England;
    (b)   (*relates to Northern Ireland*.)

"The Income Tax Acts" means all enactments relating to income tax, including any provisions of the Corporation Tax Acts which relate to income tax.

"Land" includes buildings and other structures, land covered with water, and any estate, interest, easement, servitude or right in or over land. [1st January 1979]

"Lands Clauses Acts" means—
    (a)   in relation to England and Wales, the Lands Clauses Consolidation Act 1845 and the Lands Clauses Consolidation Acts Amendment Act 1860, and any Acts for the time being in force amending those Acts; [1889]
    (b)   (*relates to Scotland*);
    (c)   (*relates to Northern Ireland*.)

"Local land charges register", in relation to England and Wales, means a register kept pursuant to section 3 of the Local Land Charges Act 1975, and "the appropriate local land charges register" has the meaning assigned by section 4 of that Act.

"London borough" means one of the boroughs so described and numbered from 1 to 12 and "outer London borough" means one of the boroughs so described and numbered from 13 to 32, subject (in each case) to any alterations made under Part IV of the Local Government Act 1972.

"Lord Chancellor" means the Lord High Chancellor of Great Britain.

"Magistrates' court" has the meaning assigned to it—
    (a)   in relation to England and Wales, by [section 148 of the Magistrates Courts Act 1980];
    (b)   (*relates to Northern Ireland*.)

"Month" means calendar month. [1850]

"National Debt Commissioners" means the Commissioners for the Reduction of the National Debt.

"Oath" and "affidavit" include affirmation and declaration, and "swear" includes affirm and declare.

"Ordnance Map" means a map made under powers conferred by the Ordnance Survey Act 1841 or the Boundary Survey (Ireland) Act 1854.

"Parliamentary Election" means the election of a Member to serve in Parliament for a constituency. [1889]

"Person" includes a body of persons corporate or unincorporate. [1889]

"Police area", "police authority" and other expressions relating to the police have the meaning or effect described—
    (a)   in relation to England and Wales, by section 62 of the Police Act 1964;
    (b)   (*relates to Scotland*.)

"The Privy Council" means the Lords and others of Her Majesty's Most Honourable Privy Council.

["Registered" in relation to nurses, midwives and health visitors, means registered in the register maintained by the United Kingdom Central Council for Nursing. Midwifery and Health Visiting by virtue of qualifications in nursing, midwifery or health visiting, as the case may be.]

"Registered medical practitioner" means a fully registered person within the meaning of [the Medical Act 1983]. [1st January 1979]

"Rules of Court" in relation to any court means rules made by the authority having power to make rules or orders regulating the practice and procedure of that court, and in Scotland includes Acts of Adjournal and Acts of Sederunt; and the power of the authority to make rules of court (as above defined) includes power to make such rules for the purpose of any Act which directs or authorises anything to be done by rules of court. [1889]

"Secretary of State" means one of Her Majesty's Principal Secretaries of State.

["The standard scale", with reference to a fine or penalty for an offence only triable summarily—

(a) in relation to England and Wales, has the meaning given by section 37 of the Criminal Justice Act 1982;

(b) *****

(c) *****]

"Statutory declaration" means a declaration made by virtue of the Statutory Declarations Act 1835.

["Statutory maximum", with reference to a fine or penalty on summary conviction for an offence—

(a) in relation to England and Wales, means the prescribed sum within the meaning of section 32 of the Magistrates' Courts Act 1980;

(b) *****

(c) *****]

"Supreme Court" means—

(a) in relation to England and Wales, the Court of Appeal and the High Court together with the Crown Court;

(b) (*relates to Northern Ireland.*)

["The Tax Acts" means the Income Tax Acts and the Corporation Tax Acts"]

"The Treasury" means the Commissioners of Her Majesty's Treasury.

"United Kingdom" means Great Britain and Northern Ireland. [12th April 1927]

"Wales" means, subject to any alteration of boundaries made under Part IV of the Local Government Act 1972, the area consisting of the counties established by section 20 of that Act. [1st April 1974]

"Water authority", in relation to England and Wales, means an authority established in accordance with section 2 of the Water Act 1973; and "water authority area", in relation to any functions of such an authority, means the area in respect of which the water authority are for the time being to exercise those functions.

"Writing" includes typing, printing, lithography, photography and other modes of representing or reproducing words in a visible form, and expressions referring to writing are construed accordingly.

Construction of certain expressions relating to children

In relation to England and Wales the following expressions and references, namely—

(a) the expression "the parental rights and duties";

(b) the expression "legal custody" in relation to a child (as defined in the Children Act 1975); and

(c) any reference to the person with whom a child (as so defined) has his home;

are to be construed in accordance with Part IV of that Act. [12th November 1975]

Construction of certain expressions relating to offences

In relation to England and Wales—

(a) "indictable offence" means an offence which, if committed by an adult, is triable on indictment, whether it is exclusively so triable or triable either way;
(b) "summary offence" means an offence which, if committed by an adult, is triable only summarily;
(c) "offence triable either way" means an offence, [other than an offence triable on indictment only by virtue of Part V of the Criminal Justice Act 1988], which, if committed by an adult, is triable either on indictment or summarily;
and the terms "indictable", "summary" and "triable either way", in their application to offences, are to be construed accordingly.

In the above definitions references to the way or ways in which an offence is triable are to be construed without regard to the effect, if any, of [section 22 of the Magistrates' Courts Act 1980] on the mode of trial in a particular case.

[*Construction of certain references to relationships*

In relation to England and Wales—
(a) references (however expressed) to any relationship betwen two persons;
(b) references to a person whose father and mother were or were not married at the time of his birth; and
(c) references cognate with references falling within paragraph (b) above
shall be construed in accordance with the Family Law Reform Act 1987.]

EMPLOYMENT PROTECTION (CONSOLIDATION) ACT 1978
(1978, c. 44)

PART VIII
RESOLUTION OF DISPUTES RELATING TO EMPLOYMENT

Industrial tribunals

128. Industrial tribunals
(1) The Secretary of State may by regulations make provision for the establishment of tribunals, to be known as industrial tribunals, to exercise the jurisdiction conferred on them by or under this Act or any other Act, whether passed before or after the Act.
(2) *****
(3) Schedule 9, which makes provision, among other things, with respect to proceedings before industrial tribunals, shall have effect.
(4) Complaints, references [applications] and appeals to industrial tribunals shall be made in accordance with regulations made under paragraph 1 of Schedule 9.

129. *****

130. Jurisdiction of referees to be exercised by tribunals
(1) There shall be referred to and determined by an industrial tribunal any question which by any statutory provision is directed (in whatsoever terms) to be determined by a referee or board of referees constituted under any of the statutory provisions specified in Schedule 10 or which is so directed to be determined in the absence of agreement to the contrary.
(2) The transfer of any jurisdiction by this section shall not affect the principles on which any question is to be determined or the persons on whom the determination is binding, or any provision which requires particular matters to be expressly dealt with or embodied in the determination, or which relates to evidence.

131. Power to confer jurisdiction on industrial tribunals in respect of damages, etc., for breach of contract of employment

(1) The appropriate Minister may by order provide that on any claim to which this section applies or any such claim of a description specified in the order, being in either case a claim satisfying the relevant condition or conditions mentioned in subsection (3), proceedings for the recovery of damages or any other sum, except damages or a sum due in respect of personal injuries, may be brought before an industrial tribunal.

(2) Subject to subsection (3), this section applies to any of the following claims, that it to say—

    (a)   a claim for damages for breach of a contract of employment or any other contract connected with employment;

    (b)   a claim for a sum due under such a contract;

    (c)   a claim for the recovery of a sum in pursuance of any enactment relating to the terms or performance of such a contract;

being in each case a claim such that a court in England and Wales or Scotland, as the case may be, would under the law for the time being in force have jurisdiction to hear and determine an action in respect of the claim.

(3)—(8) *****

Employment Appeal Tribunal

135. Employment Appeal Tribunal

(1) The Employment Appeal Tribunal established under section 87 of the Employment Protection Act 1975 shall continue in existence by that name.

(2) The Employment Appeal Tribunal (in this Act referred to as "the Appeal Tribunal") shall consist of—

    (a)   such number of judges as may be nominated from time to time by the Lord Chancellor from among the judges (other than the Lord Chancellor) of the High Court and the Court of Appeal;

    (b)   at least one judge of the Court of Session nominated from time to time by the Lord President of that Court; and

    (c)   such number of other members as may be appointed from time to time by Her Majesty on the joint recommendation of the Lord Chancellor and the Secretary of State.

(3) The members of the Appeal Tribunal appointed under subsection (2)(c) shall be persons who appear to the Lord Chancellor and the Secretary of State to have special knowledge or experience of industrial relations, either as representatives of employers or as representatives of workers (within the meaning of the Trade Union and Labour Relations Act 1974).

(4) The Lord Chancellor shall, after consultation with the Lord President of the Court of Session, appoint one of the judges nominated under subsection (2) to be President of the Appeal Tribunal.

(5) No judge shall be nominated a member of the Appeal Tribunal except with his consent.

(6) The provisions of Schedule 11 shall have effect with respect to the Appeal Tribunal and proceedings before the Tribunal.

136. Appeals to Tribunal from industrial tribunals and Certification Officer

(1) An appeal shall lie to the Appeal Tribunal on a question of law arising from any decision of, or arising in any proceedings before, an industrial tribunal under, or by virtue of, the following Acts—

    (a)   the Equal Pay Act 1970;

    (b)   the Sex Discrimination Act 1975;

    (c)   the Employment Protection Act 1975;

(d) the Race Relations Act 1976;
(e) this Act.

(2) The Appeal Tribunal shall hear appeals on questions of law arising on any proceedings before, or arising from any decision of, the Certification Officer under the following enactments—
    (a) sections 3, 4 and 5 of the Trade Union Act 1913;
    (b) section 4 of the Trade Union (Amalgamations, etc.) Act 1964.

(3) The Appeal Tribunal shall hear appeals on questions of fact or law arising in any proceedings before, or arising from any decision of, the Certification Officer under the following enactments—
    (a) section 8 of the Trade Union and Labour Relations Act 1974;
    (b) section 8 of the Employment Protection Act 1975.

(4) Without prejudice to section 13 of the Administration of Justice Act 1960 (appeal in case of contempt of court), an appeal shall lie on any question of law from any decision or order of the Appeal Tribunal with the leave of the Tribunal or of the Court of Appeal or, as the case may be, the Court of Session,—
    (a) in the case of proceedings in England and Wales, to the Court of Appeal;
    (b) in the case of proceedings in Scotland, to the Court of Session.

(5) No appeal shall lie except to the Appeal Tribunal from any decision of an industrial tribunal under the Acts listed in subsection (1) [or under section 2, 4 or 5 of the Employment Act 1980] [or section 4 or 5 of the Employment Act 1988,] or from any decision under the enactments listed in subsections (2) and (3) of the Certification Officer appointed under section 7 of the Employment Protection Act 1975.

SCHEDULE 9
INDUSTRIAL TRIBUNALS

Regulations as to tribunal procedure

1.—(1) The Secretary of State may by regulations (in this Schedule referred to as "the regulations") make such provision as appears to him to be necessary or expedient with respect to proceedings before industrial tribunals.

(2) The regulations may in particular include provision—
    (a) for determining by which tribunal any appeal, question [application] or complaint is to be determined;
    (b) for enabling an industrial tribunal to hear and determine proceedings brought by virtue of section 131 concurrently with proceedings brought before the tribunal otherwise than by virtue of that section;
    (c) for treating the Secretary of State (either generally or in such circumstances as may be prescribed by the regulations) as a party to any proceedings before an industrial tribunal, where he would not otherwise be a party to them, and entitling him to appear and to be heard accordingly;
    (d) for requiring persons to attend to give evidence and produce documents, and for authorising the administration of oaths to witnesses;
    (e) for granting to any person such discovery or inspection of documents or right to further particulars as might be granted by a county court in England and Wales or, in Scotland, for granting to any person such recovery or inspection of documents as might be granted by the sheriff;
    (f) for prescribing the procedure to be followed on any appeal, reference or complaint or other proceedings before an industrial tribunal, including provisions as to the persons entitled to appear and to be heard on behalf of parties to such proceedings, and provisions for enabling an industrial tribunal to review its decisions, and revoke or vary its orders and awards, in such circumstances as may be determined in accordance with the regulations;

(g) for the appointment of one or more assessors for the purposes of any proceedings before an industrial tribunal, where the proceedings are brought under an enactment which provides for one or more assessors to be appointed;

[(ga) for authorising an industrial tribunal to require persons to furnish information and produce documents to a person required for the purposes of section 2A(1)(b) of the Equal Pay Act 1970 to prepare a report;]

(h) for the award of costs or expenses, including any allowances payable under paragraph 10 other than allowances payable to members of industrial tribunals or assessors;

(i) for taxing or otherwise settling any such costs or expenses (and, in particular, in England and Wales, for enabling such costs to be taxed in the county court); and

(j) for the registration and proof of decisions, orders and awards of industrial tribunals.

(3) In relation to proceedings on complaints under section 67 or any other enactment in relation to which there is provision for concilation, the regulations shall include provision—

(a) for requiring a copy of any such complaint, and a copy of any notice relating to it which is lodged by or on behalf of the employer against whom the complaint is made, to be sent to a conciliation officer;

(b) for securing that the complainant and the employer against whom the complaint is made are notified that the services of a conciliation officer are available to them; and

(c) for postponing the hearing of any such complaint for such period as may be determined in accordance with the regulations for the purpose of giving an opportunity for the complaint to be settled by way of conciliation and withdrawn.

(4) In relation to proceedings under section 67—

(a) where the employee has expressed a wish to be reinstated or re-engaged which has been communicated to the employer at least seven days before the hearing of the complaint; or

(b) where the proceedings arise out of the employer's failure to permit the employee to return to work after an absence due to pregnancy or confinement,

regulations shall include provision for requiring the employer to pay the costs or expenses of any postponement or adjournment of the hearing caused by his failure, without a special reason, to adduce reasonable evidence as to the availability of the job from which the complainant was dismissed, or, as the case may be, which she held before her absence, or of comparable or suitable employment.

(5) Without prejudice to paragraph 2, the regulations may enable an industrial tribunal to sit in private for the purpose of hearing evidence which in the opinion of the tribunal relates to matters of such a nature that it would be against the interests of national security to allow the evidence to be given in public or of hearing evidence from any person which in the opinion of the tribunal is likely to consist of—

(a) information which he could not disclose without contravening a prohibition imposed by or under any enactment; or

(b) any information which has been communicated to him in confidence, or which he has otherwise obtained in consequence of the confidence reposed in him by another person; or

(c) information the disclosure of which would, for reasons other than its effect on negotiations with respect to any of the matters mentioned in section 29(1) of the Trade Union and Labour Relations Act 1974 (matters to which trade disputes relate) cause substantial injury to any undertaking of his or in which he works.

(6) The regulations may include provision authorising or requiring an industrial tribunal, in circumstances specified in the regulations, to send notice or a copy of any document so specified relating to any proceedings before the tribunal, or of any decision,

order or award of the tribunal, to any government department or other person or body so specified.

(7) Any person who without reasonable excuse fails to comply with any requirement imposed by the regulations by virtue of sub-paragraph (2)(d) [or (ga)] or any requirement with respect to the discovery, recovery or inspection of documents so imposed by virtue of sub-paragraph (2)(e) shall be liable on summary conviction to a fine not exceeding [level 3 on the standard scale].

Exclusion of Arbitration Act 1950

4. The Arbitration Act 1950 shall not apply to any proceedings before an industrial tribunal.

Right of appearance

6. Any person may appear before an industrial tribunal in person or be represented by counsel or by a solicitor or by a representative of a trade union or an employers' association or by any other person whom he desires to represent him.

Interest on sums awarded

6A. (1) The Secretary of State may by order made with the approval of the Treasury provide that sums payable in pursuance of decisions of industrial tribunals shall carry interest at such rate and between such times as may be prescribed by the order.

(2) Any interest due by virtue of such an order shall be recoverable as a sum payable in pursuance of the decision.

(3) The power conferred by sub-paragraph (1) includes power—
    (a)   to specify cases or circumstances in which interest shall not be payable;
    (b)   to provide that interest shall be payable only on sums exceeding a specified amount or falling between specified amounts;
    (c)   to make provision for the manner in which and the periods by reference to which interest is to be calculated and paid;
    (d)   to provide that any enactment shall or shall not apply in relation to interest payable by virtue of an order under sub-paragraph (1) or shall apply to it with such modifications as may be specified in the order;
    (e)   to make provision for cases where sums are payable in pursuance of decisions or awards made on appeal from industrial tribunals;
    (f)   to make such incidental or supplemental provision as the Secretary of State considers necessary.

(4) Without prejudice to the generality of sub-paragraph (3), an order under sub-paragraph (1) may provide that the rate of interest shall be the rate specified in section 17 of the Judgments Act 1838 as that enactment has effect from time to time.

Recovery of sums awarded

7. (1) Any sum payable in pursuance of a decision of an industrial tribunal in England and Wales which has been registered in accordance with the regulations shall, if a county court so orders, be recoverable by execution issued from the county court or otherwise as if it were payable under an order of that court.

(2) Applies to Scotland.

(3) In this paragraph any reference to a decision or order of an industrial tribunal—
    (a)   does not include a decision or order which, on being reviewed, has been revoked by the tribunal, and
    (b)   in relation to a decision or order which, on being reviewed, has been varied by the tribunal, shall be construed as a reference to the decision or order as so varied.

Constitution of tribunals for certain cases

8. An industrial tribunal hearing an application under section 77 or 79 may consist of a President of Industrial Tribunals, the chairman of the tribunal or a member of a panel of chairmen of such tribunals for the time being nominated by a President to hear such applications.

Remuneration for presidents and full-time chairmen of industrial tribunals

9. The Secretary of State may pay such remuneration as he may with the consent of the Minister for the Civil Service determine to the President of the Industrial Tribunals (England and Wales), the President of the Industrial Tribunals (Scotland) and any person who is a member on a full-time basis of a panel of chairmen of tribunals which is appointed in accordance with regulations under subsection (1) of section 128.

Remuneration etc. for members of industrial tribunals and for assessors and other persons

10. The Secretary of State may pay to members of industrial tribunals and to any assessors appointed for the purposes of proceedings before industrial tribunals [and to any persons required for the purposes of section 2A(1)(b) of the Equal Pay Act 1970 to prepare such reports] such fees and allowances as he may with the consent of the Minister for the Civil Service determine and may pay to any other persons such allowances as he may with the consent of that Minister determine for the purposes of, or in connection with, their attendance at industrial tribunals.

Pensions for full-time presidents or chairmen of industrial tribunals.

11. . . .

SCHEDULE 11
EMPLOYMENT APPEAL TRIBUNAL
PART I
PROVISIONS AS TO MEMBERSHIP, SITTINGS, PROCEEDINGS AND POWERS

Tenure of office of appointed members of Appeal Tribunal

1. Subject to paragraphs 2 and 3, a member of the Appeal Tribunal appointed by Her Majesty under section 135(2)(c) (in this Schedule referred to as an "appointed member") shall hold and vacate office as such a member in accordance with the terms of his appointment.

2. An appointed member may at any time resign his membership by notice in writing addressed to the Lord Chancellor and the Secretary of State.

3. (1) If the Lord Chancellor, after consultation with the Secretary of State, is satisfied that an appointed member—
   (a) has been absent from sittings of the Appeal Tribunal for a period longer than six consecutive months without the permission of the President of the Tribunals; or
   (b) has become bankrupt or made an arrangement with is creditors; or
   (c) is incapacitated by physical of mental illness; or
   (d) is otherwise unable or unfit to discharge the functions of a member;
the Lord Chancellor may declare his office as a member to be vacant and shall notify the declaration in such manner as the Lord Chancellor thinks fit; and thereupon the office shall become vacant.
   (2) (*Applies to Scotland*)

Organisation and sittings of Appeal Tribunal

12. The Appeal Tribunal shall be a superior court of record and shall have an official seal which shall be judicially noticed.

13. The Appeal Tribunal shall have a central office in London.

14. The Appeal Tribunal may sit at any time and in any place in Great Britain.

15. The Appeal Tribunal may sit, in accordance with directions given by the President of the Tribunal, either as a single tribunal or in two or more divisions concurrently.

16. With the consent of the parties to any proceedings before the Appeal Tribunal, the proceedings may be heard by a judge and one appointed member, but, in default of such consent, any proceedings before the Tribunal shall be heard by a judge and either two or four appointed members, so that in either case there are equal number of persons whose experience is as representatives of employers and whose experience is as representatives of workers.

Rules

17. (1) The Lord Chancellor, after consultation with the Lord President of the Court of Session, shall make rules with respect to proceedings before the Appeal Tribunal.
 (2) Subject to those rules, the Tribunal shall have power to regulate its own procedure.

18. Without prejudice to the generality of paragraph 17 the rules may include provisions—
 (a) with respect to the manner in which an appeal may be brought and the time within which it may be brought;
 [(aa) with respect to the manner in which an application to the Appeal Tribunal under section 5 of the Employment Act 1980 [or section 5 of the Employment Act 1988] may be made;]
 (b) for requiring persons to attend to give evidence and produce documents, and for authorising the administration of oaths to witnesses;
 (c) enabling the Appeal Tribunal to sit in private for the purpose of hearing evidence to hear which an industrial tribunal may sit in private by virtue of paragraph 1 of Schedule 9;
 [(d) for the registration and proof of any award made on an application to the Appeal Tribunal under section 5 of the Employment Act 1980 [or section 5 of the Employment Act 1988];]
 [(e) for interlocutory proceedings to be dealt with otherwise than in accordance with paragraph 16].

19. (1) Without prejudice to the generality of paragraph 17 the rules may empower the Appeal Tribunal to order a party to any proceedings before the Tribunal to pay to any other party to the proceedings the whole or part of the costs or expenses incurred by that other party in connection with the proceedings, where in the opinion of the Tribunal—
 (a) the proceedings were unnecessary, improper or vexatious, or
 (b) there has been unreasonable delay or other unreasonable conduct in bringing or conducting the proceedings.
 (2) Except as provided by sub-paragraph (1), the rules shall not enable the Appeal Tribunal to order the payment of costs or expenses by any party to proceedings before the Tribunal.

20. Any person may appear before the Appeal Tribunal in person or be represented by counsel or by a solicitor or by a representative of a trade union or an employers' association or by any other person whom he desires to represent him.

Powers of Tribunal

21. (1) For the purpose of disposing of an appeal the Appeal Tribunal may exercise any powers of the body or officer from whom the appeal was brought or may remit the case to that body or officer.

(2) Any decision or award of the Appeal Tribunal on an appeal shall have the same effect and may be enforced in the same manner as a decision or award of a body or officer from whom the appeal was brought.

[21A. (1) Any sum payable in England and Wales in pursuance of an award of the Appeal Tribunal under section 5 of the Employment Act 1980 [or section 5 of the Employment Act 1988] which has been registered in accordance with the rules shall, if a county court so orders, be recoverable by execution issued from the county court or otherwise as if it were payable under an order of that court.

(2) *(Applies to Scotland only.)*

[(3) Any sum payable in pursuance of an award of the Appeal Tribunal under section 5 of the Employment Act 1980 shall be treated as if it were a sum payable in pursuance of a decision of an industrial tribunal for the purposes of paragraph 6A of Schedule 9 (interest on industrial tribunal awards).]]

22. (1) The Appeal Tribunal shall, in relation to the attendance and examination of witnesses, the production and inspection of documents and all other matters incidental to its jurisdiction, have the like powers, rights, privileges and authority—
    (a)   in England and Wales, as the High Court;
    (b)   in Scotland, as the Court of Session.

(2) No person shall be punished for contempt of the Tribunal except by, or with the consent of, a judge.

23. (1) ...

(2) A magistrates' court shall not remit the whole or any part of a fine imposed by the Appeal Tribunal except with the consent of a judge who is a member of the Tribunal.

(3) This paragraph does not extend to Scotland.

ARBITRATION ACT 1979
(1979, c. 42)

An Act to amend the law relating to arbitration and for purposes connected therewith.   [4th April 1979]

1. Judicial review of arbitration awards

(1) In the Arbitration Act 1950 (in the Act referred to as "the principal Act") section 21 (statement of case for a decision of the High Court) shall cease to have effect and, without prejudice to the right of appeal conferred by subsection (2) below, the High Court shall not have jurisdiction to set aside or remit an award on an arbitration agreement on the ground of errors of fact or law on the face of the award.

(2) Subject to subsection (3) below, an appeal shall lie to the High Court on any question of law arising out of an award made on an arbitration agreement; and on the determination of such an appeal the High Court may by order—
    (a)   confirm, vary or set aside the award; or
    (b)   remit the award to the reconsideration of the arbitrator or umpire together with the court's opinion on the question of law which was the subject of the appeal;

and where the award is remitted under paragraph (b) above the arbitrator or umpire shall, unless the order otherwise directs, make his award within three months after the date of the order.

(3) An appeal under this section may be brought by any of the parties to the reference—
- (a) with the consent of all the other parties to the reference; or
- (b) subject to section 3 below, with the leave of the court.

(4) The High Court shall not grant leave under subsection (3)(b) above unless it considers that, having regard to all the circumstances, the determination of the question of law concerned could substantially affect the right of one or more of the parties to the arbitration agreement; and the court may make any leave which it gives conditional upon the application complying with such conditions as it considers appropriate.

(5) Subject to subsection (6) below, if an award is made and, on an application made by any of the parties to the references,—
- (a) with the consent of all the other parties to the reference, or
- (b) subject to section 3 below, with the leave of the court,

it appears to the High Court that the award does not or does not sufficiently set out the reasons for the award, the court may order the arbitrator or umpire concerned to state the reasons for his award in sufficient detail to enable the court, should an appeal be brought under this section, to consider any question of law arising out of the award.

(6) In any case where an award is made without any reason being given, the High Court shall not make an order under subsection (5) above unless it is satisfied—
- (a) that before the award was made one of the parties to the reference gave notice to the arbitrator or umpire concerned that a reasoned award would be required; or
- (b) that there is some special reason why such a notice was not given.

[(6A) Unless the High Court gives leave, no appeal shall lie to the Court of Appeal from a decision of the High Court—
- (a) to grant or refuse leave under subsection (3)(b) or (5)(b); or
- (b) to make or not to make an order under subsection (5) above.]

(7) No appeal shall lie to the Court of Appeal from a decision of the High Court on an appeal under this section unless—
- (a) the High Court or the Court of Appeal gives leave; and
- (b) it is certified by the High Court that the question of law to which its decision relates either is one of general public importance or is one which for some other special reason should be considered by the Court of Appeal.

(8) Where the award of an arbitrator or umpire is varied on appeal, the award as varied shall have effect (except for the purpose of this section) as if it were the award of the arbitrator or umpire.

2. Determination of preliminary point of law by court

(1) Subject to subsection (2) and section 3 below, on an application to the High Court made by any of the parties to a reference—
- (a) with the consent of an arbitrator who has entered on the reference or, if an umpire has entered on the reference, with his consent, or
- (b) with the consent of all the other parties,

the High Court shall have jurisdiction to determine any question of law arising in the course of the reference.

(2) The High Court shall not entertain an application under subsection (1) (a) above with respect to any question of law unless it is satisfied that—
- (a) the determination of the application might produce substantial savings in costs to the parties; and

(b) the question of law is one in respect of which leave to appeal would be likely to be given under section 1(3)(b) above.

[(2A) Unless the High Court gives leave, no appeal shall lie to the Court of Appeal from a decision of the High Court to entertain or not to entertain an application under subsection (1)(a) above.]

(3) A decision of the High Court under [subsection (1) above] shall be deemed to be a judgment of the court within the meaning of [section 16 of the Supreme Court Act 1981] (appeals to the Court of Appeal), but no appeal shall lie from such a decision unless—
    (a)   the High Court or the Court of Appeal gives leave; and
    (b)   it is certified by the High Court that the question of law to which its decision relates either is one of general public importance or is one which for some other special reason should be considered by the Court of Appeal.

3. Exclusion agreements affecting rights under sections 1 and 2

(1) Subject to the following provisions of this section and section 4 below—
    (a)   the High Court shall not, under section 1(3)(b) above, grant leave to appeal with respect to a question of law arising out of an award, and
    (b)   the High Court shall not, under section 1(5)(b) above, grant leave to make an application with respect to an award, and
    (c)   no application may be made under section 2(1)(a) above with respect to a question of law,
if the parties to the reference in question have entered into an agreement in writing (in this section referred to as an "exclusion agreement") which excludes the right of appeal under section 1 above in relation to that award or, in a case falling within paragraph (c) above, in relation to an award to which the determination of the question of law is material.

(2) An exclusion agreement may be expressed so as to relate to a particular award, to awards under a particular reference or to any other description of awards, whether arising out of the same reference or not; and an agreement may be an exclusion agreement for the purposes of this section whether it is entered into before or after the passing of this Act and whether or not it forms part of an arbitration agreement.

(3) In any case where—
    (a)   an arbitration agreement, other than a domestic arbitration agreement, provides for disputes between the parties to be referred to arbitration, and
    (b)   a dispute to which the agreement relates involves the question whether a party has been guilty of fraud, and
    (c)   the parties have entered into an exclusion agreement which is applicable to any award made on the reference of that dispute, then, except in so far as the exclusion agreement otherwise provides, the High Court shall not exercise its powers under section 24(2) of the principal Act (to take steps necessary to enable the question to be determined by the High Court) in relation to that dispute.

(4) Except as provided by subsection (1) above, sections 1 and 2 above shall have effect notwithstanding anything in any agreement purporting—
    (a)   to prohibit or restrict access to the High Court; or
    (b)   to restrict the jurisdiction of that court; or
    (c)   to prohibit or restrict the making of a reasoned award.

(5) *****

(6) An exclusion agreement shall be of no effect in relation to an award made on, or a question of law arising in the course of a reference under, an arbitration agreement which is a domestic arbitration agreement unless the exclusion agreement is entered into after the commencement of the arbitration in which the award is made or, as the case may be, in which the question of law arises.

(7) In this section "domestic arbitration agreement" means an arbitration agreement which does not provide, expressly or by implication, for arbitration in a State other than the United Kingdom and to which neither—

 (a) an individual who is a national of, or habitually resident in, any State other than the United Kingdom, nor

 (b) a body corporate which is incorporated in, or whose central management and control is exercised in, any State other than the United Kingdom,

is a party at the time the arbitration agreement is entered into.

JUSTICES OF THE PEACE ACT 1979
(1979, c. 55)

An Act to consolidate certain enactments relating to justices of the peace (including stipendiary magistrates), justices' clerks and the administrative and financial arrangements for magistrates' courts, and to matters connected therewith, with amendments to give effect to recommendations of the Law Commission. [6th December 1979]

PART I
GENERAL
Areas and commissions of the peace

1. Commission areas.

There shall in England and Wales be a commission of the peace for the following areas (in this Act referred to as "commission areas") and no others; that is to say—

 (a) every county;
 (b) every London commission area; and
 (c) the City of London.

2., 3. *****

4. Petty sessions areas.

(1) The following areas outside Greater London are petty session areas, that is to say—

 (a) every non-metropolitan county which is not divided into petty sessional divisions;
 (b) every petty sessional division of a non-metropolitan county;
 (c) every metropolitan district which is not divided into petty sessional divisions; and
 (d) every petty sessional division of a metropolitan district.

5. General form of commissions of the peace.

(1) The commission of the peace for any commission area shall be a commission under the Great Seal addressed generally, and not by name, to all such persons as may from time to time hold office as justices of the peace for the commission area.

Justices other than stipendiary magistrates

6. Appointment and removal of justices of the peace.

(1) Subject to the following provisions of this Act, justices of the peace for any commission area shall be appointed [by the Lord Chancellor by instrument on behalf and in the name of Her Majesty] and a justice so appointed may be removed from office in like manner.

(2) The preceding subsection does not apply to stipendiary magistrates and shall be without prejudice to the position of the Lord Mayor and aldermen as justices for the City of London by virtue of the charters of the City.

7. **Residence qualification.**

(1) Subject to the provisions of this section, a person shall not be appointed as a justice of the peace for a commission area in accordance with section 6 of this Act, nor act as a justice of the peace by virtue of any such appointment, unless he resides in or within fifteen miles of that area.

(2) If the Lord Chancellor is of opinion that it is in the public interest for a person to act as a justice of the peace for a particular area though not qualified to do so under subsection (1) above, he may direct that, so long as any conditions specified in the direction are satisfied, that subsection shall not apply in relation to that person's appointment as a justice of the peace for the area so specified.

(3) Where a person appointed as a justice of the peace for a commission area in accordance with section 6 of this Act is not qualified under the preceding provisions of this section to act by virtue of the appointment, he shall be removed from office as a justice of the peace in accordance with section 6 of this Act if the Lord Chancellor is of opinion that the appointment ought not to continue having regard to the probable duration and other circumstances of the want of qualification.

(4) No act or appointment shall be invalidated by reason only of the qualification or want of qualification under this section of the person acting or appointed.

8. **Supplemental list for England and Wales.**

(1) There shall be kept in the office of the Clerk of the Crown in Chancery a supplemental list for England and Wales as provided for by this Act (in this Act referred to as "the supplemental list").

(2) Subject to the following provisions of this section, there shall be entered in the supplemental list—

    (a) the name of any justice of the peace who is of the age of 70 years or over and neither holds nor has held high judicial office within the meaning of the Appellate Jurisdiction Act 1876, and

    (b) the name of any justice of the peace who holds or has held such office and is of the age of 75 years or over.

(3) A person who on the date when his name falls to be entered in the supplemental list in accordance with subsection (2) above holds office as chairman of the justices in a petty sessions area (whether by an election made, or having effect as if made, under section 17 of this Act, or, in the City of London, as Chief Magistrate or acting Chief Magistrate) shall have his name so entered on the expiry or sooner determination of the term for which he holds office on that date.

(4) The Lord Chancellor may direct that the name of a justice of the peace for any area shall be entered in the supplemental list if the Lord Chancellor is satisfied either—

    (a) that by reason of the justices's age or infirmity or other like cause it is expedient that he should cease to exercise judicial functions as a justice for that area, or

    (b) that the justice declines or neglects to take a proper part in the exercise of those functions.

(5) On a person's appointment as a justice of the peace for any area the Lord Chancellor may direct that his name shall be entered in the supplemental list, if that person is appointed a justice for that area on ceasing to be a justice for some other area.

(6) The name of a justice of the peace shall be entered in the supplemental list if he applies for it to be so entered and the application is approved by the Lord Chancellor.

(7) Nothing in this section shall apply to a person holding office as stipendiary magistrate.

9.–12. ★★★★★

Stipendiary magistrates other than metropolitan stipendiary magistrates

13. Appointment and removal of stipendiary magistrates.

(1) It shall be lawful for Her Majesty to appoint a barrister or solicitor of not less than seven years' standing to be, during Her Majesty's pleasure, a whole-time stipendiary magistrate in any commission area or areas outside the inner London area and the City of London, and to appoint more than one such magistrate in the same area or areas.

(2) A person so appointed to be a magistrate in any commission area shall by virtue of his office be a justice of the peace for that area.

(3) Any appointment of a stipendiary magistrate under this section shall be of a person recommended to Her Majesty by the Lord Chancellor, and a stipendiary magistrate appointed under this section shall not be removed from office except on the Lord Chancellor's recommendation.

(4) The number of stipendiary magistrates appointed under this section shall not at any time exceed forty or such larger number as Her Majesty may from time to time by Order in Council specify.

(5) Her Majesty shall not be recommended to make an Order in Council under subsection (4) above unless a draft of the Order has been laid before Parliament and approved by resolution of each House.

14. Retirement of stipendiary magistrates.

(1) A stipendiary magistrate appointed on or after the 25th October 1968 shall vacate his office at the end of the completed year of service in the course of which he attains the age of 70:

Provided that where the Lord Chancellor considers it desirable in the public interest to retain him in office after that time, the Lord Chancellor may from time to time authorise him to continue in office up to such age not exceeding 72 as the Lord Chancellor thinks fit.

Part II
Organisation of Functions of Justices
General provisions

17. *****

18. Rules as to chairmanship and size of bench.

(1) The number of justices (other than metropolitan stipendiary magistrates) sitting to deal with a case as a magistrates' court shall not be greater than the number prescribed by rules made under this section.

(2) Rules made under this section may make provision as to the manner in which section 17 of this Act and this section are to be administered, and in particular—

    (a) as to the arrangements to be made for securing the presence on the bench of enough, but not more than enough, justices;

    (b) as to the term of office and the procedure at an election of the chairman or a deputy chairman of the justices in a petty sessions area, and the number of deputy chairmen to be elected in any such area; and

    (c) as to the justices whom a chairman or deputy chairman of justices may request to preside at a meeting.

(3) The right of magistrates to vote at an election of the chairman or a deputy chairman of the justices in a petty sessions area may, by rules made under this section, be restricted with a view to securing that the election is made by magistrates experienced as such in the area.

(4) No rules shall be made under this section except on the advice of, or after

consultation with, the rule committee established under [section 144 of the Magistrates Courts Act 1980].

(5) Rules under this section shall be made by the Lord Chancellor by statutory instrument, which shall be subject to annulment in pursuance of a resolution of either House of Parliament.

19.–24.   *****

Justices' clerks and their staffs

25. Appointment and removal of justices' clerks.

(1) Justices' clerks shall be appointed by the magistrates' courts committee and shall hold office during the pleasure of the committee; and a magistrates' courts committee may appoint more than one justices' clerk for any area.

(2) The approval of the Secretary of State shall be required—

(a) for any decision to increase the number of justices' clerks in a petty sessions area or to have more than one justices' clerk in a new petty sessions area;

(b) for any appointment of a justices' clerk;

(c) for the removal of the justices' clerk for a petty sessional division where the magistrates for the division do not consent to the removal.

(3) A magistrates' courts committee shall consult the magistrates for any petty sessional division on the appointment or removal of a justices' clerk for the division; and the Secretary of State, before approving the appointment or removal of a justices' clerk for such a division, shall consider any representations made to him by the magistrates for the division, and before approving the removal of any such clerk shall consider any representations made to him by the clerk.

(4) The magistrates' courts committee shall inform the Secretary of State of the age, qualification and experience of any person proposed to be appointed a justices' clerk and, if the Secretary of State so requires, of any other person offering himself for the appointment.

(5) Subsection (1) to (4) above shall not apply to the inner London area.

26. Qualifications for appointment as justices' clerk.

(1) Except as provided by this section, no person shall be appointed as justices' clerk of any class or description unless either—

(a) at the time of appointment he is a barrister or solicitor of not less than five years' standing and is within any limit of age prescribed for appointments to a clerkship of that class or description, or

(b) he then is or has previously been a justices' clerk.

(2) A lower as well as an upper limit of age may be prescribed under subsection (1) above for appointments to any class or description of clerkship.

(3) A person not having the qualification as barrister or solicitor which is required by subsection (1)(a) above may be appointed a justices' clerk—

(a) if at the time of appointment he is a barrister or solicitor and has served for not less than five years in service to which this subsection applies, or

(b) if before the 1st January 1960 he had served for not less than ten years in service to which this subsection applies and, in the opinion of the magistrates' courts committee and of the Secretary of State, there are special circumstances making the appointment a proper one.

(4) Subsection (3) above applies to service in any one or more of the following capacities, that is to say, service as assistant to a justices' clerk and service before the 1st February 1969—

(a) as clerk to a stipendiary magistrate;

(b) as clerk to a magistrates' court for the inner London area or as clerk to a metropolitan stipendiary court;

(c) as clerk at one of the justice rooms of the City of London; or
(d) as assistant to any such clerk as is mentioned in paragraphs (a) to (c) above.

(5) A person may be appointed a justices' clerk notwithstanding that he is over the upper limit of age mentioned in subsection (1) of this section if he has served continuously in service to which subsection (3) above applies from a time when he was below that limit to the time of appointment.

27. *****

28. General powers and duties of justices' clerks.

(1) Rules made in accordance with [section 144 of the Magistrates Courts Act 1980] may (except in so far as any enactment passed after the 25th October 1968 otherwise directs) make provision enabling things authorised to be done by, to or before a single justice of the peace to be done instead by, to or before a justices' clerk.

(2) Any enactment (including any enactment contained in this Act) or any rule of law regulating the exercise of any jurisdiction or powers of justices of the peace, or relating to things done in the exercise or purported exercise of any such jurisdiction or powers, shall apply in relation to the exercise or purported exercise thereof by virtue of subsection (1) above by the clerk to any justices as if he were one of those justices.

(3) It is hereby declared that the functions of a justices' clerk include the giving to the justices to whom he is clerk or any of them, at the request of the justices or justice, of advice about law, practice or procedure on questions arising in connection with the discharge of their or his functions, including questions arising when the clerk is not personally attending on the justices or justice and that the clerk may at any time when he thinks he should do so, bring to the attention of the justices or justice any point of law, practice or procedure that is to may be involved in any question so arising.
In this subsection the reference to the functions of justices or a justice is a reference to any of their or his functions as justices or a justice of the peace, other than functions as a judge of the Crown Court.

(4) The enactment of subsection (3) above shall not be taken as defining or in any respect limiting the powers and duties belonging to a justices' clerk or the matters on which justices may obtain assistance from their clerk.

29., 30. *****

PART III
INNER LONDON AREA
Metropolitan stipendiary magistrates

31. Appointment removal and retirement of metropolitan stipendiary magistrates.

(1) Metropolitan stipendiary magistrates shall be appointed by Her Majesty, and Her Majesty shall from time to time appoint such number of persons as is necessary; but the number of metropolitan stipendiary magistrates shall not at any time exceed sixty or such larger number as Her Majesty may from time to time by Order in Council specify.

(2) A person shall not be qualified to be appointed a metropolitan stipendiary magistrate unless he is a barrister or solicitor of not less than seven years' standing.

(3) The Lord Chancellor shall designate one of the metropolitan stipendiary magistrates to be the chief metropolitan stipendiary magistrate.

(4) The following provisons shall apply to each metropolitan stipendiary magistrate, that is to say—
(a) he shall by virtue of his office be a justice of the peace for each of the London commission areas and for the counties of Essex, Hertfordshire, Kent and Surrey;

(b) he shall not during his continuance in office practice as a barrister or solicitor;
(c) he may be removed from office by the Lord Chancellor for inability or misbehaviour.

(5) A metropolitan stipendiary magistrate who is by virtue of his office a justice of the peace for any area mentioned in subsection (4) above shall not, by reason only of his being a justice of the peace for that area by virtue of that office, be qualified to be chosen under section 17(1) of this Act as chairman or deputy chairman of the justices for a petty sessional divison of that area or to vote under that subsection at the election of any such chairman or deputy chairman.

(6) Section 14 of this Act shall apply to metropolitan stipendiary magistrates as well as to other stipendiary magistrates in England or Wales.

(7) Her Majesty shall not be recommended to make an Order in Council under subsection (1) above unless a draft of the Order has been laid before Parliament and approved by resolution of each House.

32. *****

33. Jurisdiction of metropolitan stipendiary magistrates and lay justices.
(1) In the inner London area the jurisdiction conferred on justices of the peace by any enactment, by their commission or by the common law shall be exercisable both by metropolitan stipendiary magistrates and by justices of the peace for that area who are not metropolitan stipendiary magistrates (hereafter in this Part of this Act referred to as "lay justices").

(2) Metropolitan stipendiary magistrates shall continue to exercise the jurisdiction conferred on them as such by any enactment; and the inner London area (having taken the place of the metropolitan stipendiary courts area) shall continue to be the area for which magistrates' courts are to be held by metropolitan stipendiary magistrates.

(3) Lay justices for the inner London area may, in addition to exercising the jurisdiction mentioned in subsection (1) above, exercise the jurisdiction conferred on metropolitan stipendiary magistrates as such by any enactment except the following, that is to say—
(a) the Extradition Acts 1870 to 1935;
(b) [section 26 of the Pilotage Act 1983] (which relates to appeals by pilots against certain actions of pilotage authorities);
(c) section 25 of the Children and Young Persons Act 1933 (restrictions on persons under 18 going abroad for the purpose of performing for profit); and
(d) the Fugitive Offenders Act 1967;
but a magistrates' court consisting of lay justices for the inner London area shall not by virtue of this subsection try an information summarily or hear a complaint except when composed of at least two justices.

(4) Without prejudice to subsection (1) above, subsections (3) to (5) of section 16 of this Act shall have effect in relation to a metropolitan stipendiary magistrate as they have effect in relation to a stipendiary magistrate appointed under section 13 of this Act.

34.–43. *****

Part V
Protection of Justices and Indemnification of Justices and Justices' Clerks

44. Acts done within jurisdiction.
If apart from this section any action lies against a justice of the peace for an act done by him in the execution of his duty as such a justice, with respect to any matter within

his jurisdiction as such a justice, the action shall be as for a tort, in the nature of an action on the case; and—

(a) in the statement or particulars of claim it shall be expressly alleged that the act in question was done maliciously and without reasonable and probable cause, and

(b) if that allegation is not proved at the trial of the action, judgment shall be given for the defendant, if it is in the High Court, or, if it is in the county court, the plaintiff shall be non-suited or judgment shall be given for the defendant.

45. Acts outside or in excess of jurisdiction.

(1) This section applies—

(a) to any act done by a justice of the peace in a matter in respect of which by law he does not have jurisdiction or in which he has exceeded his jurisdiction, and

(b) to any act done under any conviction or order made or warrant issued by a justice of the peace in any such matter;

and in the following provisions of this section "the justice", in relation to any act falling within paragraph (a) above, means the justice of the peace by whom it is done, and, in relation to a conviction, order or warrant falling within paragraph (b) above, means the justice of the peace by whom the conviction or order is made or the warrant issued.

(2) Any person injured by an act to which this section applies may maintain an action against the justice without making any allegation in his statement or particulars of claim that the act complained of was done maliciously and without reasonable and probable cause.

(3) In respect of any act done under any such conviction or order as is mentioned in subsection (1)(b) above no action shall be brought against the justice until the conviction or order has been quashed, either on appeal or upon application to the High Court.

(4) In respect of any act done under any such warrant as is mentioned in subsection (1)(b) above which was issued by the justice to procure the appearance of a person (in this subsection referred to as "the complainant")—

(a) where the issue of the warrant has been followed by a conviction or order in the same manner, no action shall be brought by the complainant against the justice until the conviction or order has been quashed, either on appeal or upon application to the High Court, and

(b) where the issue of the warrant has not been followed by any such conviction or order, or the warrant was issued upon an information for an alleged indictable offence, no action shall be brought by the complainant against the justice if, before the issue of the warrant, a summons was issued and was served on the complainant (either personally or by leaving it for him with some person at his last or most usual place of abode) and he did not appear in accordance with the summons.

46. Warrant granted on a conviction or order made by another justice.

Where a conviction or order is made by a justice or justices of the peace, and another justice, in good faith and without collusion, grants a warrant of distress or warrant of commitment thereon, no action shall be brought against the justice who granted the warrant by reason of any defect in the conviction or order, or for any want of jurisdiction in the justice or justices who made it, but the action (if any) shall be brought against the justice or justices who made the conviction or order.

47. Exercise of discretionary powers.

Where by an enactment a discretionary power is given to a justice of the peace, no action shall be brought against the justice by reason of the manner in which he exercises his discretion in the execution of the power.

48. Compliance with, or confirmation on appeal to, superior court.

(1) In all cases where a justice of the peace refuses to do any act relating to the duties of his office, the party requiring the act to be done may apply to the High Court for an order of mandamus; and, if the High Court makes the order, no action or proceeding whatsoever shall be commenced or prosecuted against the justice for having obeyed the order.

(2) Where a warrant of distress or warrant of commitment is granted by a justice of the peace upon any conviction or order which, whether before or after the granting of the warrant, is confirmed on appeal, no action for anything done under warrant shall be brought against the justice by reason of any defect in the conviction or order.

49. *****

50. Where action prohibited, proceedings may be set aside.

If any action is brought in circumstances in which this Part of this Act provides that no action is to be brought, a judge of the court in which the action is brought may, on the application of the defendant and upon an affidavit as to the facts, set aside the proceedings in the action, with or without costs, as the judge thinks fit.

51. No action in county court if defendant justice objects.

No action shall be brought in the county court against a justice of the peace for anything done by him in the execution of his office as such a justice if he objects to it; and if within six days after being served with a summons in any such action the justice, or his solicitor or agent, gives written notice to the plaintiff that the justice objects to being sued in the county court in respect of the cause of action in question, all subsequent proceedings in the county court in the action shall be null and void.

52. Limitation of damages.

(1) The provisions of this section shall have effect where, in any action brought against a justice of the peace for anything done by him in the execution of his office as such a justice, the plaintiff is (apart from this section) entitled to recover damages in respect of a conviction or order, and proves the levying or payment of a penalty or sum of money under the conviction or order as part of the damages which he seeks to recover, or proves that he was imprisoned under the conviction or order and seeks to recover damages for the imprisonment, but it is also proved—

    (a) that the plaintiff was actually guilty of the offence of which he was so convicted, or that he was liable by law to pay the sum he was so ordered to pay, and

    (b) where he was imprisoned, that he had undergone no greater punishment than that assigned by law for the offence of which he was so convicted or for non-payment of the sum he was so ordered to pay.

(2) In the circumstances specified in subsection (1) above, the plaintiff shall not be entitled to recover the amount of the penalty of sum levied or paid as mentioned in that subsection or (as the case may be) to recover any sum beyond the sum of one penny as damages for the imprisonment, and shall not be entitled to any costs.

53. Indemnification of justices and justices' clerks.

(1) Subject to the provisions of this section and of section 54 below, a justice of the peace or justices' clerk may be indemnified out of local funds in respect of—

    (a) any costs reasonably incurred by him in or in connection with proceedings against him in respect of anything done or omitted in the exercise of purported exercise of the duty of his office, or in taking steps to dispute any claim which might be made in such proceedings;

    (b) any damages awarded against him or costs ordered to be paid by him in any such proceedings; or

(c) any sums payable by him in connection with a reasonable settlement of any such proceedings or claim;
and shall be entitled to be so indemnified if, in respect of the matters giving rise to the proceedings or claim, he acted reasonably and in good faith.

(2) Any question whether, or to what extent, a person is to be indemnified under this section shall be determined by the magistrates' courts committee for the area for which he acted at the material time; and a determination under this subsection with respect to any such costs or sums as are mentioned in paragraph (a) or paragraph (c) of subsection (1) above may, if the person claiming to be indemnified so requests, be made in advance before those costs are incurred or the settlement made, as the case may be:

Provided that any such determination in advance for indemnity in respect of costs to be incurred shall be subject to such limitations, if any, as the committee think proper and to the subsequent determination of the amount of the costs reasonably incurred and shall not affect any other determination which may fall to be made in connection with the proceedings or claim in question.

(3) An appeal shall lie to a person appointed for the purpose by the Lord Chancellor—

(a) on the part of the person claiming to be indemnified from any decision of the magistrates' courts committee under subsection (2) above, other than a decision to postpone until after the conclusion of the proceedings any determination with respect to his own costs or to impose limitations n making a determination in advance for indemnity in respect of such costs;

(b) on the part of the local authority, from any determination of the magistrates' courts committee under that subsection, other than a determination in advance for indemnity in respect of costs to be incurred by the person claiming to be indemnified.

(4) The Lord Chancellor may by statutory instrument make rules prescribing the procedure to be followed in any appeal under this section; and any statutory instrument made by virtue of this subsection shall be subject to annulment in pursuance of a resolution of either House of Parliament.

(5) In this section "justices' clerk" includes a person appointed by a magistrates' courts committee to assist a justices' clerk and any member of the staff of a part-time justices' clerk assisting the clerk in his duties as such; "local funds", in relation to a justice or a justices' clerk, means funds out of which any salary or allowance to which he is entitled (or, if he is entited to more than one, is entitled in the relevant capacity) is payable; and "local authority" means the authority responsible for the payment of any such salary or allowance.

(6) Subsection (5) above shall not apply to the inner London area, but in the application of the other provisions of this section to that area—

(a) for any reference to local funds there shall be substituted a reference to the metropolitan police fund;

(b) for any reference to a magistrates' courts committee there shall be substituted a reference to the committee of magistrates set up under section 35 of this Act; and

(c) for any reference to a local authority there shall be substituted a reference to the Receiver,

and "justices' clerk" includes any officer employed by the committee of magistrates.

54. Provisions as to prerogative proceedings and membership of Crown Court.

(1) Section 53 of this Act shall not apply to proceedings [on an application for judicial review] or to proceedings arising out of anything done or omitted by any person in his capacity as a member of the Crown Court.

(2) The Lord Chancellor may, if he thinks fit, defray out of moneys provided by Parliament any costs awarded against a justice or justices' clerk in proceedings [on

an application for judicial review] (other than proceedings relating to the jurisdiction of the Crown Court) or any part of such costs.

(3) In this section "justices' clerk" has the same meaning as in section 53 of this Act.

55.–62. *****

Part VII
Miscellaneous and Supplementary Provisions

63. Courses of instruction.

(1) It shall be the duty of every magistrates' courts committee, in accordance with arrangements approved by the Lord Chancellor, to make and administer schemes providing for courses of instruction for justices of the peace of their area.

(2) It shall be the duty of the committee of magistrates, in accordance with arrangements approved by the Lord Chancellor, to make and administer schemes providing for courses of instruction for justices of the peace of the inner London area.

(3) There may be paid out of moneys provided by Parliament any expenses incurred by the Lord Chancellor in providing courses of instruction for justices of the peace.

(4)–(6) *****

64. Disqualification in certain cases of justices who are members of local authorities.

(1) A justice of the peace who is a member of a local authority within the meaning of the Local Government Act 1972 or the Local Government (Scotland) Act 1973 shall not act as a member of the Crown Court or of a magistrates' court in any proceedings brought by or against, or by way of appeal from a decision of, the authority or any committee or officer of the authority.

(2) For the purposes of subsection (1) above—

 (a) any reference to a committee of a local authority includes a joint committee, joint board, joint authority or other combined body of which that authority is a member or on which it is represented; and

 (b) any reference to an officer of a local authority refers to a person employed or appointed by the authority, or by a committee of the authority, in the capacity in which he is employed or appointed to act.

(3) A justice of the peace who is a member of the Common Council of the City of London shall not act as a member of the Crown Court or of a magistrates' court in any proceedings brought by or against, or by way of appeal from a decision of, the Corporation of the City or the Common Council; and subsection (2) above shall apply for the purposes of this subsection with the substitution, for references to a local authority, of references to the Corporation or the Common Council.

(4) Nothing in this section shall prevent a justice from acting in any proceedings by reason only of their being brought by a police officer.

(5) No act shall be invalidated by reason only of the disqualification under this section of the person acting.

MAGISTRATES' COURTS ACT
(1980, c. 43)

An Act to consolidate certain enactments relating to the jurisdiction of, and the practice and procedure before, magistrates' courts and the functions of justices' clerks, and to matters connected therewith, with amendments to give effect to recommendations of the Law Commission. [1st August 1980]

Part I
Criminal Jurisdiction and Procedure
Jurisdiction to issue process and deal with charges

1. Issue of summons to accused or warrant for his arrest.

(1) Upon an information being laid before a justice of the peace for an area to which this section applies that any person has, or is suspected of having, committed an offence, the justice may, in any of the events mentioned in subsection (2) below, but subject to subsection (3) to (5) below,—

    (a) issue a summons directed to that person requiring him to appear before a magistrates' court for the area to answer to the information, or

    (b) issue a warrant to arrest that person and bring him before a magistrates' court for the area or such magistrates' court as is provided in subsection (5) below.

(2) A justice of the peace for an area to which this section applies may issue a summons or warrant under this section—

    (a) if the offence was committed or is suspected to have been committed within the area, or

    (b) if it appears to the justice necessary or expedient, with a view to the better administration of justice, that the person charged should be tried jointly with, or in the same place as, some other person who is charged with an offence, and who is in custody, or is being or is to be proceeded against, within the area, or

    (c) if the person charged resides or is, or is believed to reside or be, within the area, or

    (d) if under any enactment a magistrates' court for the area has jurisdiction to try the offence, or

    (e) if the offence was committed outside England and Wales and, where it is an offence exclusively punishable on summary conviction, if a magistrates court for the area would have jurisdiction to try the offence if the offender were before it.

(3) No warrant shall be issued under this section unless the information is in writing and substantiated on oath.

(4) No warrant shall be issued under this section for the arrest of any person who has attained the age of 17 unless—

    (a) the offence to which the warrant relates is an indictable offence or is punishable with imprisonment, or

    (b) the person's address is not sufficiently established for a summons to be served on him.

(5) Where the offence charged is not an indictable offence—

    (a) no summons shall be issued by virtue only of paragraph (c) of subsection (2) above, and

    (b) any warrant issued by virtue only of that paragraph shall require the person charged to be brought before a magistrates' court having jurisdiction to try the offence.

(6) Where the offence is an indictable offence, a warrant under this section may be issued at any time notwithstanding that a summons has previously been issued.

(7) A justice of the peace may issue a summons or warrant under this section upon an information being laid before him notwithstanding any enactment requiring the information to be laid before two or more justices.

(8) The areas to which this section applies are any county, any London commission area and the City of London.

2. Jurisdiction to deal with charges.

(1) A magistrates' court for a county, a London commission area or the City of London shall have jurisdiction to try all summary offences committed within the county, the London commission area or the City (as the case may be).

(2) Where a person charged with a summary offence appears or is brought before

a magistrates' court in answer to a summons issued under paragraph (b) of section 1(2) above, or under a warrant issued under that paragraph, the court shall have jurisdiction to try the offence.

(3) A magistrates' court for a county, a London commission area or the City of London shall have jurisdiction as examining justices over any offence committed by a person who appears or is brought before the court, whether or not the offence was committed within the county, the London commission area or the City (as the case may be).

(4) Subject to sections 18 to 22 below and any other enactment (wherever contained) relating to the mode of trial of offences triable either way, a magistrates' court shall have jurisdiction to try summarily an offence triable either way in any case in which under subsection (3) above it would have jurisdiction as examining justices.

(5) A magistrates' court shall, in the exercise of its powers under section 24 below, have jurisdiction to try summarily an indictable offence in any case in which under subsection (3) above it would have jurisdiction as examining justices.

(6) A magistrates' court for any area by which a person is tried for an offence shall have jurisdiction to try him for any summary offence for which he could be tried by a magistrates' court for any other area.

(7) Nothing in this section shall affect any jurisdiction over offences conferred on a magistrates' court by any enactment not contained in this Act.

3. *****

Committal proceedings

4. General nature of committal proceedings.
(1) The functions of examining justices may be discharged by a single justice.

(2) Examining justices shall sit in open court except where any enactment contains an express provision to the contrary and except where it appears to them as respects the whole or any part of committal proceedings that the ends of justice would not be served by their sitting in open court.

(3) Subject to subsection (4) below and section 102 below, evidence given before examining justices shall be given in the presence of the accused, and the defence shall be at liberty to put questions to any witness at the inquiry.

(4) Examining justices may allow evidence to be given before them in the absence of the accused if—
    (a) they consider that by reason of his disorderly conduct before them it is not practicable for the evidence to be given in his presence, or
    (b) he cannot be present for reasons of health but is represented by counsel or a solicitor and has consented to the evidence being given in his absence.

5. Adjournment of inquiry.
(1) A magistrates' court may, before beginning to inquire into an offence as examining justices, or at any time during the inquiry, adjourn the hearing, and if it does so shall remand the accused.

(2) The court shall when adjourning fix the time and place at which the hearing is to be resumed; and the time fixed shall be that at which the accused is required to appear or be brought before the court in pursuance of the remand [or would be required to be brought before the court but for section 128 (3A) below].

6. Discharge or committal for trial.
(1) Subject to the provisions of this and any other Act relating to the summary trial of indictable offences, if a magistrates' court inquiring into an offence as examining justices is of opinion, on consideration of the evidence and of any statement of the accused, that there is sufficient evidence to put the accused on trial by jury for any indictable offence, the court shall commit him for trial; and, if it is not of that opinion,

it shall, if he is in custody for no other cause than the offence under inquiry, discharge him.

(2) A magistrates' court inquiring into an offence as examining justices may, if satisfied that all the evidence before the court (whether for the prosecution or the defence) consists of written statements tendered to the court under section 102 below, with or without exhibits, commit the accused for trial for the offence without consideration of the contents of those statements, unless—

    (a) the accused or one of the accused [has no solicitor acting for him in the case (whether present in court or not)];

    (b) counsel or a solicitor for the accused or one of the accused, as the case may be, has requested the court to consider a submission that the statements disclose insufficient evidence to put that accused on trial by jury for the offence;

and subsection (1) above shall not apply to a committal trial under this subsection.

(3) Subject to section 4 of the Bail Act 1976 and section 41 below, the court may commit a person for trial—

    (a) in custody, that is to say, by committing him to custody there to be safely kept until delivered in due course of law, or

    (b) on bail in accordance with the Bail Act 1976, that is to say, by directing him to appear before the Crown Court for trial;

and where his release on bail is conditional on his providing one or more surety or sureties and, in accordance with section 8(3) of the Bail Act 1976, the court fixes the amount in which the surety is to be bound with a view to his entering into his recognizance subsequently in accordance with subsection (4) and (5) or (6) of that section the court shall in the meantime commit the accused to custody in accordance with paragraph (a) of this subsection.

(4) Where the court has committed a person to custody in accordance with paragraph (a) of subsection (3) above, then, if that person is in custody for no other cause, the court may, at any time before his first appearance before the Crown Court, grant him bail in accordance with the Bail Act 1976 subject to a duty to appear before the Crown Court for trial.

(5) Where a magistrates' court acting as examining justices commits any person for trial or determines to discharge him, the clerk of the court shall, on the day on which the committal proceedings are concluded or the next day, cause to be displayed in a part of the court house to which the public have access a notice—

    (a) in either case giving that person's name, address and age (if known);

    (b) in a case where the court so commits him, stating the charge or charges on which he is committed and the court to which he is committed;

    (c) in a case where the court determines to discharge him, describing the offence charged and stating that it has so determined;

but this subsection shall have effect subject to section 4 of the Sexual Offences (Amendment) Act 1976 (anonymity of complainant and accused in rape etc. cases).

(6) A notice displayed in pursuance of subsection (5) above shall not contain the name or address of any person under the age of 17 unless the justices in question have stated that in their opinion he would be mentioned in the notice apart from the preceding provisions of this subsection and should be mentioned in it for the purpose of avoiding injustice to him.

7. Place of trial on indictment.

A magistrates' court committing a person for trial shall specify the place at which he is to be tried, and in selecting that place shall have regard to—

    (a) the convenience of the defence, the prosecution and the witnesses,

    (b) the expediting of the trial, and

(c) any direction given by or on behalf of the Lord Chief Justice with the concurrence of the Lord Chancellor under section 4(5) of the Courts Act 1971.[1]

Note
[1] Courts Act 1971, s. 4(5) repealed by Supreme Court Act 1981 and replaced by s. 75(1) of that Act.

8. Restrictions on reports of committal proceedings.

(1) Except as provided by subsections (2), (3) and (8) below, it shall not be lawful to publish in Great Britain a written report, or to broadcast [or include in a cable programme] in Great Britain a report, of any committal proceedings in England and Wales containing any matter other than that permitted by subsection (4) below.

(2), (3) *****

(4) The following matters may be contained in a report of committal proceedings published [broadcast or included in a cable programme] without an order under subsection (2) above before the time authorised by subsection (3) above, that is to say—

(a) the identity of the court and the names of the examining justices;

(b) the names, addresses and occupations of the parties and witnesses and the ages of the accused and witnesses;

(c) the offence of offences, or a summary of them, with which the accused is or are charged;

(d) the names of counsel and solicitors engaged in the proceedings;

(e) any decision of the court to commit the accused or any of the accused for trial, and any decision of the court on the disposal of the case of any accused not committed;

(f) where the court commits the accused or any of the accused for trial, the charge or charges, or a summary of them, on which he is committed and the court to which he is committed;

(g) where the committal proceedings are adjourned, the date and place to which they are adjourned;

(h) any arrangements as to bail on committal or adjournment;

(i) whether legal aid was granted to the accused or any of the accused.

(5)–(10) *****

Summary trial of information

9. Procedure on trial.

(1) On the summary trial of an information, the court shall, if the accused appears, state to him the substance of the information and ask him whether he pleads guilty or not guilty.

(2) The court, after hearing the evidence and the parties, shall convict the accused or dismiss the information.

(3) If the accused pleads guilty, the court may convict him without hearing evidence.

10. Adjournment of trial.

(1) A magistrates' court may at any time, whether before or after beginning to try an information, adjourn the trial, and may do so, notwithstanding anything in this Act, when composed of a single justice.

(2) The court may when adjourning either fix the time and place at which the trial is to be resumed, or, unless it remands the accused, leave the time and place to be determined later by the court; but the trial shall not be resumed at that time and place unless the court is satisfied that the parties have had adequate notice thereof.

(3) A magistrates' court may, for the purpose of enabling inquiries to be made or of determining that most suitable method of dealing with the case, exercise its power to adjourn after convicting the accused and before sentencing him or otherwise dealing

with him; but if it does so, the adjournment shall not be for more than 4 weeks at a time unless the court remands the accused in custody and, where it so remands him, the adjournment shall not be for more than 3 weeks at a time.

(4) On adjourning the trial of an information the court may remand the accused and, where the accused has attained the age of 17, shall do so if the offence is triable either way and—

    (a) on the occasion on which the accused first appeared, or was brought, before the court to answer to the information he was in custody or, having been released on bail, surrendered to the custody of the court; or

    (b) the accused has been remanded at any time in the course of proceedings on the information;

and, where the court remands the accused, the time fixed for the resumption of the trial shall be that at which he is required to appear or be brought before the court in pursuance of the remand [or would be required to be brought before the court but for section 128 (3A) below].

11. Non-appearance of accused: general provisions.

(1) Subject to the provisions of this Act, where at the time and place appointed for the trial or adjourned trial of an information the prosecutor appears but the accused does not, the court may proceed in his absence.

(2) Where a summons has been issued, the court shall not begin to try the information in the absence of the accused unless either it is proved to the satisfaction of the court, on oath or in such other manner as may be prescribed, that the summons was served on the accused within what appears to the court to be a reasonable time before the trial or adjourned trial or the accused has appeared on a previous occasion to answer to the information.

(3) A magistrates' court shall not in a person's absence sentence him to imprisonment or detention in a [young offender institution] or make an order under section 23 of the Powers of Criminal Courts Act 1973 that a suspended sentence passed on him shall take effect.

(4) A magistrates' court shall not in a person's absence impose any disqualification on him, except on resumption of the hearing after an adjournment under section 10(3) above; and where a trial is adjourned in pursuance of this subsection the notice required by section 10(2) above shall include notice of the reason for the adjournment.

12. Non-appearance of accused: plea of guilty.

(1) Subject to subsection (7) below, this section shall apply where a summons has been issued requiring a person to appear before a magistrates' court, other than a juvenile court, to answer to an information for a summary offence, not being an offence for which the accused is liable to be sentenced to be imprisoned for a term exceeding 3 months, and the clerk of the court is notified by or on behalf of the prosecutor that the following documents have been served upon the accused with the summons, that is to say—

    (a) a notice containing such statement of the effect of this section as may be prescribed; and

    (b) a concise statement in the prescribed form of such facts relating to the charge as will be placed before the court by or on behalf of the prosecutor if the accused pleads guilty without appearing before the court.

(2) Subject to subsections (3) to (5) below, where the clerk of the court receives a notification in writing purporting to be given by the accused or by a solicitor acting on his behalf that the accused desires to plead guilty without appearing before the court, the clerk of the court shall inform the prosecutor of the receipt of the notification and if at the time and place appointed for the trial or adjourned trial of the information

the accused does not appear and it is proved to the satisfaction of the court, on oath or in such other manner as may be prescribed, that the notice and statement of facts referred to in subsection (1) above have been served upon the accused with the summons, then—

    (a) subject to section 11(3) and (4) above, the court may proceed to hear and dispose of the case in the absence of the accused, whether or not the prosecutor is also absent, in like manner as if both parties had appeared and the accused had pleaded guilty; or

    (b) if the court decides not to proceed as aforesaid, the court shall adjourn or futher adjourn the trial for the purpose of dealing with the information as if the notification aforesaid had not been given.

(3) If at any time before the hearing the clerk of the court receives an intimation in writing purporting to be given by or on behalf of the accused that he wishes to withdraw the notification aforesaid, the clerk of the court shall inform the prosecutor thereof and the court shall deal with the information as if this section had not been passed.

(4) Before accepting the plea of guilty and convicting the accused in his absence under subsection (2) above, the court shall cause the notification and statement of facts aforesaid, including any submission received with the notification which the accused wishes to be brought to the attention of the court with a view to mitigation of sentence, to be read out before the court [by the clerk of the court].

(5) If the court proceeds under subsection (2) above to hear and dispose of the case in the absence of the accused, the court shall not permit any statement to be made by or on behalf of the prosecutor with respect to any facts relating to the offence charged other than the statement of facts aforesaid except on a resumption of the trial after an adjournment under section 10(3) above.

(6) In relation to an adjournment by reason of the requirements of paragraph (b) of subsection (2) above or to an adjournment on the occasion of the accused's conviction in his absence under that subsection, the notice required by section 10(2) above shall include notice of the reason for the adjournment.

(7) The Secretary of State may by order made by statutory instrument provide that this section shall not apply in relation to such offences (in addition to an offence for which the accused is liable to be sentenced to be imprisoned for a term exceeding 3 months) as may be specified in the order, and any order under this subsection—

    (a) may vary or revoke any previous order thereunder; and
    (b) shall not be made unless a draft thereof has been approved by resolution of each House of Parliament.

(8) Any such notice or statement as is mentioned in subsection (1) above may be served in Scotland with a summons which is so served under the Summary Jurisdiction (Process) Act 1881.

[(9) Where the clerk of the court has received such a notification as is mentioned in subsection (2) above but the accused nevertheless appears before the court at the time and place appointed for the trial or adjourned trial the court may, if the accused consents, proceed under this section as if he were absent.]

(10)–(12) *****

13. Non-appearance of accused: issue of warrant.

(1) Subject to the provisions of this section, where the court, instead of proceeding in the absence of the accused, adjourns or further adjourns the trial, the court may, if the information has been substantiated on oath, issue a warrant for his arrest.

(2) Where a summons has been issued, the court shall not issue a warrant under this section unless either it is proved to the satisfaction of the court, on oath or in such other manner as may be prescribed, that the summons was served on the accused

within what appears to the court to be a reasonable time before the trial or adjourned trial or the accused has appeared on a previous occasion to answer to the information.

(3) A warrant for the arrest of any person who has attained the age of 17 shall not be issued under this section unless—

(a) the offence to which the warrant relates is punishable with imprisonment; or

(b) the court, having convicted the accused, proposes to impose a disqualification on him.

(4) This section shall not apply to an adjournment by reason of the requirements of paragraph (b) of subsection (2) of section 12 above or to an adjournment on the occasion of the accused's conviction in his absence under that subsection.

(5) Where the court adjourns the trial—

(a) after having, either on that or on a previous occasion, received any evidence or convicted the accused without hearing evidence on his pleading guilty under section 9(3) above; or

(b) after having on a previous occasion convicted the accused without hearing evidence on his pleading guilty under section 12(2) above,

the court shall not issue a warrant under this section unless it thinks it undesirable, by reason of the gravity of the offence, to continue the trial in the absence of the accused.

14. Proceedings invalid where accused did not know of them.

(1) Where a summons has been issued under section 1 above and a magistrates' court has begun to try the information to which the summons relates, then, if—

(a) the accused, at any time during or after the trial, makes a statutory declaration that he did not know of the summons or the proceedings until a date specified in the declaration, being a date after the court has begun to try the information; and

(b) within 21 days of that date the declaration is served on the clerk to the justices,

without prejudice to the validity of the information, the summons and all subsequent proceedings shall be void.

(2) For the purposes of subsection (1) above a statutory declaration shall be deemed to be duly served on the clerk to the justices if it is delivered to him, or left at his office, or is sent in a registered letter or by the recorded delivery service addressed to him at his office.

(3) If on the application of the accused it appears to a magistrates' court (which for this purpose may be composed of a single justice) that it was not reasonable to expect the accused to serve such a statutory declaration as is mentioned in subsection (1) above within the period allowed by that subsection, the court may accept service of such a declaration by the accused after that period has expired; and a statutory declaration accepted under this subsection shall be deemed to have been served as required by that subsection.

(4) Where any proceedings have become void by virtue of subsection (1) above, the information shall not be tried again by any of the same justices.

15. Non-appearance of prosecutor.

(1) Where at the time and place appointed for the trial or adjourned trial of an information the accused appears or is brought before the court and the prosecutor does not appear, the court may dismiss the information or, if evidence has been received on a previous occasion, proceed in the absence of the prosecutor.

(2) Where, instead of dismissing the information or proceeding in the absence of the prosecutor, the court adjourns the trial, it shall not remand the accused in custody

unless he has been brought from custody or cannot be remanded on bail by reason of his failure to find sureties.

16. Non-appearance of both parties.
Subject to section 11(3) and (4) and to section 12 above, where at the time and place appointed for the trial or adjourned trial of an information neither the prosecutor nor the accused appears, the court may dismiss the information or, if evidence has been received on a previous occasion, proceed in their absence.

Offences triable on indictment or summarily

17. Certain offences triable either way.
(1) The offences listed in Schedule 1 to this Act shall be triable either way.
(2) Subsection (1) above is without prejudice to any other enactment by virtue of which any offence is triable either way.

18. Initial procedure on information against adult for offence triable either way.
(1) Sections 19 to 23 below shall have effect where a person who has attained the age of 17 appears or is brought before a magistrates' court on an information charging him with an offence triable either way.
(2) Without prejudice to section 11(1) above, everything that the court is required to do under sections 19 to 22 below must be done before any evidence is called and, subject to subsection (3) below and section 23 below, with the accused present in court.
(3) The court may proceed in the absence of the accused in accordance with such of the provisions of sections 19 to 22 below as are applicable in the circumstances if the court considers that by reason of his disorderly conduct before the court it is not practicable for the proceedings to be conducted in his presence; and the subsections (3) to (5) of section 23 below, so far as applicable, shall have effect in relation to proceedings conducted in the absence of the accused by virtue of this subsection (references in those subsections to the person representing the accused being for this purpose read as references to the person, if any, representing him).
(4) A magistrates' court proceeding under section 19 to 23 below may adjourn the proceedings at any time, and on doing so on any occasion when the accused is present may remand the accused, and shall remand him if—
    (a) on the occasion on which he first appeared, or was brought, before the court to answer to the information he was in custody or, having been released on bail, surrendered to the custody of the court; or
    (b) he has been remanded at anytime in the course of proceedings on the information;
and where the court remands the accused, the time fixed for the resumption of the proceedings shall be that at which he is required to appear or be brought before the court in pursuance of the remand [or would be required to be brought before the court but for section 128(3A) below].
(5) The functions of a magistrates' court under sections 19 to 23 below may be discharged by a single justice, but the foregoing provision shall not be taken to authorise the summary trial of an information by a magistrates' court composed of less than two justices.

19. Court to begin by considering which mode of trial appears more suitable.
(1) The court shall consider whether, having regard to the matters mentioned in subsection (3) below and any representations made by the prosecutor or the accused, the offence appears to the court more suitable for summary trial or for trial on indictment.

(2) Before so considering, the court—

(a) shall cause the charge to be written down, if this has not already been done, and read to the accused; and

(b) shall afford first the prosecutor and then the accused an opportunity to make representations as to which mode of trial would be more suitable.

(3) The matters to which the court is to have regard under subsection (1) above are the nature of the case; whether the circumstances make the offence one of serious character; whether the punishment which a magistrates' court would have power to inflict for it would be adequate; and any other circumstances which appear to the court to make it more suitable for the offence to be tried in one way rather than the other.

(4) If the prosecution is being carried on by the Attorney-General, the Solicitor General or the Director of Public Prosecutions and he applies for the offence to be tried on indictment, the preceding provisons of this section and sections 20 to 21 below shall not apply, and the court shall proceed to inquire into the information as examining justices.

[(5) The power of the Director of Public Prosecutions under subsection (4) above to apply for an offence to be tried on indictment shall not be exercised without the consent of the Attorney-General].

20. Procedure where summary trial appears more suitable.

(1) If, where the court has considered as required by section 19(1) above, it appears to the court that the offence is more suitable for summary trial, the following provisions of this section shall apply (unless excluded by section 23 below).

(2) The court shall explain to the accused in ordinary language—

(a) that it appears to the court more suitable for him to be tried summarily for the offence, and that he can either consent to be so tried or, if he wishes, be tried by a jury; and

(b) that if he is tried summarily and is convicted by the court, he may be committed for sentence to the Crown Court under section 38 below if the convicting court, on obtaining information about his character and antecedents, is of opinion that they are such that greater punishment should be inflicted than the convicting court has power to inflict for the offence.

(3) After explaining to the accused as provided by subsection (2) above the court shall ask him whether he consents to be tried summarily or wishes to be tried by a jury, and—

(a) if he consents to be tried summarily, shall proceed to the summary trial of the information;

(b) if he does not so consent, shall proceed to inquire into the information as examining justices.

21. Procedure where trial on indictment appears more suitable.

If, where the court has considered as required by section 19(1) above, it appears to the court that the offence is more suitable for trial on indictment, the court shall tell the accused that the court has decided that it is more suitable for him to be tried for the offence by a jury, and shall proceed to inquire into the information as examining justices.

22. Certain offences triable either way to be tried summarily if value involved is small.

(1) If the offence charged by the information is one of those mentioned in the first column of Schedule 2 to this Act (in this section referred to as "schedule offences") then, subject to subsection (7) below, the court shall, before proceeding in accordance with section 19 above, consider whether, having regard to any representations made

by the prosecutor or the accused, the value involved (as defined in subsection (10) below) appears to the court to exceed the relevant sum.

For the purposes of this section the relevant sum is [£2000.]

(2) If, where subsection (1) above applies, it appears to the court clear that, for the offence charged, the value involved does not exceed the relevant sum, the court shall proceed as if the offence were triable only summarily, and sections 19 to 21 above shall not apply.

(3) If, where subsection (1) above applies, it appears to the court clear that, for the offence charged, the value involved exceeds that relevant sum, the court shall thereupon proceed in accordance with section 19 above in the ordinary way without further regard to the provisions of this section.

(4) If, where subsection (1) above applies, it appears to the court for any reason not clear whether, for the offence charged, the value involved does or does not exceed the relevant sum, the provisions of subsection (5) and (6) below shall apply.

(5) The court shall cause the charge to be written down, if this has not already been done, and read to the accused, and shall explain to him in ordinary language—

(a) that he can, if he wishes, consent to be tried summarily for the offence and that if he consents to be so tried, he will definitely be tried in that way; and

(b) that if he is tried summarily and is convicted by the court, his liability to imprisonment or a fine will be limited as provided in section 33 below.

(6) After explaining to the accused as provided by subsection (5) above the court shall ask him whether he consents to be tried summarily and—

(a) if he so consents, shall proceed in accordance with subsection (2) above as if that subsection applied;

(b) if he does not so consent, shall proceed in accordance with subsection (3) above as if that subsection applied.

(7) *****

(8) Where a person is convicted by a magistrates' court of a scheduled offence, it shall not be open to him to appeal to the Crown Court against the conviction on the ground that the convicting court's decision as to the value involved was mistaken.

(9) If, where subsection (1) above applies, the offence charged is one with which the accused is charged jointly with a person who has not attained the age of 17, the reference in that subsection to any representations made by the accused shall be read as including any representations made by the person under 17.

(10) In this section "the value involved", in relation to any scheduled offence, means the value indicated in the second column of Schedule 2 to this Act, measured as indicated in the third column of that Schedule; and in that Schedule "the material time" means the time of the alleged offence.

23. Power of court with consent of legally represented accused, to proceed in his absence.

(1) Where—

(a) the accused is represented by counsel or a solicitor who in his absence signifies to the court the accused's consent to the proceedings for determining how he is to be tried for the offence being conducted in his absence; and

(b) the court is satisfied that there is good reason for proceeding in the absence of the accused,

the following provisions of this section shall apply.

(2) Subject to the following provisions of this section, the court may proceed in the absence of the accused in accordance with such of the provisions of sections 19 to 22 above as are applicable in the circumstances.

(3) If, in a case where subsection (1) of section 22 above applies, it appears to

the court as mentioned in subsection (4) of that section, subsections (5) and (6) of that section shall not apply and the court—

    (a) if the accused's consent to be tried summarily has been or is signified by the person representing him, shall proceed in accordance with subsection (2) of that section as if that subsection applied; or

    (b) if that consent has not been and is not so signified, shall proceed in accordance with subsection (3) of that section as if that subsection applied.

(4) If, where the court has considered as required by section 19(1) above, it appears to the court that the offence is more suitable for summary trial then—

    (a) if the accused's consent to be tried summarily has been or is signified by the person representing him, section 20 above shall not apply, and the court shall proceed to the summary trial of the information; or

    (b) if that consent has not been and is not so signified, section 20 above, it appears to the court that the offence is more suitable for trial on indictment, section 21 above shall not apply, and the court shall proceed to inquire into the information as examining justices and may adjourn the hearing without remanding the accused.

24. Summary trial of information against child or young person for indictable offence.

(1) Where a person under the age of 17 appears or is brought before a magistrates' court on an information charging him with an indictable offence other than homicide, he shall be tried summarily unless—

    (a) he has attained the age of 14 and the offence is such as is mentioned in subsection (2) of section 53 of the Children and Young Persons Act 1933 (under which young persons convicted on indictment of certain grave crimes may be sentenced to be detained for long periods) and the court considers that if he is found guilty of the offence it ought to be possible to sentence him in pursuance of that subsection; or

    (b) he is charged jointly with a person who has attained the age of 17 and the court considers it necessary in the interests of justice to commit them both for trial;

and accordingly in a case falling within paragraph (a) or (b) of this subsection the court shall commit the accused for trial if either it is of opinion that there is sufficient evidence to put him on trial or it has power under section 6(2) above so to commit him without consideration of the evidence.

(2) Where, in a case falling within subsection (1)(b) above, a magistrates' court commits a person under the age of 17 for trial for an offence with which he is charged jointly with a person who has attained that age, the court may also commit him for trial for any other indictable offence with which he is charged at the same time (whether jointly with the person who has attained that age or not) if that other offence arises out of circumstances which are the same as or connected with those giving rise to the first-mentioned offence.

(3) If on trying a person summarily in pursuance of subsection (1) above the court finds him guilty, it may impose a fine of an amount not exceeding [£400] or may exercise the same powers as it could have exercised if he had been found guilty of an offence for which, but for section [1(1) of the Criminal Justice Act 1982, it could have sentenced him to imprisonment for a term not exceeding—

    (a) the maximum term of imprisonment for the offence on conviction on indictment; or

    (b) six months;

whichever is the less.]

(4) In relation to a person under the age of 14 subsection (3) above shall have effect as if for the words [£400] there were substituted the words [£100]; but this

subsection shall cease to have effect on the coming into force of section 4 of the Children and Young Persons Act 1969 (which prohibits criminal proceedings against children).

25. Power to change from summary trial to committal proceedings, and vice versa.

(1) Subsections (2) to (4) below shall have effect where a person who has attained the age of 17 appears or is brought before a magistrates' court on an information charging him with an offence triable either way.

(2) Where the court has (otherwise than in pursuance of section 22(2) above) begun to try the information summarily, the court may, at any time before the conclusion of the evidence for the prosecution, discontinue the summary trial and proceed to inquire into the information as examining justices and, on doing so, may adjourn the hearing without remanding the accused.

(3) Where the court has begun to inquire into the information as examining justices, then, if at any time during the inquiry it appears to the court, having regard to any representations made in the presence of the accused by the prosecutor, or made by the accused, and to the nature of the case, that the offence is after all more suitable for summary trial, the court may, after doing so provided in subsection (4) below, ask the accused whether he consents to be tried summarily and, if he so consents, may [subject to sub-section (3A) below proceed to try the information summarily.]

[(3A) Where the prosecution is being carried on by the Attorney General or the Solicitor General, the court shall not exercise the power conferred by subsection (3) above without his consent and, where the prosecution is being carried on by the Director of Public Prosecutions, shall not exercise that power if the Attorney General directs that it should not be exercised.]

(4) Before asking the accused under subsection (3) above whether he consents to be tried summarily, the court shall in ordinary language—

(a) explain to him that it appears to the court more suitable for him to be tried summarily for the offence, but that this can only be done if he consents to be so tried; and

(b) unless it has already done so, explain to him, as provided in section 20(2)(b) above, about the court's power to commit to the Crown Court for sentence.

(5) Where a person under the age of 17 appears or is brought before a magistrates' court on an information charging him with an indictable offence other than homicide, and the court—

(a) has begun to try the information summarily on the footing that the case does not fall within paragraph (a) or (b) of section 24(1) above and must therefore be tried summarily as required by the said section 24(1); or

(b) has begun to inquire into the case as examining justices on the footing that the case does so fall,

subsection (6) or (7) below, as the case may be, shall effect.

(6) If, in a case falling within subsection (5)(a) above, it appears to the court at any time before the conclusion of the evidence for the prosecution that the case is after all one which under the said section 24(1) ought not to be tried summarily, the court may discontinue the summary trial and proceed to inquire into the information as examining justices and, on doing so, may adjourn the hearing without remanding the accused.

(7) If, in a case falling within subsection (5)(b) above, it appears to the court at any time during the inquiry that the case is after all one which under the said section 24(1) ought to be tried summarily, the court may proceed to try the information summarily.

26. Power to issue summons to accused in certain circumstances.
(1) Where—

(a) in the circumstances mentioned in section 23(1)(a) above the court is not satisfied that there is good reason for proceeding in the absence of the accused; or

(b) subsection (4)(b) or (5) of section 23 or subsection (2) or (6) of section 25 above applies, and the court adjourns the hearing in pursuance of that subsection without remanding the accused,

the justice or any of the justices of which the court is composed may issue a summons directed to the accused requiring his presence before the court.

(2) If the accused is not present at the time and place appointed—

(a) in a case within subsection (1)(a) above, for the proceedings under section 19(1) or 22(1) above, as the case may be; or

(b) in a case within subsection (1)(b) above, for the resumption of the hearing, the court may issue a warrant for his arrest.

27. Effect of dismissal of information for offence triable either way.
Where on the summary trial of an information for an offence triable either way the court dismisses the information, the dismissal shall have the same effect as an acquittal on indictment.

28. Using in summary trial evidence given in committal proceedings.
Where under section 25(3) or (7) above a magistrates' court, having begun to inquire into an information as examining justices, proceeds to try the information summarily, then, subject to sections 102(9) and 103(3) below, any evidence already given before the court shall be deemed to have been given in and for the purposes of the summary trial.

Power to remit person under 17 for trial to juvenile court

29. Power of magistrates' court to remit a person under 17 for trial to a juvenile court in certain circumstances.
(1) Where—

(a) a person under the age of 17 ("the juvenile") appears or is brought before a magistrates' court other than a juvenile court on an information jointly charging him and one or more other persons with an offence; and

(b) that other person, or any of those other persons, has attained that age,

subsection (2) below shall have effect notwithstanding proviso (a) in section 46(1) of the Children and Young Persons Act 1933 (which would otherwise require the charge against the juvenile to be heard by a magistrates' court other than a juvenile court).

In the following provisions of this section "the older accused" means such one or more of the accused as have attained the age of 17.

(2) If—

(a) the court proceeds to the summary trial of the information in the case of both or all of the accused, and the older accused or each of the older accused pleads guilty; or

(b) the court—

(i) in the case of the older accused or each of the older accused, proceeds to inquire into the information as examining justices and either commits him for trial or discharges him; and

(ii) in the case of the juvenile, proceeds to the summary trial of the information,

then, if in either situation the juvenile pleads not guilty, the court may before any evidence is called in his case remit him for trial to a juvenile court acting for the same place as the remitting court or for the place where he habitually resides.

(3) A person remitted to a juvenile court under subsection (2) above shall be brought before and tried by a juvenile court accordingly.

(4) Where a person is so remitted to a juvenile court—
   (a)   he shall have no right of appeal against the order of remission; and
   (b)   the remitting court may give such directions as appear to be necessary with respect to his custody or for his release on bail until he can be brought before the juvenile court.

(5) The preceding provisions of this section shall apply in relation to a corporation as if it were an individual who has attained the age of 17.

Remand for medical examination

30. Remand for medical examination.
(1) If, on the trial by a magistrates' court of an offence punishable on summary conviction with imprisonment, the court is satisfied that the accused did the act or made the omission charged but is of opinion that an inquiry ought to be made into his physical or mental condition before the method of dealing with him is determined, the court shall adjourn the case to enable a medical examination and report to be made and shall remand him; but the adjournment shall not be for more than 3 weeks at a time where the court remands him in custody nor for more than 4 weeks at a time where it remands him on bail.

(2) Where on an adjournment under subsection (1) above the accused is remanded on bail, the court shall impose conditions under paragraph (d) of section 3(6) of the Bail Act 1976 and the requirements imposed as conditions under that paragraph shall be or shall include requirements that the accused—
   (a)   undergo medical examination by a duly qualified medical practitioner or, where the inquiry is into his mental condition and the court so direct, two such practitioners; and
   (b)   for that purpose attend such an institution or place, or on such practititioner, as the court directs and, where the inquiry is into his mental condition, comply with any other directions which may be given to him for that purpose by any person specified by the court or by a person of any class so specified.

(3) . . .

Powers in respect of offenders

31. General limit on power of magistrates' court to impose imprisonment.
(1) Without prejudice to section 133 below, a magistrates' court shall not have power to impose imprisonment [or detention in a young offender institution] for more than 6 months in respect of any one offence.

(2) Unless expressly excluded, subsection (1) above shall apply even if the offence in question is one for which a person would otherwise be liable on summary conviction to imprisonment for more than 6 months.

(3) Any power of a magistrates' court to impose a term of imprisonment for non-payment of a fine, or for want of sufficient distress to satisfy a fine, shall not be limited by virtue of subsection (1) above.

(4) In subsection (3) above "fine" includes a pecuniary penalty but does not include a pecuniary forfeiture or pecuniary compensation.

32. Penalties on summary conviction for offences triable either way.

(1) On summary conviction of any of the offences triable either way listed in Schedule 1 to this Act a person shall be liable to imprisonment for a term not exceeding 6 months or to a fine not exceeding the prescribed sum or both, except that—

    (a) a magistrates' court shall not have power to impose imprisonment for an offence so listed if the Crown Court would not have that power in the case of an adult convicted of it on indictment;

    (b) on summary conviction of an offence consisting in the incitement to commit an offence triable either way a person shall not be liable to any greater penalty than he would be liable to on summary conviction of the last-mentioned offence; and

    (c) . . .

(2) For any offence triable either way which is not listed in Schedule 1 to this Act, being an offence under a relevant enactment, the maximum fine which may be imposed on summary conviction shall by virtue of this subsection be the prescribed sum unless the offence is one for which by virtue of an enactment other than this subsection a larger fine may be imposed on summary conviction.

(3) Where, by virtue of any relevant enactment, a person summarily convicted of an offence triable either way would, apart from this section, be liable to a maximum fine of one amount in the case of a first conviction and of a different amount in the case of a second or subsequent conviction, subsection (2) above shall apply irrespective of whether the conviction is a first, second or subsequent one.

(4) Subsection (2) above shall not affect so much of any enactment as (in whatever words) makes a person liable on summary conviction to a fine not exceeding a specified amount for each day on which a continuing offence is continued after conviction or the occurrence of any other specified event.

(5) *****

(6) Where, as regard any offence triable either way, there is under any enactment (however framed or worded) a power by subordinate instrument to restrict the amount of the fine which on summary conviction can be imposed in respect of that offence—

    (a) subsection (2) above shall not affect that power or override any restriction imposed in the exercise of that power; and

    (b) the amount to which that fine may be restricted in the exercise of that power shall be any amount less than the maximum fine which could be imposed on summary conviction in respect of the offence apart from any restriction so imposed.

(7) Where there is under any relevant enactment (however framed or worded) a power by subordinate instrument to impose penal provisions, being a power which allows the creation of offences triable either way—

    (a) the maximum fine which may in the exercise of that power be authorised on summary conviction in respect of an offence triable either way shall by virtue of this subsection be the prescribed sum unless some larger maximum fine can be authorised on summary conviction in respect of such an offence by virtue of an enactment other than this subsection; and

    (b) subsection (2) above shall not override any restriction imposed in the exercise of that power on the amount of the fine which on summary conviction can be imposed in respect of an offence triable either way created in the exercise of the power.

(8) *****

(9) In this section—

"fine" includes a pecuniary penalty but does not include a pecuniary forfeiture or pecuniary compensation;

"the prescribed sum" means [£2000] or such sum as is for the time being substituted in this definition by an order in force under section 143(1) below;

"relevant enactment" means an enactment contained in the Criminal Law Act 1977 or in any Act passed before, or in the same Session as, that Act.

33. Maximum penalties on summary conviction in pursuance of section 22.
(1) Where in pursuance of subsection (2) of section 22 above a magistrates' court proceeds to the summary trial of an information, then, if the accused is summarily convicted of the offence—
    (a) the court shall not have power to impose on him in respect of that offence imprisonment for more than 3 months or a fine greater than £500; and
    (b) section 38 below shall not apply as regards that offence.
(2) In subsection (1) above "fine' includes a pecuniary penalty but does not include a pecuniary forfeiture or pecuniary compensation.

34. *****

35. Fixing amount of fine.
In fixing the amount of a fine, a magistrates' court shall take into consideration among other things the means of the person on whom the fine is imposed so far as they appear or are known to the court.

36. Restriction on fines in respect of young persons.
(1) Where a person under 17 years of age is found guilty by a magistrates' court of an offence for which, apart from this section, the court would have power to impose a fine of an amount exceeding [£400] the amount of any fine imposed by the court shall not exceed [£400].
(2) In relation to a person under the age of 14 subsection (1) above shall have effect as if for the words [£400], in both the places where they occur, there were substituted the words "£100"; but this subsection shall cease to have effect on the coming into force of section 4 of the Children and Young Persons Act 1969 (which prohibits criminal proceedings against children).

37. *****

38. Committal for sentence on summary trial of offence triable either way.
Where on the summary trial of an offence triable either way (not being an offence as regards which this section is excluded by section 33 above) a person who is not less than 17 years old is convicted of the offence, then, if on obtaining information about his character and antecedents the court is of opinion that they are such that greater punishment should be inflicted for the offence than the court has power to inflict, the court may, in accordance with section 56 of the Criminal Justice Act 1967, commit him in custody or on bail to the Crown Court for sentence in accordance with the provisions of section 42 of the Powers of Criminal Courts Act 1973.

39. Cases where magistrates' court may remit offender to another such court for sentence.
(1) Where a person who has attained the age of 17 ("the offender") has been convicted by a magistrates' court ("the convicting court") of an offence to which this section applies ("the instant offence") and—
    (a) it appears to the convicting court that some other magistrates' court ("the other court") has convicted him of another such offence in respect of which the other court has neither passed sentence on him nor committed him to the Crown Court for sentence nor dealt with him in any other way; and
    (b) the other court consents to his being remitted under this section to the other court,
the convicting court may remit him to the other court to be dealt with in respect of the instant offence by the other court instead of by the convicting court.

(2) The offender, if remitted under this section, shall have no right of appeal against the order of remission.

(3) Where the convicting court remits the offender to the other court under this section, it shall adjourn the trial of the information charging him with the instant offence, and—

(a) section 128 below and all other enactments (whenever passed) relating to remand or the granting of bail in criminal proceedings shall have effect in relation to the convicting court's power or duty to remand the offender on that adjournment as if any reference is to be brought or appear after remand were a reference to the court to which he is being remitted; and

(b) subject to subsection (4) below, the other court may deal with the case in any way in which it would have power to deal with it (including, where applicable, the remission of the offender under this section to another magistrates' court in respect of the instant offence) if all proceedings relating to that offence which took place before the convicting court had taken place before the other court.

(4) Nothing in this section shall preclude the convicting court from making any order which it has power to make under section 28 of the Theft Act 1968 (orders for restitution) by virtue of the offender's conviction of the instant offence.

(5) Where the convicting court has remitted the offender under this section to the other court, the other court may remit him back to the convicting court; and the provisions of subsection (3) above (so far as applicable) shall apply with the necessary modifications in relation to any remission under this subsection.

(6) This section applies to—

(a) any offence punishable with imprisonment; and

(b) any offence in respect of which the convicting court has a power or duty to order the offender to be disqualified under [section 34 or 36 of the Road Traffic Offenders Act 1988] (disqualification for certain motoring offences);

and in this section "conviction" includes a finding under section 30(1) above that the person in question did the act or made the omission charged, and "convicted" shall be construed accordingly.

40. Restriction on amount payable under compensation order of magistrates' court.

(1) The compensation to be paid under a compensation order made by a magistrates' court in respect of any offence of which the court has convicted the offender shall not exceed [£2000] and the compensation or total compensation to be paid under a compensation order or compensation orders made by a magistrates's court in respect of any offence or offences taken into consideration in determining sentence shall not exceed the difference (if any) between the amount or total amount which under the preceeding provisions of this subsection is the maximum for the offence or offences of which the offender has been convicted and the amount or total amounts (if any) which are in fact ordered to be paid in respect of that offence or those offences.

(2) In subsection (1) above "compensation order" has the meaning assigned to it by section 35(1) of the Powers of Criminal Courts Act 1973.

Miscellaneous

41. *****

42. Restriction on justices sitting after dealing with bail.

(1) A justice of the peace shall not take part in trying the issue of an accused's guilt on the summary trial of an information if in the course of the same proceedings

the justice has been informed, for the purpose of determining whether the accused shall be granted bail, that he has one or more previous convictions.

(2) For the purposes of this section any committal proceedings from which the proceedings on the summary trial arose shall be treated as part of the trial.

[43. **Bail on arrest**

(1) Where a person has been granted bail under the Police and Criminal Evidence Act 1984 subject to a duty to appear before a magistrates' court, the court before which he is to appear may appoint a later time as the time at which he is to appear and may enlarge the recognizance of any sureties for him at that time.

(2) The recognizance of any surety for any person granted bail subject to a duty to attend at a police station may be enforced as if it were conditioned for his appearance before a magistrates' court for the petty sessions area in which the police station named in the recognizance is situated.]

[43A. **Functions of magistrates' court where a person in custody is brought before it with a view to his appearance before the Crown Court**

(1) Where a person in custody in pursuance of a warrant issued by the Crown Court with a view to his appearance before the Crown Court is brought before a magistrates' court in pursuance of section 81(5) of the Supreme Court Act 1981—

　　(a)　the magistrates' court shall commit him in custody or release him on bail until he can be brought or appear before the Crown Court at the time and place appointed by the Crown Court;

　　(b)　if the warrant is endorsed for bail, but the person in custody is unable to satisfy the conditions endorsed, the magistrates' court may vary those conditions, if satisfied that it is proper to do so.

(2) A magistrates' court shall have jurisdiction under subsection (1) whether or not the offence was committed, or the arrest was made, within the court's area.]

44.–50.　*****

PART II
CIVIL JURISDICTION AND PROCEDURE
Jurisdiction to issue summons and deal with complaints

51. **Issue of summons on complaint.**
Subject to the provisions of this Act, where a complaint is made to a justice of the peace acting for any petty sessions area upon which a magistrates' court acting for that area has power to make an order against any person, the justice may issue a summons directed to that person requiring him to appear before a magistrates' court acting for that area to answer to the complaint.

52. **Jurisdiction to deal with complaints**
Where no express provison is made by any Act or the rules specifying what magistrates' courts shall have jurisdiction to hear a complaint, a magistrates' court shall have such jurisdiction if the complaint relates to anything done within the commission area for which the court is appointed or anything left undone that ought to have been done there, or ought to have been done either there or elsewhere, or relates to any other matter arising within that area.

In this section "commission area" has the same meaning as in the Justices of the Peace Act 1979.

53.–57.　*****

Civil debt

58. Money recoverable summarily as civil debt.
(1) A magistrates' court shall have power to make an order on complaint for the payment of any money recoverable summarily as a civil debt.
(2) *****

59. *****

60. Revocation, variation, etc., of orders for periodical payment.
Where a magistrates' court has made an order for the periodical payment of money, the court may, by order on complaint, revoke, revive or vary the order.

The power to vary an order by virtue of this section shall include power to suspend the operation of any provision of that order temporarily and to revive the operation of any provision so suspended.

61., 62. *****

63. Orders other than for payment of money
(1) Where under any Act passed after 31st December 1879 a magistrates' court has power to require the doing of anything other than the payment of money, or to prohibit the doing of anything, any order of the court for the purpose of exercising that power may contain such provisions for the manner in which anything is to be done, for the time within which anything is to be done, or during which anything is not to be done, and generally for giving effect to the order, as the court thinks fit.

(2) The court may by order made on complaint suspend or rescind any such order as aforesaid.

(3) Where any person disobeys an order of a magistrates' court made under an Act passed after 31st December 1879 to do anything other than the payment of money or to abstain from doing anything the court may—

    (a)   order him to pay a sum not exceeding £50 for every day during which he is in default or a sum not exceeding [£2000] or

    (b)   commit him to custody until he has remedied his default or for a period not exceeding 2 months;

but a person who is ordered to pay a sum for every day during which he is in default or who is committed to custody until he has remedied his default shall not by virtue of this section be ordered to pay more than £1,000 or be committed for more than 2 months in all for doing or abstaining from doing the same thing contrary to the order (without prejudice to the operation of this section in relation to any subsequent default).

(4) Any sum ordered to be paid under subsection (3) above shall for the purposes of this Act be treated as adjudged to be paid by a conviction of a magistrates' court.

(5) The preceding provisions of this section shall not apply to any order for the enforcement of which provision is made by any other enactment.

Costs

64. Power to award costs and enforcement of costs.
(1) On the hearing of a complaint, a magistrates' court shall have power in its discretion to make such order as to costs—

    (a)   on making the order for which the complaint is made, to be paid by the defendant to the complainant;

Magistrates' Courts Act 1980

    (b)   on dismissing the complaint, to be paid by the complainant to the defendant, as it thinks just and reasonable; but if the complaint is for an order for the periodical payment of money, or for the revocation, revival or variation of such an order, or for the enforcement of such an order, the court may, whatever adjudication it makes, order either party to pay the whole or any part of the other's costs.

(2)—(5) *****

Domestic proceedings

65. Meaning of domestic proceedings.

(1) In this Act "domestic proceedings" means proceedings under any of the following enactments, that is to say—
- (a)   the Maintenance Orders (Facilities for Enforcement) Act 1920;
- (b)   section 43 or section 44 of the National Assistance Act 1948;
- (c)   section 3 of the Marriage Act 1949;
- (d)   the Affiliation Proceedings Act 1957;
- (e)   the Guardianship of Minors Act 1971 and 1973;
- [(ee) Section 35 of the Matrimonial Causes Act 1973;]
- (f)   Part I of the Maintenance Orders (Reciprocal Enforcement) Act 1972;
- (g)   Part II of the Children Act 1975;
- (h)   the Adoption Act 1976, except proceedings under section 34 of that Act;
- (i)   section 18 or section 19 of the Supplementary Benefits Act 1976;
- (j)   Part I of the Domestic Proceedings and Magistrates' Courts Act 1978;
- (k)   section 47, 49 or 50 of the Child Care Act 1980;
- (l)   section 60 of this Act;

except that, subject to subsection (2) below, it does not include—

    (i)   proceedings for the enforcement of any order made, confirmed or registered under any of those enactments;

    (ii)   proceedings for the variation of any provision for the periodical payment of money contained in an order made, confirmed or registered under any of those enactments; or

    (iii)   proceedings on an information in respect of the commission of an offence under any of those enactments.

(2) The court before which there fall to be heard any of the following proceedings, that is to say—

    (a)   proceedings (whether under this Act or any other enactment) for the enforcement of any order made, confirmed or registered under any of the enactments specified in paragraphs (a) to (k) of subsection (1) above;

    (b)   proceeding (whether under this Act or any other enactment) for the variation of any provision for the making of periodical payments contained in an order made, confirmed or registered under any of those enactments;

    (c)   proceedings for an attachment of earnings order to secure maintenance payments within the meaning of the Attachment of Earnings Act 1971 or for the discharge or variation of such an order; or

    (d)   proceedings for the enforcement of a maintenance order which is registered in a magistrates' court under Part II of the Maintenance Orders Act 1950 or Part I of the Maintenance Orders Act 1958 or for the variation of the rate of payments specified by such an order.

may if it thinks fit order that those proceedings and any other proceedings being heard therewith shall, notwithstanding anything in subsection (1) above, be treated as domestic proceedings for the purposes of this Act.

(3) Where the same parties are parties—

    (a)   to proceedings which are domestic proceedings by virtue of subsection (1) above, and

(b) to proceedings which the court has power to treat as domestic proceedings by virtue of subsection (2) above.
and the proceedings are heard together by a magistrates' court, the whole of those proceedings shall be treated as domestic proceedings for the purposes of this Act.

(4) No appeal shall lie from the making of, or refusal to make, an order under subsection (2) above.

(5) (spent)

66. Composition of magistrates' courts for domestic proceedings: general.

(1) Subject to the provisions of this section, a magistrates' court when hearing domestic proceedings shall be composed of not more than 3 justices of the peace, including, so far as practicable, both a man and a woman.

(2) Subsection (1) above shall not apply to a magistrates' court for an inner London petty sessions area, and, notwithstanding anything in section 67 below, for the purpose of exercising jurisdiction to hear domestic proceedings such a court shall be composed of—

(a) a metropolitan stipendiary magistrate as chairman and one or 2 lay justices who are members of the domestic court panel for that area; or

(b) 2 or 3 lay justices who are members of that panel;

or, if it is not practicable for such a court to be so composed, the court shall for that purpose be composed of a metropolitan stipendiary magistrate sitting alone.

(3) Where in pursuance of subsection (2) above a magistrates' court includes lay justices it shall, so far as practicable, include both a man and a woman.

(4) In the preceding provisions of this section "lay justices" means justices of the peace for the inner London area who are not metropolitan stipendiary magistrates.

(5) In this section "inner London petty sessions area" means the City of London or any petty sessional division of the inner London area.

67. Domestic courts and panels.

(1) Magistrates' courts constituted in accordance with the provisions of this section and sitting for the purpose of hearing domestic proceedings shall be known as domestic courts.

(2) A justice shall not be qualified to sit as a member of a domestic court unless he is a member of a domestic court panel, that is to say a panel of justices specially appointed to deal with domestic proceedings.

(3) Without prejudice to the generality of the power to make rules under section 144 below relating to the procedure and practice to be followed in magistrates' courts, provision may be made by such rules with respect to any of the following matters, that is to say—

(a) the formation and revision of domestic court panels and the eligibility of justices to be members of such panels;

(b) the appointment of persons as chairmen of domestic courts; and

(c) the composition of domestic courts.

(4)—(8) *****

68. *****

69.

(1) The business of magistrates' courts shall, so far as is consistent with the due dispatch of business, be arranged in such manner as may be requisite for separating the hearing and determination of domestic proceedings from other business.

(2)–(7) *****

70. *****

71. Newspaper reports of domestic proceedings.
(1) In the case of domestic proceedings in a magistrates' court (other than proceedings under the Adoption Act 1976) it shall not be lawful for the proprietor, editor or publisher of a newspaper or periodical to print or publish, or cause or procure to be printed or published, in it any particulars of the proceedings other than the following, that is to say—
    (a)   the names, addresses and occupations of the parties and witnesses;
    (b)   the grounds of the application, and a concise statement of the charges, defences and counter-charges in support of which evidence has been given;
    (c)   submission on any point of law arising in the course of the proceedings and the decision of the court on the submissions;
    (d)   the decision of the court, and any observations made by the court in giving it.
(2)–(6) *****

72. *****

73. Examination of witnesses by court.
Where in any domestic proceedings, or in any proceedings for the enforcement or variation of an order made in domestic proceedings, it appears to a magistrates' court that any party to the proceedings who is not legally represented is unable effectively to examine or cross-examine a witness, the court shall ascertain from that party what are the matters about which the witness may be able to depose or on which the witness ought to be cross-examined, as the case may be, and shall put, or cause to be put, to the witness such questions in the interests of that party as may appear to the court to be proper.

74. Reasons for decisions in domestic proceedings
(1) The power to make rules conferred by section 144 below shall, without prejudice to the generality of subsection (1) of that section, include power to make provision for the recording by a magistrates' court, in such manner as may be prescribed by the rules, of reasons for a decision made in such domestic proceedings or class of domestic proceedings as may be so prescribed, and for making available a copy of any record made in accordance with those rules of the reasons for a decision of a magistrates' court to any person who requests a copy thereof for the purposes of an appeal against that decision or for the purpose of deciding whether or not to appeal against that decision.
(2) A copy of any record made by virtue of this section of the reasons for a decision of a magistrates' court shall, if certified by such officer of the court as may be prescribed, be admissible as evidence of those reasons.

75.–96. *****

PART IV
WITNESSES AND EVIDENCE
Procuring attendance of witness

97. Summons to witness and warrant for his arrest
(1) Where a justice of the peace for any county, any London commission area or the City of London is satisfied that any person in England or Wales is likely to be able to give material evidence, or produce any document or thing likely to be material evidence, at any inquiry into an indictable offence by a magistrates' court for that county, that London commission area or the City (as the case may be) or at the summary

trial of an information or hearing of a complaint by such a court and that that person will not voluntarily attend as a witness or will not voluntarily produce the document or thing, the justice shall issue a summons directed to that person requiring him to attend before the court at the time and place appointed in the summons to give evidence or to produce the document or thing.

(2) If a justice of the peace is satisfied by evidence on oath of the matters mentioned in subsection (1) above, and also that it is probable that a summons under that subsection would not procure the attendance of the person in question, the justice may instead of issuing a summons issue a warrant to arrest that person and bring him before such a court as aforesaid at a time and place specified in the warrant; but a warrant shall not be issued under this subsection where the attendance is required for the hearing of a complaint.

(3) On the failure of any person to attend before a magistrates' court in answer to a summons under this section, if—

    (a) the court is satisfied by evidence on oath that he is likely to be able to give material evidence or produce any document or thing likely to be material evidence in the proceedings; and

    (b) it is proved on oath, or in such other manner as may be prescribed, that he has been duly served with the summons, and that a reasonable sum has been paid or tendered to him for costs and expenses; and

    (c) it appears to the court that there is no just excuse for the failure,

the court may issue a warrant to arrest him and bring him before the court at a time and place specified in the warrant.

(4) If any person attending or brought before a magistrates' court refuses without just excuse to be sworn or give evidence, or to produce any document or thing, the court may commit him to custody until the expiration of such period not exceeding 7 days as may be specified in the warrant or until he sooner gives evidence or produces the document or thing.

Evidence generally

98. Evidence on oath.
Subject to the provisions of any enactment or rule of law authorising the reception of unsworn evidence, evidence given before a magistrates' court shall be given on oath.

99., 100. *****

101. Onus of proving exceptions, etc.
Where the defendant to an information or complaint relies for his defence on any exception, exemption, proviso, excuse or qualification, whether or not it accompanies the description of the offence or matter of complaint in the enactment creating the offence or on which the complaint is founded, the burden of proving the exception, exemption, proviso, excuse or qualification shall be on him; and this notwithstanding that the information or complaint contains an allegation negativing the exception, exemption, proviso, excuse or qualification.

Evidence in criminal cases

102. Written statements before examining justices.
(1) In committal proceedings a written statement by any person shall, if the conditions mentioned in subsection (2) below are satisfied, be admissible as evidence to the like extent as oral evidence to the like effect by that person.

(2) The said conditions are—

(a) the statement purports to be signed by the person who made it;

(b) the statement contains a declaration by that person to the effect that it is true to the best of his knowledge and belief that he made the statement knowing that, if it were tendered in evidence, he would be liable to prosecution if he wilfully stated in it anything which he knew to be false or did not believe to be true;

(c) before the statement is tendered in evidence, a copy of the statement is given, by or on behalf of the party proposing to tender it, to each of the other parties to the proceedings; and

(d) none of the other parties, before the statement is tendered in evidence at the committal proceedings, objects to the statement being so tendered under this section.

(3) The following provisions shall also have effect in relation to any written statement tendered in evidence under this section, that is to say—

(a) if the statement is made by a person under 21 years old, it shall give his age;

(b) if it is made by a person who cannot read it, it shall be read to him before he signs it and shall be accompanied by a declaration by the person who so read the statement to the effect that it was so read; and

(c) if it refers to any other document as an exhibit, the copy given to any other party to the proceedings under subsection (2)(c) above shall be accompanied by a copy of that document or by such information as may be necessary in order to enable the party to whom it is given to inspect that document or a copy thereof.

(3A)...

(4) Notwithstanding that a written statement made by any person may be admissable in committal proceedings by virtue of this section, the court before which the proceedings are held may, of its own motion or on the application of any party to the proceedings, require that person to attend before the court and give evidence.

(5) So much of any statement as is admitted in evidence by virtue of this section shall, unless the court commits the accused for trial by virtue of section 6(2) above or the court otherwise directs, be read aloud at the hearing, and where the court so directs an account shall be given orally of so much of any statement as is not read aloud.

(6) Any document or object referred to as an exhibit and identified in a written statement tendered in evidence under this section shall be treated as if it had been produced as an exhibit and identitied in court by the maker of the statement.

(7) Subsection (3) of section 13 of the Criminal Justice Act 1925 (reading of deposition as evidence at the trial) shall apply to any written statement tendered in evidence in committal proceedings under this section as it applies to a deposition taken in such proceedings, but in its application to any such statement that subsection shall have effect as if paragraph (b) thereof were omitted.

(8) In section 2(2) of the Administration of Justice (Miscellaneous Provisions) Act 1933 (procedure for preferring bills of indictment) the reference in proviso (i) to facts disclosed in any deposition taken before a justice in the presence of the accused shall be construed as including a reference to facts disclosed in any such written statement as aforesaid [and section 40 of the Criminal Justice Act 1988 ... shall be given a corresponding construction.]

(9) Section 28 above shall not apply to any such statement as aforesaid.

(10) A person whose written statement is tendered in evidence in committal proceedings under this section shall be treated for the purposes of section 1 of the Criminal Procedure (Attendance of Witnesses) Act 1965 (witness orders) as a witness who has been examined by the court.

103. *****

104. Proof of previous convictions.
Where a person is convicted of a summary offence by a magistrates' court, other than a juvenile court, and—
    (a)   it is proved to the satisfaction of the court, on oath or in such other manner as may be prescribed, that not less than 7 days previously a notice was served on the accused in the prescribed form and manner specifying any alleged previous conviction of the accused of a summary offence proposed to be brought to the notice of the court in the event of his conviction of the offence charged; and
    (b)   the accused is not present in person before the court,
the court may take account of any such previous conviction so specified as if the accused had appeared and admitted it.

105. *****

Offences

106. False written statements tendered in evidence.
(1) If any person in a written statement tendered in evidence in criminal proceedings by virtue of section 102 above wilfully makes a statement material in those proceedings which he knows to be false or does not believe to be true, he shall be liable on conviction on indictment to imprisonment for a term not exceeding 2 years or a fine or both.

(2) The Perjury Act 1911 shall have effect as if this section were contained in this Act.

107. False statements in declaration proving service, etc.
If, in any solemn declaration, certificate or other writing made or given for the purpose of its being used in pursuance of the rules as evidence of the service of any document or the handwriting or seal of any person, a person makes a statement that he knows to be false in a material particular, or recklessly makes any statement that is false in a material particular, he shall be liable on summary conviction to imprisonment for a term not exceeding 6 months or a fine not exceeding [level 3 on the standard scale] or both.

PART V
APPEAL AND CASE STATED
Appeal

108. Right of appeal to the Crown Court.
(1) A person convicted by a magistrates' court may appeal to the Crown Court—
    (a)   if he pleaded guilty, against his sentence;
    (b)   if he did not, against the conviction or sentence.

[(1A) Section 13 of the Powers of the Criminal Courts Act 1973 (. . .) shall not prevent an appeal under this section, whether against conviction or otherwise.]

(2) A person sentenced by a magistrates' court for an offence in respect of which a probation order or an order for conditional discharge has been previously made may appeal to the Crown Court against the sentence.

(3) In this section "sentence" includes any order made on conviction by a magistrates' court, not being—
    (a)   . . .
    (b)   an order for the payment of costs;

(c) an order under section 2 of the Protection of Animals Act 1911 (which enables a court to order the destruction of an animal); or

(d) an order made in pursuance of any enactment under which the court has no discretion as to the making of the order or its terms.

109. Abandonment of appeal.

(1) Where notice to abandon an appeal has been duly given by the appellant—

(a) the court against whose decision the appeal was brought may issue process for enforcing that decision, subject to anything already suffered or done under it by the appellant; and

(b) the said court may, on the application of the other party to the appeal, order the appellant to pay to that party such costs as appear to the court to be just and reasonable in respect of expenses properly incurred by that party in connection with the appeal before notice of the abandonment was given to that party.

(2) In this section "appeal" means an appeal from a magistrates' court to the Crown Court, and the reference to a notice to abandon an appeal is a reference to a notice shown to the satisfaction of the magistrates' court to have been given in accordance with Crown Court rules.

110. Enforcement of decision of the Crown Court.

After the determination by the Crown Court of an appeal from a magistrates' court the decision appealed against as confirmed or varied by the Crown Court, or any decision of the Crown Court substituted for the decision appealed against, may, without prejudice to the powers of the Crown Court to enforce the decision, be enforced—

(a) by the issue by the court by which the decision appealed against was given of any process that it could have issued if it had decided the case as the Crown Court decided it;

(b) so far as the nature of any process already issued to enforce the decision appealed against permits, by that process;

and the decision of the Crown Court shall have effect as if it had been made by the magistrates' court against whose decision the appeal is brought.

Case stated

111. Statement of case by magistrates' court.

(1) Any person who was a party to any proceeding before a magistrates' court or is aggrieved by the conviction, order, determination or other proceeding of the court may question the proceeding on the ground that it is wrong in law or is in excess of jurisdiction by applying to the justices composing the court to state a case for the opinion of the High Court on the question of law or jurisdiction involved; but a person shall not make an application under this section in respect of a decision against which he has a right of appeal to the High Court or which by virtue of any enactment passed after 31st December 1879 is final.

(2) An application under subsection (1) above shall be made within 21 days after the day on which the decision of the magistrates' court was given.

(3) For the purpose of subsection (2) above, the day on which the decision of the magistrates' court is given shall, where the court has adjourned the trial of an information after conviction, be the day on which the court sentences or otherwise deals with the offender.

(4) On the making of an application under this section in respect of a decision any right of the applicant to appeal against the decision to the Crown Court shall cease.

(5) If the justices are of opinion that an application under this section is frivolous,

they may refuse to state a case, and, if the applicant so requires, shall give him a certificate stating that the application has been refused; but the justices shall not refuse to state a case if the application is made by or under the direction of the Attorney General.

(6) Where justices refuse to state a case, the High Court may, on the application of the person who applied for the case to be stated, make an order of mandamus requiring the justices to state a case.

112. Effect of decision of High Court on case stated by magistrates' court.
Any conviction, order, determination or other proceeding of a magistrates' court varied by the High Court on an appeal by case stated, and any judgement or order of the High Court on such an appeal, may be enforced as if it were a decision of the magistrates' court from which the appeal was brought.

Supplemental provisions as to appeal and case stated

113. Bail on appeal or case stated.
(1) Where a person has given notice of appeal to the Crown Court against the decision of a magistrates' court or has applied to a magistrates' court to state a case for the opinion of the High Court, then, if he is in custody, the magistrates' court may grant him bail.
(2) *****
(3) Subsection (1) above shall not apply where the accused has been committed to the Crown Court for sentence under section 37 or 38 above.
(4) *****

114. *****

Part VI
Recognizances
Recognizances to keep the peace or be of good behaviour

115. Binding over to keep the peace or be of good behaviour.
(1) The power of a magistrates' court on the complaint of any person to adjudge any other person to enter into a recognizance, with or without sureties, to keep the peace or to be of good behaviour towards the complainant shall be exercised by order on complaint.
(2) Where a complaint is made under this section, the power of the court to remand the defendant under subsection (5) of section 55 above shall not be subject to the restrictions imposed by subsection (6) of that section.
(3) If any person ordered by a magistrates' court under subsection (1) above to enter into a recognizance, with or without sureties, to keep the peace or to be of good behaviour fails to comply with the order, the court may commit him to custody for a period not exceeding 6 months or until he sooner complies with the order.

116. *****

Other provisions

117. Warrant endorsed for bail
(1) A justice of the peace on issuing a warrant for the arrest of any person may grant him bail by endorsing the warrant for bail, that is to say, by endorsing the warrant with a direction in accordance with subsection (2) below.

(2) A direction for bail endorsed on a warrant under subsection (1) above shall—
    (a)   in the case of bail in criminal proceedings, state that the person arrested is to be released on bail subject to a duty to appear before such magistrates' court and at such time as may be specified in the endorsement;
    (b)   in the case of bail otherwise than in criminal proceedings, state that the person arrested is to be released on bail on his entering into such a recognizance (with or without sureties) conditioned for his appearance before a magistrates' court as may be specified in the endorsement;
and the endorsement shall fix the amounts in which any sureties and, in a case falling within paragraph (b) above, that person is or are to be bound.
    (3)   *****

118., 119. *****

120. Forfeiture of recognizance.
(1) Where a recognizance to keep the peace or to be of good behaviour has been entered into before a magistrates' court or any recognizance is conditioned for the appearance of a person before a magistrates' court or for his doing any other thing connected with a proceeding before a magistrates' court, and the recognizance appears to the court to be forfeited, the court may, subject to subsection (2) below, declare the recognizance to be forfeited and adjudged the persons bound thereby, whether as principal or sureties, or any of them, to pay the sum in which they are respectively bound.
(2) Where a recognizance is conditioned to keep the peace or to be of good behaviour, the court shall not declare it forfeited except by order made on complaint.
(3) The court which declares the recognizance to be forfeited may, instead of adjudging any person to pay the whole sum in which he is bound, adjudge him to pay part only of the sum or remit the sum.
(4) Payment of any sum adjudged to be paid under this section, including any costs awarded against the defendant, may be enforced, any such sum shall be applied, as if it were a fine and as if the adjudication were a summary conviction of an offence not punishable with imprisonment and so much of section 85(1) above as empowers a court to remit fines shall not apply to the sum but so much thereof as relates to remission after a term of imprisonment has been imposed shall so apply; but at any time before the issue of a warrant of commitment to enforce payment of the sum, or before the sale of goods under a warrant of distress to satisfy the sum, the court may remit the whole or part of the sum either absolutely or on such conditions as the court thinks just.
(5) A recognizance such as is mentioned in this section shall not be enforced otherwise than in accordance with this section, and accordingly shall not be transmitted to the Crown Court nor shall its forfeiture be certified to that Court.

PART VII
MISCELLANEOUS AND SUPPLEMENTARY
Constitution and place of sitting of magistrates' courts

121. Constitution and place of sitting of court.
(1) A magistrates' court shall not try an information summarily or hear a complaint except when composed of at least 2 justices unless the trial or hearing is one that by virtue of any enactment may take place before a single justice.
(2) A magistrates' court shall not hold an inquiry into the means of an offender for the purposes of section 82 above [or determine under that section at a hearing

at which the offender is not present whether to issue a warrant of commitment] except when composed of at least 2 justices.

(3) A magistrates' court shall not—

    (a) try summarily an information for an indictable offence or hear a complaint except when sitting in a petty-sessional court-house;

    (b) try an information for a summary offence or hold an inquiry into the means of an offender for the purposes of section 82 above, or impose imprisonment, except when sitting in a petty-sessional court-house or an occasional court-house.

(4) Subject to the provisions of any enactment to the contrary, where a magistrates' court is required by this section to sit in a petty-sessional or occasional court-house, it shall sit in open court.

(5) A magistrates' court composed of a single justice, or sitting in an occasional court-house, shall not impose imprisonment for a period exceeding 14 days or order a person to pay more than £1.

(6) Subject to the provisions of subsection (7) below, the justices composing the court before which any proceedings take place shall be present during the whole of the proceedings; but, if during the course of the proceedings any justice absents himself, he shall cease to act further therein and, if the remaining justices are enough to satisfy the requirements of the preceding provisions of this section, the proceedings may continue before a court composed of those justices.

(7) Where the trial of an information is adjourned after the accused has been convicted and before he is sentenced or otherwise dealt with, the court which sentences or deals with him need not be composed of the same justices as that which convicted him; but, where among the justices composing the court which sentences or deals with an offender there are any who were not sitting when he was convicted, the court which sentences or deals with the offender shall before doing so make such inquiry into the facts and circumstances of the case as will enable the justices who were not sitting when the offender was convicted to be fully acquainted with those facts and circumstances.

(8) This section shall have effect subject to the provisions of this Act relating to domestic proceedings.

Appearance by counsel or solicitor

122. Appearance by counsel or solicitor

(1) A party to any proceedings before a magistrates' court may be represented by counsel or solicitor.

(2) Subject to subsection (3) below, an absent party so represented shall be deemed not to be absent.

(3) Appearance of a party by counsel or solicitor shall not satisfy any provision of any enactment or any condition of a recognizance expressly requiring his presence.

123.–126. *****

Limitation of time

127. Limitation of time.

(1) Except as otherwise expressly provided by any enactment and subject to subsection (2) below, a magistrates' court shall not try an information or hear a complaint unless the information was laid, or the complaint made, within 6 months from the time when the offence was committed, or the matter of complaint arose.

(2) Nothing in—

    (a) subsection (1) above; or

    (b) subject to subsection (4) below, any other enactment (however framed or

worded) which, as regards any offence to which it applies, would but for this section impose a time-limit on the power of a magistrates' court to try an information summarily or impose a limitation on the time for taking summary proceedings,
shall apply in relation to any indictable offence.

(3) Without prejudice to the generality of paragraph (b) of subsection (2) above, that paragraph includes enactments which impose a time-limit that applies only in certain circumstances (for example, where the proceedings are not instituted by or with the consent of the Director of Public Prosecutions or some other specified authority).

(4) Where, as regards any indictable offence, there is imposed by any enactment (however framed or worded, and whether falling within subsection (2)(b) above or not) a limitation on the time for taking proceedings on indictment for that offence no summary proceedings for that offence shall be taken after the latest time for taking proceedings on indictment.

Remand

128. Remand in custody or on bail

(1) Where a magistrates' court has power to remand any person, then, subject to section 4 of the Bail Act 1976 and to any other enactment modifying that power, the court may—

    (a) remand him in custody, that is to say, commit him to custody to be brought before the court [, subject to subsection (3A) below,] at the end of the period of remand or at such earlier time as the court may require; or

    (b) where it in inquiring into or trying as offence alleged to have been committed by that person or has convicted him of an offence, remand him on bail in accordance with the Bail Act 1976, that is to say, by directing him to appear as provided in subsection (4) below; or

    (c) except in a case falling within paragraph (b) above, remand him on bail by taking from him a recognizance (with or without sureties) conditioned as provided in that subsection;

and may, in a case falling within paragraph (c) above, instead of taking recognizances in accordance with that paragraph, fix the amount of the recognizances with a view to their being taken subsequently in accordance with section 119 above.

[(1A) Where—

    (a) on adjourning a case under section 5, 10(1) or 18(4) above the court proposes to remand or further remand a person in custody; and

    (b) he is before the court; and

    (c) he has attained the age of 17; and

    (d) he is legally represented in that court,

it shall be the duty of the court—

        (i) to explain the effect of subsections (3A) and (3B) below to him in ordinary language; and

        (ii) to inform him in ordinary language that, notwithstanding the procedure for a remand without his being brought before a court, he would be brought before a court for the hearing and determination of at least every fourth application for his remand, and of every application for his remand heard at a time when it appeared to the court that he had no solicitor acting for him in the case.

(1B) For the purposes of subsection (1A) above a person is to be treated as legally represented in a court if, but only if, he has the assistance of counsel or a solicitor to represent him in the proceedings in that court.

(1C) After explaining to an accused as provided by subsection (1A) above the court shall ask him whether he consents to the hearing and determination of such applications in his absence.]

(2) *****

(3) Where a person is brought before the court after remand, the court may further remand him.

[(3A) Subject to subsection (3B) below, where a person has been remanded in custody, and the remand was not a remand under section 128A below for a period exceeding 8 clear days, the court may further remand him (otherwise than in the exercise of the power conferred by that section) on an adjournment under section 5, 10(1) or 18(4) above without his being brought before it if it is satisfied—

    (a) that he gave his consent, either in response to a question under subsection (1C) above or otherwise, to the hearing and determination in his absence of any application for his remand on an adjournment of the case under any of those provisions; and

    (b) that he has not by virtue of this subsection been remanded wihout being brought before the court on more than two such applications immediately preceding the application which the court is hearing; and

    (c) that he had attained the age of 17 years when he gave his consent to the hearing and determination of such applications in his absence; and

    (d) that he has not withdrawn his consent to their being so heard and determined.

(3B) The court may not exercise the power conferred by subsection (3A) above if it appears to the court, on an application for a further remand being made to it, that the person to whom the application relates has no solicitor acting for him in the case (whether present in court or not).

(3C) Where—

    (a) a person has been remanded in custody on an adjournment of a case under section 5, 10(1) or 18(4) above; and

    (b) an application is subsequently made for his further remand on such an adjournment; and

    (c) he is not brought before the court which hears and determines the application; and

    (d) that court is not satisfied as mentioned in subsection (3A) above,

the court shall adjourn the case and remand him in custody for the period for which it stands adjourned.

(3D) An adjournment under subsection (3C) above shall be for the shortest period that appears to the court to make it possible for the accused to be brought before it.

(3E) Where—

    (a) on an adjournment of a case under section 5, 10(1) or 18(4) above a person has been remanded in custody without being brought before the court; and

    (b) it subsequently appears—

        (i) to the court which remanded him in custody; or

        (ii) to an alternative magistrates' court to which he is remanded under section 130 below,

that he ought not to have been remanded in custody in his absence, the court shall require him to be brought before it at the earliest time that appears to the court to be possible.]

(4) Where a person is remanded on bail under subsection (1) above the court may, where it remands him on bail in accordance with the Bail Act 1976 direct him to appear or, in any other case, direct that his recognizance be conditioned for his appearance—

    (a) before that court at the end of the period of remand; or

    (b) at every time and place to which during the course of the proceedings the hearing may be from time to time adjourned;

and, where it remands him on bail conditionally on his providing a surety during an inquiry into an offence alleged to have been committed by him, may direct that the recognizance of the surety be conditioned to secure that the person so bailed appears—

(c) at every time and place to which during the course of the proceedings the hearing may be from time to time adjourned and also before the Crown Court in the event of the person so bailed being committed for trial there.

(5) *****

(6) Subject to the provisions of section 128A and 129 below, a magistrates' court shall not remand a person for a period exceeding 8 clear days, except that—

(a) if the court remands him on bail, it may remand him for a longer period if he and the other party consent;

(b) where the court adjourns a trial under section 10(3) or 30 above, the court may remand him for the period of the adjournment;

(c) where a person is charged with an offence triable either way, then, if it falls to the court to try the case summarily but the court is not at the time so constituted, and sitting in such a place, as will enable it to proceed with the trial, the court may remand him until the next occasion on which it will be practicable for the court to be so constituted, and to sit in such a place, as aforesaid, notwithstanding that the remand is for a period exceeding 8 clear days.

(7) *****

[(8) *****]

Remands in custody for more than eight days

[**128A.**

(1) The Secretary of State may by order made by statutory instrument provide that this section shall have effect—

(a) in an area specified in the order; or
(b) in proceedings of a description so specified,

in relation to any accused person ("the accused") who has attained the age of 17.

(2) A magistrates' court may remand the accused in custody for a period exceeding 8 clear days if—

(a) it has previously remanded him in custody for the same offence; and
(b) he is before the court,

but only if, after affording the parties an opportunity to make representations, it has set a date on which it expects that it will be possible for the next stage in the proceedings, other than a hearing relating to a further remand in custody or on bail, to take place, and only—

(i) for a period ending not later than that date; or
(ii) for a period of 28 clear days,

whichever is the less.

(3) Nothing in this section affects the right of the accused to apply for bail during the period of the remand.

(4) A statutory instrument containing an order under this section shall not be made unless a draft of the instrument has been laid before Parliament and been approved by a resolution of each House.]

129. Further remand.

(1) If a magistrates' court is satisfied that any person who has been remanded is unable by reason of illness or accident to appear or be brought before the court at the expiration of the period for which he was remanded, the court may, in his absence, remand him for a further time; and section 128(6) above shall not apply.

(2) Notwithstanding anything in section 128(1) above, the power of a court under subsection (1) above to remand a person on bail for a further time—

(a) where he was granted bail in criminal proceedings, includes power to enlarge the recognizance of any surety for him to a later time;

(b) where he was granted bail otherwise than in criminal proceedings, may be exercised by enlarging his recognizance and those of any sureties for him to a later time.

(3) Where a person remanded on bail is bound to appear before a magistrates' court at any time and the court has no power to remand him under subsection (1) above, the court may in his absence—

(a) where he was granted bail in criminal proceedings, appoint a later time as the time at which he is to appear and enlarge the recognizances of any sureties for him to that time;

(b) where he was granted bail otherwise than in criminal proceedings, enlarge his recognizance and those of any sureties for him to a later time;

and the appointment of the time or the enlargement of his recognizance shall be deemed to be a further demand.

(4) Where a magistrates' court commits a person for trial on bail and the recognizance of any surety for him has been conditioned in accordance with paragraph (a) of subsection (4) of section 128 above the court may, in the absence of the surety, enlarge his recognizance so that he is bound to secure that the person so committed for trial appears also before the Crown Court.

130., 131. *****

Restrictions on imprisonment

132. Minimum term
A magistrates' court shall not impose imprisonment for less than 5 days.

133. Consecutive terms of imprisonment.
(1) A magistrates' court imposing imprisonment [or detention in a young offender institution] on any person may order that the term of imprisonment shall commence on the expiration of any other term of imprisonment [or detention in a young offender institution] imposed by that or any other court; but where a magistrates' court imposes two or more terms of imprisonment [or detention in a young offender institution] to run consecutively the aggregate of such terms shall not, subject to the provisions of this section, exceed 6 months.

(2) If two or more of the terms imposed by the court are imposed in respect of an offence triable either way which was tried summarily otherwise than in pursuance of section 22(2) above, the aggregate of the term so imposed and any other terms imposed by the court may exceed 6 months but shall not, subject to the following provisions of this section, exceed 12 months.

[(2A) In relation to the imposition of terms of detention in a young offender institution subsection (2) above shall have effect as if the reference to an offence triable either way were a reference to such an offence or an offence triable only on indictment.]

(3) The limitations imposed by the preceding subsections shall not operate to reduce the aggregate of the terms that the court may impose in respect of any offences below the term which the court has power to impose in respect of any one of those offences.

(4) Where a person has been sentenced by a magistrates' court to imprisonment and a fine for the same offence, a period of imprisonment imposed for non-payment of the fine, or for want of sufficient distress to satisfy the fine, shall not be subject to the limitations imposed by the preceding subsections.

(5) For the purposes of this section a term of imprisonment shall be deemed to be imposed in respect of an offence if it is imposed as a sentence or in default of

payment of a sum adjudged to be paid by the conviction or for want of sufficient distress to satisfy such a sum.

134.–147. *****

Interpretation

148.

(1) In this Act the expression "magistrates' court" means any justice or justices of the peace acting under any enactment or by virtue of his or their commission or under the common law.

(2) Except where the contrary is expressed, anything authorised or required by this Act to be done by, to or before the magistrates' court by, to or before which any other thing was done, or is to be done, may be done by, to or before any magistrates' court acting for the same petty sessions area as that court.

*****

SCHEDULE 1
Offences Triable Either Way by Virtue of Section 17

1. Offences at common law of public nuisance.
2. Offences under section 8 of the Disorderly Houses Act 1751 (appearing to be keeper of bawdy house etc.).
3. Offences consisting in contravention of section 13 of the Statutory Declarations Act 1835 (administration by a person of an oath etc. touching matters in which he has no jurisdiction).
4. *****
5. Offences under the following provisions of the Offences against the Person Act 1861—
    - (a) section 16 (threats to kill);
    - (b) section 20 (inflicting bodily injury, with or without a weapon);
    - (c) section 26 (not providing apprentices or servants with food etc.);
    - (d) section 27 (abandoning or exposing child);
    - (e) section 34 (doing or omitting to do anything so as to endanger railway passengers);
    - (f) section 36 (assaulting a clergyman at a place of worship etc.);
    - (g) section 38 (assault with intent to resist apprehension);
    - (h) section 47 (assault occasioning bodily harm);
    - (i) section 57 (bigamy);
    - (j) section 60 (concealing the birth of a child).
6. *****
7. Offences under section 13 of the Debtors Act 1869 (transactions intended to defraud creditors).
8., 9. *****
10. Offences under section 22 of the Electric Lighting Act 1882 (injuring works with intent to cut off electricity supply).
11.–13. *****
14. All offences under the Perjury Act 1911 except offences under—
    - (a) section 1 (perjury in judicial proceedings);
    - (b) section 3 (false statements etc. with reference to marriage);
    - (c) section 4 (false statements etc. as to births or deaths).
15. The following offences under the Forgery Act 1913—

(a) offences under paragraph (a) of section 2(2) (forgery of valuable security etc.) in relation to—
 (i) any document being an accountable receipt, release, or discharge, or any receipt or other instrument evidencing the payment of money, or the delivery of any chattel personal; or
 (ii) any document being an authority or request for the payment of money or for the delivery or transfer of goods and chattels, where the amount of money or the value of the goods or chattels does not exceed £1,000;
 (b) offences under section 4 (forgery of documents in general); and
 (c) offences under paragraph (a) of section 7 (demanding property on forged documents), where the amount of the money or the value of the property in respect of which the offence is committed does not exceed £1,000.

16.-21. *****

22. Offences under the following provisions of the Post Office Act 1953—
 (a) section 53 (unlawfully taking away or opening mail bag);
 (b) section 55 (fraudulent retention of mail bag or postal packet);
 (c) section 57 (stealing, embezzlement, destruction etc. by officer of Post Office of postal packet);
 (d) section 58 (opening or delaying of postal packets by officers of the Post Office).

23. Offences under the following provisions of the Sexual Offences Act 1956—
 (a) section 6 (unlawful sexual intercourse with a girl under 16);
 (b) section 13 (indecency between men);
 (c) section 26 (permitting a girl under 16 to use premises for sexual intercourse).

24., 25. . . .

26. The following offences under the Criminal Law Act 1967—
 (a) offences under section 4(1) (assisting offenders); and
 (b) offences under section 5(1) (concealing arrestable offences and giving false information),
where the offence to which they relate is triable either way.

27. Offences under section 4(1) of the Sexual Offences Act 1967 (procuring others to commit homosexual acts).

28. All indictable offences under the Theft Act 1968 except:—
 (a) robbery, aggravated burglary, blackmail and assault with intent to rob;
 (b) burglary comprising the commission of, or an intention to commit, an offence which is triable only on indictment;
 (c) burglary in a dwelling if any person in the dwelling was subjected to violence or the threat of violence.

29. Offences under the following provisions of the Criminal Damage Act 1971—
section 1(1) (destroying or damaging property);
section 1(1) and (3) (arson);
section 2 (threats to destroy or damage property);
section 3 (possessing anything with intent to destroy or damage property).

30. *****

31. Uttering any forged document the forgery of which is an offence listed in this Schedule.

32. Committing an indecent assault upon a person whether male or female.

33. Aiding, abetting, counselling or procuring the commission of any offence listed in the preceding paragraphs of this Schedule except paragraph 26.

34. . . .

35. Any offence consisting in the incitement to commit an offence triable either way except an offence mentioned in paragraph 33.

NOTE: Only a selection of the offences in Schedule 1 are printed: for illustrative purposes.

SCHEDULE 2

OFFENCES FOR WHICH THE VALUE INVOLVED IS RELEVANT TO THE MODE OF TRIAL

Offence	Value involved	How measured

1. Offences under section 1 of the Criminal Damage Act 1971 (destroying or damaging property), excluding any offence committed by destroying or damaging property by fire.	As regards property alleged to have been destroyed, its value.
	
	As regards property alleged to have been damaged, the value of the alleged damage.
		What the property would probably have cost to buy in the open market at the material time.
		
		(a) If immediately after the material time the damage was capable of repair—
		  (i) what would probably then have been the market price for the repair of the damage, or
		  (ii) what the property alleged to have been damaged would probably have cost to buy in the open market at the material time,
		  whichever is the less; or
		(b) if immediately after the material time the damage was beyond repair, what the said property would probably have cost to buy in the open market at the material time.

2. The following offences, namely— (a) aiding, abetting, counselling or procuring the commission of any offence mentioned in paragraph 1 above; (b) attempting to commit any offence so mentioned; and (c) inciting another to commit any offence so mentioned.	The value indicated in paragraph 1 above for the offence alleged to have been aided, abetted, counselled or procured, or attempted or incited.	As for the corresponding entry in paragraph 1 above.

CONTEMPT OF COURT ACT 1981
(1981, c. 49)

An Act to amend the law relating to contempt of court and related matters.

[27th July 1981]

Strict liability

1. The strict liability rule.

In this Act "the strict liability rule" means the rule of law whereby conduct may be treated as a contempt of court as tending to interfere with the course of justice in particular legal proceedings regardless of intent to do so.

2. Limitation of scope of strict liability.

(1) The strict liability rule applies only in relation to publications, and for this purpose "publication" includes any speech, writing, broadcast [cable programme] or other communication in whatever form, which is addressed to the public at large or any section of the public.

(2) The strict liability rule applies only to a publication which creates a substantial risk that the course of justice in the proceedings in question will be seriously impeded or prejudiced.

(3) The strict liability rule applies to a publication only if the proceedings in question are active within the meaning of this section at the time of publication.

(4) Schedule 1 applies for determining the times at which proceedings are to be treated as active within the meaning of this section.

3. Defence of innocent publication or distribution.

(1) A person is not guilty of contempt of court under the strict liability rule as the publisher of any matter to which that rule applies if at the time of publication (having taken all reasonable care) he does not know and has no reason to suspect that relevant proceedings are active.

(2) A person is not guilty of contempt of court under the strict liability rule as the distributor of a publication containing any such matter if at the time of distribution (having taken all reasonable care) he does not know that it contains such matter and has no reason to suspect that it is likely to do so.

(3) The burden of proof of any fact tending to establish a defence afforded by this section to any person lies upon that person.

(4) *****

4. Contemporary reports of proceedings.

(1) Subject to this section a person is not guilty of contempt of court under the strict liability rule in respect of a fair and accurate report of legal proceedings held in public, published contemporaneously and in good faith.

(2) In any such proceedings the court may, where it appears to be necessary for avoiding a substantial risk of prejudice to the administration of justice in those proceedings, or in any other proceedings pending or imminent, order that the publication of any report of the proceedings, or any part of the proceedings be postponed for such period as the court thinks necessary for that purpose.

(3) For the purposes of subsection (1) of this section and of section 3 of the Law of Libel Amendment Act 1888 (privilege) a report of proceedings shall be treated as published contemporaneously—

    (a) in the case of a report of which publication is postponed pursuant to an order under subsection (2) of this section, if published as soon as practicable after that order expires;

    (b) in the case of a report of committal proceedings of which publication is permitted by virtue only of subsection (3) of section 8 of the Magistrates' Court Act 1980, if published as soon as practicable after publication is so permitted.

(4) *****

5. Discussion of public affairs.

A publication made as or as part of a discussion in good faith of public affairs or other matters of general public interest is not to be treated as a contempt of court under the strict liability rule if the risk of impediment or prejudice to particular legal proceedings is merely incidental to the discussion.

6. Savings.

Nothing in the foregoing provisions of this Act—

    (a)   prejudices any defence available at common law to a charge of contempt of court under the strict liability rule;

    (b)   implies that any publication is punishable as contempt of court under that rule which would not be so punishable apart from those provisions;

    (c)   restricts liability for contempt of court in respect of conduct intended to impede or prejudice the administration of justice.

7. Consent required for institution of proceedings.

Proceedings for a contempt of court under the strict liability rule (other than Scottish proceedings) shall not be instituted except by or with the consent of the Attorney General or on the motion of a court having jurisdiction to deal with it.

Other aspects of law and procedure

8. Confidentiality of jury's deliberations.

(1) Subject to subsection (2) below, it is a contempt of court to obtain, disclose or solicit any particulars of statements made, opinions expressed, arguments advanced or votes cast by members of a jury in the course of their deliberations in any legal proceedings.

(2) This section does not apply to any disclosure of any particulars—

    (a)   in the proceedings in question for the purpose of enabling the jury to arrive at their verdict, or in connection with the delivery of that verdict, or

    (b)   in evidence in any subsequent proceedings for an offence alleged to have been committed in relation to the jury in the first mentioned proceedings,

or to the publication of any particulars so disclosed.

(3) Proceedings for a contempt of court under this section (other than Scottish proceedings) shall not be instituted except by or with the consent of the Attorney General or on the motion of a court having jurisdiction to deal with it.

9. Use of tape recorders.

(1) Subject to subsection (4) below, it is a contempt of court—

    (a)   to use in court, or bring into court for use, any tape recorder or other instrument for recording sound, except with the leave of the court;

    (b)   to publish a recording of legal proceedings made by means of any such instrument, or any recording derived directly or indirectly from it, by playing it in the hearing of the public or any section of the public, or to dispose of it or any recording so derived, with a view to such publication;

    (c)   to use any such recording in contravention of any conditions of leave granted under paragraph (a).

(2) Leave under paragraph (a) of subsection (1) may be granted or refused at the discretion of the court, and if granted may be granted subject to such conditions as the court thinks proper with respect to the use of any recording made pursuant to the leave; and where leave has been granted the court may at the like discretion withdraw or amend it either generally or in relation to any particular part of the proceedings.

(3) Without prejudice to any other power to deal with an act of contempt under paragraph (a) of subsection (1), the court may order the instrument, or any recording made with it, or both, to be forfeited; and any object so forfeited shall (unless the court otherwise determines on application by a person appearing to be the owner) be sold or otherwise disposed of in such manner as the court may direct.

(4) This section does not apply to the making or use of sound recordings for purposes of official transcripts of proceedings.

10. Sources of information.

No court may require a person to disclose, nor is any person guilty of contempt of court for refusing to disclose, the source of information contained in a publication for which he is responsible, unless it be established to the satisfaction of the court that disclosure is necessary in the interests of justice or national security or for the prevention of disorder or crime.

11. Publication of matters exempted from disclosure in court.

In any case where a court (having power to do so) allows a name or other matter to be withheld from the public in proceedings before the court, the court may give such directions prohibiting the publication of that name or matter in connection with the proceedings as appear to the court to be necessary for the purpose for which it was so withheld.

12. Offences of contempt of magistrates' courts.

(1) A magistrates' court has jurisdiction under this section to deal with any person who—

    (a) wilfully insults the justice or justices, any witness before or officer of the court or any solicitor or counsel having business in the court, during his or their sitting or attendance in court or in going to or returning from the court; or

    (b) wilfully interrupts the proceedings of the court or otherwise misbehaves in court.

(2) In any such case the court may order any officer of the court, or any constable, to take the offender into custody and detain him until the rising of the court; and the court may, if it thinks fit, commit the offender to custody for a specified period not exceeding one month or impose on him a fine not exceeding [£1,000], or both.

(3) ... [Repealed Criminal Justice Act 1982.]

(4) A magistrates' court may at any time revoke an order of committal made under subsection (2) and, if the offender is in custody, order his discharge.

(5) The following provisions of the Magistrates' Courts Act 1980 apply in relation to an order under this section as they apply in relation to a sentence on conviction or finding of guilty of an offence, namely; section 36 (restriction on fines in respect of young persons); sections 75 to 91 (enforcement); section 108 (appeal to Crown Court); section 136 (overnight detention in default of payment); and section 142(1) (power to rectify mistakes).

13. ... [Repealed Legal Aid Act 1988.]

Penalties for contempt and kindred offences

14. Proceedings in England and Wales.

(1) In any case where a court has power to commit a person to prison for contempt of court and (apart from this provision) no limitation applies to the period of committal, the committal shall (without prejudice to the power of the court to order his earlier discharge) be for a fixed term, and that term shall not on any occasion exceed two years in the case of committal by a superior court, or one month in the case of committal by an inferior court.

(2) In any case where an inferior court has power to fine a person for contempt

of court and (apart from this provision) no limit applies to the amount of the fine, the fine shall not on any occasion exceed [£1,000].

[(2A) In the exercise of jurisdiction to commit for contempt of court or any kindred offence the court shall not deal with the offender by making an order under section 17 of the Criminal Justice Act 1982 (an attendance centre order) if it appears to the court after considering any available evidence, that he is under 17 years of age.]

(3) ... [Repealed Criminal Justice Act 1982.]

(4) Each of the superior courts shall have the like power to make a hospital order or guardianship order under [section 37 of the Mental Health Act 1983] or an order interim hospital order under [section 38 of that Act] in the case of a person suffering from mental illness or severe mental impairment who could otherwise be committed to prison for contempt of court as the Crown Court has under that section in the case of a person convicted of an offence.

[(4A) Each of the superior courts shall have the like power to make an order under [section 35 of the said Act of 1983] (remand for report on accused's mental condition) where there is reason to suspect that a person who could be committed to prison for contempt of court is suffering from mental illness or severe mental impairment as the Crown Court has under that section in the case of an accused person within the meaning of that section.]

[(4A)[1] For the purpose of the preceding provisions of this section a county court shall be treated as a superior court and not as an inferior court.]

(5) The enactments specified in Part III of Schedule 2 shall have effect subject to the amendments set out in that Part, being amendments relating to the penalties and procedure in respect of certain offences of contempt in coroners' courts, county courts and magistrates' courts.

Note
[1]Two subsections 4A erroneously inserted by Parliamentary draftsman.

15. *****

16. Enforcement of fines imposed by certain superior courts.

(1) Payment of a fine for contempt of court imposed by a superior court, other than the Crown Court or one of the courts specified in subsection (4) below, may be enforced upon the order of the court—

(a) in like manner as a judgment of the High Court for the payment of money; or

(b) in like manner as a fine imposed by the Crown Court.

(2) Where payment of a fine imposed by an court falls to be enforced as mentioned in paragraph (a) of subsection (1)—

(a) the court shall, if the fine is not paid in full forthwith or within such time as the court may allow, certify to Her Majesty's Remembrancer the sum payable;

(b) Her Majesty's Remembrancer shall thereupon proceed to enforce payment of that sum as if it were due to him as a judgment debt;

(c) ... [Repealed SCA 1981.]

(3) Where payment of a fine imposed by any court falls to be enforced as mentioned in paragraph (b) of subsection (1), the provisions of sections 31 and 32 of the Powers of Criminal Courts Act 1973 shall apply as they apply to a fine imposed by the Crown Court.

(4) Subsection (1) of this section does not apply to fines imposed by the criminal division of the Court of Appeal or by the House of Lords on appeal from that division.

(5) The Fines Act 1833 shall not apply to a fine to which subsection (1) of this section applies.

(6) ...

17. Disobedience to certain orders of magistrates' courts.

(1) The powers of a magistrates' court under subsection (3) of section 63 of the Magistrates' Courts Act 1980 (punishment of fine or committal for disobeying an order to do anything other than the payment of money or to abstain from doing anything) may be exercised either of the court's own motion or by order on complaint.

(2) In relation to the exercise of those powers the provisions of the Magistrates' Court Act 1980 shall apply subject to the modifications set out in Schedule 3 to this Act.

Supplemental

18. (Relates to Northern Ireland).

19. Interpretation.

In this Act—

["cable programme" means a programme included in a cable programme service;]
"court" includes any tribunal or body exercising the judicial power of the State, and "legal proceedings" shall be construed accordingly;
"publication" has the meaning assigned by subsection (1) of section 2, and "publish" (except in section 9) shall be construed accordingly;
"Scottish proceedings" means proceeding before any court, including the Courts-Martial Appeal Court, the Restrictive Practices Court and the Employment Appeal Tribunal, sitting in Scotland, and includes proceedings before the House of Lords in the exercise of any appellate jurisdiction over proceedings in such a court;
"the strict liability rule" has the meaning assigned by section 1;
"superior court" means the Court of Appeal, the High Court, the Crown Court, the Courts-Martial Appeal Court, the Restrictive Practices Court, the Employment Appeal Tribunal and any other court exercising in relation to its proceedings powers equivalent to those of the High Court, and includes the House of Lords in the exercise of its appellate jurisdiction.

20. Tribunals of Inquiry.

(1) In relation to any tribunal to which the Tribunals of Inquiry (Evidence) Act 1921 applies, and the proceedings of such a tribunal, the provisions of this Act (except subsection (3) of section 9) apply as they apply in relation to courts and legal proceedings; and references to the course of justice or the administration of justice in legal proceedings shall be construed accordingly.

(2) The proceedings of a tribunal established under the said Act shall be treated as active within the meaning of section 2 from the time when the tribunal is appointed until its report is presented to Parliament.

21. *****

SCHEDULE 1
TIMES WHEN PROCEEDINGS ARE ACTIVE FOR PURPOSES OF
SECTION 2

Preliminary

1. In this Schedule "criminal proceedings" means proceedings against a person in respect of an offence, not being appellate proceedings or proceedings commenced by motion for committal or attachment in England and Wales or Northern Ireland; and "appellate proceedings" means proceedings on appeal from or for the review of the decision of a court in any proceedings.

2. Criminal, appellate and other proceedings are active within the meaning of section 2 at the times respectively prescribed by the following paragraphs of this Schedule; and in relation to proceedings in which more than one of the steps described in any

Contempt of Court Act 1981

of those paragraphs is taken, the reference in that paragraph is a reference to the first of those steps.

Criminal proceedings

3. Subject to the following provisions of this Schedule, criminal proceedings are active from the relevant initial step specified in paragraph 4 until concluded as described in paragraph 5.

4. The initial steps of criminal proceedings are:—
    (a)   arrest without warrant;
    (b)   the issue, or in Scotland the grant, of a warrant for arrest;
    (c)   the issue of a summons to appear, or in Scotland the grant of a warrant to cite;
    (d)   the service of an indictment or other document specifying the charge;
    (e)   except in Scotland, oral charge.

5. Criminal proceedings are concluded—
    (a)   by acquittal or, as the case may be, by sentence;
    (b)   by any other verdict, finding, order or decision which puts an end to the proceedings;
    (c)   by discontinuance or by operation of law.

6. The reference in paragraph 5(a) to sentence includes any order or decision consequent on conviction of finding of guilt which disposes of the case, either absolutely or subject to future events, and a deferment of sentence under section 1 of the Powers of Criminal Courts Act 1973, section 219 or 432 of the Criminal Procedure (Scotland) Act 1975 or Article 14 of the Treatment of Offenders (Northern Ireland) Order 1976.

7. Proceedings are discontinued within the meaning of paragraph 5(c)—
    (a)   in England and Wales or Northern Ireland, if the charge or summons is withdrawn or a *nolle prosequi* entered;
    [(aa)   in England and Wales, if they are discontinued by virtue of section 23 of the Prosecution of Offences Act 1985;]
    (b)   in Scotland, if the proceedings are expressly abandoned by the prosecutor or are deserted *simpliciter*;
    (c)   in the case of proceedings in England and Wales or Northern Ireland commenced by arrest without warrant, if the person arrested is released, otherwise than on bail, without having been charged.

8. Criminal proceedings before a court-martial or standing civilian court are not concluded until the completion of any review of finding or sentence.

9. Criminal proceedings in England and Wales or Northern Ireland cease to be active if an order is made for the charge to lie on the file, but become active again if leave is later given for the proceedings to continue.

[9A. Where proceedings in England and Wales have been discontinued by virtue of section 23 of the Prosecution of Offences Act 1985, but notice is given by the accused under subsection (7) of that section to the effect that he wants the proceedings to continue, they become active again with the giving of that notice.]

10. Without prejudice to paragraph 5(b) above, criminal proceedings against a person cease to be active—
    (a)   if the accused is found to be under a disability such as to render him unfit to be tried or unfit to plead or, in Scotland, is found to be insane in bar of trial; or
    (b)   if a hospital order is made in his case under paragraph (b) of subsection (2) of section 51(5) of the Mental Health Act 1983 or [Article 57(5) of the Mental Health (Northern Ireland) Order 1986] or, in Scotland, where a transfer order ceased to have effect by virtue of section 73(1) of the Mental Health (Scotland) Act 1984,

but became active again if they are later resumed.

11. Criminal proceedings against a person which become active on the issue or the grant of a warrant for his arrest cease to be active at the end of the period of twelve months beginning with the date of the warrant unless he has been arrested within that period, but become active again if he is subsequently arrested.

Other proceedings at first instance

12. Proceedings other than criminal proceedings and appellate proceedings are active from the time when arrangements for the hearing are made or, if no such arrangements are previously made, from the time the hearing begins, until the proceedings are disposed of or discontinued or withdrawn; and for the purposes of this paragraph any motion or application made in or for the purposes of any proceedings, and any pre-trial review in the county court, is to be treated as a distinct proceeding.

13. In England and Wales or Northern Ireland arrangements for the hearing of proceedings to which paragraph 12 applies are made within the meaning of that paragraph—

    (a)   in the case of proceedings in the High Court for which provision is made by rules of court for setting down for trial, when the case is set down;

    (b)   in the case of any proceedings, when a date for the trial or hearing is fixed.

14. In Scotland arrangements for the hearing of proceedings to which paragraph 12 applies are made within the meaning of that paragraph—

    (a)   in the case of an ordinary action in the Court of Session or in the sheriff court, when the Record is closed;

    (b)   in the case of a motion or application, when it is enrolled or made;

    (c)   in any other case, when the date for a hearing is fixed or a hearing is allowed.

Appellate proceedings

15. Appellate proceedings are active from the time when they are commenced—

    (a)   by application for leave to appeal or apply for review, or by notice of such an application;

    (b)   by notice of appeal or of application for review;

    (c)   by other originating process,

until disposed of or abandoned, discontinued or withdrawn.

16. Where, in appellate proceedings relating to criminal proceedings, the court—

    (a)   remits the case to the court below; or

    (b)   orders a new trial or a *venire de novo*, or in Scotland grants authority to bring a new prosecution,

any further or new proceedings which result shall be treated as active from the conclusion of the appellate proceedings.

*****

SUPREME COURT ACT 1981
(1981, c. 54)

An Act to consolidate with amendments the Supreme Court of Judicature (Consolidation) Act 1925 and other enactments relating to the Supreme Court in England and Wales and the administration of justice therein; to repeal certain obsolete or unnecessary enactments so relating; to amend Part VIII of the Mental Health Act 1959, the Courts-Martial (Appeals) Act 1968, the Arbitration Act 1979 and the law relating to county courts; and for connection purposes. [28 July 1978]

PART I
CONSTITUTION OF SUPREME COURT

The Supreme Court

1. The Supreme Court

(1) The Supreme Court of England and Wales shall consist of the Court of Appeal, the High Court of Justice and the Crown Court, each having such jurisdiction as is conferred on it by or under this or any other Act.

(2) The Lord Chancellor shall be president of the Supreme Court.

2. The Court of Appeal

(1) The Court of Appeal shall consist of ex-officio judges and not more than [twenty eight] ordinary judges.

(2) The following shall be ex-officio judges of the Court of Appeal—
    (a) the Lord Chancellor;
    (b) any person who has been Lord Chancellor;
    (c) any Lord of Appeal in Ordinary who at the date of his appointment was, or was qualified for appointment as, an ordinary judge of the Court of Appeal or held an office within paragraphs (d) to (g);
    (d) the Lord Chief Justice;
    (e) the Master of the Rolls;
    (f) the President of the Family Division; and
    (g) the Vice-Chancellor;
but a person within paragraph (b) or (c) shall not be required to sit and act as a judge of the Court of Appeal unless at the Lord Chancellor's request he consents to do so.

(3) The ordinary judges of the Court of Appeal (including the vice-president, if any, of either division) shall be styled "Lords Justices of Appeal".

(4) Her Majesty may by Order in Council from time to time amend subsection (1) so as to increase or further increase the maximum number of ordinary judges of the Court of Appeal.

(5) No recommendations shall be made to Her Majesty in Council to make an Order under subsection (4) unless a draft of the Order has been laid before Parliament and approved by resolution of each House of Parliament.

(6) The Court of Appeal shall be taken to be duly constituted notwithstanding any vacancy in the office of Lord Chancellor, Lord Chief Justice, Master of the Rolls, President of the Family Division or Vice-Chancellor.

3. Divisions of Court of Appeal

(1) There shall be two divisions of the Court of Appeal, namely the criminal division and the civil division.

(2) The Lord Chief Justice shall be president of the criminal division of the Court of Appeal, and the Master of the Rolls shall be president of the civil division of that court.

(3) The Lord Chancellor may appoint one of the ordinary judges of the Court of Appeal as vice-president of both divisions of that court, or one of those judges as vice-president of the criminal division and another of them as vice-president of the civil division.

(4) When sitting in a court of either division of the Court of Appeal in which no ex-officio judge of the Court of Appeal is sitting, the vice-president (if any) of that division shall preside.

(5) Any number of courts of either division of the Court of Appeal may sit at the same time.

The High Court

4. High Court

(1) The High Court shall consist of—
    (a)   the Lord Chancellor;
    (b)   the Lord Chief Justice;
    (c)   the President of the Family Division;
    (d)   the Vice-Chancellor; and
    (e)   not more than [eighty five] puisne judges of that court.

(2) The puisne judges of the High Court shall be styled "Justices of the High Court".

(3) All the judges of the High Court shall, except where this Act expressly provides otherwise, have in all respects equal power, authority and jurisdiction.

(4) Her Majesty may by Order in Council from time to time amend subsection (1) so as to increase or further increase the maximum number of puisne judges of the High Court.

(5) No recommendation shall be made to Her Majesty in Council to make an Order under subsection (4) unless a draft of the Order has been laid before Parliament and approved by resolution of each House of Parliament.

(6) The High Court shall be taken to be duly constituted notwithstanding any vacancy in the office of Lord Chancellor, Lord Chief Justice, President of the Family Division or Vice-Chancellor.

5. Divisions of High Court

(1) There shall be three divisions of the High Court namely—
    (a)   the Chancery Division, consisting of the Lord Chancellor, who shall be president thereof, the Vice-Chancellor, who shall be vice-president thereof, and such of the puisne judges as are for the time being attached thererto in accordance with this section;
    (b)   the Queen's Bench Division, consisting of the Lord Chief Justice, who shall be president thereof, and such of the puisne judges as are for the time being so attached thereto; and
    (c)   the Family Division, consisting of the President of the Family Division and such of the puisne judges as are for the time being so attached thereto.

(2) The puisne judges of the High Court shall be attached to the various Divisions by direction of the Lord Chancellor; and any such judge may with his consent be transferred from one Division to another by direction of the Lord Chancellor, but shall be so transferred only with the concurrence of the senior judge of the Division from which it is proposed to transfer him.

(3) Any judge attached to any Division may act as an additional judge of any other Division at the request of the Lord Chancellor made with the concurrence of the senior judge of each of those Divisions.

(4) Nothing in this section shall be taken to prevent a judge of any Division (whether nominated under section 6(2) or not) from sitting, whenever required, in a divisional court of another Division or for any judge of another Division.

(5) Without prejudice to the provisions of this Act relating to the distribution of business in the High Court, all jurisdiction vested in the High Court under this Act shall belong to all the Divisions alike.

6. The Patents, Admiralty and Commercial Courts

(1) There shall be—
    (a)   as part of the Chancery Division, a Patents Court; and

(b) as parts of the Queen's Bench Division, an Admiralty Court and a Commercial Court.

(2) The judges of the Patents Court, of the Admiralty Court and of the Commercial Court shall be such of the puisne judges of the High Court as the Lord Chancellor may from time to time nominate to be judges of the Patents Court, Admiralty Judges and Commercial Judges respectively.

7. Power to alter Divisions or transfer certain courts to different Divisions

(1) Her Majesty may from time to time, on a recommendation of the judges mentioned in subsection (2), by Order in Council direct that—

(a) any increase or reduction in the number of Divisions of the High Court; or

(b) the transfer of any of the courts mentioned in section 6(1) to a different Division,

be carried into effect in pursuance of the recommendation.

(2) Those judges are the Lord Chancellor, the Lord Chief Justice, the Master of the Rolls, the President of the Family Division and the Vice-Chancellor.

(3) An Order in Council under this section may include such incidental, supplementary or consequential provisions as appear to Her Majesty necessary or expedient, including amendments of provisions referring to particular Divisions contained in this Act or any other statutory provision.

(4) Any Order in Council under this section shall be subject to annulment in pursuance of a resolution of either House of Parliament.

The Crown Court

8. The Crown Court

(1) The jurisdiction of the Crown Court shall be exercisable by—

(a) any judge of the High Court; or

(b) any Circuit judge or Recorder; or

(c) subject to and in accordance with the provisions of sections 74 and 75(2), a judge of the High Court, Circuit judge or Recorder sitting with not more than four justices of the peace,

and any such persons when exercising the jurisdiction of the Crown Court shall be judges of the Crown Court.

(2) A justice of the peace shall not be disqualified from acting as a judge of the Crown Court for the reason that the proceedings are not at a place within the area for which he was appointed as a justice, or because the proceedings are not related to that area in any other way.

(3) When the Crown Court sits in the City of London it shall be known as the Central Criminal Court; and the Lord Mayor of the City and any Alderman of the City shall be entitled to sit as judges of the Central Criminal Court with any judge of the High Court or any Circuit judge or Recorder.

Other provisions

9. Assistance for transaction of judicial business of Supreme Court

(1) A person within any entry in column 1 of the following Table may at any time, at the request of the appropriate authority, act—

(a) as a judge of a relevant court specified in the request; or

(b) if the request relates to a particular division of a relevant court so specified, as a judge of that court in that division.

TABLE

1 *Judge or ex-judge*	2 *Where competent to act on request*
1. A judge of the Court of Appeal.	The High Court and the Crown Court.
2. A person who has been a judge of the Court of Appeal.	The Court of Appeal, the High Court and the Crown Court
3. A puisne judge of the High Court.	The Court of Appeal.
4. A person who has been a puisne judge of the High Court.	The Court of Appeal, the High Court and the Crown Court.
5. A Circuit judge.	The High Court.
[6. A Recorder.	The High Court,]

(2) In subsection (1)—
"the appropriate authority"—
    (a)   in the case of a request to a judge of the High Court to act in the criminal division of the Court of Appeal as a judge of that court, means the Lord Chief Justice or, at any time when the Lord Chief Justice is unable to make such a request himself or there is a vacancy in the office of Lord Chief Justice, the Mater of the Rolls;
    (b)   in any other case means the Lord Chancellor;
"relevant court", in the case of a person within any entry in column 1 of the Table, means a court specified in relation to that entry in column 2 of the Table.

(3) In the case of—
    (a)   a request under subsection (1) to a Lord Justice of Appeal to act in the High Court; or
    (b)   any request under that subsection to a puisne judge of the High Court or a Circuit judge,
it shall be the duty of the person to whom the request is made to comply with it.

(4) Without prejudice to section 24 of the Courts Act 1971 (temporary appointment of deputy Circuit judges and assistant Recorders), if it appears to the Lord Chancellor that it is expedient as a temporary measure to make an appointment under this subsection in order to facilitate the disposal of business in the High Court or the Crown Court, he may appoint a person qualified for appointment as a puisne judge of the High Court to be a deputy judge of the High Court during such period or on such occasions as the Lord Chancellor thinks fit; and during the period or on the occasions for which a person is appointed as a deputy judge under this subsection, he may act as a puisne judge of the High Court.

(5) Every person while acting under this section shall, subject to subsection (6), be treated for all purposes as, and accordingly may perform any of the functions of, a judge of the court in which he is acting.

(6) A person shall not by virtue of subsection (5)—
    (a)   be treated as a judge of the court in which he is acting for the purposes of section 98(2) or of any statutory provision relating to—
        (i)   the appointment, retirement, removal or disqualification of judges of that court;
        (ii)   the tenure of office and oaths to be taken by such judges; or
        (iii)   the remuneration, allowances or pensions of such judges; or
    (b)   subject to subsection (7), be treated as having been a judge of a court in which he has acted only under this section.

(7) Notwithstanding the expiry of any period for which a person is authorised by virtue of subsection (1) or (4) to act as a judge of a particular court—
    (a)   he may attend at that court for the purpose of continuing to deal with, giving judgment in, or dealing with any ancillary matter relating to, any case begun before him while acting as a judge of that court; and

Supreme Court Act 1981

    (b)   for that purpose, and for the purpose of any proceedings arising out of any such case or matter, he shall be treated as being or, as the case may be, having been a judge of that court.

    (8) Such remuneration and allowances as the Lord Chancellor may, with the concurrence of the Minister for the Civil Service, determine may be paid out of money provided by Parliament—
- (a)   to any person who has been—
  - (i)   a Lord of Appeal in Ordinary; or
  - (ii)   a judge of the Court of Appeal; or
  - (iii)   a judge of the High Court,

and is by virtue of subsection (1) acting as mentioned in that subsection;
- (b)   to any deputy judge of the High Court appointed under subsection (4).

10. Appointment of judges of Supreme Court

    (1) Whenever the office of Lord Chief Justice, Master of the Rolls, President of the Family Division or Vice-Chancellor is vacant, Her Majesty may by letters patent appoint a qualified person to that office;

    (2) Subject to the limits on numbers for the time being imposed by sections 2(1) and 4(1), Her Majesty may from time to time by letters patent appoint qualified persons as Lords Justices of Appeal or as puisne judges of the High Court.

    (3) No person shall be qualified for appointment—
- (a)   as Lord Chief Justice, Master of the Rolls, President of the Family Division or Vice-Chancellor, unless he is qualified for appointment as a Lord Justice of Appeal or is a judge of the Court of Appeal;
- (b)   as a Lord Justice of Appeal, unless he is a barrister of at least fifteen years' standing or a judge of the High Court; or
- (c)   as a puisne judge of the High Court, unless he is a barrister of at least ten years' standing.

    (4) Every person appointed to an office mentioned in subsection (1) or as a Lord Justice of Appeal or puisne judge of the High Court shall, as soon as may be after his acceptance of office, take the oath of allegiance and the judicial oath, as set out in the Promissory Oaths Act 1868, in the presence of the Lord Chancellor.

11. Tenure of office of judges of Supreme Court

    (1) This section applies to the office of any judge of the Supreme Court except the Lord Chancellor.

    (2) A person appointed to an office to which this section applies shall vacate it on the day on which he attains the age of seventy-five years unless by virtue of this section he has ceased to hold it before then.

    (3) A person appointed to an office to which this section applies shall hold that office during good behaviour, subject to a power of removal by Her Majesty on an address presented to Her by both Houses of Parliament.

    (4) A person holding an office within section 2(2)(d) to (g) shall vacate that office on becoming Lord Chancellor or a Lord of Appeal in Ordinary.

    (5) A Lord Justice of Appeal shall vacate that office on becoming an ex-officio judge of the Court of Appeal.

    (6) A puisne judge of the High Court shall vacate that office on becoming a judge of the Court of Appeal.

    (7) A person who holds an office to which this section applies may at any time resign it by giving the Lord Chancellor notice in writing to that effect.

    (8) The Lord Chancellor, if satisfied by means of a medical certificate that a person holding an office to which this section applies—
- (a)   is disabled by permanent infirmity from the performance of the duties of his office; and
- (b)   is for the time being incapacitated from resigning his office,

may, subject to subsection (9), by instrument under his hand declare that person's office to have been vacated; and the instrument shall have the like effect for all purposes as if that person had on the date of the instrument resigned his office.

(9) A declaration under subsection (8) with respect to a person shall be of no effect unless it is made—

(a) in the case of any of the Lord Chief Justice, the Master of the Rolls, the President of the Family Division and the Vice-Chancellor, with the concurrence of two others of them;

(b) in the case of a Lord Justice of Appeal, with the concurrence of the Master of the Rolls;

(c) in the case of a puisne judge of any Division of the High Court, with the concurrence of the senior judge of that Division.

(10) Subsection (2) shall not apply to a person who held an office to which this section applies on 17th December 1959 and did not elect under section 3 of the Judicial Pensions Act 1959 that the corresponding provision in that Act should apply to him.

12. Salaries etc. of judges of Supreme Court

(1) Subject to subsections (2) and (3), there shall be paid to judges of the Supreme Court, other than the Lord Chancellor, such salaries as may be determined by the Lord Chancellor with the concurrence of the Minister for the Civil Service,

(2)—(4) *****

(5) Salaries payable under this section shall be charged on and paid out of the Consolidated Fund.

(6) *****

(7) Pensions shall be payable to or in respect of the judges mentioned in subsection (1) in accordance with section 2 of the Judicial Pensions Act 1981.

13., 14. *****

PART II
JURISDICTION
THE COURT OF APPEAL

15. General jurisdiction of Court of Appeal

(1) The Court of Appeal shall be a superior court of record.

(2) Subject to the provisions of this Act, there shall be exercisable by the Court of Appeal—

(a) all such jurisdiction (whether civil or criminal) as is conferred on it by this or any other Act; and

(b) all such other jurisdiction (whether civil or criminal) as was exercisable by it immediately before the commencement of this Act.

(3) For all purposes of or incidental to—

(a) the hearing and determination of any appeal to the civil division of the Court of Appeal; and

(b) the amendment, execution and enforcement of any judgment or order made on such an appeal,

the Court of Appeal shall have all the authority and jurisdiction of the court or tribunal from which the appeal was brought.

(4) It is hereby declared that any provision in this or any other Act which authorises or requires the taking of any steps for the execution or enforcement of a judgment or order of the High Court applies in relation to a judgment or order of the civil division of the Court of Appeal as it applies in relation to a judgment or order of the High Court.

16. Appeals from High Court

(1) Subject as otherwise provided by this or any other Act (and in particular to the provision in section 13(2)(a) of the Administration of Justice Act 1969 excluding appeals to the Court of Appeal in cases where leave to appeal from the High Court directly to the House of Lords is granted under Part II of that Act), the Court of Appeal shall have jurisdiction to hear and determine appeals from any judgment or order of the High Court.

(2) An appeal from a judgment or order of the High Court when acting as a prize court shall not be to the Court of Appeal, but shall be to Her Majesty in Council in accordance with the Prize Acts 1864 to 1944.

17. Applications for new trial

(1) Where any cause or matter, or any issue in any cause or matter, has been tried in the High Court, any application for a new trial thereof, or to set aside a verdict, finding or judgment therein, shall be heard and determined by the Court of Appeal except where rules of court made in pursuance of subsection (2) provide otherwise.

(2) As regards cases where the trial was by a judge alone and no error of the court at the trial is alleged, or any prescribed class of such cases, rules of court may provide that any such application as is mentioned in subsection (1) shall be heard and determined by the High Court.

(3) Nothing in this section shall alter the practice in bankruptcy.

18. Restrictions on appeals to Court of Appeal

(1) No appeal shall lie to the Court Appeal—

    (a) except as provided by the Administration of Justice Act 1960, from any judgment of the High Court in any criminal cause or matter;

    (b) from any order of the High Court or any other court or tribunal allowing an extension of time for appealing from a judgment or order;

    (c) from any order, judgment or decision of the High Court or any other court or tribunal which, by virtue of any provision (however expressed) of this or any other Act, is final;

    (d) from a decree absolute of divorce or nullity of marriage, by a party who, having had time and opportunity to appeal from the decree nisi on which that decree was founded, has not appealed from the decree nisi;

    (e) without the leave of the divisional court in question or of the Court of Appeal, from the determination by a divisional court of any appeal to the High Court;

    (f) without the leave of the court or tribunal in question, from any order of the High Court or any other court or tribunal made with the consent of the parties or relating only to costs which are by law left to the discretion of the court or tribunal;

    (g) except as provided by the Arbitration Act 1979, from any decision of the High Court—

        (i) on an appeal under section 1 of that Act on a question of law arising out of an arbitration award; or

        (ii) under section 2 of that Act on a question of law arising in the course of a reference;

    (h) without the leave of the court or tribunal in question or of the Court of Appeal, from any interlocutory order or interlocutory judgment made or given by the High Court or any other court or tribunal, except in the following cases, namely—

        (i) where the liberty of the subject or the custody, education or welfare of a minor is concerned;

        (ii) where an applicant for access to a minor is refused all access to the minor;

        (iii) where an injunction or the appointment of a receiver is granted or refused;

(iv) in the case of a decision determining the claim of any creditor, or the liability of any contributory or of any director or other officer, under the law relating to companies;

(v) in the case of a decree nisi in a matrimonial cause, or a judgment or order in an admiralty action determining liability;

(vi) in such case as may be described.

(2) For the purposes of subsection (1)(h)—

(a) an order refusing unconditional leave to defend an action shall not be treated as an interlocutory order; and

(b) "education" includes training and religious instruction.

THE HIGH COURT
General jurisdiction

19. General jurisdiction

(1) The High Court shall be a superior court of record.

(2) Subject to the provisions of this Act, there shall be exercisable by the High Court—

(a) all such jurisdiction (whether civil or criminal) as is conferred on it by this or any other Act; and

(b) all such other jurisdiction (whether civil or criminal) as was exercisable by it immediately before the commencement of this Act (including jurisdiction conferred on a judge of the High Court by any statutory provision).

(3) Any jurisdiction of the High Court shall be exercised only by a single judge of that court, except in so far as it is—

(a) by or by virtue of rules of court or any other statutory provision required to be exercised by a divisional court; or

(b) by rules of court made exercisable by a master, registrar or other officer of the court, or by any other person.

(4) The specific mention elsewhere in this Act of any jurisdiction covered by subsection (2) shall not derogate from the generality of that subsection.

20.—24. *****

Other particular fields of jurisdiction

25. Probate jurisdiction of High Court

(1) Subject to the provisions of Part V, the High Court shall, in accordance with section 19(2), have the following probate jurisdiction, that is to say all such jurisdiction in relation to probates and letters of administration as it had immediately before the commencement of this Act, and in particular all such contentious and non-contentious jurisdiction as it then had in relation to—

(a) testamentary causes or matters;

(b) the grant, amendment or revocation of probates and letters of administration; and

(c) the real and personal estate of deceased persons.

(2) Subject to the provisions of Part V, the High Court shall, in the exercise of its probate jurisdiction, perform all such duties with respect to the estates of deceased persons as fell to be performed by it immediately before the commencement of this Act.

26. Matrimonial jurisdiction of High Court

The High Court shall, in accordance with section 19(2), have all such jurisdiction in relation to matrimonial causes and matters as was immediately before the commencement of the Matrimonial Causes Act 1857 vested in or exercisable by any ecclesiastical court or person in England or Wales in respect of—

(a) divorce a mensa et thoro (renamed judicial separation by that Act);
(b) nullity of marriage . . .; and
(c) any matrimonial cause or matter except marriage licences.

27. *****

28. Appeals from Crown Court and inferior courts
(1) Subject to subsection (2), any order, judgment or other decision of the Crown Court may be questioned by any party to the proceedings, on the ground that it is wrong in law or is in excess of jurisdiction, by applying to the Crown Court to have a case stated by that court for the opinion of the High Court.

(2) Subsection (1) shall not apply to—
 (a) a judgment or other decision of the Crown Court relating to trial on indictment; or
 (b) any decision of that court under the Betting, Gaming and Lotteries Act 1963, the Licensing Act 1964 [the Gaming Act 1968 or the Local Government (Miscellaneous Provisions) Act 1982] which, by any provision of any of those Acts, is to be final.

(3) Subject to the provisions of this Act and to rules of court, the High Court shall, in accordance with section 19(2), have jurisdiction to hear and determine—
 (a) any application, or any appeal (whether by way of case stated or otherwise), which it has power to hear and determine under or by virtue of this or any other Act; and
 (b) all such other appeals as it had jurisdiction to hear and determine immediately before the commencement of this Act.

29. Orders of mandamus, prohibition and certiorari
(1) The High Court shall have jurisdiction to make orders of mandamus, prohibition and certiorari in those classes of cases in which it had power to do so immediately before the commencement of this Act.

(2) Every such order shall be final, subject to any right of appeal therefrom.

(3) In relation to the jurisdiction of the Crown Court, other than its jurisdiction in matters relating to trial on indictment, the High Court shall have all such jurisdiction to make orders of mandamus, prohibition or certiorari as the High Court possesses in relation to the jurisdiction of an inferior court.

(4) The power of the High Court under any enactment to require justices of the peace or a judge or officer of a county court to do any act relating to the duties of their respective offices, or to require a magistrates' court to state a case for the opinion of the High Court, in any case where the High Court formerly had by virtue of any enactment jurisdiction to make a rule absolute, or an order, for any of those purposes, shall be exercisable by order of mandamus.

(5) In any enactment—
 (a) references to a writ of mandamus, of prohibition or of certiorari shall be read as references to the corresponding order; and
 (b) references to the issue or award of any such writ shall be read as references to the making of the corresponding order.

30. Injunctions to restrain persons from acting in offices in which they are not entitled to act
(1) Where a person not entitled to do so acts in an office to which this section applies, the High Court may—
 (a) grant an injunction restraining him from so acting; and
 (b) if the case so requires, declare the office to be vacant,

(2) This section applies to any substantive office of a public nature and permanent

character which is held under the Crown or which has been created by any statutory provision or royal charter.

31. Application for judicial review

(1) An application to the High Court for one or more of the following forms of relief, namely—

    (a)   an order of mandamus, prohibition or certiorari;

    (b)   a declaration or injunction under subsection (2); or

    (c)   an injunction under section 30 restraining a person not entitled to do so from acting in an office to which that section applies,

shall be made in accordance with rules of court by a procedure to be known as an application for judicial review.

(2) A declaration may be made or an injunction granted under this subsection in any case where an application for judicial review, seeking that relief, has been made and the High Court considers that, having regard to—

    (a)   the nature of the matters in respect of which relief may be granted by orders of mandamus, prohibition or certiorari;

    (b)   the nature of the persons and bodies against whom relief may be granted by such orders; and

    (c)   all the circumstances of the case,

it would be just and convenient for the declaration to be made or of the injunction to be granted, as the case may be.

(3) No application for judicial review shall be made unless the leave of the High Court has been obtained in accordance with rules of court; and the court shall not grant leave to make such an application unless it considers that the applicant has a sufficient interest in the matter to which the application relates.

(4) On an application for judicial review the High Court may award damages to the applicant if—

    (a)   he has joined with his application a claim for damages arising rom any matter to which the application relates; and

    (b)   the court is satisfied that, if the claim had been made in an action begun by the applicant at the time of making his application, he would have been awarded damages.

(5) If, on an application for judicial review seeking an order of certiorari, the High Court quashes the decision to which the application relates, the High Court may remit the matter to the court, tribunal or authority concerned, with a direction to reconsider it and reach a decision in accordance with the findings of the High Court.

(6) Where the High court considers that there has been undue delay in making an application for judicial review, the court may refuse to grant—

    (a)   leave for the making of the application; or

    (b)   any relief sought on the application,

if it considers that the granting of the relief sought would be likely to cause substantial hardship to, or substantially prejudice the rights of, any person or would be detrimental to good administration.

(7) Subsection (6) is without prejudice to any enactment or rule of court which has the effect of limiting the time within which an application for judicial review may be made.

Powers

32. Orders for interim payment

(1) As regards proceedings pending in the High Court, provision may be made by rules of court for enabling the court, in such circumstances as may be prescribed, to make an order requiring a party to the proceedings to make an interim payment

of such amount as may be specified in the order, with provision for the payment to be made to such other party to the proceedings as may be so specified or, if the order so provides, by paying it into court.

(2) Any rules of court which make provision in accordance with subsection (1) may include provision for enabling a party to any proceedings who, in pursuance of such an order, has made an interim payment to recover the whole or part of the amount of the payment in such circumstances, and from such other party to the proceedings, as may be determined in accordance with the rules.

(3) Any rules made by virtue of this section may include such incidental, supplementary and consequential provisions as the rule-making authority may consider necessary or expedient.

(4) Nothing in this section shall be construed as affecting the exercise of any power relating to costs, including any power to make rules of court relating to costs.

(5) In this section "interim payment", in relation to a party to any proceedings, means a payment on account of any damages, debt or other sum (excluding any costs) which that party may be held liable to pay to or for the benefit of another party to the proceedings if a final judgment or order of the court in the proceedings is given or made in favour of that other party.

[32A. **Orders for provisional damage for personal injuries**

(1) This section applies to an action for damages for personal injuries in which there is proved or admitted to be a chance that at some definite or indefinite time in the future the injured person will, as a result of the act or omission which gave rise to the cause of action, develop some serious disease or suffer some serious deterioration in his physical or mental condition.

(2) Subject to subsection (4) below, as regards any action for damages to which this section applies in which a judgment is given in the High Court, provision may be made by rules of court for enabling the court, in such circumstances as may be prescribed, to award the injured person—

(a) damages assessed n the assumption that the injured person will not develop the disease or suffer the deterioration in his condition; and

(b) further damages at a future date if he develops the disease or suffers the deterioration.

(3) Any rules made by virtue of this section may include such incidental, supplementary and consequential provisions as the rule-making authority may consider necessary or expedient.

(4) Nothing in this section shall be construed—

(a) as affecting the exercise of any power relating to costs, including any power to make rules of court relating to costs; or

(b) as prejudicing any duty of the court under any enactment or rule of law to reduce or limit the total damages which would have been recoverable apart from any such duty.]

33. **Powers of High Court exercisable before commencement of action**

(1) On the application of any person in accordance with rules of court, the High Court shall, in such circumstances as may be specified in the rules, have power to make an order providing for any one or more of the following matters, that is to say—

(a) the inspection, photographing, preservation, custody and detention of property which appears to the court to be property which may become the subject-matter of subsequent proceedings in the High court, or as to which any question may arise in any such proceedings; and

(b) the taking of samples of any such property as is mentioned in paragraph (a), and the carrying out of any experiment on or with any such property.

(2) On the application, in accordance with rules of court, of a person who appears

to the High court to be likely to be a party to subsequent proceedings in that court in which a claim in respect of personal injuries to a person, or in respect of a person's death, is likely to be made, the High Court shall, in such circumstances as may be specified in the rules, have power to order a person who appears to the court to be likely to be a party to the proceedings and to be likely to have or have had in his possession, custody or power any documents which are relevant to an issue arising or likely to arise out of that claim—

    (a)   to disclose whether those documents are in his possession, custody or power; and

    (b)   to produce such of those documents as are in his possession, custody or power to the applicant or, on such conditions as may be specified in the order—

        (i)   to the applicant's legal advisers; or

        (ii)   to the applicant's legal advisers and any medical or other professional adviser of the applicant; or

        (iii)   if the applicant has no legal adviser, to any medical or other professional adviser of the applicant.

34. Power of High Court to order disclosure of documents, inspection of property etc in proceedings for personal injuries or death

(1) This section applies to any proceedings in the High Court in which a claim is made in respect of personal injuries to a person, or in respect of a person's death.

(2) On the application, in accordance with rules of court, of a party to any proceedings to which this section applies, the High Court shall, in such circumstances as may be specified in the rules, have power to order a person who is not a party to the proceedings and who appears to the court to be likely to have in his possession, custody or power any documents which are relevant to an issue arising out of the said claim—

    (a)   to disclose whether those documents are in his possession, custody or power; and

    (b)   to produce such of those documents, as are in his possession, custody or power to the applicant or, on such conditions as may be specified in the order—

        (i)   to the applicant's legal advisers; or

        (ii)   to the applicant's legal advisers and any medical or other professional adviser of the applicant; or

        (iii)   if the applicant has no legal adviser, to any medical or other professional adviser of the applicant.

(3) On the application, in accordance with rules of court, of a party to any proceedings to which this section applies, the High Court shall, in such circumstances as may be specified in the rules, have power to make an order providing for any one or more of the following matters, that is to say—

    (a)   the inspection, photographing, preservation, custody and detention of property which is not the property of, or in the possession of, any party to the proceedings but which is the subject-matter of the proceedings or as to which any question arises in the proceedings;

    (b)   the taking of samples of any such property as is mentioned in paragraph (a) and the carrying out of any experiment on or with any such property.

(4) The preceding provisions of this section are without prejudice to the exercise by the High Court of any power to make orders which is exercisable apart from those provisions.

35. Provisions supplementary to ss 33 and 34

(1) The High Court shall not make an order under section 33 or 34 if it considers that compliance with the order, if made, would be likely to be injurious to the public interest.

(2) Rules of court may make provision as to the circumstances in which an order

under section 33 or 34 can be made; and any rules making such provision may include such incidental, supplementary and consequential provisions as the rulemaking authority may consider necessary or expedient.

(3) Without prejudice to the generality of subsection (2), rules of court shall be made for the purpose of ensuring that the costs of and incidental to proceedings for an order under section 33(2) or 34 incurred by the person against whom the order is sought shall be awarded to that person unless the court otherwise directs.

(4) Sections 33(2) and 34 and this section bind the Crown; and section 33(1) binds the Crown so far as it relates to property as to which it appears to the court that it may become the subject-matter of subsequent proceedings involving a claim in respect of personal injuries to a person or in respect of a person's death.

In this subsection references to the Crown do not include references to Her Majesty in Her private capacity or to Her Majesty in right of Her Duchy of Lancaster or to the Duke of Cornwall.

(5) In sections [32A], 33 and 34 and this section—

"property" includes any land, chattel or other corporeal property of any description;

"personal injuries" includes any disease and any impairment of a person's physical or mental condition.

[**35A. Power of High Court to award interest on debts and damages**

(1) Subject to rules of court, in proceedings (whenever instituted) before the High Court for the recovery of a debt or damages there may be included in any sum for which judgment is given simple interest, at such rate as the court thinks fit or as rules of court may provide, on all or any part of the debt or damages in respect of which judgment is given, or payment is made before judgment, for all or any part of the period between the date when the cause of action arose and—

    (a) in the case of any sum paid before judgment, the date of the payment; and

    (b) in the case of the sum for which judgment is given, the date of the judgment.

(2) In relation to a judgment given for damages for personal injuries or death which exceed £200 subsection (1) shall have effect—

    (a) with the substitution of "shall be included" for "may be included"; and

    (b) with the addition of "unless the court is satisfied that there are special reasons to the contrary" after "given", where first occurring.

(3) Subject to rules of court, where—

    (a) there are proceedings (whenever instituted) before the High Court for the recovery of a debt; and

    (b) the defendant pays the whole debt to the plaintiff (otherwise than in pursuance of a judgment in the proceedings),

the defendant shall be liable to pay the plaintiff simple interest at such rate as the court thinks fit or as rules of court may provide on all or any part of the debt for all or any part of the period between the date when the cause of action arose and the date of the payment.

(4) Interest in respect of a debt shall not be awarded under this section for a period during which, for whatever reason, interest on the debt already runs.

(5) Without prejudice to the generality of section 84, rules of court may provide for a rate of interest by reference to the rate specified in section 17 of the Judgments Act 1838 as that section has effect from time to time or by reference to a rate for which any other enactment provides.

(6) Interest under this section may be calculated at different rates in respect of different periods.

(7) In this section "plaintiff" means the person seeking the debt or damages and "defendant" means the person from whom the plaintiff seeks the debt or damages

and "personal injuries" includes any disease and any impairment of a person's physical or mental condition.

(8) Nothing in this section affects the damages recoverable for the dishonour of a bill of exchange.]

36. Subpoena issued by High Court to run throughout United Kingdom

(1) If in any cause or matter in the High court it appears to the court that it is proper to compel the personal attendance at any trial of a witness who may not be within the jurisdiction of the court, it shall be lawful for the court, if in the discretion of the court it seems fit so to do, to order that a writ of subpoena ad testificandum or writ of subpoena duces tecum shall issue in special form commanding the witness to attend the trial wherever he shall be within the United Kingdom; and the service of any such writ in any part of the United Kingdom shall be as valid and effectual for all purposes as if it had been served within the jurisdiction of the High Court.

(2) Every such writ shall have at its foot a statement to the effect that it is issued by the special order of the High Court, and no such writ shall issue without such a special order.

(3) If any person served with a writ issued under this section does not appear as required by the writ, the High Court, on proof to the satisfaction of the court of the service of the writ and of the default, may transmit a certificate of the default under the seal of the court or under the hand of a judge of the court—

    (a)   if the service was in Scotland, to the Court of Session at Edinburgh; or

    (b)   if the service was in Northern Ireland, to the High Court of Justice in Northern Ireland at Belfast;

and the court to which the certificate is sent shall thereupon proceed against and punish the person in default in like manner as if that person had neglected or refused to appear in obedience to process issued out of that court.

(4) No court shall in any case proceed against or punish any person for having made such default as aforesaid unless it is shown to the court that a reasonable and sufficient sum of money to defray the expenses of coming and attending to give evidence and of returning from giving evidence was tendered to that person at the time when the writ was served upon him.

(5) Nothing in this section shall affect—

    (a)   the power of the High Court to issue a commission for the examination of witnesses out of the jurisdiction of the court in any case in which, notwithstanding this section, the court thinks fit to issue such a commission; or

    (b)   the admissibility at any trial of any evidence which, if this section had not been enacted, would have been admissible on the ground of a witness being outside the jurisdiction of the court.

(6) In this section references to attendance at a trial include references to attendance before an examiner or commissioner appointed by the High Court in any cause or matter in that court, including an examiner or commissioner appointed to take evidence outside the jurisdiction of the court.

37. Powers of High Court with respect to injunctions and receivers

(1) The High Court may by order (whether interlocutory or final) grant an injunction or appoint a receiver in all cases in which it appears to the court to be just and convenient to do so.

(2) Any such order may be made either unconditionally or on such terms and conditions as the court thinks just.

(3) The power of the High Court under subsection (1) to grant an interlocutory injunction restraining a party to any proceedings from removing from the jurisdiction of the High Court, or otherwise dealing with, assets located within that jurisdiction

shall be exercisable in cases where that party is, as well as in cases where he is not, domiciled, resident or present within that jurisdiction.

(4) The power of the High Court to appoint a receiver by way of equitable execution shall operate in relation to all legal estates and interests in land; and that power—

    (a)   may be exercised in relation to an estate or interest in land whether or not a charge has been imposed on that land under section 1 of the Charging Orders Act 1979 for the purpose of enforcing the judgment, order or award in question; and

    (b)   shall be in addition to, and not in derogation of, any power of any court to appoint a receiver in proceedings for enforcing such a charge.

(5) Where an order under the said section 1 imposing a charge for the purpose of enforcing a judgment, order or award has been, or has effect as if, registered under section 6 of the Land Charges Act 1972, subsection (4) of the said section 6 (effect of non-registration of writs and orders registrable under that section) shall not apply to an order appointing a receiver made either—

    (a)   in proceedings for enforcing the charge; or

    (b)   by way of equitable execution of the judgment, order or award or, as the case may be, of so much of it as requires payment of moneys secured by the charge.

38. Relief against forfeiture for non-payment of rent

(1) In any action in the High Court for the forfeiture of a lease for non-payment of rent, the court shall have power to grant relief against forfeiture in a summary manner, and may do so subject to the same terms and conditions as to the payment of rent, costs or otherwise as could have been imposed by it in such an action immediately before the commencement of this Act.

(2) Where the lessee or a person deriving title under him is granted relief under this section, he shall hold the demised premises in accordance with the terms of the lease without the necessity for a new lease.

39. Execution of instrument by person nominated by High Court

(1) Where the High Court has given or made a judgment or order directing a person to execute any conveyance, contract or other document, or to indorse any negotiable instrument, then, if that person—

    (a)   neglects or refuses to comply with the judgment or order; or

    (b)   cannot after reasonable inquiry be found, the High Court may, on such terms and conditions, if any, as may be just, order that the conveyance, contract or other document shall be executed, or that the negotiable instrument shall be indorsed, by such person as the court may nominate for that purpose.

(2) A conveyance, contract, document or instrument executed or indorsed in pursuance of an order under this section shall operate, and be for all purposes available, as if it had been executed or indorsed by the person originally directed to execute or indorse it.

40. Attachment of debts

(1) Subject to any order for the time being in force under subsection (4), this section applies to the following accounts, namely—

    (a)   any deposit account with a bank or other deposit-taking institution; and

    (b)   any withdrawable share account with any deposit-taking institution.

(2) In determining whether, for the purposes of the jurisdiction of the High Court to attach debts for the purpose of satisfying judgments or orders for the payment of money, a sum standing to the credit of a person in an account to which this section applies is a sum due or accruing to that person and, as such, attachable in accordance with rules of court, any condition mentioned in subsection (3) which applies to the account shall be disregarded.

(3) Those conditions are—

(a) any condition that notice is required before any money or share is withdrawn;
(b) any condition that a personal application must be made before any money or share is withdrawn;
(c) any condition that a deposit book or share-account book must be produced before any money or share is withdrawn; or
(d) any other prescribed condition.

(4) The Lord Chancellor may by order make such provision as he thinks fit, by way of amendment of this section or otherwise, for all or any of the following purposes, namely—
(a) including in, or excluding from, the accounts to which this section applies accounts of any description specified in the order;
(b) excluding from the accounts to which this section applies all accounts with any particular deposit-taking institution so specified or with any deposit-taking institution of a description so specified.

(5) Any order under subsection (4) shall be made by statutory instrument subject to annulment in pursuance of a resolution of either House of Parliament.

(6) In this section "deposit-taking institution" means any person carrying on a business which is a deposit-taking business for the purposes of the Banking Act 1979.

40A. *****

41. Wards of court

(1) Subject to the provisions of this section, no minor shall be made a ward of court except by virtue of an order to that effect made by the High Court.

(2) Where an application is made for such an order in respect of a minor, the minor shall become a ward of court on the making of the application, but shall cease to be a ward of court at the end of such period as may be prescribed unless within that period an order has been made in accordance with the application.

(3) The High Court may, either upon an application in that behalf or without such an application, order that any minor who is for the time being a ward of court shall cease to be a ward of court.

42. Restriction of vexatious legal proceedings

(1) If, on an application made by the Attorney-General under this section, the High Court is satisfied that any person has habitually and persistently and without any reasonable ground—
(a) instituted vexatious civil proceedings, whether in the High Court or any inferior court, and whether against the same person or against different persons; or
(b) made vexatious applications in any civil proceedings, whether in the High Court or any inferior court, and whether instituted by him or another, [or
(c) instituted vexatious prosecutions (whether against the same person or different persons),]
the court may, after hearing that person or giving him an opportunity of being heard, [make a civil proceedings order, a criminal proceedings order or an all proceedings order.]

[(1A) In this section—
"civil proceedings order" means an order that—
(a) no civil proceedings shall without the leave of the High Court be instituted in any court by the person against whom the order is made;
(b) any civil proceedings instituted by him in any court before the making of the order shall not be continued by him without the leave of the High Court; and
(c) no application (other than one for leave under this section) shall be made by him, in any civil proceedings instituted in any court by any person, without the leave of the High Court;

"criminal proceedings order" means an order that—
  (a) no information shall be laid before a justice of the peace by the person against whom the order is made without the leave of the High Court; and
  (b) no application for leave to prefer a bill of indictment shall be made by him without the leave of the High Court; and
"all proceedings order" means an order which has the combined effect of the two other orders.]

(2) An order under subsection (1) may provide that it is to cease to have effect at the end of a specified period, but shall otherwise remain in force indefinitely.

(3) Leave for the institution or continuance of, or for the making of an application in, any civil proceedings by a person who is the subject of an order for the time being in force under subsection (1) shall not be given unless the High Court is satisfied that the proceedings or application are not an abuse of the process of the court in question and that there are reasonable grounds for the proceedings or application.

[(3A) Leave for the laying of an information or for an application for leave to prefer a bill of indictment by a person who is the subject of an order for the time being in force under subsection (1) shall not be given unless the High Court is satisfied that the institution of the prosecution is not an abuse of the criminal process and that there are reasonable grounds for the institution of the prosecution by the applicant.]

(4) No appeal shall lie from a decision of the High Court refusing leave.

(5) A copy of any order made under subsection (1) shall be published in the London Gazette.

43. Power of High Court to vary sentence on certiorari

(1) Where a person who has been sentenced for an offence—
  (a) by a magistrates' court; or
  (b) by the Crown Court after being convicted of the offence by a magistrates' court and committed to the Crown Court for sentence; or
  (c) by the Crown Court on appeal against conviction or sentence,
applies to the High Court in accordance with section 31 for an order of certiorari to remove the proceedings of the magistrates' court or the Crown Court into the High Court, then, if the High Court determines that the magistrates' court or the Crown Court had no power to pass the sentence, the High Court may, instead of quashing the conviction, amend it by substituting for the sentence passed any sentence which the magistrates' court or, in a case within paragraph (b), the Crown Court had power to imposed.

(2) Any sentence passed by the High Court by virtue of this section in substitution for the sentence passed in the proceedings of the magistrates' court or the Crown Court shall, unless the High Court otherwise directs, begin to run from the time when it would have begun to run if passed in those proceedings; but in computing the term of the sentence, any time during which the offender was released on bail in pursuance of section 37(1)(d) of the Criminal Justice Act 1948 shall be disregarded.

(3) Subsections (1) and (2) shall, with the necessary modifications, apply in relation to any order of a magistrates' court or the Crown Court which is made on, but does not form part of, the conviction of an offender as they apply in relation to a conviction and sentence.

44. *****

THE CROWN COURT

45. General jurisdiction of Crown Court

(1) The Crown Court shall be a superior court of record.

(2) Subject to the provisions of this Act, there shall be exercisable by the Crown Court—

(a) all such appellate and other jurisdiction as is conferred on it by or under this or any other Act; and

(b) all such other jurisdiction as was exercisable by it immediately before the commencement of this Act.

(3) Without prejudice to subsection (2), the jurisdiction of the Crown Court shall include all such powers and duties as were exercisable or fell to be performed by it immediately before the commencement of this Act.

(4) Subject to section 8 of the Criminal Procedure (Attendance of Witnesses) Act 1965 (substitution in criminal cases of procedure in that Act for procedure by way of subpoena) and to any provision contained in or having effect under this Act, the Crown Court shall, in relation to the attendance and examination of witnesses, any contempt of court, the enforcement of its orders and all other matters incidental to its jurisdiction, have the like powers, rights, privileges and authority as the High Court.

(5) The specific mention elsewhere in this Act of any jurisdiction covered by subsections (2) and (3) shall not derogate from the generality of those subsections.

46. Exclusive jurisdiction of Crown Court in trial on indictment

(1) All proceedings on indictment shall be brought before the Crown Court.

(2) The jurisdiction of the Crown Court with respect of proceedings on indictment shall include jurisdiction in proceedings on indictment for offences wherever committed, and in particular proceedings on indictment for offences within the jurisdiction of the Admiralty of England.

47. Sentences and other orders of Crown Court when dealing with offenders

(1) A sentence imposed, or other order made, by the Crown Court when dealing with an offender shall take effect from the beginning of the day on which it is imposed, unless the court otherwise directs.

(2) Subject to the following provisions of this section, a sentence imposed, or other order made, by the Crown Court when dealing with an offender may be varied or rescinded by the Crown Court within the period of twenty-eight days beginning with the day on which the sentence or other order was imposed or made or, where subsection (3) applies, within the time allowed by that subsection.

(3) Where two or more persons are jointly tried on an indictment, then, subject to the following provisions of this section, a sentence imposed, or other order made by the Crown Court on conviction of any of those persons on the indictment may be varied or rescinded by the Crown Court not later than the expiration of whichever is the shorter of the following periods, that is—

(a) the period of twenty-eight days beginning with the date of conclusion of the joint trial;

(b) the period of fifty-six days beginning with the day on which the sentence or other order was imposed or made.

For the purposes of this subsection the joint trial is concluded on the latest of the following dates, that is any date on which any of the persons jointly tried is sentenced, or is acquitted, or on which a special verdict is brought in.

(4) A sentence or other order shall not be varied or rescinded under this section except by the court constituted as it was when the sentence or other order was imposed or made, or, where that court comprised one or more justices of the peace, a court so constituted except for the omission of any one or more of those justices.

(5) Where a sentence or other order is varied under this section, the sentence or other order, as so varied, shall take effect from the beginning of the day on which it was originally imposed or made, unless the court otherwise directs:

Provided that for the purposes of section 18(2) of the Criminal Appeal Act 1968 (time limit for notice of appeal or of application for leave to appeal) [and for the purposes of paragraph 1 of Schedule 3 to the Criminal Justice Act 1988 (time limit for notice of an application for leave to refer a case under section 36 of that Act)] the sentence or other order shall be regarded as imposed or made on the day on which it is so varied.

(6) Crown Court Rules—

    (a)   may, as respects cases where two or more persons are tried separately on the same or related facts alleged in one or more indictments, provide for extending the period fixed by subsection (2);

    (b)   may, subject to the preceding provisions of this section, prescribe the cases and circumstances in which, and the time within which, any order or other decision made by the Crown Court may be varied or rescinded by that court.

(7) In this section—

"order" does not include a [contribution order made under section 23 of the Legal Aid Act 1988];

"sentence" includes a recommendation for deportation made when dealing with an offender.

48. Appeals to Crown Court

(1) The Crown Court may, in the course of hearing any appeal, correct any error or mistake in the order or judgment incorporating the decision which is the subject of the appeal.

(2) On the termination of the hearing of an appeal the Crown Court—

    (a)   may confirm, reverse or vary [any part of the decision appealed against including a determination not to impose a separate penalty in respect of an offence]; or

    (b)   may remit the matter with its opinion thereon to the authority whose decision is appealed against; or

    (c)   may make such other order in the matter as the court thinks just, and by such order exercise any power which the said authority might have exercised.

(3) Subsection (2) has effect subject to any enactment relating to any such appeal which expressly limits or restricts the powers of the court on the appeal.

(4) If the appeal is against a conviction or a sentence, the preceding provisions of this section shall be construed as including power to award any punishment, whether more or less severe than that awarded by the magistrates' court whose decision is appealed against, if that is a punishment which that magistrates' court might have awarded.

(5) This section applies whether or not the appeal is against the whole of the decision.

(6) In this section "sentence" includes any order made by a court when dealing with an offender, including—

    (a)   a hospital order under [Part III of the Mental Health Act 1983], with or without [a restriction order, and an interim hospital order under [that Act]]; and

    (b)   a recommendation for deportation made when dealing with an offender.

[(7) The fact that an appeal is pending against an interim hospital order under [the said Act of 1983] shall not affect the power of the magistrates' court that made it to renew or terminate the order or to deal with the appellant on its termination; and where the Crown Court quashes such an order but does not pass any sentence or make any other order in its place the Court may direct the appellant to be kept in custody or released on bail pending his being dealt with by that magistrates' court.

(8) Where the Crown Court makes an interim hospital order by virtue of subsection (2)—

    (a)   the power of renewing or terminating the order and of dealing with the appellant on its termination shall be exercisable by the magistrates' court whose decision is appealed against and not by the Crown Court; and

    (b)   that magistrates' court shall be treated for the purposes of [section 38(7) of the said Act of 1983] (absconding offenders) as the court that made the order.]

GENERAL PROVISIONS
Law and equity

49. Concurrent administration of law and equity

(1) Subject to the provisions of this or any other Act, every court exercising jurisdiction in England or Wales in any civil cause or matter shall continue to administer law and equity on the basis that, wherever there is any conflict or variance between the rules of equity and the rules of the common law with reference to the same matter, the rules of equity shall prevail.

(2) Every such court shall give the same effect as hitherto—

    (a) to all equitable estates, titles, rights, reliefs, defences and counterclaims, and to all equitable duties and liabilities; and

    (b) subject thereto, to all legal claims and demands and all estates, titles, rights, duties, obligations and liabilities existing by the common law or by any custom or created by any statute,

and, subject to the provisions of this or any other Act, shall so exercise its jurisdiction in every cause or matter before it as to secure that, as far as possible, all matters in dispute between the parties are completely and finally determined, and all multiplicity of legal proceedings with respect to any of those matters is avoided.

(3) Nothing in this Act shall affect the power of the Court of Appeal or the High Court to stay any proceedings before it, where it thinks fit to do so, either of its own motion or on the application of any person, whether or not a party to the proceedings.

50. Power to award damages as well as, or in substitution for, injunction or specific performance

Where the Court of Appeal or the High Court has jurisdiction to entertain an application for an injunction or specific performance, it may award damages in addition to, or in substitution for, an injunction or specific performance.

Costs

51. Costs in civil division of Court of Appeal and High Court

(1) Subject to the provisions of this or any other Act and to rules of court, the costs of and incidental to all proceedings in the civil division of the Court of Appeal and in the High Court, including the administration of estates and trusts, shall be in the discretion of the court, and the court shall have full power to determine by whom and to what extent the costs are to be paid.

(2) Nothing in subsection (1) shall alter the practice in any criminal cause or matter, or in bankruptcy.

(3) Provision may be made by rules of court for regulating any matters relating to the costs of proceedings in the civil division of the Court of Appeal or in the High Court, including the administration of estates and trusts.

52. Costs in Crown Court

(1) Crown Court Rules may authorise the Crown Court to award costs and may regulate any matters relating to costs of proceedings in that court, and in particular may make provision as to—

    (a) any discretion to award costs;

    (b) the taxation of costs, or the fixing of a sum instead of directing a taxation, and as to the officer of the court or other person by whom costs are to be taxed;

    (c) a right of appeal from any decision on the taxation of costs, whether to a Taxing Master of the Supreme Court or to any other officer or authority;

    (d) a right of appeal to the High Court, subject to any conditions specified in the rules, from any decision on an appeal brought by virtue of paragraph (c);

    (e) the enforcement of an order for costs; and

(f) the charges or expenses or other disbursements which are to be treated as costs for the purposes of the rules.

(2) The costs to be dealt with by rules made in pursuance of this section may, where an appeal is brought to the Crown Court from the decision of a magistrates' court, or from the decision of any other court or tribunal, include costs in the proceedings in that court or tribunal.

(3) Nothing in this section authorises the making of rules about the payment of costs out of central funds, whether under the [Part II of the Prosecution of Offences Act 1985] or otherwise, but rules made in pursuance of this section may make any such provision as [in relation to costs of proceedings in the Crown Court, is contained in section 18 of that Act or in regulations made under section 19 of that Act (awards of party and party costs in criminal proceedings).]

(4) Rules made in pursuance of this section may amend or repeal all or any of the provisions of any enactment about costs between party and party in criminal or other proceedings in the Crown Court, being an enactment passed before, or contained in, the [Part II of the Prosecution of Offences Act 1985].

(5) Rules made in pursuance of this section shall have effect subject to the provisions of section 41 of, and Schedule 9 to, the Administration of Justice Act 1970 (method of enforcing orders for costs).

PART III
PRACTICE AND PROCEDURE
THE COURT OF APPEAL
Distribution of business

53. Distribution of business between civil and criminal divisions

(1) Rules of court may provide for the distribution of business in the Court of Appeal between the civil and criminal divisions, but subject to any such rules business shall be distributed in accordance with the following provisions of this section.

(2) The criminal division of the Court of Appeal shall exercise—
    (a) all jurisdiction of the Court of Appeal under Parts I and II of the Criminal Appeal Act 1968;
    (b) the jurisdiction of the Court of Appeal under section 13 of the Administration of Justice Act 1960 (appeals in cases of contempt of court) in relation to appeals from orders and decisions of the Crown Court;
    (c) all other jurisdiction expressly conferred on that division by this or any other Act; and
    (d) the jurisdiction to order the issue of writs of venire de novo.

(3) The civil division of the Court of Appeal shall exercise the whole of the jurisdiction of that court not exercisable by the criminal division.

(4) Where any class of proceedings in the Court of Appeal is by any statutory provision assigned to the criminal division of that court, rules of court may provide for any enactment relating to—
    (a) appeals to the Court of Appeal under Part I of the Criminal Appeal Act 1968; or
    (b) any matter connected with or arising out of such appeals,
to apply in relation to proceedings of that class or, as the case may be, to any corresponding matter connected with or arising out of such proceedings, as it applies in relation to such appeals or, as the case may be, to the relevant matter within paragraph (b), with or without prescribed modifications in either case.

Composition of court

54. Court of civil division

(1) This section relates to the civil division of the Court of Appeal; and in this section "court", except where the context otherwise requires, means a court of that division.

(2) A court shall be duly constituted for the purpose of exercising any of its jurisdiction if it consists of an uneven number of judges not less than three.

(3) Where—

    (a) part of any proceedings before a court has been heard by an uneven number of judges greater than three; and

    (b) one or more members of the court are unable to continue,

the court shall remain duly constituted for the purpose of those proceedings so long as the number of members (whether even or uneven) is not reduced to less than three.

(4) A court shall, if it consists of two judges, be duly constituted for the purpose of—

    (a) hearing and determining any appeal against an interlocutory order or interlocutory judgment;

    (b) hearing and determining any appeal against a decision of a single judge acting by virtue of section 58(1);

    (c) hearing and determining any appeal where all the parties have before the hearing filed a consent to the appeal being heard and determined by two judges;

    (d) hearing the remainder of, and determining, any appeal where part of it has been heard by three or more judges of whom one or more are unable to continue and all the parties have consented to the remainder of the appeal being heard, and the appeal being determined, by two remaining judges; or

    (e) hearing and determining an appeal of any such description or in any such circumstances not covered by paragraphs (a) to (d) as may be prescribed for the purposes of this subsection by an order made by the Lord Chancellor with the concurrence of the Master of the Rolls.

(5) Where—

    (a) an appeal has been heard by a court consisting of an even number of judges; and

    (b) the members of the court are equally divided, the case shall, on the application of any party to the appeal, be re-argued before and determined by an uneven number of judges not less than three, before any appeal to the House of Lords.

(6) An application to the civil division of the Court of Appeal for leave to appeal to that court may be determined by a single judge of that court, and no appeal shall lie from a decision of a single judge acting under this subsection.

(7) In any cause or matter pending before the civil division of the Court of Appeal a single judge of that court may at any time during vacation make an interim order to prevent prejudice to the claims of any parties pending an appeal.

(8) Subsections (1) and (2) of section 70 (assessors in the High Court) shall apply in relation to causes and matters before the civil division of the Court of Appeal as they apply in relation to causes and matters before the High Court.

(9) Subsections (3) and (4) of section 70 (scientific advisers to assist the Patents Court in proceedings under the Patents Act 1949 and the Patents Act 1977) shall apply in relation to the civil division of the Court of Appeal and proceedings on appeal from any decision of the Patents Court in proceedings under those Acts as they apply in relation to the Patents Court and proceedings under those Acts.

(10) Any order under subsection (4) shall be made by statutory instrument subject to annulment in pursuance of a resolution of either House of Parliament.

55. Court of criminal division

(1) This section relates to the criminal division of the Court of Appeal; and in this section "court" means a court of that division.

(2) A court shall be duly constituted for the purpose of exercising any of its jurisdiction if it consists of an uneven number of judges not less than three.

(3) Where—

(a) part of any proceedings before a court has been heard by an uneven number of judges greater than three; and

(b) one or more members of the court are unable to continue,

the court shall remain duly constituted for the purpose of those proceedings so long as the number of members (whether even or uneven) is not reduced to less than three.

(4) A court shall, if it consists of two judges, be duly constituted for every purpose except—

(a) determining an appeal against—
  (i) conviction; or
  (ii) a verdict of not guilty by reason of insanity; or
  (iii) a finding of a jury under section 4 of the Criminal Procedure (Insanity) Act 1964 (unfitness to plead) that a person is under a disabilty;

(b) determining an application for leave to appeal to the House of Lords; and

(c) refusing an application for leave to appeal to the criminal division against conviction or any such verdict or finding as is mentioned in paragraph (a)(ii) or (iii), other than an application which has been refused by a single judge.

(5) Where an appeal has been heard by a court consisting of an even number of judges and the members of the court are equally divided, the case shall be re-argued before and determined by an uneven number of judges not less than three.

56. Judges not to sit on appeal from their own judgments, etc

(1) No judge shall sit as a member of the civil division of the Court of Appeal on the hearing of, or shall determine any application in proceedings incidental or preliminary to, an appeal from a judgment or order made in any case by himself or by any court of which he was a member.

(2) No judge shall sit as a member of the criminal division of the Court of Appeal on the hearing of, or shall determine any application in proceedings incidental or preliminary to, an appeal against—

(a) a conviction before himself or a court of which he was a member; or

(b) a sentence passed by himself or such a court.

Sittings and vacations

57. Sittings and vacations

(1) Sittings of the Court of Appeal may be held, and any other business of the Court of Appeal may be conducted, at any place in England or Wales.

(2) Subject to rules of court—

(a) the places at which the Court of Appeal sits outside the Royal Courts of Justice; and

(b) the days and times at which the Court of Appeal sits at any place outside the Royal Courts of Justice,

shall be determined in accordance with directions given by the Lord Chancellor.

(3), (4) *****

Other provisions

58. Exercise of incidental jurisdiction in civil division

(1) Any jurisdiction exercisable in any proceedings incidental to any cause or matter pending before the civil division of the Court of Appeal and not involving the

determination of an appeal may, if and so far as rules of court so provide, be exercised (with or without a hearing) by a single judge of that court, whether in court or in chambers, or by the registrar of civil appeals.

(2) Rules of court may provide for decisions of a single judge or the registrar of civil appeals acting by virtue of subsection (1) to be called in question in such manner as may be prescribed; but, except as may be provided by rules of court, no appeal shall lie from a decision of a single judge or that registrar so acting.

(3) For the purposes of subsection (1) the making of an interlocutory order having the effect of preventing an appeal from reaching the stage of being heard and determined shall not be treated as a determination of the appeal.

59. Form of judgment of court of criminal division
Any judgment of a court of the criminal division of the Court of Appeal on any question shall, except where the judge presiding over the court states that in his opinion the question is one of law on which it is convenient that separate judgments should be pronounced by the members of the court, be pronounced by the judge presiding over the court or by such other member of the court as he directs and, except as aforesaid, no judgment shall be separately pronounced on any question by any member of the court.

60. Rules of court, and decisions of Court of Appeal, as to whether judgment or order is final or interlocutory
(1) Rules of court may provide for orders or judgments of any prescribed description to be treated for any prescribed purpose connected with appeals to the Court of Appeal as final or as interlocutory.

(2) No appeal shall lie from a decision of the Court of Appeal as to whether a judgment or order is, for any purpose connected with an appeal to that court, final or interlocutory.

THE HIGH COURT

Distribution of business

61. Distribution of business among Divisions
(1) Subject to any provision made by or under this or any other Act (and in particular to any rules of court made in pursuance of subsection (2) and any order under subsection (3)), business in the High Court of any description mentioned in Schedule 1, as for the time being in force, shall be distributed among the Divisions in accordance with that Schedule.

(2) Rules of court may provide for the distribution of business in the High Court among the Divisions; but any rules made in pursuance of this subsection shall have effect subject to any orders for the time being in force under subsection (3).

(3) Subject to subsection (5), the Lord Chancellor may by order—
    (a) direct that any business in the High Court which is not for the time being assigned by or under this or any other Act to any Division be assigned to such Division as may be specified in the order;
    (b) if at any time it appears to him desirable to do so with a view to the more convenient administration of justice, direct that any business for the time being assigned by or under this or any other Act to any Division be assigned to such other Division as may be specified in the order; and
    (c) amend Schedule 1 so far as may be necessary in consequence of provision made by order under paragraph (a) or (b).

(4) The powers conferred by subsection (2) and subsection (3) include power to assign business of any description of two or more Divisions concurrently.

Supreme Court Act 1981

(5) No order under subsection (3)(b) relating to any business shall be made without the concurrence of the senior judge or—
    (a)   the Division or each of the Divisions to which the business is for the time being assigned; and
    (b)   the Division or each of the Divisions to which the business is to be assigned by the order.

(6) Subject to rules of court, the fact that a cause or matter commenced in the High Court falls within a class of business assigned by or under this Act to a particular Division does not make it obligatory for it to be allocated or transferred to that Division.

(7) Without prejudice to subsections (1) to (5) and section 63, rules of court may provide for the distribution of the business (other than business required to be heard by a divisional court) in any Division of the High Court among the judges of that Division.

(8) Any order under subsection (3) shall be made by statutory instrument, which shall be laid before Parliament after being made.

62. Business of Patents, Admiralty and Commercial Courts

(1) The Patents Court shall take such proceedings relating to patents as are within the jurisdiction conferred on it by the Patents Act 1977, and such other proceedings relating to patents or other matters as may be prescribed.

(2) The Admiralty Court shall take Admiralty business, that is to say causes and matters assigned to the Queen's Bench Division and involving the exercise of the High Court's Admiralty jurisdiction or its jurisdiction as a prize court.

(3) The Commercial Court shall take such causes and matters as may in accordance with rules of court be entered in the commercial list.

63. Business assigned to specially nominated judges

(1) Any business assigned, in accordance with this or any other Act or rules of court, to one or more specially nominated judges of the High Court may—
    (a)   during vacation; or
    (b)   during the illness or absence of that judge or any of those judges; or
    (c)   for any other reasonable cause,
be dealt with by any judge of the High Court named for that purpose by the Lord Chancellor.

(2) If at any time it appears to the Lord Chancellor desirable to do so with a view to the more convenient administration of justice, he may by order direct that business of any description which is for the time being assigned, in accordance with this or any other Act or rules of court, to one or more specially nominated judges of the High Court shall cease to be so assigned and may be dealt with by any one or more judges of the High Court.

(3) An order under subsection (2) shall not be made in respect of any business without the concurrence of the senior judge of the Division to which the business is for the time being assigned.

64. Choice of Division by plaintiff

(1) Without prejudice to the power of transfer under section 65, the person by whom any cause or matter is commenced in the High Court shall in the prescribed manner allocate it to whichever Division he thinks fit.

(2) Where a cause or matter is commenced in the High Court, all subsequent interlocutory or other steps or proceedings in the High Court in that cause or matter shall be taken in the Division to which the cause or matter is for the time being allocated (whether under subsection (1) or in consequence of its transfer under section 65).

65. Power of transfer

(1) Any cause or matter may at any time and at any stage thereof, and either with or without application from any of the parties, be transferred, by such authority and in such manner as rules of court may direct, from one Division or judge of the High Court to another Division or judge thereof.

(2) The transfer of a cause or matter under subsection (1) to a different Division or judge of the High Court shall not affect the validity of any steps or proceedings taken or order made in that cause or matter before the transfer.

Divisional courts

66. Divisional courts of High Court

(1) Divisional courts may be held for the transaction of any business in the High Court which is, by or by virtue of rules of court or any other statutory provision, required to be heard by a divisional court.

(2) Any number of divisional courts may sit at the same time.

(3) A divisional court shall be constituted of not less than two judges.

(4) Every judge of the High Court shall be qualified to sit in any divisional court.

(5) The judge who is, according to the order of precedence under this Act, the senior of the judges constituting a divisional court shall be the president of the court.

Mode of conducting business

67. Proceedings in court and in chambers

Business in the High Court shall be heard and disposed of in court except in so far as it may, under this or any other Act, under rules of court or in accordance with the practice of the court, be dealt with in chambers.

68. Exercise of High Court jurisdiction otherwise than by judges of that court

(1) Provision may be made by rules of court as to the cases in which jurisdiction of the High Court may be exercised by—

    (a) such [Circuit judges, deputy Circuit judges or Recorders] as the Lord Chancellor may from time to time nominate to deal with official referees' business; or

    (b) special referees; or

    (c) masters, registrars, district registrars or other officers of the court.

(2) Without prejudice to the generality of subsection (1), rules of court may in particular—

    (a) authorise the whole of any cause or matter, or any question or issue therein, to be tried before any such person as is mentioned in that subsection; or

    (b) authorise any question arising in any cause or matter to be referred to any such person for inquiry and report.

(3) Rules of court shall not authorise the exercise of powers of attachment and committal by any such person as is mentioned in subsecton (1)(b) or (c).

(4) Subject to subsection (5), the decision of any such person as is mentioned in subsection (1) may be called in question in such manner as may be prescribed by rules of court, whether by appeal to the Court of Appeal, or by an appeal or application to a divisional court or a judge in court or a judge in chambers, or by an adjournment to a judge in court or a judge in chambers.

(5) Rules of court may provide either generally or to a limited extent for decisions of [persons] nominated under subsection (1)(a) being called in question only by appeal on a question of law.

(6) The cases in which jurisdiction of the High Court may be exercised by [persons] nominated under subsection (1)(a) shall be known as "official referees' business"; and, subject to rules of court, the distribution of official referees' business among [persons]

so nominated shall be determined in accordance with directions given by the Lord Chancellor.

(7) Any reference to an official referee in any enactment, whenever passed, or in rules of court or any other instrument or document, whenever made, shall, unless the context otherwise requires, be construed as, or (where the context requires) as including, a reference to a [person] nominated under subsection (1)(a).

69. Trial by jury

(1) Where, on the application of any party to an action to be tried in the Queen's Bench Division, the court is satisfied that there is in issue—

    (a)   a charge of fraud against that party; or

    (b)   a claim in respect of libel, slander, malicious prosecution or false imprisonment; or

    (c)   any question or issue of a kind prescribed for the purposes of this paragraph, the action shall be tried with a jury, unless the court is of opinion that the trial requires any prolonged examination of documents or accounts or any scientific or local investigation which cannot conveniently be made with a jury.

(2) An application under subsection (1) must be made not later than such time before the trial as may be prescribed.

(3) An action to be tried in the Queen's Bench Division which does not by virtue of subsection (1) fall to be tried with a jury shall be tried without a jury unless the court in its discretion orders it to be tried with a jury.

(4) Nothing in subsections (1) to (3) shall affect the power of the court to order, in accordance with rules of court, that different questions of fact arising in any action be tried by different modes of trial; and where any such order is made, subsection (1) shall have effect only as respects questions relating to any such charge, claim, question or issue as is mentioned in that subsection.

(5) Where for the purpose of disposing of any action or other matter which is being tried in the High Court by a judge with a jury it is necessary to ascertain the law of any other country which is applicable to the facts of the case, any question as to the effect of the evidence given with respect to that law shall, instead of being submitted to the jury, be decided by the judge alone.

70. Assessors and scientific advisers

(1) In any cause or matter before the High Court the court may, if it thinks it expedient to do so, call in the aid of one or more assessors specially qualified, and hear and dispose of the cause or matter wholly or partially with their assistance.

(2)—(4) *****

Sittings and vacations

71. Sittings and vacations

(1) Sittings of the High Court may be held, and any other business of the High Court may be conducted, at any place in England or Wales.

(2) Subject to rules of court—

    (a)   the places at which the High Court sits outside the Royal Courts of Justice; and

    (b)   the days and times when the High Court sits at any place outside the Royal Courts of Justice,

shall be determined in accordance with directions given by the Lord Chancellor.

(3)—(5) *****

72. *****

THE CROWN COURT
Composition of court

73. General provisions

(1) Subject to the provisions of section 8(1)(c), 74 and 75(2) as respects courts comprising justices of the peace, all proceedings in the Crown Court shall be heard and disposed of before a single judge of that court.

(2) Crown Court Rules may authorise or require a judge of the High Court, Circuit judge or Recorder, in such circumstances as are specified by the rules, at any stage to continue with any proceedings with a court from which any one or more of the justices initially constituting the court has withdrawn, or is absent for any reason.

(3) Where a judge of the High Court, Circuit judge or Recorder sits with justices of the peace he shall preside, and—

(a) the decision of the Crown Court may be a majority decision; and

(b) if the members of the court are equally divided, the judge of the High Court, Circuit judge or Recorder shall have a second and casting vote.

74. Appeals and committals for sentence

(1) On any hearing by the Crown Court—

(a) of any appeal; or

(b) of proceedings on committal to the Crown Court for sentence,

the Crown Court shall consist of a judge of the High Court or a Circuit judge or a Recorder who, subject to the following provisions of this section, shall sit with not less than two nor more than four justices of the peace.

(2) Crown Court Rules may, with respect to hearings falling within subsection (1)—

(a) prescribe the number of justices of the peace constituting the court (within the limits mentioned in that subsection); and

(b) prescribe the qualifications to be possessed by any such justices of the peace;

and the rules may make different provision for different descriptions of cases, different places of sitting or other different circumstances.

(3) Crown Court Rules may authorise or require a judge of the High Court, Circuit judge or Recorder, in such circumstances as are specified by the rules, to enter on, or at any stage to continue with, any proceedings with a court not comprising the justices required by subsections (1) and (2).

(4) The Lord Chancellor may from time to time, having regard to the number of justices, or the number of justices with any prescribed qualifications, available for service in the Crown Court, give directions providing that, in such descriptions of proceedings as may be specified by the Lord Chancellor, the provisions of subsections (1) and (2) shall not apply.

(5) Directions under subsection (4) may frame descriptions of proceedings by reference to the place of trial, or by reference to the time of trial, or in any other way.

(6) No decision of the Crown Court shall be questioned on the ground that the court was not constituted as required by or under subsections (1) and (2) unless objection was taken by or on behalf of a party to the proceedings not later than the time when the proceedings were entered on, or when the alleged irregularity began.

(7) Crown Court Rules may make provision as to the circumstances in which—

(a) a person concerned with a decision appealed against is to be disqualified from hearing the appeal;

(b) a person concerned with the committal of a person to the Crown Court for sentence is to be disqualified from hearing proceedings on the committal; and

(c) proceedings on the hearing of an appeal or on committal to the Crown

Supreme Court Act 1981

Court for sentence are to be valid notwithstanding that any person taking part in them is disqualified.

Distribution of business

75. Allocation of cases according to composition of court, etc
(1) The cases or classes of cases in the Crown Court suitable for allocation respectively to a judge of the High Court and to a Circuit Judge or Recorder, and all other matters relating to the distribution of Crown Court business, shall be determined in accordance with directions given by or on behalf of the Lord Chief Justice with the concurrence of the Lord Chancellor.
(2) Subject to section 74(1), the cases or classes of cases in the Crown Court suitable for allocation to a court comprising justices of the peace (including those by way of trial on indictment which are suitable for allocation to such a court) shall be determined in accordance with directions given by or on behalf of the Lord Chief Justice with the concurrence of the Lord Chancellor.

76. Committal for trial: alteration of place of trial
(1) Without prejudice to the provisions of this Act about the distribution of Crown Court business, the Crown Court may give directions, or further directions, altering the place of any trial on indictment, whether by varying the decision of a magistrates' court under section 7 of the Magistrates' Courts Act 1980 or [by substituting some other place for the place specified in a notice under section 4 of the Criminal Justice Act 1987 (notices of transfer from magistrates' court to Crown Court) or by varying] a previous decision of the Crown Court.
(2) Directions under section (1) may be given on behalf of the Crown Court by an officer of the court.
[(2A) Where a preparatory hearing has been ordered under section 7 of the Criminal Justice Act 1987, directions altering the place of trial may be given under subsection (1) at any time before the jury are sworn]
(3) The defendant or the prosecutor, if dissatisifed with the place of trial as fixed by the magistrates' court, or by the Crown Court, may apply to the Crown Court for a direction, or further direction, varying the place of trial; and the court shall take the matter into consideration and may comply with or refuse the application, or give a direction not in compliance with the application, as the court thinks fit.
(4) An application under subsection (3) shall be heard in open court by a judge of the High Court.

77. Committal for trial: date of trial
(1) Crown Court Rules shall prescribe the minimum period which may elapse between a person's committal for trial [or the giving of a notice of transfer under section 4 of the Criminal Justice Act 1987] and the beginning of the trial; and such rules may make different provision for different places of trial and for other different circumstances.
(2) The trial of a person committed by a magistrates' court—
    (a) shall not begin until the prescribed minimum period has expired except with his consent and the consent of the prosecutor; . . . .
(3) For the purposes of this section the prescribed minimum [period] shall begin with the date of committal for trial and the trial shall be taken to begin when the defendant is arraigned.

Sittings

78. Sittings
(1) Any Crown Court business may be conducted at any place in England or Wales,

and the sittings of the Crown Court at any place may be continuous or intermittent or occasional.

(2) Judges of the Crown Court may sit simultaneously to take any number of different cases in the same or different places, and may adjourn cases from place to place at any time.

(3) The places at which the Crown Court sits, and the days and times at which the Crown Court sits at any place, shall be determined in accordance with directions given by the Lord Chancellor.

Other provisions

79. Practice and procedure in connection with indictable offences and appeals

(1) All enactments and rules of law relating to procedure in connection with indictable offences shall continue to have effect in relation to proceedings in the Crown Court.

(2) Without prejudice to the generality of subsection (1), that subsection applies in particular to—

    (a) the practice by which, on any one indictment, the taking of pleas, the trial by jury and the pronouncement of judgment may respectively be by or before different judges;

    (b) the release, after respite of judgment, of a convicted person on recognizance to come up for judgment if called on, but meanwhile to be of good behaviour;

    (c) the manner of trying any question relating to the breach of a recognizance;

    (d) the manner of execution of any sentence on conviction, or the manner in which any other judgment or order given in connection with trial on indictment may be enforced.

(3) The customary practice and procedure with respect to appeals to the Crown Court, and in particular any practice as to the extent to which an appeal is by way of rehearing of the case, shall continue to be observed.

80. Process to compel appearance

(1) Any direction to appear and any condition of a recognizance to appear before the Crown Court, and any summons or order to appear before that court, may be so framed as to require appearance at such time and place as may be directed by the Crown Court, and if a time or place is specified in the direction, condition, summons or order, it may be varied by any subsequent direction of the Crown Court.

(2) Where an indictment has been signed although the person charged has not been committed for trial, the Crown Court may issue a summons requiring that person to appear before the Crown Court, or may issue a warrant for his arrest.

(3) Section 4 of the Summary Jurisdiction (Process) Act 1881 (execution of process of English courts in Scotland) shall apply to process issued under this section as it applies to process issued under the Magistrates' Courts Act 1980 by a magistrates' court.

81. Bail

(1) The Crown Court may grant bail to any person—

    (a) who has been committed in custody for appearance before the Crown Court [or in relation to whose case a notice of transfer has been given under section 4 of the Criminal Justice Act 1987]; or

    (b) who is in custody pursuant to a sentence imposed by a magistrates' court, and who has appealed to the Crown Court against his conviction or sentence; or

    (c) who is in the custody of the Crown Court pending the disposal of his case by that court; or

    (d) who, after the decision of his case by the Crown Court, has applied to that court for the statement of a case for the High Court on that decision; or

    (e) who has applied to the High Court for an order of certiorari to remove

Supreme Court Act 1981

proceedings in the Crown Court in his case into the High Court, or has applied to the High Court for leave to make such an application; [or

(f) to whom the Crown Court has granted a certificate under section 1(2) or 11(1A) of the Criminal Appeal Act 1968 or under subsection (1B) below;] [or

(g) who has been remanded in custody by a magistrates' court on adjourning a case under—

    (i)   section 5 (adjournment of inquiry into offence);

    (ii)   section 10 (adjournment of trial);

    (iii)   section 18 (initial procedure on information against adult for offence triable either way); or

    (iv)   section 30 (remand for medical examination),

of the Magistrates' Courts Act 1980;]

and the time during which a person is released on bail under any provision of this subsection shall not count as part of any term of imprisonment or detention under his sentence.

[(1A) The power conferred by subsection (1)(f) does not extend to a case to which section 12 or 15 of the Criminal Appeal Act 1968 (appeal against verdict of not guilty by reason of insanity or against finding of disability) applies.

(1B) A certificate under this subsection is a certificate that a case is fit for appeal on a ground which involves a question of law alone.

(1C) The power conferred by subsection (1)(f) is to be exercised—

(a) where the appeal is under section 1 or 9 of the Criminal Appeal Act 1968, by the judge who tried the case; and

(b) where it is under section 10 of that Act, by the judge who passed the sentence.

(1D) The power may only be exercised within twenty-eight days from the date of the conviction appealed against, or in the case of appeal against sentence, from the date on which sentence was passed or, in the case of an order made or treated as made on conviction, from the date of the making of the order.

(1E) The power may not be exercised if the appellant has made an application to the Court of Appeal for bail in respect of the offence or offences to which the appeal relates.

(1F) It shall be a condition of bail granted in the exercise of the power that, unless a notice of appeal has previously been lodged in accordance with subsection (1) of section 18 of the Criminal Appeal Act 1968—

(a) such a notice shall be so lodged within the period specified in subsection (2) of that section; and

(b) not later than 14 days from the end of that period, the appellant shall lodge with the Crown Court a certificate from the registrar of criminal appeals that a notice of appeal was given within that period.

(1G) If the Crown Court grants bail to a person in the exercise of the power, it may direct him to appear—

(a) if a notice of appeal is lodged within the period specified in section 18(2) of the Criminal Appeal Act 1968 at such time and place as the Court of Appeal may require and

(b) if no such notice is lodged within that period at such time and place as the Crown Court may require.]

[(1H) Where the Crown Court grants a person bail under subsection (1)(g) it may direct him to appear at a time and place which the magistrates' court could have directed and the recognizance of any surety shall be conditioned accordingly.

(1J) The Crown Court may only grant bail to a person under subsection (1)(g) if the magistrates' court which remanded him in custody has certified under section 5(6A) of the Bail Act 1976 that it heard full argument on his application for bail before it refused the application.]

(2) Provision may be made by Crown Court Rules as respects the powers of the Crown Court relating to bail, including any provision—

    (a)   except in the case of bail in criminal proceedings (within the meaning of the Bail Act 1976), allowing the court instead of requiring a person to enter into a recognizance, to consent to his giving other security;

    (b)   allowing the court to direct that a recognizance shall be entered into or other security given before a magistrates' court or a justice of peace, or, if the rules so provide, a person of such other description as is specified in the rules;

    (c)   prescribing the manner in which a recognizance is to be entered into or other security given, and the persons by whom and the manner in which the recognizance or security may be enforced;

    (d)   authorising the recommittal, in such cases and by such courts or justices as may be prescribed by the rules, of persons released from custody in pursuance of the powers;

    (e)   making provision corresponding to sections 118 and 119 of the Magistrates' Courts Act 1980 (varying or dispensing with requirements as to sureties, and postponement of taking recognizances).

(3) Any reference in any enactment to a recognizance shall include, unless the context otherwise requires, a reference to any other description of security given instead of a recognizance, whether in pursuance of subsection (2)(a) or otherwise.

(4) The Crown Court, on issuing a warrant for the arrest of any person, may endorse the warrant for bail, and in any such case—

    (a)   the person arrested under the warrant shall, unless the CrownCourt otherwise directs, be taken to a police station; and

    (b)   the officer in charge of the station shall release him from custody if he, and any sureties required by the endorsement and approved by the officer, enter into recognizances of such amount as may be fixed by the endorsement:

Provided that in the case of bail in criminal proceedings (within the meaning of the Bail Act 1976) the person arrested shall not be required to enter into a recognizance.

(5) A person in custody in pursuance of a warrant issued by the Crown Court with a view to his appearance before that court shall be brought forthwith before either the Crown Court or a magistrates' court.

(6) A magistrates' court shall have jurisdiction, and a justice of the peace may act, under or in pursuance of rules under subsection (2) whether or not the offence was committed, or the arrest was made, within the court's area, or the area for which he was appointed.

82.   *****

83. Right of audience for solicitors

(1) The Lord Chancellor may at any time direct that solicitors may appear in, conduct, defend and address the court in any proceedings in the Crown Court, or proceedings in the Crown Court of any description specified in the direction.

(2) A direction under this section may have effect as respects all places where the Crown Court sits, or as respects a specified area, region or circuit, or as respects one or more specified places where the Crown Court sits.

(3) In considering whether to exercise his powers under this section as respects any one or more places where the Crown Court sits, the Lord Chancellor shall have regard to any shortage of counsel in the area in question, any rights of audience formerly exercised by solicitors at any court of quarter sessions in the locality in question, and to any other circumstances affecting the public interest.

(4) Any direction given under this section may be subject to such conditions and restrictions as appear to the Lord Chancellor to be necessary or expedient.

RULES OF COURT

84. Power to make rules of court

(1) Rules of court may be made for the purpose of regulating and prescribing the practice and procedure to be followed in the Supreme Court.

(2) Without prejudice to the generality of subsection (1), the matters about which rules of court may be made under this section include all matters of practice and procedure in the Supreme Court which were regulated or prescribed by rules of court immediately before the commencement of this Act.

(3)—(9) *****

85., 86 *****

Note. — These sections respectively make provision for the constitution of a Rule Committee for the Supreme Court and Crown Court.

87.—137. *****

138. Effect of writs of execution against goods

(1) Subject to subsection (2), a writ of fieri facias or other writ of execution against goods issued from the High Court shall bind the property in the goods of the execution debtor as from the time when the writ is delivered to the sheriff to be executed.

(2) Such a writ shall not prejudice the title to any goods of the execution debtor acquired by a person in good faith and for valuable consideration unless he had, at the time when he acquired his title—

(a) notice that that writ or any other such writ by virtue of which the goods of the execution debtor might be seized or attached had been delivered to and remained unexecuted in the hands of the sheriff; or

(b) notice that an application for the issue of a warrant of execution against the goods of the execution debtor had been made to the registrar of a county court and that the warrant issued on the application either—

(i) remained unexecuted in the hands of the registrar of the court from which it was issued; or

(ii) had been sent for execution to, and received by, the registrar of another county court, and remained unexecuted in the hands of the registrar of that court.

(3) For the better manifestation of the time mentioned in subsection (1), it shall be the duty of the sheriff (without fee) on receipt of any such writ as is there mentioned to endorse on its back the hour, day, month and year when he received it.

(4) For the purposes of this section—

(a) "property" means the general property in goods, and not merely a special property;

(b) "sheriff" includes any officer charged with the enforcement of a writ of execution;

(c) any reference to the goods of the execution debtor includes a reference to anything else of his that may lawfully be seized in execution; and

(d) a thing shall be treated as done in good faith if it is in fact done honestly, whether it is done negligently or not.

139. *****

140. Enforcement of fines and forfeited recognizances

(1) Payment of a fine imposed, or sum due under a recognizance forfeited, by the High Court or the civil division of the Court of Appeal may be enforced upon the order of the court—

(a) in like manner as a judgment of the High Court for the payment of money; or

(b) in like manner as a fine imposed by the Crown Court.

(2) Where payment of a fine or other sum falls to be enforced as mentioned in paragraph (a) of subsection (1) upon an order of the High Court or the civil division of the Court of Appeal under that subsection—

(a) the court shall, if the fine or other sum is not paid in full forthwith or within such time as the court may allow, certify to Her Majesty's Remembrancer the sum payable; and

(b) Her Majesty' Remembrancer shall thereupon proceed to enforce payment of that sum as if it were due to him as a judgment debt.

(3) Where payment of a fine or other sum falls to be enforced as mentioned in paragraph (b) of subsection (1) upon an order of the High Court or the civil division of the Court of Appeal under that subsection, the provisions of sections 31 and 32 of the Powers of Criminal Courts Act 1973 shall apply to that fine or other sum as they apply to a fine imposed by the Crown Court.

(4) Where payment of a fine or other sum has become enforceable by Her Majesty's Remembrancer by virtue of this section or section 16 of the Contempt of Court Act 1981, any payment received by him in respect of that fine or other sum shall be dealt with by him in such manner as the Lord Chancelor may direct.

(5) In this section, and in sections 31 and 32 of the Powers of Criminal Courts Act 1973 as extended by this section, "fine" includes a penalty imposed in civil proceedings.

141.—150. ***** (**Note.** — 143, 144 and 149 have been repealed)

151. Interpretation of this Act, and rules of construction for other Acts and documents

(1) In this Act, unless the context otherwise requires—

"action" means any civil proceedings commenced by writ or in any other manner prescribed by rules of court;

"appeal", in the context of appeals to the civil division of the Court of Appeal, includes—

(a) an application for a new trial, and

(b) an application to set aside a verdict, finding or judgment in any cause or matter in the High Court which has been tried, or in which any issue has been tried, by a jury;

"cause" means any action or any criminal proceedings;

"Division", where it appears with a capital letter, means a division of the High Court;

"judgment" includes a decree;

"jurisdiction" includes powers;

"matter" means any proceedings in court not in a cause;

"party", in relation to any proceedings, includes any person who pursuant to or by virtue of rules of court or any other statutory provision has been served with notice of, or has intervened in, those proceedings;

"prescribed" means—

(a) except in relation to fees, prescribed by rules of court; and

(b) in relation to fees, prescribed by an order under section 130;

"senior judge", where the reference is to the senior judge of a Division, means—

(a) in the case of the Chancery Division, the Vice Chancellor;

(b) in any other case, the President of the Division in question;

"solicitor" means a solicitor of the Supreme Court;

"statutory provision" means any enactment, whenever passed, or any provision contained in subordinate legislation (as defined in section 21(1) of the Interpretation Act 1978), whenever made;

"this or any other Act" includes an Act passed after this Act.

(2) Section 128 contains definitions of expressions used in Part V and in the other provisions of this Act relating to probate causes and matters.

(3) Any reference in this Act to rules of court under any provision of this or any other Act which confers on the Supreme Court Rule Committee or the Crown Court Rule Committee power to make rules of court.

(4) Except where the context otherwise requires, in this or any other Act—

"Criminal Appeal Rules" means rules of court made by the Crown Court Rule Committee in relation to the criminal division of the Court of Appeal;

"Crown Court Rules" means rules of court made by the Crown Court Rule Committee in relation to the Crown Court;

"divisional court" (with or without capital letters) means a divisional court constituted under section 66;

"judge of the Supreme Court" means—

    (a)   a judge of the Court of Appeal other than an ex-officio judge within paragraph (b) or (c) of section 2(2), or

    (b)   a judge of the High Court,

and accordingly does not include, as such, a judge of the Crown Court;

"official referees' business" has the meaning given by section 68(6);

"Rules of the Supreme Court" means rules of court made by the Supreme Court Rule Committee.

(5) The provisions of Schedule 4 (construction of references to superseded courts and officers) shall have effect.

SCHEDULES

Section 61(1), (3)

SCHEDULE 1
DISTRIBUTION OF BUSINESS IN HIGH COURT

Chancery Division

1. To the Chancery Division are assigned all causes and matters relating to—
    (a) the sale, exchange or partition of land, or the raising of charges on land;
    (b) the redemption or foreclosure of mortgages;
    (c) the execution of trusts;
    (d) the administration of the estates of deceased persons;
    (e) bankruptcy;
    (f) the dissolution of partnerships or the taking of partnership or other accounts;
    (g) the rectification, setting aside or cancellation of deeds or other instruments in writing;
    (h) probate business, other than non-contentious or common form business;
    (i) patents, trade marks, registered designs [, copyright or design right];
    (j) the appointment of a guardian of a minor's estate,

and all causes and matters involving the exercise of the High Court's jurisdiction under the enactments relating to companies.

Queen's Bench Division

2. To the Queen's Bench Division are assigned—
    (a) applications for writs of habeas corpus, except applications made by a parent or guardian of a minor for such a writ concerning the custody of the minor;
    (b) applications for judicial review:
    (c) all causes and matters involving the exercise of the High Court's Admiralty jurisdiction or its jurisdiction as a prize court; and

(d) all causes and matters entered in the commercial list.

Family Division

3. To the Family Division are assigned—
    (a) all matrimonial causes and matters (whether at first instance or on appeal);
    (b) all causes and matters (whether at first instance or on appeal) relating to—
        (i) legitimacy;
        (ii) the wardship, guardianship, custody or maintenance of minors (including proceedings about access), except proceedings solely for the appointment of a guardian of a minor's estate;
        (iii) . . . adoption;
        (iv) non-contentious or common form probate business;
    (c) applications for consent to the marriage of a minor [or for a declaration under section 27B(5) of the Marriage Act 1949];
    (d) proceedings on appeal under section 13 of the Administration of Justice Act 1960 from an order or decision made under section 63(3) of the Magistrates' Courts Act 1980 to enforce an order of a magistrates' court made in matrimonial proceedings or with respect to the guardianship of a minor;
    (e) [applications under Part III of the Family Law Act 1986.]

Sections 88 to 95

SCHEDULE 2
LIST OF OFFICES IN SUPREME COURT FOR PURPOSES OF PART IV

PART I

	1. Office		*2. Persons qualified*
1.	Permanent Secretary to the Lord Chancellor and Clerk of the Crown in Chancery.	1.	Barrister of not less than 10 years' standing.
2.	Official Solicitor.	2.	Solicitor of not less than 10 years' standing.

PART II

	1. Office		*2. Persons qualified*
1.	Master, Queen's Bench Division.	1.	Barrister or solicitor of not less than 10 years' standing.
2.	Queen's coroner and attorney and master of the Crown Office.	2.	Barrister or solicitor of not less than 10 years' standing.
3.	Admiralty Registrar.	3.	Barrister or solicitor of not less than 10 years' standing.
4.	Master, Chancery Division.	4.	Barrister or solicitor of not less than 10 years' standing.
5.	Registrar in Bankruptcy of the High Court.	5.	Barrister or solicitor of not less than 10 years' standing
6.	Taxing Master of the Supreme Court.	6.	Barrister or solicitor of not less than 10 years' standing.
7.	Registrar, Principal Registry of the Family Division.	7.—	(1) Barrister or solicitor of not less than 10 years' standing. (2) District probate registrar who either— (a) is of not less than 5 years' standing; or (b) has, during so much of

			the 10 years immediately preceding his appointment as he has not been a district probate registrar, served as a clerk in the Principal Registry or a district probate registry.
			(3) Clerk who has served not less than 10 years in the Principal Registry or a district probate registry.
8.	Registrar of criminal appeals.	8.—	(1) Barrister or solicitor of not less than 10 years' standing.
			(2) Assistant or deputy assistant registrar of criminal appeals.
9.	Registrar of civil appeals.	9.	Barrister or solicitor of not less than 10 years' standing.
10.	Master of the Court of Protection.	10.—	(1) Barrister or solicitor of not less than 10 years' standing.
			(2) ...
11.	...	11.	...

CRIMINAL JUSTICE ACT 1982
(1982, c. 48)

An Act to make further provision as to the sentencing and treatment of offenders (including provision as to the enforcement of fines and the standardisation of fines and of certain other sums specified in enactments relating to the powers of criminal courts);

[28 October 1982]

PART I
TREATMENT OF YOUNG OFFENDERS

Custody and detention of persons under 21

1. General restriction on custodial sentences

(1) Subject to subsection (2) below, no court shall pass a sentence of imprisonment on a person under 21 years of age or commit such a person to prison for any reason.

(2) Nothing in subsection (1) above shall prevent the committal to prison of a person under 21 years of age who is remanded in custody or committed in custody for trial or sentence.

(3) No court shall pass a sentence of Borstal training.

[(3A) Subject to section 53 of the Children and Young Persons Act 1933 (punishment of certain grave crimes), the only custodial orders that a court may make where a person under 21 years of age is convicted or found guilty of an offence are—
   (a) a sentence of detention in a young offender institution under section 1A below; and
   (b) a sentence of custody for life under section 8 below.]

[(4) A court may not—
   (a) pass a sentence of detention in a young offender institution; or
   (b) pass a sentence of custody for life under section 8(2) below, unless it is satisfied—
      (i) that the circumstances, including the nature and the gravity of the offence, are such that if the offender were aged 21 or over the court would pass a sentence of imprisonment; and
      (ii) that he qualifies for a custodial sentence.

(4A) An offender qualifies for a custodial sentence if—

(a) he has a history of failure to respond to non-custodial penalties and is unable or unwilling to respond to them; or

(b) only a custodial sentence would be adequate to protect the public from serious harm from him; or

(c) the offence of which he has been convicted or found guilty was so serious that a non-custodial sentence for it cannot be justified.]

(5) No court shall commit a person under 21 years of age to be detained under section 9 below unless it is of the opinion that no other method of dealing with him is appropriate.

(6) For the purposes of any provision of this Act which requires the determination of the age of a person by the court or the Secretary of State his age shall be deemed to be that which it appears to the court or the Secretary of State (as the case may be) to be after considering any available evidence.

[1A. **Detention in a young offender institution**

(1) Subject to section 8 below and to section 53 of the Children and Young Persons Act 1933, where—

(a) a male offender under 21 but not less than 14 years of age or a female offender under 21 but not less than 15 years of age is convicted of an offence which is punishable with imprisonment in the case of a person aged 21 or over; and

(b) the court is satisfied of the matters referred to in section 1(4) above,

the sentence that the court is to pass is a sentence of detention in a young offender institution.

(2) Subject to section 1B(1) and (2) below, the maximum term of detention in a young offender institution that a court may impose for an offence is the same as the maximum term of imprisonment that it may impose for that offence.

(3) Subject to subsection (4) below and section 1B(3) below, a court shall not pass a sentence for an offender's detention in a young offender institution for less than 21 days.

(4) A court may pass a sentence of detention in a young offender institution for less than 21 days for an offence under section 15(11) below.

(5) Subject to section 1B(4) below, where—

(a) an offender is convicted of more than one offence for which he is liable to a sentence of detention in a young offender institution; or

(b) an offender who is serving a sentence of detention in a young offender institution is convicted of one or more further offences for which he is liable to such a sentence.

the court shall have the same power to pass consecutive sentences of detention in a young offender institution as if they were sentences of imprisonment

(6) Where an offender who—

(a) is serving a sentence of detention in a young offender institution; and

(b) is aged over 21 years,

is convicted of one or more further offences for which he is liable to imprisonment, the court shall have the power to pass one or more sentences of imprisonment to run consecutively upon the sentence of detention in a young offender institution.

1B. **Special provision for offenders under 17**

(1) In the case of a male offender under 15 the maximum term of detention in a young offender institution that a court may impose is whichever is the lesser of—

(a) the maximum term of imprisonment the court may impose for the offence; and

(b) 4 months.

(2) In the case of an offender aged 15 or 16 the maximum term of detention in a young offender institution that a court may impose is whichever is the lesser of—

(a) the maximum term of imprisonment the court may impose for the offence; and
(b) 12 months.

(3) Where an offender is a female under 17 a court shall not pass a sentence for her detention in a young offender institution whose effect would be that she would be sentenced to a total term of four months or less.

(4) A court shall not pass a sentence of detention in a young offender institution on an offender whose effect would be that the offender would be sentenced to a total term which exceeds—
    (a) if the offender is male and under 15, 4 months; and
    (b) if the offender is aged 15 or 16, 12 months.

(5) Where the total term of detention in a young offender institution to which an offender is sentenced exceeds—
    (a) in the case of a male offender under 15, 4 months; and
    (b) in the case of an offender aged 15 or 16, 12 months,
so much of the term as exceeds 4 or 12 months, as the case may be, shall be treated as remitted.

(6) In this section 'total term' means—
    (a) in the case of an offender sentenced (whether or not on the same occasion) to two or more terms of detention in a young offender institution which are consecutive or wholly or partly concurrent, the aggregate of those terms;
    (b) in the case of any other offender, the term of the sentence of detention in a young offender institution in question.

1C. Accommodation of offenders sentenced to detention in a young offender institution

(1) Subject to section 22(2)(b) of the Prison Act 1952 (removal to hospital etc.), an offender sentenced to detention in a young offender institution shall be detained in such an institution unless a direction under this section is in force in relation to him.

(2) The Secretary of State may from time to time direct that an offender sentenced to detention in a young offender institution shall be detained in a prison or remand centre instead of a young offender institution, but if he is under 17 at the time of the direction, only for a temporary purpose.]

2. Social inquiry reports etc.

(1) For the purpose of determining whether there is any appropriate method of dealing with a person under 21 years of age other than a method whose use in the case of such a person is restricted by section 1(4) or (5) above the court shall obtain and consider information about the circumstances and shall take into account any information before the court which is relevant to his character and his physical and mental condition.

(2) Subject to subsection (3) below, the court shall in every case obtain a social inquiry report for the purpose of determining whether there is any appropriate method of dealing with a person other than a method whose use is restricted by section 1(4) above.

(3) Subsection (2) above does not apply if, in the circumstances of the case, the court is of the opinion that it is unnecessary to obtain a social inquiry report.

[(4) Where—
    (a) the Crown Court passes a sentence of detention in a young offender institution or a sentence of custody for life under section 8(2) below, or
    (b) a magistrates' court passes a sentence of detention in a young offender institution,
it shall be its duty—

(i) to state in open court that it is satisfied that he qualifies for a custodial sentence under one or more of the paragraphs of section 1(4A) above, the paragraph or paragraphs in question and why it is so satisfied; and

(ii) to explain to the offender in open court and in ordinary language why it is passing a custodial sentence on him.]

(5) Where a magistrates' court deals with a person under 21 years of age by a method whose use in the case of such a person is restricted by section 1(5) above, it shall state in open court the reason for its opinion that no other method of dealing with him is appropriate.

(6) Where a magistrates' court deals with a person under 21 years of age by a method whose use in the case of such a person is restricted by section 1(4) above without obtaining a social inquiry report, it shall state in open court the reason for its opinion that it was unnecessary to obtain such a report.

(7) A magistrates' court shall cause a reason stated under subsection (4), (5) or (6) above to be specified in the warrant of commitment and to be entered in the register.

(8) No sentence or order shall be invalidated by the failure of a court to comply with subsection (2) above, but any other court on appeal from that court shall obtain a social inquiry report if none was obtained by the court below, unless it is of the opinion that in the circumstances of the case it is unnecessary to do so.

(9) In determining whether it should deal with the appellant by a method different from that by which the court below dealt with him the court hearing the appeal shall consider any social inquiry report obtained by it or by the court below.

(10) In this section "social inquiry report" means a report about a person and his circumstances made by a probation officer or by a social worker of a local authority social services department.

3. Restriction on imposing custodial sentences on persons under 21 not legally represented.

(1) A magistrates' court on summary conviction or the Crown Court on committal for sentence or on conviction on indictment shall not—

(a) make a detention centre order under section 4 below;
(b) pass a youth custody sentence under section 6 below;
(c) pass a sentence of custody for life under section 8(2) below; or
(d) make an order for detention under section 53(2) of the Children and Young Persons Act 1933,

in respect of or on a person who is not legally represented in that court, unless either—

(i) he applied for legal aid and the application was refused on the ground that it did not appear his means were such that he required assistance; or

(ii) having been informed of his right to apply for legal aid and had the opportunity to do so, he refused or failed to apply.

(2) For the purposes of this section a person is to be treated as legally represented in a court if, but only if, he has the assistance of counsel or a solicitor to represent him in the proceedings in that court at some time after he is found guilty and before he is sentenced, and in subsection (1)(i) and (ii) above "legal aid" means legal aid for the purposes of proceedings in that court, whether the whole proceedings or the proceedings on or in relation to sentence; but in the case of a person committed to the Crown Court for sentence or trial, it is immaterial whether he applied for legal aid in the Crown Court to, or was informed of his right to apply by, that court or the court which committed him.

4.—7. *****

8. Custody for life

(1) Where a person under the age of 21 is convicted of murder or any other offence the sentence for which is fixed by law as imprisonment for life, the court shall sentence him to custody for life unless he is liable to be detained under section 53(1) of the Children and Young Persons Act 1933 (detention of persons under 18 convicted of murder).

(2) Where a person aged 17 years or over but under the age of 21 is convicted of any other offence for which a person aged 21 years or over would be liable to imprisonment for life, the court shall, if it considers that a custodial sentence for life would be appropriate, sentence him to custody for life.

9. Detention of persons aged 17 to 20 for default or contempt.

(1) In any case where, but for section 1(1) above, a court would have power—

(a) to commit a person under 21 but not less than 17 years of age to prison for default in payment of a fine or any other sum of money; or

(b) to make an order fixing a term of imprisonment in the event of such a default by such a person; or

(c) to commit such a person to prison for contempt of court or any kindred offence,

the court shall have power, subject to section 1(5) above, to commit him to be detained under this section or, as the case may be, to make an order fixing a term of detention under this section in the event of default, for a term not exceeding the term of imprisonment.

(2) For the purposes of subsection (1) above, the power of a court to order a person to be imprisoned under section 23 of the Attachment of Earnings Act 1971 shall be taken to be a power to commit him to prison.

10.—34. *****(Note. — 14 and 34 repealed)

PART III
FINES ETC.

Abolition of enhanced penalties

35. Abolition of enhanced penalties on subsequent conviction of summary offences under Acts of Parliament.

(1) Subject to subsection (3) below, this section applies where under an Act a person convicted of a summary offence—

(a) is liable to a fine or maximum fine of one amount in the case of a first conviction and of a different amount in the case of a second or subsequent conviction; or

(b) is liable to imprisonment for a longer term in the case of a second or subsequent conviction; or

(c) is only liable to imprisonment in the case of a second or subsequent conviction.

(2) Where this section applies, a person guilty of such an offence shall be liable on summary conviction—

(a) to a fine or, as the case may be, a maximum fine of an amount not exceeding the greatest amount;

(b) to imprisonment for a term not exceeding the longest or only term,

to which he would have been liable before this section came into force if his conviction had satisfied the conditions required for the imposition of a fine or maximum fine of that amount or imprisonment for that term.

(3) This section does not apply to offences under—

(a) sections 33 to 36 of the Sexual Offences Act 1956 (brothel-keeping and prostitution); and

(b) section 1(2) of the Street Offences Act 1959 (loitering and soliciting for the purpose of prostitution).

36. Abolition of enhanced penalties under subordinate instruments

(1) This section applies where an Act (however framed or worded) confers power by subordinate instrument to make a person, as regards any summary offence (whether or not created by the instrument), liable on conviction—

(a) to a fine or maximum fine of one amount in the case of a first conviction and of a different amount in the case of a second or subsequent conviction; or

(b) to imprisonment for a longer term in the case of a second or subsequent conviction; or

(c) to imprisonment only in the case of a second or subsequent conviction.

(2) Any such Act shall have effect as if it conferred power by subordinate instrument to make a person liable—

(a) to a fine or, as the case may be, a maximum fine of an amount not exceeding the greatest amount;

(b) to imprisonment for a term not exceeding the longest or only term,

to which he would have been liable before this section came into force if his conviction had satisfied the conditions required for the imposition of a fine or maximum fine of that amount or imprisonment for that term.

Introduction of standard scale of fines

37. The standard scale of fines for summary offences

(1) There shall be a standard scale of fines for summary offences, which shall be known as "the standard scale".

(2) The scale at the commencement of this section is shown below.

Level on the scale	Amount of fine
1	[£50]
2	[£100]
3	[£400]
4	[£1,000]
5	[£2,000]

(3) Where any enactment (whether contained in an Act passed before or after this Act) provides—

(a) that a person convicted of a summary offence shall be liable on conviction to a fine or a maximum fine by reference to a specified level on the standard scale; or

(b) confers power by subordinate instrument to make a person liable on conviction of a summary offence (whether or not created by the instrument) to a fine or maximum fine by reference to a specified level on the standard scale,

it is to be construed as referring to the standard scale for which this section provides as that standard scale has effect from time to time by virtue either of this section or of an order under section 143 of the Magistrates' Courts Act 1980.

Increase of fines

38. General increase of fines for summary offences under Acts of Parliament

(1) Subject to subsection (5) below and to section 39(1) below, this section applies to any enactment contained in an Act passed before this Act (however framed or worded) which, as regards any summary offence created not later than 29th July 1977 (the date

of the passing of the Criminal Law Act 1977), makes a person liable on conviction to a fine or maximum fine which—
  (a) is less than £1,000; and
  (b) was not altered by section 30 or 31 of the Criminal Law Act 1977; and
  (c) has not been altered since 29th July 1977 or has only been altered since that date by section 35 above.

(2) Subject to subsection (7) below, where an enactment to which this section applies provides on conviction of a summary offence for a fine or maximum fine in respect of a specified quantity or a specified number of things, that fine or maximum fine shall be treated for the purposes of this section as being the fine or maximum fine for the offence.

(3) Where an enactment to which this section applies provides for different fines or maximum fines in relation to different circumstances or persons of different descriptions, they are to be treated separately for the purposes of this section.

(4) An enactment in which section 31(6) and (7) of the Criminal Law Act 1977 (pre-1949 enactments) produced the same fine or maximum fine for different convictions shall be treated for the purposes of this section as if there were omitted from it so much of it as before 29th July 1977 had the effect that a person guilty of an offence under it was liable on summary conviction to a fine or maximum fine less than the highest fine or maximum fine to which he would have been liable if his conviction had satisfied the conditions required for the imposition of the highest fine or maximum fine.

(5) This section shall not affect so much of any enactment as (in whatever words) makes a person liable on summary conviction to a fine or maximum fine for each period of a specified length during which a continuing offence is continued.

(6) The fine or maximum fine for an offence under an enactment to which this section applies shall be increased to the amount at the appropriate level on the standard scale unless it is an enactment in relation to which section 39(2) below provides for some other increase.

(7) Where an enactment to which this section applies provides on conviction of a summary offence for a fine or maximum fine in respect of a specified quantity or a specified number of things but also specifies an alternative fine or maximum fine, subsection (6) above shall have effect to increase—
  (a) the alternative fine; and
  (b) any amount that the enactment specifies as the maximum which a fine under it may not exceed,
as well as the fine or maximum fine which it has effect to increase by virtue of subsection (2) above.

(8) Subject to subsection (9) below, the appropriate level on the standard scale for the purposes of subsections (6) and (7) above is the level on that scale next above the amount of the fine or maximum fine that falls to be increased.

(9) If the amount of the fine or maximum fine that falls to be increased is £400 or more but less than £500, the appropriate level if £1,000.

(10) Where section 35 above applies, the amount of the fine or maximum fine that falls to be increased is to be taken to be the fine or maximum fine to which a person is liable by virtue of that section.

COUNTY COURTS ACT 1984
(1984, c. 28)

An Act to consolidate certain enactments relating to county courts   [26 June 1984]

PART I
CONSTITUTION AND ADMINISTRATION
County courts and districts

1. County courts to be held for districts

(1) For the purposes of this Act, England and Wales shall be divided into districts, and a court shall be held under this Act for each district at one or more places in it; and throughout the whole of each district the court so held for the district shall have such jurisdiction and powers as are conferred by this Act and any other enactment for the time being in force.

(2) Every court so held shall be called a county court and shall be a court or record and shall have a seal.

(3) *****

2.—4. *****

Judges

5. Judges of county courts

(1) Every Circuit judge shall, by virtue of his office, be capable of sitting as a judge for any county court district in England and Wales, and the Lord Chancellor shall assign one or more Circuit judges to each district and may from time to time vary the assignment of Circuit judges among the districts.

(2) Subject to any directions given by or on behalf of the Lord Chancellor, in any case where more than one Circuit judge is assigned to a district under subsection (1), any function conferred by or under this Act on the judge for a district may be exercised by any of the Circuit judges for the time being assigned to that district.

(3) The following, that is—
every judge of the Court of Appeal,
every judge of the High Court,
every Recorder,
shall, by virtue of his office, be capable of sitting as a judge for any county court district in England and Wales and, if he consents to do so, shall sit as such a judge at such times and on such occasions as the Lord Chancellor considers desirable.

(4) Notwithstanding that he is not for the time being assigned to a particular district, a Circuit judge—

(a) shall sit as a judge of that district at such times and on such occasions as the Lord Chancellor may direct; and

(b) may sit as a judge of that district in any case where it appears to him that the judge of that district is not, or none of the judges of that district is, available to deal with the case.

Registrars, assistant registrars and deputy registrars

6. Registrars

(1) Subject to the provisions of this section, there shall be a registrar for each district, who shall be appointed by the Lord Chancellor and paid such salary as the Lord Chancellor may, with the concurrence of the Treasury, direct.

(2) The Lord Chancellor may, if he thinks fit, appoint a person to be registrar for two or more districts.

(3) The Lord Chancellor may, if he thinks fit, appoint two or more persons to

County Courts Act 1984

execute jointly the office of registrar for a district and may, in any case where joint registrars are appointed, give directions with respect to the division between them of the duties of the office.

(4) The Lord Chancellor may, as he thinks fit, on the death, resignation or removal of a joint registrar, either appoint another person to be joint registrar in his place or give directions that the continuing registrar shall act as sole registrar or, as the case may be, that the continuing registrars shall execute jointly the office of registrar.

(5) The registrar for any district shall be capable of acting, in any other district for the registrar of that other district.

7., 8.   *****

9. Qualifications
No person shall be appointed a registrar, assistant registrar or deputy registrar unless he is a solicitor of at least 7 years' standing.

10. Restrictions on practice as solicitor of registrars and assistant registrars
(1) Subject to subsection (2), a registrar or assistant registrar shall not directly or indirectly practise as a solicitor or as an agent for a solicitor.

(2) If in any case the Lord Chancellor thinks it expedient so to do, he may authorise a registrar or assistant registrar to practise as a solicitor or as an agent for a solicitor, either subject to such restrictions as may be specified in the authorisation or without restrictions.

(3) A registrar with respect to whom an authorisation has been given under subsection (2) is in this Act referred to as a "part-time registrar", and an assistant registrar with respect to whom an authorisation has been so given is referred to as a "part-time assistant registrar".

(4) The Lord Chancellor may revoke an authorisation under subsection (2) by giving notice to the part-time registrar or part-time assistant registrar to whom it applies.

(5) A part-time registrar shall not, by virtue of section 6(5), act as registrar in relation to any proceedings in which he is, either by himself or his partner, directly or indirectly engaged as solicitor or agent for any party.

11. Tenure of office
(1) This subsection applies—
    (a)   to the office of registrar or assistant registrar; and
    (b)   to the office of part-time registrar or part-time assistant registrar.

(2) Subject to the following provisions of this section, a person who holds an office to which subsection (1) applies shall vacate his office at the end of the completed year of service in which he attains the age of 72 years.

(3) Where the Lord Chancellor considers it desirable in the public interest to retain in office a person who holds an office to which subsection (1) applies after the time when he would otherwise retire in accordance with subsection (2), the Lord Chancellor may from time to time authorise the continuance in office of that person until such date, not being later than the date on which that person attains the age of 75 years, as he thinks fit.

(4) A person appointed to an office to which subsection (1) applies shall hold that office during good behaviour.

(5) The power to remove such a person from his office on account of misbehaviour shall be exercisable by the Lord Chancellor.

(6) The Lord Chancellor may also remove such a person from his office on account of inability to perform the duties of his office.

12.—14. *****

PART II
JURISDICTION AND TRANSFER OF PROCEEDINGS
Actions of contract and tort

15. General jurisdiction in actions of contract and tort

(1) Subject to subsection (2), a county court shall have jurisdiction to hear and determine any action founded on contract or tort where the debt, demand or damage claimed does not exceed the county court limit whether on balance of account or otherwise.

(2) A county court shall not, except as in this Act provided, have jurisdiction to hear and determine—

    (a)   any action for the recovery of land; or

    (b)   any action in which the title to any hereditament or to any toll, fair, market or franchise is in question; or

    (c)   any action for libel or slander.

(3) A county court shall have jurisdiction to hear and determine any action where the debt or demand claimed consists of a balance not exceeding the county court limit after a set-off of any debt or demand claimed or recoverable by the defendant from the plaintiff, being a set-off admitted by the plaintiff in the particulars of his claim or demand.

16. Money recoverable by statute

A county court shall have jurisdiction to hear and determine an action for the recovery of a sum recoverable by virtue of any enactment for the time being in force, if—

    (a)   it is not provided by that or any other enactment that such sums shall only be recoverable in the High Court or shall only be recoverable summarily; and

    (b)   the amount claimed in the action does not exceed the county court limit.

17. Abandonment of part of claim to give court jurisdiction

(1) Where a plaintiff has a cause of action for more than the county court limit in which, if it were not for more than the county court limit, a county court would have jurisdiction, the plaintiff may abandon the excess, and thereupon a county court shall have jurisdiction to hear and determine the action, but the plaintiff shall not recover in the action an amount exceeding the county court limit.

(2) Where the court has jurisdiction to hear and determine an action by virtue of this section, the judgment of the court in the action shall be in full discharge of all demands in respect of the cause of action, and entry of the judgment shall be made accordingly.

18. Jurisdiction by agreement in certain actions

If the parties to any action, other than an action which, if commenced in the High Court, would have been assigned to the Chancery Division or to the Family Division or have involved the exercise of the High Court's Admiralty jurisdiction, agree, by a memorandum signed by them or by their respective solicitors, that a county court specified in the memorandum shall have jurisdiction in the action, that court shall have jurisdiction to hear and determine the action accordingly.

19. Limitation of recoverable costs of actions of contract or tort commenced in High Court which could have been commenced in county court

(1) Subject to subsections (2) to (4) and section 29, where an action founded on contract or tort is commenced in the High Court which could have been commenced in the county court the costs (if any) of the proceedings in the High Court to which the plaintiff is entitled shall be determined in accordance with section 20.

(2) Neither this section nor section 20 affects any question as to costs if it appears to the High Court that there was reasonable ground for supposing the amount recoverable

in respect of the plaintiff's claim to be in excess of the amount recoverable in an action commenced in the county court.

(3) The High Court, if satisfied—

(a) that there was sufficient reason for bringing the action in the High Court; or

(b) that the defendant or one of the defendants objected to the transfer of the action to a county court;

may make an order allowing the costs or any part of the costs on the High Court scale or on such one of the county court scales as it may direct,

(4) Neither this section nor section 20 applies in the case of proceedings by the Crown.

20. Rules for limitation of recoverable costs

(1) If the plaintiff in an action for the recovery of goods to which this section applies recovers an aggregate amount less than the higher limit, he shall not be entitled to recover any more costs of the action than those to which he would have been entitled if the action had been brought in the county court.

(2) If the plaintiff in an action to which this section applies, other than one for the recovery of goods, recovers a sum less than the higher limit, he shall not be entitled to recover any most costs of the action than those to which he would have been entitled if the action had been brought in the county court.

(3) Where a plaintiff is entitled to costs on a county court scale only, the taxing master shall have the same power of directing on what county court scale costs are to be allowed, and of allowing any item of costs, as the judge would have had if the action had been brought in a county court.

(4) If the plaintiff in an action for the recovery of goods to which this section applies recovers an aggregate amount less than the lower limit, he shall not be entitled to recover any costs of the action.

(5) If the plaintiff in an action to which this section applies, other than one for the recovery of goods, recovers a sum less than the lower limit, he shall not be entitled to recover any costs of the action.

(6) For the purposes of this section a plaintiff shall be treated as recovering the full amount recoverable in respect of his claim without regard to any deduction made in respect of contributory negligence on his part or otherwise in respect of matters not falling to be taken into account in determining whether the action could have been commenced in the county court.

(7) In this section "action for the recovery of goods" means an action brought to enforce a right to recover possession of goods or to enforce such a right and to claim payment of a debt or other demand or damages.

(8) The aggregate amount mentioned in subsections (1) and (4) includes the value—

(a) of any goods ordered in the action to be delivered to the plaintiff; and

(b) of any goods so ordered to be delivered of which the value is in the alternative ordered to be paid to him.

(9) In this section—

"the higher limit" means, subject to section 145, £3,000;

"the lower limit" means, subject to section 145, £600.

Recovery of land and cases where title in question

21. Actions for recovery of land and actions where title is in question

(1) A county court shall have jurisdiction to hear and determine any action for the recovery of land where the net annual value for rating of the land does not exceed the county court limit.

(2) A county court shall have jurisdiction to hear and determine any action in which

the title to any hereditament comes in question, being an action which would otherwise be within the jurisdiction of the court,—

    (a)   in the case of an easement or licence, if the net annual value for rating of the hereditament in respect of which the easement or licence is claimed, or on, through over or under which the easement or licence is claimed, does not exceed the county court limit; or

    (b)   in any other case, if the net annual value for rating of the hereditament in question does not exceed the county court limit.

(3) Where a mortgage of land consists of or includes a dwelling-house and no part of the land is situated in Greater London then, subject to subsection (4), if a county court has jurisdiction by virtue of this section to hear and determine an action in which the mortgagee under that mortgage claims possession of the mortgaged property, no court other than a county court shall have jurisdiction to hear and determine that action.

(4) Subsection (3) shall not apply to an action for foreclosure or sale in which a claim for possession of the mortgaged property is also made.

(5) If an action in which the mortgagee under a mortgage of land claims possession of the mortgaged property would, by virtue of this section, be within the jurisdiction of a county court had that claim been the only claim made in the action, a county court shall have jurisdiction to hear and determine the action notwithstanding that a claim is also made in the action for payment by the mortgagor of the amount owing in respect of the mortgage or for payment of that amount by any person who guaranteed the debt secured by the mortgage and that by reason of the amount claimed the last mentioned claim is not within the jurisdiction of a county court.

(6) Nothing in subsection (5) shall be taken as empowering a county court to hear and determine an action for foreclosure or sale which is not within the jurisdiction of a county court.

(7) In this section—

"dwelling-house" includes any building or part of a building which is used as a dwelling;

"mortgage" includes a charge and "mortgagor" and "mortgagee" shall be construed accordingly;

"mortgagor" and "mortgagee" includes any person deriving title under the original mortgagor or mortgagee.

(8) The fact that part of the premises comprised in a dwelling-house is used as a shop or office or for business, trade or professional purposes shall not prevent the dwelling-house from being a dwelling-house for the purposes of this section.

(9) This section does not apply to a mortgage securing an agreement which is a regulated agreement within the meaning of the Consumer Credit Act 1974.

22. Injunctions and declarations relating to land

(1) Subject to the provisions of this section, a county court shall have the same jurisdiction as the High Court to grant an injunction or declaration in respect of, or relating to, any land, or the possession, occupation, use or enjoyment of any land.

(2) This section only applies where the net annual value for rating of the relevant land does not exceed the county court limit for section 21.

(3) In this section "land" includes any hereditament, and in the case of an easement or licence the relevant land for the purposes of subsection (2) is the land in respect of which the easement or licence is claimed or on, through, over or under which the easement or licence is claimed.

Equity proceedings

23. Equity jurisdiction

A county court shall have all the jurisdiction of the High Court to hear and determine—

(a) proceedings for the administration of the estate of a deceased person, where the estate does not exceed in amount or value the county court limit;

(b) proceedings—

  (i) for the execution of any trust, or
  (ii) for a declaration that a trust subsists, or
  (iii) under section 1 of the Variation of Trusts Act 1958,

where the estate or fund subject, or alleged to be subject, to the trust does not exceed in amount or value the county court limit;

(c) proceedings for foreclosure or redemption of any mortgage or for enforcing any charge or lien, where the amount owing in respect of the mortgage, charge or lien does not exceed the county court limit;

(d) proceedings for the specific performance, or for the rectification, delivery up or cancellation, of any agreement for the sale, purchase or lease of any property, where, in the case of a sale or purchase, the purchase money, or in the case of a lease, the value of the property, does not exceed the county court limit;

(e) proceedings relating to the maintenance or advancement of a minor, where the property of the minor does not exceed in amount or value the county court limit;

(f) proceedings for the dissolution or winding-up of any partnership (whether or not the existence of the partnerships is in dispute), where the whole assets of the partnership do not exceed in amount or value the county court limit;

(g) proceedings for relief against fraud or mistake, where the damage sustained or the estate or fund in respect of which relief is sought does not exceed in amount or value the county court limit.

24. *****

Family provision proceedings

25. Jurisdiction under Inheritance (Provision for Family and Dependants) Act 1975.

A county court shall have jurisdiction to hear and determine any application for an order under section 2 of the Inheritance (Provision for Family and Dependants) Act 1975 (including any application for permission to apply for such an order and any application made, in the proceedings on an application for such an order, for an order under any other provision of that Act) where it is shown to the satisfaction of the court that the value at the date of the death of the deceased of all property included in his net estate for the purposes of that Act by virtue of paragraph (a) of the definition of "net estate" in section 25(1) of that Act does not exceed the county court limit.

26.—31. *****

[32. Contentious probate jurisdiction

(1) Where—

(a) an application for the grant or revocation of probate or administration has been made through the principal registry of the Family Division or a district probate registry under section 105 of the Supreme Court Act 1981; and

(b) it is shown to the satisfaction of a county court that the value at the date of the death of the deceased of his net estate does not exceed the county court limit,

the county court shall have the jurisdiction of the High Court in respect of any contentious matter arising in connection with the grant or revocation.

(2) In subsection (1) "net estate", in relation to a deceased person, means the estate of that person exclusive of any property he was possessed of or entitled to as a trustee

and not beneficially, and after making allowances for funeral expenses and for debts and liabilities.]

33. Effect of order of judge in probate proceedings
Where an order is made by a county court for the grant or revocation of probate or administration, in pursuance of any jurisdiction conferred upon [the court] by section 32—

    (a)   the registrar of the county court shall transmit to the principal registry of the Family Division or a district probate registry, as he thinks convenient, a certificate under the seal of the court certifying that the order has been made; and

    (b)   on the application of a party in favour of whom the order has been made, probate or administration in compliance with the order shall be issued from the registry to which the certificate was sent or, as the case may require, the probate or letters of administration previously granted shall be recalled or varied by, as the case may be, a registrar of the principal registry of the Family Division or the district probate registrar according to the effect of the order.

Miscellaneous provisions as to jurisdiction

34. Proceedings beyond jurisdiction
(1) Subject to subsection (2), where any proceedings are commenced in a county court in which a county court has no jurisdiction, the court shall, unless it is given jurisdiction by a jurisdiction agreement, order that the proceedings be transferred to the High Court.

(2) Where, on the application of any defendant, it appears to the court that the plaintiff or one of the plaintiffs knew or ought to have known that the court had no jurisdiction in the proceedings, the court may, if it thinks fit, instead of ordering that the proceedings be transferred, order that they be struck out.

(3) In this section "jurisdiction agreement" means an agreement under section 18, 24 or 27(6).

35. Division of causes of action
It shall not be lawful for any plaintiff to divide any cause of action for the purpose of bringing two or more actions in one or more of the county courts.

36. No action on judgment of High Court
No action shall be brought in a county court on any judgment of the High Court.

Exercise of jurisdiction and ancillary jurisdiction

37. Persons who may exercise jurisdiction of court
(1) Any jurisdiction and powers conferred by this or any other Act—
    (a)   on a county court; or
    (b)   on the judge of a county court,
may be exercised by any judge of the court.

(2) Subsection (1) applies to jurisdiction and powers conferred on all county courts or judges of county courts or on any particular county court or the judge of any particular county court.

38. General ancillary jurisdiction
(1) Every county court, as regards any cause of action for the time being within its jurisdiction,—
    (a)   shall grant such relief, redress or remedy or combination of remedies, either absolute or conditional; and
    (b)   shall give such and the like effect to every ground of defence or counterclaim equitable or legal,

as ought to be granted or given in the like case by the High Court and in as full and ample a manner.

(2) For the purposes of this section it shall be assumed (notwithstanding any enactment to the contrary) that any proceedings which can be commenced in a county court could be commenced in the High Court.

39. Ancillary powers of judge
A judge shall have jurisdiction in any pending proceedings to make any order or exercise any authority or jurisdiction which, if it related to an action or proceeding pending in the High Court, might be made or exercised by a judge of the High Court in chambers.

Transfer of proceedings

40. Transfer of proceedings to county court
(1) At any stage in any proceedings to which this section applies, the High Court may, in accordance with rules of the Supreme Court, either of its own motion or on the application of any party to the proceedings, order the transfer of the whole or any part of the proceedings to a county court if—

    (a)   the parties consent to the transfer; or

    (b)   the High Court is satisfied—

        (i)   that, after allowance has been made for any payment, set-off or other amount admitted to be due, the amount remaining in dispute in respect of the claim is within the monetary limit of the jurisdiction of the county court; or

        (ii)   that the amount recoverable in respect of the claim is likely to be within the monetary limit of the jurisdiction of the county court; or

        (iii)   in the case of proceedings not involving an unliquidated claim, that the subject matter of the proceedings is or is likely to be within the limits of the jurisdiction of the county court; or

    (c)   where only a counterclaim remains in dispute, the High Court considers that the amount recoverable in respect of the counterclaim is likely to be within the monetary limit of the jurisdiction of the county court; or

    (d)   the High Court considers that the proceedings are not likely to raise any important question of law or fact and are suitable for determination by a county court.

(2) Subject to subsection (3), this section applies to all proceedings commenced in the High Court which a county court would, apart from any limitation by reason of amount or value or annual value, have jurisdiction to hear and determine if commenced in that court.

(3) This section does not apply to the following proceedings, namely—

    (a)   matrimonial causes;

    (b)   applications relating to the adoption or custody of, or access to, minors (including applications relating to guardianship or custodianship).

(4) This section applies to all proceedings transferred to the High Court under section 41 or 42.

(5) An order for the transfer to a county court of any proceedings by or against the Crown in the High Court shall not be made without the consent of the Crown.

(6) Proceedings transferred under this section shall be transferred to such county court as the High Court considers to be convenient to the parties.

(7) Where proceedings are ordered to be transferred from the High Court to a county court—

    (a)   any party may lodge with the registrar of the county court named in the order, or cause to be lodged with him, the order and the writ, or copies of them, and such other documents (if any) as the High Court may direct; and

    (b)   the proper officer of the Supreme Court shall, on the application of that party and on the production of the order and the filing of a copy of it, send by post to the registrar of the county court all pleadings, affidavits and other documents filed in the High Court relating to the proceedings.

(8) Subject to subsection (9), on the documents mentioned in subsection (7) being so lodged or sent, the proceedings shall be transferred to the county court.

(9) The transfer shall not affect any right of appeal from the order directing the transfer, or the right to enforce in the High Court any judgment signed, or order made, in that court before the transfer.

(10) Where proceedings are transferred to a county court under this section, the county court shall have jurisdiction—
    (a)   to hear and determine those proceedings; and
    (b)   to award any relief, including any amount of damages, which could have been awarded by the High Court.

41. Transfer to High Court by order of High Court

(1) If at any stage in proceedings commenced in a county court or transferred to a county court under section 40, the High Court thinks it desirable that the proceedings, or any part of them, should be heard and determined in the High Court, it may order the transfer to the High Court of the proceedings or, as the case may be, of that part of them.

(2) The power conferred by subsection (1) is without prejudice to section 29 of the Supreme Court Act 1981 (power of High Court to issue prerogative orders).

42. Transfer to High Court by order of county court

(1) At any stage in any proceedings to which this section applies, the county court may, either of its own motion or on the application of any party to the proceedings, order the transfer of the whole or any part of the proceedings to the High Court if—
    (a)   the court considers that some important question of law or fact is likely to arise; or
    (b)   the court considers that one or other of the parties is likely to be entitled in respect of a claim or counter-claim to an amount exceeding the amount recoverable in the county court; or
    (c)   any counterclaim or set-off and counterclaim of a defendant involves matters beyond the jurisdiction of the county court.

(2) Where—
    (a)   the county court has ordered that the proceedings on a counterclaim or set-off and counterclaim be transferred to the High Court, but the proceedings on the plaintiff's claim and the defence other than any set-off are heard and determined in the county court; and
    (b)   judgment on the claim is given for the plaintiff,
execution of the judgment shall, unless the High Court at any time otherwise orders, be stayed until the proceedings transferred to the High Court have been concluded.

(3) This section applies to all proceedings commenced in a county court which the High Court would have jurisdiction to hear and determine if they were commenced in it, other than—
    (a)   matrimonial causes;
    (b)   applications relating to the adoption or custody of, or access to, minors (including applications relating to guardianship or custodianship).

(4) This section applies to all proceedings transferred to a county court under section 40.

43. Jurisdiction to deal with counterclaim or set-off and counterclaim.

If the condition specified in section 42(1)(c) is satisfied, but—
    (a)   no application is made for an order under that section; or
    (b)   an application for such an order is made but is refused,

County Courts Act 1984   247

the county court shall have jurisdiction to deal with the counter-claim or set-off and counterclaim.

44. Transfer of interpleader proceedings from High Court to county court
If it appears to the High Court that any proceedings in the High Court by way of interpleader, in which the amount or value of the matter in dispute does not exceed the county court limit, may be more conveniently heard and determined in a county court, the High Court may at any time order that that proceedings be transferred to any county court in which proceedings might have been brought by any party to the interpleader against any other party to it if there had been a trust to be executed concerning the matter in question.

45. Costs in transferred cases
(1) Where an action, counterclaim or matter is ordered to be transferred—
    (a)   from the High Court to a county court; or
    (b)   from a county court to the High Court; or
    (c)   from one county court to another county court,
the costs of the whole proceedings both before and after the transfer shall, subject to any order of the court which ordered the transfer, be in the discretion of the court to which the proceedings are transferred; and that court shall have power to make orders with respect to the costs and as to the scales on which the costs of the several parts of the proceedings are to be taxed, and the costs of the whole proceedings shall be taxed in that court.

(2) The costs of so much of the proceedings in any action transferred from the High court to a county court as takes place in the High Court before the transfer shall be subject to section 19, and the powers of the High Court under section 19(3) to make an order allowing costs on the High Court scale or on any county court scale shall, subject to any order of the High Court, be exercisable by the county court.

PART III
PROCEDURE

46.—50. *****

51. Orders for provisional damages for personal injuries
(1) This section applies to an action for damages for personal injuries in which there is proved or admitted to be a chance that at some definite or indefinite time in the future the injured person will, as a result of the act or omission which gave rise to the cause of action, develop some serious disease or suffer some serious deterioration in his physical or mental condition.

(2) Subject to subsection (4), as regards any action for damages to which this section applies in which a judgment is given in the county court, provision may be made by county court rules for enabling the court, in such circumstances as may be prescribed, to award the injured person—
    (a)   damages assessed on the assumption that the injured person will not develop the disease or suffer the deterioration in his condition; and
    (b)   further damages at a future date if he develops the disease or suffers the deterioration.

(3) Any rules made by virtue of this section may include such incidental, supplementary and consequential provisions as the rule committee may consider necessary or expedient.

(4) Nothing in this section shall be construed—
    (a)   as affecting the exercise of any power relating to costs, including any power to make county court rules relating to costs; or
    (b)   as prejudicing any duty of the court under any enactment or rule of law

to reduce or limit the total damages which would have been recoverable apart from any such duty.

(5) In this section "personal injuries" includes any disease and any impairment of a person's physical or mental condition.

52.—59. *****

Right of audience

60. Right of audience

(1) In any proceedings in a county court any of the following persons may address the court—

    (a)   any party to the proceedings;

    (b)   a barrister retained by or on behalf of any party;

    (c)   a solicitor acting generally in the proceedings for a party to them (in this subsection referred to as a "solicitor on the record");

    (d)   any solicitor employed by a solicitor on the record;

    (e)   any solicitor engaged as an agent by a solicitor on the record;

    (f)   any solicitor employed by a solicitor so engaged; and

    (g)   any other person allowed by leave of the court to appear instead of any party;

but a court may refuse to hear a person claiming to address the court as a solicitor unless that person has signed and delivered to the court a statement of his name and place of business and the name of the firm (if any) of which he is a member.

(2) Where an action is brought in a county court by a local authority for either or both of the following—

    (a)   the recovery of possession of a house belonging to the authority;

    (b)   the recovery of any rent, mesne profits, damages or other sum claimed by the authority in respect of the occupation by any person of such a house,

then, in so far as the proceedings in the action are heard by the registrar, any officer of the authority authorised by the authority in that behalf, not being a person entitled to address the court by virtue of subsection (1), may address the registrar as if he were a person so entitled.

(3) In this section—

"local authority" means a county council, a district council, [the Broads Authority,] a London borough council [a joint authority established by part IV of the Local Government Act 1985] or the Common Council of the City of London; and

"house" includes a part of a house, a flat or any other dwelling and also includes any yard, garden, outhouse or appurtenance occupied with a house or part of a house or with a flat or other dwelling,

and any reference to the occupation of a house by a person includes a reference to anything done by that person, or caused or permitted by him to be done, in relation to the house as occupier of the house, whether under a tenancy or licence or otherwise.

61. Right of audience by direction of Lord Chancellor

(1) The Lord Chancellor may at any time direct that such categories of persons in relevant legal employment as may be specified in the direction may address the court in any proceedings in a county court, or in proceedings in a county court of such description as may be so specified.

(2) In subsection (1), "relevant legal employment" means employment which consists of or includes giving assistance in the conduct of litigation to a solicitor whether in private practice or not.

(3) A direction under this section may be given subject to such conditions and restrictions as appear to the Lord Chancellor to be necessary or expedient, and may

be expressed to have effect as respects every county court or as respects a specified county court or as respects one or more specified places where a county court sits.

(4) The power to give directions conferred by this section includes a power to vary or rescind any direction given under this section.

Mode of trial

62. General power of judge to determine questions of law and fact
Subject to the provisions of this Act and of county court rules, the judge of a county court shall be the sole judge in all proceedings brought in the court, and shall determine all questions of fact as well as of law.

63. *****

64. Reference to arbitration
(1) County court rules—
    (a) may prescribe cases in which proceedings are (without any order of the court) to be referred to arbitration, and
    (b) may prescribe the manner in which and the terms on which cases are to be so referred, and
    (c) may, where cases are so referred, require other matters within the jurisdiction of the court in dispute between the parties also to be referred to arbitration.

(2) County court rules—
    (a) may prescribe cases in which proceedings may be referred to arbitration by order of the court, and
    (b) may authorise the court also to order other matters in dispute between the parties and within the jurisdiction of the court to be so referred.

(3) On a reference under subsection (1) or (2) the award of the arbitrator, arbitrators or umpire shall be entered as the judgment in the proceedings and shall be as binding and effectual to all intents, subject to subsecton (4), as if it had been given by the judge.

(4) The judge may, if he thinks fit, on application made to him within such time as may be prescribed, set aside the award, or may, with the consent of the parties, revoke the reference or order another reference to be made in the manner specified in this section.

(5) In this section "award" includes an interim award.

65. *****

Juries

66. Trial by jury
(1) In the following proceedings in a county court the trial shall be without a jury—
    (a) Admiralty proceedings;
    (b) proceedings arising—
        (i) under Part I, II or III of the Rent (Agriculture) Act 1976, or
        (ii) under any provision of the Rent Act 1977 other than a provision contained in Part V, sections 103 to 106 or Part IX, or
        (iii) under Part I of the Protection from Eviction Act 1977; [or
        (iv) under Part I of the Housing Act 1988]
    (c) any appeal to the county court under the Housing Act 1985.

(2) In all other proceedings in a county court the trial shall be without a jury unless the court otherwise orders on an application made in that behalf by any party to the proceedings in such manner and within such time before the trial as may be prescribed.

(3) Where, on any such application, the court is satisfied that there is in issue—

(a) a charge of fraud against the party making the application; or
(b) a claim in respect of libel, slander, malicious prosecution or false imprisonment; or
(c) any question or issue of a kind prescribed for the purposes of this paragraph,
the action shall be tried with a jury, unless the court is of opinion that the trial requires any prolonged examination of documents or accounts or any scientific or local investigation which cannot conveniently be made with a jury.

(4) There shall be payable, in respect of the trial with a jury of proceedings in a county court, such fees as may be prescribed by the fees orders.

67. Impanelling and swearing of jury
At the county court where proceedings are to be tried with a jury, eight jurymen shall be impanelled and sworn as occasion requries to give their verdicts in the proceedings brought before them, and being once sworn need not be re-sworn in each trial.

68. Duty of judge to determine foreign law in jury trials
Where, for the purpose of disposing of any proceedings which are being tried in a county court by the judge with a jury, it is necessary to ascertain the law of any other country which is applicable to the facts of the case, any question as to the effect of the evidence given with respect to that law shall, instead of being submitted to the jury, be decided by the judge alone.

Interest on debts and damages

69. Power to award interest on debts and damages
(1) Subject to county court rules, in proceedings (whenever instituted) before a county court for the recovery of a debt or damages there may be included in any sum for which judgment is given simple interest, at such rate as the court thinks fit or as may be prescribed, on all or any part of the debt or damages in respect of which judgment is given, or payment is made before judgment, for all or any part of the period between the date when the cause of action arose and—
(a) in the case of any sum paid before judgment, the date of the payment; and
(b) in the case of the sum for which judgment is given, the date of the judgment.

(2) In relation to a judgment given for damages for personal injuries or death which exceed £200 subsection (1) shall have effect—
(a) with the substitution of "shall be included" for "may be included"; and
(b) with the addition of "unless the court is satisfied that there are special reasons to the contrary" after "given", where first occurring.

(3) Subject to county court rules, where—
(a) there are proceedings (whenever instituted) before a county court for the recovery of a debt; and
(b) the defendant pays the whole debt to the plaintiff (otherwise than in pursuance of a judgment in the proceedings),
the defendant shall be liable to pay the plaintiff simple interest, at such rate as the court thinks fit or as may be prescribed, on all or any part of the debt for all or any part of the period between the date when the cause of action arose and the date of the payment.

(4) Interest in respect of a debt shall not be awarded under this section for a period during which, for whatever reason, interest on the debt already runs.

(5) Interest under this section may be calculated at different rates in respect of different periods.

(6) In this section "plaintiff" means the person seeking the debt or damages and "defendant" means the person from whom the plaintiff seeks the debt or damages and

County Courts Act 1984

"personal injuries" includes any disease and any impairment of a person's physical or mental condition.

(7) Nothing in this section affects the damages recoverable for the dishonour of a bill of exchange.

(8) In determining whether an amount exceeds—
- (a) the county court limit for the purposes of any provision of this Act; or
- (b) an amount specified in any provision of this Act,

no account shall be taken of the provisions of this section or of anything done under it.

Judgments and orders

70. Finality of judgments and orders

Every judgment and order of a county court shall, except as provided by this or any other Act or as may be prescribed, be final and conclusive between the parties.

71. Satisfaction of judgments and orders for payment of money

(1) Where a judgment is given or an order is made by a county court under which a sum of money of any amount is payable, whether by way of satisfaction of the claim or counterclaim in the proceedings or by way of costs or otherwise, the court may, as it thinks fit, order the money to be paid either—
- (a) in one sum, whether forthwith or within such period as the court may fix; or
- (b) by such instalments payable at such times as the court may fix.

(2) If at any time it appears to the satisfaction of the court that any party to any proceedings is unable from any cause to pay any sum recovered against him (whether by way of satisfaction of the claim or counterclaim in the proceedings or by way of costs or otherwise) or any instalment of such a sum, the court may, in its discretion, suspend or stay any judgment or order given or made in the proceedings for such time and on such terms as the court thinks fit, and so from time to time until it appears that the cause of inability has ceased.

72. Set-off in cases of cross judgments in county courts and High Court

(1) Where one person has obtained a judgment or order in a county court against another person, and that other person has obtained a judgment or order against the first-mentioned person in the same or in another county court or in the High Court, either such person may, in accordance with rules of court, give notice in writing to the court or the several courts as the case may be, and may apply to the court or any of the said courts in accordance with rules of court for leave to set off any sums, including costs, payable under the several judgments or orders.

(2) Upon any such application, the set-off may be allowed in accordance with the practice for the time being in force in the High Court as to the allowance of set-off and in particular in relation to any solicitor's lien for costs.

(3) Where the cross judgments or orders have not been obtained in the same court, a copy of the order made on any such application shall be sent by the proper officer of the court to which the application is made to the proper officer of the other court.

73. *****

74. Interest on judgment debts etc

(1) The Lord Chancellor may by order made with the concurrence of the Treasury provide that any sums to which this subsection applies shall carry interest at such rate and between such times as may be prescribed by the order.

(2) The sums to which subsection (1) applies are—
- (a) sums payable under judgments or orders given or made in a county court, including sums payable by instalments; and

(b) sums which by virtue of any enactment are, if the county court so orders, recoverable as if payable under an order of that court, and in respect of which the county court has so ordered.

(3) The payment of interest due under subsection (1) shall be enforceable as a sum payable under the judgment or order.

(4) The power conferred by subsection (1) includes power—

(a) to specify the descriptions of judgment or order in respect of which interest shall be payable;

(b) to provide that interest shall be payable only on sums exceeding a specified amount;

(c) to make provision for the manner in which and the periods by reference to which the interest is to be calculated and paid;

(d) to provide that any enactment shall or shall not apply in relation to interest payable under subsection (1) or shall apply to it with such modifications as may be specified in the order; and

(e) to make such incidental or supplementary provisions as the Lord Chancellor considers appropriate.

(5) Without prejudice to the generality of subsection (4), an order under subsection (1) may provide that the rate of interest shall be the rate specified in section 17 of the Judgments Act 1838 as that enactment has effect from time to time.

(6) The power to make an order under subsection (1) shall be exercisable by statutory instrument subject to annulment in pursuance of a resolution of either House of Parliament.

General rules of procedure

75. County court rules

(1) The rule committee may make county court rules regulating the practice of the courts and forms of proceedings in them and prescribing scales of costs to be paid to counsel and solicitors.

(2) The power to make county court rules shall extend to all matters of procedure or practice, or matters relating to or concerning the effect or operation in law of any procedure or practice, in any case within the cognisance of county courts as to which rules of the Supreme Court have been or might lawfully be made for cases within the cognisance of the High Court.

(3)—(10) *****

76. Application of practice of High Court

In any case not expressly provided for by or in pursuance of this Act, the general principles of practice in the High Court may be adopted and applied to proceedings in a county court.

PART IV
APPEALS ETC.
Appeals

77. Appeals: general provisions

(1) Subject to the provisions of this section and the following provisions of this Part of this Act, if any party to any proceedings in a county court is dissatisfied with the determination of the judge or jury, he may appeal from it to the Court of Appeal in such manner and subject to such conditions as may be provided by the rules of the Supreme Court.

(2) The Lord Chancellor may by order prescribe classes of proceedings in which there is to be no right of appeal under this section without the leave either of the judge of the county court or of the Court of Appeal.

(3) An order under subsection (2)—
  (a) may classify proceedings according to the nature of those proceedings;
  (b) may classify proceedings according to the amount or value or annual value of the money or other property which is the subject of those proceedings or according to whether that amount or value or annual value exceeds a specified fraction of the relevant county court limit;
  (c) may provide that the order shall not apply to determinations made before such date as may be specified in the order; and
  (d) may make different provision for different classes of proceedings.

(4) The power to make an order under subsection (2) shall be exercisable by statutory instrument subject to annulment in pursuance of a resolution of either House of Parliament.

(5) Subject to the provisions of this section and the following provisions of this Part of this Act, where an appeal is brought under subsection (1) in any action, an appeal may be brought under that subsection in respect of any claim or counterclaim in the action notwithstanding that there could have been no such appeal if that claim had been the subject of a separate action.

(6) In proceedings in which either the plaintiff or the defendant is claiming possession of any premises this section shall not confer any right of appeal on any question of fact if by virtue of—
  (a) section 13(4) of the Landlord and Tenant Act 1954; or
  (b) Cases III to IX in Schedule 4 to the Rent (Agriculture) Act 1976; or
  (c) section 98 of the Rent Act 1977, as it applies to Cases 1 to 6 and 8 and 9 in Schedule 15 to that Act, or that section as extended or applied by any other enactment; or
  (d) section 99 of the Rent Act 1977, as it applies to Cases 1 to 6 and 9 in Schedule 15 to that Act; or
  (e) section 84(2)(a) of the Housing Act 1985; or
  (ee) section 7 of the Housing Act 1988, as it applies to the grounds in Part II of Schedule 2 to that Act; or]
  (f) any other enactment,
the court can only grant possession on being satisfied that it is reasonable to do so.

(7) This section shall not—
  (a) confer any right of appeal from any judgment or order where a right of appeal is conferred by some other enactment; or
  (b) take away any right of appeal from any judgment or order where a right of appeal is so conferred,
and shall have effect subject to any enactment other than this Act.

(8) In this section—
"enactment" means an enactment whenever passed; and
"the relevant county court limit" means, in relation to proceedings of any description, the sum by reference to which the question whether a county court has jurisdiction to hear and determine the proceedings falls to be decided.

78. *****

79. Agreement not to appeal
(1) No appeal shall lie from any judgment, direction, decision or order of a judge of county courts if, before the judgment, direction, decision or order is given or made, the parties agree, in writing signed by themselves or their solicitors or agents, that it shall be final.
(2) . . .

80. Judge's note on appeal

(1) At the hearing of any proceedings in a county court in which there is a right of appeal or from which an appeal may be brought with leave, the judge shall, at the request of any party, make a note—
    (a)   of any question of law raised at the hearing; and
    (b)   of the facts in evidence in relation to any such question; and
    (c)   of his decision on any such question and of his determination of the proceedings.

(2) Where such a note has been taken, the judge shall (whether notice of appeal has been served or not), on the application of any party to the proceedings, and on payment by that party of such fee as may be prescribed by the fees orders, furnish him with a copy of the note, and shall sign the copy, and the copy so signed shall be used at the hearing of the appeal.

81. Powers of Court of Appeal on appeal from county court

(1) On the hearing of an appeal, the Court of Appeal may draw any inference of fact and either—
    (a)   order a new trial on such terms as the court thinks just; or
    (b)   order judgment to be entered for any party; or
    (c)   make a final or other order on such terms as the court thinks proper to ensure the determinaton on the merits of the real question in controversy between the parties.

(2) Subject to any rules of the Supreme Court, on any appeal from a county court the Court of Appeal may reverse or vary, in favour of a party seeking to support the judgment or order of the county court in whole or in part, any determinations made in the county court on questions of fact, notwithstanding that the appeal is an appeal on a point of law only, or any such determinations on points of law, notwithstanding that the appeal is an appeal on a question of fact only.

(3) Subsection (2) shall not enable the Court of Appeal to reverse or vary any determination, unless the party dissatisfied with the determination would have been entitled to appeal in respect of it if aggrieved by the judgment or order.

82. Decision of Court of Appeal on probate appeals to be final

No appeal shall lie from the decision of the Court of Appeal on any appeal from a county court in any probate proceedings.

Certiorari and prohibition

83. Stay of proceedings in case of certiorari or prohibition

(1) The grant by the High Court or leave to make an application for an order of certiorari or prohibition to a county court shall, if the High Court so directs, operate as a stay of the proceedings in question until the determination of the application, or until the High Court otherwise orders.

(2) Where any proceedings are so stayed, the judge of the county court shall from time to time adjourn the hearing of the proceedings to such day as he thinks fit.

84. Prohibition

(1) Where an application is made to the High Court for an order of prohibition addressed to any county court, the matter shall be finally disposed of by order.

(2) Upon any such application, the judge of the county court shall not be served with notice of it, and shall not, except by the order of a judge of the High Court—
    (a)   be required to appeal or be heard; or
    (b)   be liable to any order for the payment of the costs of the application;
but the application shall be proceeded with and heard in the same manner in all respects as an appeal duly brought from a decision of the judge, and notice of the application

shall be given to or served upon the same parties as in the case of an order made or refused by a judge in a matter within his jurisdiction.

PART V
ENFORCEMENT OF JUDGMENTS AND ORDERS

85.—111.   *****

PART VI
ADMINISTRATION ORDERS

112.—117.   *****

PART VIII
COMMITTALS

118. Power to commit for contempt
(1) If any person—
    (a)   wilfully insults the judge of a county court, or any juror or witness, or any officer of the court during his sitting or attendance in court, or in going to or returning from the court; or
    (b)   wilfully interrupts the proceedings of a county court or otherwise misbehaves in court;
any officer of the court, with or without the assistance of any other person, may, by order of the judge, take the offender into custody and detain him until the rising of the court, and the judge may, if he thinks fit,—
      (i)   make an order committing the offender for a specified period not exceeding one month to prison; or
      (ii)   impose upon the offender, for every offence, a fine of an amount not exceeding £1,000, or may both make such an order and impose such a fine.
(2) The judge may at any time revoke an order committing a person to prison under this section and, if he is already in custody, order his discharge.

119.—122.   *****

PART VIII
RESPONSIBILITY AND PROTECTION OF OFFICERS

123.—127.   *****

PART IX
MISCELLANEOUS AND GENERAL

128.—141.   *****

142. Power to enforce undertakings of solicitors
A county court shall have the same power to enforce an undertaking given by a solicitor in relation to any proceedings in that court as the High Court has to enforce an undertaking so given in relation to any proceedings in the High Court.

143.—145.   *****

146.   *****

147. Interpretation
(1) In this Act, unless the context otherwise requires—
"action" means any proceedings in a county court which may be commenced as prescribed by plaint;
"Admiralty county court" means a county court appointed to have Admiralty jurisdiction by order under this Act;

"Admiralty proceedings" means proceedings in which the claim would not be within the jurisdiction of a county court but for sections 26 and 27;

"bailiff" includes a registrar;

"the county court limit" means—

    (a) in relation to any enactment contained in this Act for which a limit is for the time being specified by an Order under section 145, that limit,

    (b) (subject to paragraph (a)), in sections 21(1), 21(2)(a) and (b) and 139(2), £1000, and

    (c) in relation to any enactment contained in this Act and not within paragraph (a) or (b), the county court limit for the time being specified by any other Order in Council or order defining the limit of county court jurisdiction for the purposes of that enactment;

"county court rules" means rules made under section 75;

"court" and "county court" mean a court held for a district under this Act;

"deposit-taking institution" means any person carrying on a business which is a deposit-taking business for the purposes of the [Banking Act 1987];

"district" and "county court district" means a district for which a court is to be held under section 2;

"fees orders" means orders made under section 128;

"hearing" includes trial, and "hear" and "heard" shall be construed accordingly;

"hereditament" includes both a corporeal and an incorporeal hereditament;

"judge", in relation to a county court, means a judge assigned to the district of that court under subsection (1) of section 5 and any person sitting as a judge for that district under subsection (3) or (4) of that section;

"judgment summons" means a summons issued on the application of a person entitled to enforce a judgment or order under section 5 of the Debtors Act 1869 requiring a person, or where two or more persons are liable under the judgment or order, requiring any one or more of them, to appear and be examined on oath as to his or their means;

"landlord", in relation to any land, means the person entitled to the immediate reversion or, if the property therein is held in joint tenancy, any of the persons entitled to the immediate reversion;

"matrimonial cause" has the meaning assigned to it by section 10(1) of the Matrimonial Causes Act 1967;

"matter" means every proceeding in a county court which may be commenced as prescribed otherwise than by plaint;

"officer", in relation to a court, means any registrar, deputy registrar or assistant registrar of that court, and any clerk, bailiff, usher or messenger in the service of that court;

"part-time registrar" and "part-time assistant registrar" have the meaning assigned to them by section 10(3);

"party" includes every person served with notice of, or attending, any proceeding, whether named as a party to that proceeding or not;

"prescribed" means prescribed by county court rules;

"probate proceedings" means proceedings brought in a county court by virtue of section 32 or transferred to that court under section 40;

"proceedings" includes both actions and matters;

"registrar" and "registrar of a county court" mean a registrar appointed for a district under this Act, or in a case where two or more registrars are appointed jointly, either or any of those registrars;

"return day" means the day appointed in any summons or proceeding for the appearance of the defendant or any other day fixed for the hearing of any proceedings;

"the rule committee" means the committee constituted under section 75;

"ship" includes any description of vessel used in navigation;

"solicitor" means solicitor of the Supreme Court;
"standard scale" has the meaning given by section 75 of the Criminal Justice Act 1982; and
"statutory maximum" has the meaning given by section 74 of that Act.

(2) For the purposes of this Act, the net annual value for rating of any property shall be determined as at the time when the relevant proceedings are commenced, except in a case where it is otherwise expressly provided, and, subject to subsection (3), by reference to the valuation list in force at the time in question.

(3) Where the property of which the value is in question does not consist of one or more hereditaments having at the time in question a separate net annual value for rating, the property or such part of it as does not consist—

(a) shall, for the purpose of entitling a county court to exercise jurisdiction (but not for any other purpose), be taken to have a net annual value for rating not exceeding that of any such hereditament of which at the time in question it forms part; and

(b) subject to paragraph (a), shall be taken to have a net annual value for rating equal to its value by the year.

148.—151. *****

MATRIMONIAL AND FAMILY PROCEEDINGS ACT 1984
(1984, c. 42)
PART V
FAMILY BUSINESS: DISTRIBUTION AND TRANSFER
Preliminary

32. What is family business
In this Part of this Act—

"family business" means business of any description which in the High Court is for the time being assigned to the Family Division and to no other Division by or under section 61 of (and Schedule 1 to) the Supreme Court Act 1981;

"family proceedings" means proceedings which are family business;

"matrimonial cause" means an action for divorce, nullity of marriage, [or judicial separation . . .];

and "the 1973 Act" means the Matrimonial Causes Act 1973.

Jurisdiction of county courts in matrimonial causes and matters

33. Jurisdiction of county courts in matrimonial causes
(1) The Lord Chancellor may by order designate any county court as a divorce county court and any court so designated shall have jurisdiction to hear and determine any matrimonial cause, except that it shall have jurisdiction to try such a cause only if it is also designated in the order as a court of trial.

In this Part of this Act "divorce county court" means a county court so designated.

(2) The jurisdiction conferred by this section on a divorce county court shall be exercisable throughout England and Wales, but rules of court may provide for a matrimonial cause pending in one such court to be heard and determined in another or partly in that and partly in another.

(3) Every matrimonial cause shall be commenced in a divorce county court and shall be heard and determined in that or another such court unless or except to the extent it is transferred to the High Court under section 39 below or section 41 of the County Courts Act 1984 (transfer to High Court by order of High Court).

(4) The Lord Chancellor may by order designate a divorce county court as a court for the exercise of jurisdiction in matrimonial matters arising under Part III of this Act.

(5) The power to make an order under subsection (1) or (4) above shall be exercisable by statutory instrument.

34. Jurisdiction of divorce county courts as respects financial relief and protection of children

(1) Subject to subsections (2) and (3) below, a divorce county court shall have the following jurisdiction, namely—

    (a) jurisdiction to exercise any power exercisable under Part II or Part III of the 1973 Act in connection with any petition, decree or order pending in or made by such a court and to exercise any power under section 27 or 35 of that Act;

    (b) if designated by an order under section 33(4) above, jurisdiction to exercise any power under Part III of this Act.

(2) Any proceedings for the exercise of a power which a divorce county court has jurisdiction to exercise by virtue of subsection (1)(a) or (b) above shall be commenced in such divorce county court as may be prescribed by rules of court.

(3) A divorce county court shall not by virtue of subsection (1)(a) above have jurisdiction to exercise any power under section 32, 33, 36 or 38 of the 1973 Act; but nothing in this section shall prejudice the exercise by a county court of any jurisdiction conferred on county courts by any of those sections.

(4) Nothing in this section shall affect the jurisdiction of a magistrates' court under section 35 of the 1973 Act.

35. Consideration of agreements or arrangements

Any provision to be made by rules of court for the purposes of section 7 of the 1973 Act with respect to any power exercisable by the court on an application made before the presentation of a petition shall confer jurisdiction to exercise the power on divorce county courts.

36. Assignment of Circuit judges to matrimonial proceedings

The jurisdiction conferred by the preceding provisions of this Part of this Act on divorce county courts, so far as it is exercisable by judges of such courts, shall be exercised by such Circuit judges as the Lord Chancellor may direct.

Distribution and transfer of family business and proceedings

37. Directions as to distribution and transfer of family business and proceedings

The President of the Family Division may, with the concurrence of the Lord Chancellor, give directions with respect to the distribution and transfer between the High Court and county courts of family business and family proceedings.

38. Transfer of family proceedings from High Court to county court

(1) At any stage in any family proceedings in the High Court the High Court may, if the proceedings are transferable under this section, either of its own motion or on the application of any party to the proceedings, order the transfer of the whole or any part of the proceedings to a county court.

(2) The following family proceedings are transferable to a county court under this section, namely—

    (a) all family proceedings commenced in the High Court which are within the jurisdiction of a county court or divorce county court;

    (b) wardship proceedings, except applications for an order that a minor be made, or cease to be, a ward of court; and

    (c) all family proceedings transferred from a county court to the High Court under section 39 below or section 41 of the County Courts Act 1984 (transfer to High Court by order of High Court) [and

(d) all matrimonial causes and matters transferred from a county court otherwise than as mentioned in paragraph (c) above.]

(3) Proceedings transferred under this section shall be transferred to such county court or, in the case of a matrimonial cause or matter within the jurisdiction of a divorce county court only, such divorce county court as the High Court directs.

(4) The transfer shall not affect any right of appeal from the order directing the transfer, or the right to enforce in the High Court any judgment signed, or order made, in that Court before the transfer.

(5) Where proceedings are transferred to a county court under this section, the county court—

    (a) if it has no jurisdiction apart from this paragraph, shall have jurisdiction to hear and determine those proceedings;

    (b) shall have jurisdiction to award any relief which could have been awarded by the High Court.

39. Transfer of family proceedings to High Court from county court

(1) At any stage in any family proceedings in a county court, the county court may, if the proceedings are transferable under this section, either of its own motion or on the application of any party to the proceedings, order the transfer of the whole or any part of the proceedings to the High Court.

(2) The following family proceedings are transferable to the High Court under this section, namely—

    (a) all family proceedings commenced in a county court or divorce county court; and

    (b) all family proceedings transferred from the High Court to a county court or divorce county court under section 38 above.

POLICE AND CRIMINAL EVIDENCE ACT 1984
(1984, c. 60)

81. Advance notice of expert evidence in Crown Court

(1) Crown Court rules may make provision for—

    (a) requiring any party to proceedings before the court to disclose to the other party or parties any expert evidence which he proposes to adduce in the proceedings; and

    (b) prohibiting a party who fails to comply in respect of any evidence with any requirement imposed by virtue of paragraph (a) above from adducing that evidence without the leave of the court.

(2) Crown Court Rules made by virtue of this section may specify the kinds of expert evidence to which they apply and may exempt facts or matters of any description specified in the rules.

PROSECUTION OF OFFENCES ACT 1985
(1985, c. 23)

An Act to provide for the establishment of a Crown Prosecution Service for England and Wales; to make provision as to costs in criminal cases; to provide for the imposition of time limits in relation to preliminary stages of criminal proceedings; to amend section 42 of the Supreme Court Act 1981 and section 3 of the Children and Young Persons Act 1969; to make provision with respect to consents to prosecutions; to repeal section 9 of the Perjury Act 1911; and for connected purposes. [23 May 1985]

PART I
THE CROWN PROSECUTION SERVICE
Constitution and functions of Service

1. The Crown Prosecution Service

(1) There shall be a prosecuting service for England and Wales (to be known as the "Crown Prosecution Service") consisting of—

    (a)   the Director of Public Prosecutions, who shall be head of the Service;

    (b)   the Chief Crown Prosecutors, designated under sub-section (4) below, each of whom shall be the member of the Service responsible to the Director for supervising the operation of the Service in his area; and

    (c)   the other staff appointed by the Director under this section.

(2) The Director shall appoint such staff for the Service as, with the approval of the Treasury as to numbers, remuneration and other terms and conditions of service, he considers necessary for the discharge of his functions.

(3) The Director may designate any member of the Service who is a barrister or solicitor for the purposes of this subsection, and any person so designated shall be known as a Crown Prosecutor.

(4) The Director shall divide England and Wales into areas and, for each of those areas, designate a Crown Prosecutor for the purposes of this subsection and any person so designated shall be known as a Chief Crown Prosecutor.

(5) The Director may, from time to time, vary the division of England and Wales made for the purposes of subsection (4) above.

(6) Without prejudice to any functions which may have been assigned to him in his capacity as a member of the Service, every Crown Prosecutor shall have all the powers of the Director as to the institution and conduct of proceedings but shall exercise those powers under the direction of the Director.

(7) Where any enactment (whenever passed);

    (a)   prevents any step from being taken without the consent of the Director or without his consent or the consent of another; or

    (b)   requires any step to be taken by or in relation to the Director;

any consent given by or, as the case may be, step taken by or in relation to, a Crown Prosecutor shall be treated, for the purposes of that enactment, as given by or, as the case may be, taken by or in relation to the Director.

2. The Director of Public Prosecutions

(1) The Director of Public Prosecutions shall be appointed by the Attorney General.

(2) The Director must be a barrister or solicitor of not less than ten years' standing.

(3) There shall be paid to the Director such remuneration as the Attorney General may, with the approval of the Treasury, determine.

3. Functions of the Director

(1) The Director shall discharge his functions under this or any other enactment under the superintendence of the Attorney General.

(2) It shall be the duty of the Director [subject to any provisions contained in the Criminal Justice Act 1987]—

    (a)   to take over the conduct of all criminal proceedings, other than specified proceedings, instituted on behalf of a police force (whether by a member of that force or by any other person);

    (b)   to institute and have the conduct of criminal proceedings in any case where it appears to him that—

        (i)   the importance or difficulty of the case makes it appropriate that proceedings should be instituted by him; or

        (ii)   it is otherwise appropriate for proceedings to be instituted by him;

Prosecution of Offences Act 1985

(c) to take over the conduct of all binding over proceedings instituted on behalf of a police force (whether by a member of that force or by another person);

(d) to take over the conduct of all proceedings begun by summons issued under section 3 of the Obscene Publications Act 1959 (forfeiture of obscene articles);

(e) to give, to such extent as he considers appropriate, advice to police forces on all matters relating to criminal offences;

(f) to appear for the prosecution, when directed by the court to do so, on any appeal under—

(i) section 1 of the Administration of Justice Act 1960 (appeal from the High Court in criminal cases);

(ii) Part I or Part II of the Criminal Appeal Act 1968 (appeals from the Crown Court to the criminal division of the Court of Appeal and thence to the House of Lords); or

(iii) section 108 of the Magistrates' Courts Act 1980 (right of appeal to Crown Court) as it applies, by virtue of subsection (5) of section 12 of the Contempt of Court Act 1981, to orders made under section 12 (contempt of magistrates' courts); and

(g) to discharge such other functions as may from time to time be assigned to him by the Attorney General in pursuance of this paragraph.

(3) In this section—
"the court" means—

(a) in the case of an appeal to or from the criminal division of the Court of Appeal, that division;

(b) in the case of an appeal from a Divisional Court of the Queen's Bench Division, the Divisional Court; and

(c) in the case of an appeal against an order of a magistrates' court, the Crown Court;

"police force" means any police force maintained by a police authority under the Police Act 1964 and any other body of constables for the time being specified by order made by the Secretary of State for the purposes of this section; and

"specified proceedings" means proceedings which fall within any category for the time being specified by order made by the Attorney General for the purposes of this section.

(4) The power to make orders under subsection (3) above shall be exercisable by statutory instrument subject to annulment in pursuance of a resolution of either House of Parliament.

4. Crown Prosecutors

(1) Crown Prosecutors shall have, in any court, the rights of audience enjoyed by solicitors holding practising certificates and shall have such additional rights of audience in the Crown Court as may be given by virtue of subsection (3) below.

(2) The reference in subsection (1) above to rights of audience enjoyed in any court by solicitors includes a reference to rights enjoyed in the Crown Court by virtue of any direction given by the Lord Chancellor under section 83 of the Supreme Court Act 1981.

(3) For the purpose of giving Crown Prosecutors additional rights of audience in the Crown Court, the Lord Chancellor may give any such direction as respects Crown Prosecutors as he could give under section 83 of the Act of 1981 in respect of solicitors.

(4)—(6) . . .

5. Conduct of prosecutions on behalf of the Service

(1) The Director may at any time appoint a person who is not a Crown Prosecutor but who is—

(a) a solicitor; or

(b) a barrister who is a member of the staff of a public authority;
to institute or take over the conduct of such criminal proceedings as the Director may assign to him.

(2) Any person conducting proceedings assigned to him under this section shall have all the powers of a Crown Prosecutor but shall exercise those powers subject to any instructions given to him by a Crown Prosecutor.

6. Prosecutions instituted and conducted otherwise than by the Service

(1) Subject to subsection (2) below, nothing in this Part shall preclude any person from instituting any criminal proceedings or conducting any criminal proceedings to which the Director's duty to take over the conduct of proceedings does not apply.

(2) Where criminal proceedings are instituted in circumstances in which the Director is not under a duty to take over their conduct, he may nevertheless do so at any stage.

7. Delivery of recognizances etc. to Director

(1) Where the Director or any Crown Prosecutor gives notice to any justice of the peace that he has instituted, or is conducting, any criminal proceedings, the justice shall—

(a) at the prescribed time and in the precribed manner; or

(b) in a particular case, at the time and in the manner directed by the Attorney General;

send him every recognizance, information, certificate, deposition, document and thing connected with those proceedings which the justice is required by law to deliver to the appropriate officer of the Crown Court.

(2) The Attorney General may make regulations for the purpose of supplementing this section; and in subsection (1) above "prescribed" means prescribed by the regulations.

(3) The Director or, as the case may be, Crown Prosecutor shall—

(a) subject to the regulations, cause anything which is sent to him under subsection (1) above to be delivered to the appropriate officer of the Crown Court; and

(b) be under the same obligation (on the same payment) to deliver to an applicant copies of anything so sent as that officer.

(4) It shall be the duty of every justices' clerk to send to the Director, in accordance with the regulations, a copy of the information and of any depositions and other documents relating to any case in which—

(a) a prosecution for an offence before the magistrates' court to which he is clerk is withdrawn or is not proceeded with within a reasonable time;

(b) the Director does not have the conduct of the proceedings; and

(c) there is some ground for suspecting that there is no satisfactory reason for the withdrawal or failure to proceed.

Reports

8. Reports to Director by chief officers of police

(1) The Attorney General may make regulations requiring the chief officer of any police force to which the regulations are expressed to apply to give to the Director information with respect to every offence of a kind prescribed by the regulations which is alleged to have been committed in his area and in respect of which it appears to him that there is a prima facie case for proceedings.

(2) The regulations may also require every such chief officer to give to the Director such information as the Director may require with respect to such cases or classes of case as he may from time to time specify.

9. Reports by Director to Attorney General

(1) As soon as practicable after 4th April in any year the Director shall make to the Attorney General a report on the discharge of his functions during the year ending with that date.

(2) The Attorney General shall lay before Parliament a copy of every report received by him under subsection (1) above and shall cause every such report to be published.

(3) The Director shall, at the request of the Attorney General, report to him on such matters as the Attorney General may specify.

Guidelines

10. Guidelines for Crown Prosecutors

(1) The Director shall issue a Code for Crown Prosecutors giving guidance on general principles to be applied by them—
    (a)   in determining, in any case—
        (i)   whether proceedings for an offence should be instituted, whether they should be discontinued; or
        (ii)   what charges should be preferred; and
    (b)   in considering, in any case, representations to be made by them to any magistrates' court about the mode of trial suitable for that case.

(2) The Director may from time to time make alterations in the Code.

(3) The provisions of the Code shall be set out in the Director's report under section 9 of this Act for the year in which the Code is issued; and any alteration in the Code shall be set out in his report under that section for the year in which the alteration is made.

11.—14. *****

15. Interpretation of Part I

(1) In this Part—
"binding over proceedings" means any proceedings instituted (whether by way of complaint under section 115 of the Magistrates' Court Act 1980 or otherwise) with a view to obtaining from a magistrates' court an order requiring a person to enter into a recognizance to keep the peace or to be of good behaviour;
"Director" means the Director of Public Prosecutions;
"police force' has the same meaning as in section 3 of this Act;
"prosecution functions" means functions which by virtue of this Part become functions of the Director;
"public authority" has the same meaning as in section 17 of this Act;
"Service" means the Crown Prosecution Service; and
"solicitor" means a solicitor of the Supreme Court.

(2) For the purposes of this Part, proceedings in relation to an offence are instituted—
    (a)   where a justice of the peace issues a summons under section 1 of the Magistrates' Courts Act 1980, when the information for the offence is laid before him;
    (b)   where a justice of the peace issues a warrant for the arrest of any person under that section, when the information for the offence is laid before him;
    (c)   where a person is charged with the offence after being taken into custody without a warrant, when he is informed of the particulars of the charge;
    (d)   where a bill of indictment is preferred under section 2 of the Administration of Justice (Miscellaneous Provisions) Act 1933 in a case falling within paragraph (b) of subsection (2) of that section, when the bill of indictment is preferred before the court;
and where the application of this subsection would result in there being more than one time for the institution of the proceedings, they shall be taken to have been instituted at the earliest of those times.

(3) For the purposes of this Part, references to the conduct of any proceedings include references to the proceedings being discontinued and to the taking of any steps (including the bringing of appeals and making of representations in respect of applications for bail) which may be taken in relation to them.

(4) For the purposes of sections 3(2)(b), 5, 6 and 7(1) of this Act, binding over proceedings shall be taken to be criminal proceedings.

(5) For the purposes of section 5 of this Act, proceedings begun by summons issued under section 3 of the Obscene Publications Act 1959 (forfeiture of obscene articles) shall be taken to be criminal proceedings.

(6) The functions which become functions of the Director by virtue of this Part shall be treated as transferred functions for the purposes of section 95 of the Employment Protection (Consolidation) Act 1978 (effect of certain provisions where functions are transferred to the Crown) but shall not be so treated for the purposes of paragraph 1(2) of Schedule 3 to the Pensions (Increase) Act 1971 (meaning of "last employing authority").

(7) The person who, immediately before the commencement of section 2 of this Act, holds the office of Director shall be treated on the commencement of that section as holding that office in pursuance of an appointment made by the Attorney General.

PART II
COSTS IN CRIMINAL CASES
Award of costs out of central funds

16. Defence costs

(1) Where—
  (a) an information laid before a justice of the peace for any area, charging any person with an offence, is not proceeded with;
  (b) a magistrates' court inquiring into an indictable offence as examining justices determines not to commit the accused for trial;
  (c) a magistrates' court dealing summarily with an offence dismisses the information;
that court or, in a case falling within paragraph (a) above, a magistrates' court for that area, may make an order in favour of the accused for a payment to be made out of central funds in respect of his costs (a "defendant's costs order").

(2) Where—
  (a) any person is not tried for an offence for which he has been indicted or committted for trial; or
  [(aa) a notice of transfer is given under section 4 of the Criminal Justice Act 1987 but a person in relation to whose case it is given is not tried on a charge to which it relates; or]
  (b) any person is tried on indictment and acquitted on any count in the indictment;
the Crown Court may make a defendant's cost order in favour of the accused.

(3) Where a person convicted of an offence by a magistrates' court appeals to the Crown Court under section 108 of the Magistrates' Courts Act 1980 (right of appeal against conviction or sentence) and, in consequence of the decision on appeal—
  (a) his conviction is set aside; or
  (b) a less severe punishment is awarded;
the Crown Court may make a defendant's costs order in favour of the accused.

(4) Where the Court of Appeal—
  (a) allows an appeal under Part I of the Criminal Appeal Act 1968 against—
    (i) conviction;
    (ii) a verdict of not guilty by reason of insanity; or

(iii) a finding under section 4 of the Criminal Procedure (Insanity) Act 1964 that the appellant is under disability;

[(aa) directs under section 8(1B) of the Criminal Appeal Act 1968 the entry of a judgment and verdict of acquittal;]

(b) on an appeal under that Part against conviction—
    (i) substitutes a verdict of guilty of another offence;
    (ii) in a case where a special verdict has been found, orders a different conclusion on the effect of that verdict to be recorded; or
    (iii) is of the opinion that the case falls within paragraph (a) or (b) of section 6(1) of that Act (cases where the court substitutes a finding of insanity or unfitness to plead); or

(c) on an appeal under that Part against sentence, exercises its powers under section 11(3) of that Act (power where the court considers that the appellant should be sentenced differently for an offence for which he was dealt with by the court below);

the court may make a defendant's costs order in favour of the accused.

[(4A)The court may also make a defendant's costs order in favour of the accused on an appeal under section 9(11) of the Criminal Justice Act 1987 (appeals against orders or rulings at preparatory hearings).]

(5) Where—

(a) any proceedings in a criminal cause or matter are determined before a Divisional Court of the Queen's Bench Division;

(b) the House of Lords determines an appeal, or application for leave to appeal, from such a Divisional Court in a criminal cause or matter;

(c) the Court of Appeal determines an application for leave to appeal to the House of Lords under Part II of the Criminal Appeal Act 1968; or

(d) the House of Lords determines an appeal, or application for leave to appeal, under Part II of that Act;

the court may make a defendant's costs order in favour of the accused.

(6) A defendant's costs order shall, subject to the following provisions of this section, be for the payment out of central funds, to the person in whose favour the order is made, of such amount as the court considers reasonably sufficient to compensate him for any expenses properly incurred by him in the proceedings.

(7) Where a court makes a defendant's costs order but is of the opinion that there are circumstanes which make it inappropriate that the person in whose favour the order is made should recover the full amount mentioned in subsection (6) above, the court shall—

(a) assess what amount would, in its opinion, be just and reasonable; and
(b) specify that amount in the order.

(8) . . .

(9) Subject to subsection (7) above, the amount to be paid out of central funds in pursuance of a defendant's costs order shall—

(a) be specified in the order, in any case where the court considers it appropriate for the amount to be so specified and the person in whose favour the order is made agrees the amount; and

(b) in any other case, be determined in accordance with regulations made by the Lord Chancellor for the purposes of this section.

(10) Subsection (6) above shall have effect, in relation to any case falling within subsection (1)(a) or (2)(a) above, as if for the words "in the proceedings" there were substituted the words "in or about the defence".

(11) Where a person ordered to be retried is acquitted at his retrial, the costs which may be ordered to be paid out of central funds under this section shall include—

(a) any costs which, at the original trial, could have been ordered to be so paid under this section if he had been acquitted; and

(b) if no order was made under this section in respect of his expenses on appeal, any sums for the payment of which such an order could have been made.

17. Prosecution costs

(1) Subject to subsection (2) below, the court may—

    (a) in any proceedings in respect of an indictable offence; and

    (b) in any proceedings before a Divisional Court of the Queen's Bench Division or the House of Lords in respect of a summary offence;

order the payment out of central funds of such amount as the court considers reasonably sufficient to compensate the prosecutor for any expenses properly incurred by him in the proceedings.

(2) No order under this section may be made in favour of—

    (a) a public authority; or

    (b) a person acting—

        (i) on behalf of a public authority; or

        (ii) in his capacity as an official appointed by such an authority.

(3) Where a court makes an order under this section but is of the opinion that there are circumstances which make it inappropriate that the prosecution should recover the full amount mentioned in subsection (1) above, the court shall—

    (a) assess what amount would, in its opinion, be just and reasonable; and

    (b) specify that amount in the order.

(4) Subject to subsection (3) above, the amount to be paid out of central funds in pursuance of an order under this section shall—

    (a) be specified in the order, in any case where the court considers it appropriate for the amount to be so specified and the prosecutor agrees the amount; and

    (b) in any other case, be determined in accordance with regulations made by the Lord Chancellor for the purposes of this section.

(5) Where the conduct of proceedings to which subsection (1) above applies is taken over by the Crown Prosecution Service, that subsection shall have effect as if it referred to the prosecutor who had the conduct of the proceedings before the intervention of the Service and to expenses incurred by him up to the time of intervention.

(6) In this section "public authority" means—

    (a) a police force within the meaning of section 3 of this Act;

    (b) the Crown Prosecution Service or any other government department;

    (c) a local authority or other authority or body constituted for purposes of—

        (i) the public service or of local government; or

        (ii) carrying on under national ownership any industry or undertaking or part of an industry or undertaking; or

    (d) any other authority or body whose members are appointed by Her Majesty or by any Minister of the Crown or government department or whose revenues consist wholly or mainly of money provided by Parliament.

Award of costs against accused

18. Award of costs against accused

(1) Where—

    (a) any person is convicted of an offence before a magistrates' court;

    (b) the Crown Court dismisses an appeal against such a conviction or against the sentence imposed on that conviction; or

    (c) any person is convicted of an offence before the Crown Court;

the court may make such order as to the costs to be paid by the accused to the prosecutor as it considers just and reasonable.

(2) Where the Court of Appeal dismisses—

(a) an appeal or application for leave to appeal under Part I of the Criminal Appeal Act 1968; or

(b) an application by the accused for leave to appeal to the House of Lords under Part II of that Act; [or

(c) an appeal or application for leave to appeal under section 9(11) of the Criminal Justice Act 1987;]

it may make such order as to the costs to be paid by the accused, to such person as may be named in the order, as it considers just and reasonable.

(3) The amount to be paid by the accused in pursuance of an order under this section shall be specified in the order.

(4) Where any person is convicted of an offence before a magistrates' court and—

(a) under the conviction the court orders payment of any sum as a fine, penalty, forfeiture or compensation; and

(b) the sum so ordered to be paid does not exceed £5;

the court shall not order the accused to pay any costs under this section unless in the particular circumstances of the case it considers it right to do so.

(5) Where any person under the age of seventeen is convicted of an offence before a magistrates' court, the amount of any costs ordered to be paid by the accused under this section shall not exceed the amount of any fine imposed on him.

(6) Costs ordered to be paid under subsection (2) above may include the reasonable cost of any transcript of a record of proceedings made in accordance with rules of court made for the purposes of section 32 of the Act of 1968.

Other awards

19. Provision for orders as to costs in other circumstances

(1) The Lord Chancellor may by regulations make provision empowering magistrates' courts, the Crown Court and the Court of Appeal, in any case where the court is satisfied that one party to criminal proceedings has incurred costs as a result of an unnecessary or improper act or omission by, or on behalf of, another party to the proceedings, to make an order as to the payment of those costs.

(2) Regulations made under subsection (1) above may, in particular—

(a) allow the making of such an order at any time during the proceedings;

(b) make provision as to the account to be taken, in making such an order, of any other order as to costs which has been made in respect of the proceedings [or any grant of representation for the purposes of the proceedings which has been made under the Legal Aid Act 1988];

(c) make provision as to the account to be taken of any such order in the making of any other order as to costs in respect of the proceedings; and

(d) contain provisions similar to those in section 18(4) and (5) of this Act.

(3) The Lord Chancellor may by regulations make provision for the payment out of central funds, in such circumstances and in relation to such criminal proceedings as may be specified, or such sums as appear to the court to be reasonably necessary—

(a) to compensate any witness in the proceedings for the expense, trouble or loss of time properly incurred in or incidental to his attendance;

(b) to cover the proper expenses of an interpreter who is required because of the accused's lack of English;

(c) to compensate a duly qualified medical practitioner who—

(i) makes a report otherwise than in writing for the purpose of section 30 of the Magistrates' Courts Act 1980 (remand for medical examination); or

(ii) makes a written report to a court in pursuance of a request to which section 32(2) of the Criminal Justice Act 1967 (report by medical practitioner on medical condition of offender) applies;

for the expenses properly incurred in or incidental to his reporting to the court.

(4) The Court of Appeal may order the payment out of central funds of such sums as appear to it to be reasonably sufficient to compensate an appellant who is not in custody and who appears before it on, or in connection with, his appeal under Part I of the Criminal Appeal Act 1968.

(5) The Lord Chancellor may by regulations provide that any provision made by or under this Part which would not otherwise apply in relation to any category of proceedings in which an offender is before a magistrates' court or the Crown Court shall apply in relation to proceedings of that category, subject to any specified modifications.

20. *****

21. Interpretation, etc.

(1) In this Part—

"defendant's costs order" has the meaning given in section 16 of this Act;

["legally assisted person", in relation to any proceedings, means a person to whom representation under the Legal Aid Act 1988 has been granted for the purposes of the proceedings;]

"proceedings" includes—
    (a) proceedings in any court below; and
    (b) in relation to the determination of an appeal by any court, any application made to that court for leave to bring the appeal; and

"witness" means any person properly attending to give evidence, whether or not he gives evidence or is called at the instance of one of the parties or of the court, but does not include a person attending as a witness to character only unless the court has certified that the interests of justice required his attendance.

(2) Except as provided by or under this Part no costs shall be allowed on the hearing or determination of, or of any proceedings preliminary or incidental to, an appeal to the Court of Appeal under Part I of the Criminal Appeal Act 1968.

(3) Subject to rules of court made under section 53(1) of the Supreme Court Act 1981 (power by rules to distribute business of Court of Appeal between its civil and criminal divisions), the jurisdiction of the Court of Appeal, under this Part, or under regulations made under this Part, shall be exercised by the criminal division of that Court; and references in this Part to the Court of Appeal shall be construed as references to that division.

(4) For the purposes of sections 16 and 17 of this Act, the costs of any party to proceedings shall be taken to include the expense of compensating any witness for the expenses, trouble or loss of time properly incurred in or incidental to his attendance.

[(4A) Where one party to any proceedings is a legally assisted person then—
    (a) for the purposes of sections 16 and 17 of this Act, his costs shall be taken not to include either the expenses incurred on his behalf by the Legal Aid Board or the Lord Chancellor or, if he is liable to make a contribution under section 23 of the Legal Aid Act 1988, any sum paid or payable by way of contribution; and
    (b) for the purposes of sections 18 and 19 of this Act, his costs shall be taken to include the expenses incurred on his behalf by the Legal Aid Board or the Lord Chancellor (without any deduction on account of any contribution paid or payable under section 23 of the Legal Aid Act 1988) but, if he is liable to make such a contribution his costs shall be taken not to include any sum paid or payable by way of contribution.]

(5) Where, in any proceedings in a criminal cause or matter or in either of the cases mentioned in subsection (6) below, an interpreter is required because of the accused's lack of English, the expenses properly incurred on his employment shall not be treated as costs of any party to the proceedings.

(6) The cases are—
    (a) where an information charging the accused with an offence is laid before

a justice of the peace for any area but not proceeded with and the expenses are incurred on the employment of the interpreter for the proceedings on the information; and

(b) where the accused is committed for trial but not tried and the expenses are incurred on the employment of the interpreter for the proceedings in the Crown Court.

PART III
MISCELLANEOUS

22. *****

23. Discontinuance of proceedings in magistrates' courts

(1) Where the Director of Public Prosecutions has the conduct of proceedings for an offence, this section applies in relation to the preliminary stages of those proceedings.

(2) In this section, "preliminary stage" in relation to proceedings for an offence does not include—

(a) in the case of a summary offence, any stage of the proceedings after the court has begun to hear evidence for the prosecution at the trial;

(b) in the case of an indictable offence, any stage of the proceedings after—

(i) the accused has been committed for trial; or

(ii) the court has begun to hear evidence for the prosecution at a summary trial of the offence.

(3) Where, at any time during the preliminary stages of the proceedings, the Director gives notice under this section to the clerk of the court that he does not want the proceedings to continue, they shall be discontinued with effect from the giving of that notice but may be revived by notice given by the accused under subsection (7) below.

(4) Where, in the case of a person charged with an offence after being taken into custody without a warrant, the Director gives him notice, at a time when no magistrates' court has been informed of the charge, that the proceedings against him are discontinued, they shall be discontinued with effect from the giving of that notice.

(5) The Director shall, in any notice given under subsection (3) above, give reasons for not wanting the proceedings to continue.

(6) On giving any notice under subsection (3) above the Director shall inform the accused of the notice and of the accused's right to require the proceedings to be continued; but the Director shall not be obliged to give the accused any indication of his reasons for not wanting the proceedings to continue.

(7) Where the Director has given notice under subsection (3) above, the accused shall, if he wants the proceedings to continue, give notice to that effect to the clerk of the court within the prescribed period; and where notice is so given the proceedings shall continue as if no notice had been given by the Director under subsection (3) above.

(8) Where the clerk of the court has been so notified by the accused he shall inform the Director.

(9) The discontinuance of any proceedings by virtue of this section shall not prevent the institution of fresh proceedings in respect of the same offence.

(10) In this section "prescribed" means prescribed by rules made under section 144 of the Magistrates' Courts Act 1980.

ADMINISTRATION OF JUSTICE ACT 1985
(1985, c. 61)

An Act to make further provision with respect to the administration of justice and matters connected therewith; to amend the Solicitors Act 1974; to regulate the provision of solicitors' services in the case of incorporated practices; to regulate the provision of conveyancing services by persons practising as licensed conveyancers; to make further provision with respect to complaints relating to the provision of legal aid services; to amend the law relating to time limits for actions for libel and slander; and to make further provision with respect to arbitrations and proceedings in connection with European patents.

[30 October 1985]

1.—10. *****

PART II
LICENSED CONVEYANCING

11. Provision of conveyancing services by licensed conveyancers

(1) The provisions of this Part shall have effect for the purposes of regulating the provision of conveyancing services by persons who hold licences in force under this Part.

(2) In this Part—
"licence" means a licence to practise as a licensed conveyancer;
"licensed conveyancer" means a person who holds a licence in force under this Part; and references in this Part to practising as a licensed conveyancer are references to providing, as the holder of such a licence, conveyancing services in accordance with the licence.

(3) References in this Part to conveyancing services are references to the preparation of transfers, conveyances, contracts and other documents in connection with, and other services ancillary to, the disposition or acquisition of estates or interests in land; and for the purposes of this subsection—
 (a) "disposition"—
  (i) does not include a testamentary disposition or any disposition in the case of such a lease as is referred to in section 54(2) of the Law of Property Act 1925 (short leases); but
  (ii) subject to that, includes in the case of leases both their grant and their assignment; and
 (b) "acquisition" has a corresponding meaning.

(4) Section 22(1) of the Solicitors Act 1974 (restriction on person preparing certain instruments when not qualified to act as a solicitor) shall not apply to any act done by a licensed conveyancer in the course of the provision of any conveyancing services if he is not precluded from providing those services as a licensed conveyancer by any conditions imposed as mentioned in section 16(3)(a).

The Council for Licensed Conveyancers

12. Establishment of the Council

(1) For the purposes of this Part there shall be a body to be known as the Council for Licensed Conveyancers.

(2) It shall be the general duty of the Council to ensure that the standards of competence and professional conduct among persons who practise as licensed conveyancers are sufficient to secure adequate protection for consumers, and that the conveyancing services provided by such persons are provided both economically and efficiently.

(3) *****

13.—19. *****

Code of conduct

20. Rules as to professional practice, conduct and discipline

(1) The Council shall, in pursuance of its general duty referred to in section 12(2),

make rules for regulating the professional practice, conduct and discipline of licensed conveyancers.

(2) Rules made by the Council under this section may provide for regulating the association of licensed conveyancers with other persons in connection with the provision of conveyancing services to members of the public.

21. *****

INSOLVENCY ACT 1986
(1986, c. 45)

375. Appeals etc. from courts exercising insolvency jurisdiction

(1) Every court having jurisdiction for the purposes of the Parts in this Group may review, rescind or vary any order made by it in the exercise of that jursidction.

(2) An appeal from a decision made in the exercise of jurisdiction for the purposes of those Parts by a county court or by a registrar in bankruptcy of the High Court lies to a single judge of the High Court; and an appeal from a decision of that judge on such an appeal lies, with the leave of the judge or of the Court of Appeal, to the Court of Appeal.

(3) A county court is not, in the exercise of its jurisdiction for the purposes of those Parts, to be subject to be restrained by the order of any other court, and no appeal lies from its decision in the exercise of that jurisdiction except as provided by this section.

EUROPEAN COMMUNITIES (AMENDMENT) ACT 1986
(1986, c. 58)

An Act to amend the European Communities Act 1972 so as to include in the definition of "the Treaties" and "the Community Treaties" certain provisions of the Single European Act signed at Luxembourg and The Hague on 17th and 28th February 1986 and extend certain provisions relating to the European Court to any court attached thereto; and to amend references to the Assembly of the European Communities and approve the Single European Act. [7 November 1986]

1., 2. *****

3. Provisions relating to European Assembly

(1) Subject to subsection (2) below and to the repeals and revocations made by section 4(3) below, any enactment or instrument passed or made before the day on which the Single European Act enters into force shall have effect on and after that day with the substitution—

(a) of a reference to the (or, as the case may be, a) European Parliament for any reference (however worded) to the (or an) Assembly of the European Communities; and

(b) of the words "European Parliament" for the word "Assembly" and for the words "European Assembly" wherever that word or those words are used adjectivally with reference to the European Assembly (together with, where necessary, the consequential substitution of "a" for "an").

(2) The provisions on which subsection (1) above operates do not include that subsection itself or subsection (3) below or the long title of this Act but, subject to those exceptions, include—

(a) the long titles of Acts passed before the day mentioned in subsection (1) above;

(b) any provision of an Act or instrument passed or made before that day specifying how that Act or instrument may be cited; and

(c) so much of any Act or instrument so passed or made as uses a mode of citation authorised by another such Act or instrument to refer to that other Act or instrument.

(3) On and after the day mentioned in subsection (1) above the enactments and instruments amended by this section shall have effect as if the Assembly of the European Communities had always been named the European Parliament.

(4) For the purposes of section 6 of the European Assembly Elections Act 1978 the Single European Act is hereby approved.

4. *****

CRIMINAL JUSTICE ACT 1987
(1987, c. 38)

An Act to make further provision for the investigation of and trials for fraud; and for connected purposes. [15 May 1987]

1.—3. *****

Transfer of cases to Crown Court

4. Notices of transfer and designated authorities

(1) If—
    (a) a person has been charged with an indictable offence; and
    (b) in the opinion of an authority designated by subsection (2) below or of one of such an authority's officers acting on the authority's behalf the evidence of the offence charged—
        (i) would be sufficient for the person charged to be committed for trial; and
        (ii) reveals a case of fraud of such seriousness and complexity that it is appropriate that the management of the case should without delay be taken over by the Crown Court; and

    (c) before the magistrates' court in whose jurisdiction the offence has been charged begins to inquire into the case as examining justices the authority or one of the authority's officers acting on the authority's behalf gives the court a notice (in this Act referred to as a 'notice of transfer') certifying that opinion,
the functions of the magistrates' court shall cease in relation to the case, except as provided by section 5(3) [, (7A)] and (8) below and by [section 20(4) of the Legal Aid Act 1988.]

(2) The authorities mentioned in subsection (1) above (in this Act referred to as 'designated authorities') are—
    (a) the Director of Public Prosecutions;
    (b) the Director of the Serious Fraud Office;
    (c) the Commissioners of Inland Revenue;
    (d) the Commissioners of Customs and Excise; and
    (e) the Secretary of State.

(3) A designated authority's decision to give notice of transfer shall not be subject to appeal or liable to be questioned in any court.

5. *****

[6. **Applications for dismissal**

(1) Where notice of transfer has been given, any person to whom the notice relates, at any time before he is arraigned (and whether or not an indictment has been preferred against him), may apply orally or in writing to the Crown Court sitting at the place specified by the notice of transfer as the proposed place of trial for the charge, or any of the charges, in the case to be dismissed; and the judge shall dismiss a charge (and accordingly quash a count relating to it in any indictment preferred against the applicant) if it appears to him that the evidence against the applicant would not be sufficient for a jury properly to convict him.

(2) No oral application may be made under subsection (1) above unless the applicant has given the Crown Court sitting at the place specified by the notice of transfer as the proposed place of trial written notice of his intention to make the application.

(3) Oral evidence may be given on such an application only with the leave of the judge or by his order, and the judge shall give leave or make an order only if it appears to him, having regard to any matters stated in the application for leave, that the interests of justice require him to do so.

(4) If the judge gives leave permitting, or makes an order requiring, a person to give oral evidence, but he does not do so, the judge may disregard any document indicating the evidence that he might have given.

(5) Dismissal of the charge, or all the charges, against the applicant shall have the same effect as a refusal by examining magistrates to commit for trial, except that no further proceedings may be brought on a dismissed charge except by means of the preferment of a voluntary bill of indictment.

(6) Crown Court Rules may make provision for the purposes of this section and, without prejudice to the generality of this subsection—

    (a)   as to the time or stage in the proceedings at which anything required to be done is to be done (unless the court grants leave to do it at some other time or stage);

    (b)   as to the contents and form of notices or other documents;

    (c)   as to the manner in which evidence is to be submitted; and

    (d)   as to persons to be served with notices or other material.]

Preparatory hearings

7. **Power to order preparatory hearing**

(1) Where it appears to a judge of the Crown Court that the evidence on an indictment reveals a case of fraud of such seriousness and complexity that substantial benefits are likely to accrue from a hearing (in this Act referred to as a 'preparatory hearing') before the jury are sworn, for the purpose of—

    (a)   identifying issues which are likely to be material to the verdict of the jury;

    (b)   assisting their comprehension of any such issues;

    (c)   expediting the proceedings before the jury; or

    (d)   assisting the judge's management of the trial,

he may order that such a hearing shall be held.

(2) A judge may make an order under subsection (1) above on the application either of the prosecution or of the person indicted or, if the indictment charges a number of persons, any of them, or of his own motion.

(3) If a judge orders a preparatory hearing, he may also order the prosecution to prepare and serve any documents that appear to him to be relevant and whose service could be ordered at the preparatory hearing by virtue of this part of this Act or Crown Court Rules.

(4) Where—

    (a)   a judge has made an order under subsection (3) above; and

    (b)   the prosecution have complied with it,

the judge may order the person indicted or, if the indictment charges a number of persons, any of them to prepare and serve any documents that appear to him to be relevant and whose service could be so ordered at the preparatory hearing.

(5) An order under this section may specify the time within which it is to be complied with, but Crown Court Rules may make provision as to the minimum or maximum time that may be specified for compliance.

8. Commencement of trial and arraignment
(1) If a judge orders a preparatory hearing, the trial shall begin with that hearing.
(2) Arraignment shall accordingly take place at the start of the preparatory hearing.

9., 10. *****

CORONERS ACT 1988
(1988, c. 13)

An Act to consolidate the Coroners Acts 1887 to 1980 and certain related enactments, with amendments to give effect to recommendations of the Law Commission.

[10 May 1988]

Coroners

1. Appointment of coroners
(1) Coroners shall be appointed for each coroner's district in a metropolitan county or Greater London, for each non-metropolitan county and for the City and shall be so appointed by the relevant council, that is to say—
    (a) in the case of a coroner's district consisting of or included in a metropolitan district or London borough, the council of that district or borough;
    (b) in the case of a coroner's district consisting of two or more metropolitan districts or London boroughs, such one of the councils of those districts or boroughs as may be designed by an order made by the Secretary of State by statutory instrument;
    (c) in the case of a non-metropolitan county, the council of that county; and
    (d) in the case of the City, the Common Council.

(2) A relevant council falling within paragraph (a) or (b) of subsection (1) above shall not appoint a coroner except with the approval of the Secretary of State; and a relevant council falling within paragraph (b) of that subsection shall not appoint a coroner except after consultation with the other council or councils in question.

(3) Subject to subsection (2) above, where a vacancy occurs in the office of coroner, the relevant council shall—
    (a) immediately give notice of the vacancy to the Secretary of State;
    (b) within three months of the vacancy occurring or within such further period as the Secretary of State may allow, appoint a person to that office; and
    (c) immediately after making the appointment, give notice of the appointment to the Secretary of State.

2. Qualifications for appointment as coroner
(1) No person shall be qualified to be appointed as coroner unless he is a barrister, solicitor or legally qualified medical practitioner of not less than five years' standing in his profession.

(2) A person shall, so long as he is a councillor of a metropolitan district or London borough, and for six months after he ceases to be one, be disqualified for being a coroner for a coroner's district which consists of, includes or is included in that metropolitan district or London borough.

(3) A person shall, so long as he is an alderman or a councillor of a non-metropolitan

county, and for six months after he ceases to be one, be disqualified for being a coroner for that county.

(4) A person shall, so long as he is an alderman of the City or a common councillor, and for six months after he ceases to be one, be disqualified for being a coroner for the City.

3. Terms on which coroners hold office

(1) The provisions of Schedule 1 to this Act shall have effect with respect to the payment of salaries and the grant of pensions to coroners.

(2) Except as authorised by this or any other Act, a coroner shall not take any fee or remuneration in respect of anything done by him in the execution of his office.

(3) A coroner may resign his office by giving notice in writing to the relevant council, but the resignation shall not take effect unless and until it is accepted by that council.

(4) The Lord Chancellor may, if he thinks fit, remove any coroner from office for inability or misbehaviour in the discharge of his duty.

(5) A coroner who is guilty of corruption, wilful neglect of his duty or misbehaviour in the discharge of his duty shall be guilty of an offence and liable on conviction on indictment to imprisonment for a term not exceeding two years or to a fine or to both.

(6) Where a coroner is convicted of an offence under subsection (5) above, the court may, unless his offence as coroner is annexed to any other office, order that he be removed from office and be disqualified for acting as coroner.

4. *****

5. Jurisdiction of coroners

(1) Subject to subsection (3) and sections 7 and 13 to 15 below, an inquest into a death shall be held only by the coroner within whose district the body lies.

(2) Subject to subsection (3) and section 13 below, a coroner shall hold inquests only within his district.

(3) A coroner may act as coroner for another district in the same administrative area—

(a) during the illness, incapacity or unavoidable absence of the coroner for that district; or

(b) where there is a vacancy in the office of coroner for that district;

and the inquisition returned in respect of an inquest held under this subsection shall certify the cause of the coroner's holding the inquest and shall be conclusive evidence of any matter stated in it which falls within paragraph (a) or (b) above.

6., 7. *****

Inquests: general

8. Duty to hold inquest

(1) Where a coroner is informed that the body of a person ("the deceased") is lying within his district and there is reasonable cause to suspect that the deceased—

(a) has died a violent or an unnatural death;

(b) has died a sudden death of which the cause is unknown; or

(c) has died in prison or in such a place or in such circumstances as to require an inquest under any other Act,

then, whether the cause of death arose within his district or not, the coroner shall as soon as practicable hold an inquest into the death of the deceased either with or, subject to subsection (3) below, without a jury.

(2) In the case of an inquest with a jury—

(a) the coroner shall summon by warrant not less than seven nor more than eleven persons to appear before him at a specified time and place, there to inquire as jurors into the death of the deceased; and

(b) when not less than seven jurors are assembled, they shall be sworn by or before the coroner diligently to inquire into the death of the deceased and to give a true verdict according to the evidence.

(3) If it appears to a coroner, either before he proceeds to hold an inquest or in the course of an inquest begun without a jury, that there is reason to suspect—

(a) that the death occured in prison or in such a place or in such circumstances as to require an inquest under any other Act;

(b) that the death occurred while the deceased was in police custody, or resulted from an injury caused by a police officer in the purported execution of his duty;

(c) that the death was caused by an accident, poisoning or disease notice of which is required to be given under any Act to a government department, to any inspector or other officer of a government department or to an inspector appointed under section 19 of the Health and Safety at Work etc. Act 1974; or

(d) that the death occurred in circumstances the continuance or possible recurrence of which is prejudicial to the health or safety of the public or any section of the public,

he shall proceed to summon a jury in the manner required by subsection (2) above.

(4) If it appears to a coroner, either before he proceeds to hold an inquest or in the course of an inquest begun without a jury, that there is any reason for summoning a jury, he may proceed to summon a jury in the manner required by subsection (2) above.

(5) In the case of an inquest or any part of an inquest held without a jury, anything done by or before the coroner alone shall be as validly done as if it had been done by or before the coroner and a jury.

(6) Where an inquest is held into the death of a prisoner who dies within a prison, neither a prisoner in the prison nor any person engaged in any sort of trade or dealing with the prison shall serve as a juror at the inquest.

9. Qualifications of jurors

(1) A person shall not be qualified to serve as a juror at an inquest held by a coroner unless he is for the time being qualified to serve as a juror in the Crown Court, the High Court and county courts in accordance with section 1 of the Juries Act 1974.

(2) If a person serves on a jury knowing that he is ineligible for such service under Group A, B or C in Part I of Schedule 1 to that Act, he shall be guilty of an offence and liable on summary conviction to a fine not exceeding level 3 on the standard scale.

(3) If a person serves on a jury knowing that he is disqualified for such service under Part II of that Schedule, he shall be guilty of an offence and liable on summary conviction to a fine not exceeding level 5 on the standard scale.

(4) The appropriate officer may at any time put or cause to be put to any person who is summoned under section 8 above such questions as he thinks fit in order to establish whether or not the person is qualified to serve as a juror at an inquest.

(5) Where a question is put to any person under subsection (4) above, if that person—

(a) refuses without reasonable excuse to answer;

(b) gives an answer which he knows to be false in a material particular; or

(c) recklessly gives an answer which is false in a material particular,

he shall be guilty of an offence and liable on summary conviction to a fine not exceeding level 3 on the standard scale.

(6) If any person—

(a) duly summoned as a juror at an inquest makes, or causes or permits to be made on his behalf, any false representation to the coroner or the appropriate officer with the intention of evading service as such juror; or

(b) makes or causes to be made on behalf of another person who has been

so summoned any false representation to the coroner or the appropriate officer with the intention of enabling that other person to evade such service,
he shall be guilty of an offence and liable on summary conviction to a fine not exceeding level 3 on the standard scale.

(7) A coroner may authorise a person to perform the functions conferred on the appropriate officer by subsection (4) above and references in this section to the appropriate officer shall be construed as references to the person so authorised.

10. Attendance of jurors and witnesses

(1) Where a person duly summoned as a juror at an inquest—

(a) does not, after being openly called three times, appear to the summons; or

(b) appears to the summons but refuses without reasonable excuse to serve as a juror,

the coroner may impose on that person a fine not exceeding £400.

(2) Where a person duly summoned to give evidence at an inquest—

(a) does not, after being openly called three times, appear to the summons; or

(b) appears to the summons but refuses without lawful excuse to answer a question put to him,

the coroner may impose on that person a fine not exceeding £400.

(3) The powers conferred upon a coroner by this section shall be in addition to and not in derogation of any other power which the coroner may possess—

(a) for compelling any person to appear and give evidence before him in any inquest or other proceeding; or

(b) for punishing any person for contempt of court in not so appearing and giving evidence;

but a person shall not be fined by the coroner under this section and also be punished under any such other power.

(4) Notwithstanding anything in the foregoing provisions of this section, a juror shall not be liable to any penalty for non-attendance on a coroner's jury unless the summons requiring him to attend was duly served on him no later than six days before the day on which he was required to attend.

11. Proceedings at inquest

(1) It shall not be obligatory for a coroner holding an inquest into a death to view the body; and the validity of such an inquest shall not be questioned in any court on the ground that the coroner did not view the body.

(2) The coroner shall, at the first sitting of the inquest, examine on oath concerning the death all persons who tender evidence as to the facts of the death and all persons having knowledge of those facts whom he considers it expedient to examine.

(3) In the case of an inquest held with a jury, the jury shall, after hearing the evidence—

(a) give their verdict and certify it by an inquisition; and

(b) inquire of and find the particulars for the time being required by the Births and Deaths Registration Act 1953 (in this Act referred to as "the 1953 Act") to be registered concerning the death.

(4) In the case of an inquest held without a jury, the coroner shall, after hearing the evidence—

(a) give his verdict and certify it by an inquisition; and

(b) inquire of and find the particulars for the time being required by the 1953 Act to be registered concerning the death.

(5) An inquisition—

(a) shall be in writing under the hand of the coroner and, in the case of an inquest held with a jury, under the hands of the jurors who concur in the verdict;
(b) shall set out, so far as such particulars have been proved—
  (i) who the deceased was; and
  (ii) how, when and where the deceased came by his death; and
(c) shall be in such form as the Lord Chancellor may by rules made by statutory instrument from time to time prescribe.

(6) At a coroner's inquest into the death of a person who came by his death by murder, manslaughter or infanticide, the purpose of the proceedings shall not include the finding of any person guilty of the murder, manslaughter or infanticide; and accordingly a coroner's inquisition shall in no case charge a person with any of those offences.

(7) When an inquest into a death is held, the coroner shall, within five days after the finding of the inquest is given, send to the registrar of deaths a certificate under his hand—
(a) giving information concerning the death;
(b) specifying the finding with respect to the particulars which under the 1953 Act are required to be registered concerning the death and with respect to the cause of death; and
(c) specifying the time and place at which the inquest was held.

(8) In the case of an inquest into the death of a person who is proved—
(a) to have been killed on a railway; or
(b) to have died in consequence of injuries received on a railway,
the coroner shall within seven days after holding the inquest, make a return of the death, including the cause of death, to the Secretary of State in such form as he may require; and in this subsection "railway" has the same meaning as in the Railway Regulation Act 1842.

12. Failure of jury to agree

(1) This section applies where, in the case of an inquest held with a jury, the jury fails to agree on a verdict.

(2) If the minority consists of not more than two, the coroner may accept the verdict of the majority, and the majority shall, in that case, certify the verdict under section 11(3) above.

(3) In any other case of disagreement the coroner may discharge the jury and issue a warrant for summoning another jury and, in that case, the inquest shall proceed in all respects as if the proceedings which terminated in the disagreement had not taken place.

CRIMINAL JUSTICE ACT 1988
(1988, c. 33)

[29 July 1988]

PART IV
REVIEWS OF SENTENCING

35. Scope of Part IV

(1) A case to which this Part of this Act applies may be referred to the Court of Appeal under section 36 below.

(2) Subject to Rules of Court, the jurisdiction of the Court of Appeal under section 36 below shall be exercised by the criminal division of the Court, and references to the Court of Appeal in this Part of this Act shall be construed as references to that division.

(3) This Part of this Act applies to any cause in which sentence is passed on a person—
    (a)   for an offence triable only on indictment; or
    (b)   for an offence of a description specified in an order under this section.
(4), (5) *****
(6) In this Part of this Act 'sentence' has the same meaning as in the Criminal Appeal Act 1968, except that it does not include an interim hospital order under Part III of the Mental Health Act 1983, and 'sentencing' shall be construed accordingly.
(7)—(11) *****

36. Reviews of sentencing

(1) If it appears to the Attorney General—
    (a)   that the sentencing of a person in a proceeding in the Crown Court has been unduly lenient; and
    (b)   that the case is one to which this Part of this Act applies,
he may, with the leave of the Court of Appeal, refer the case to them for them to review the sentencing of that person; and on such a reference the Court of Appeal may—
    (i)   quash any sentence passed on him in the proceeding; and
    (ii)   in place of it pass such sentence as they think appropriate for the case and as the court below had power to pass when dealing with him.

(2) Without prejudice to the generality of subsection (1) above, the condition specified in paragraph (a) of that subsection may be satisfied if it appears to the Attorney General that the judge erred in law as to his powers of sentencing.

(3) For the purposes of this Part of this Act any two or more sentences are to be treated as passed in the same proceeding if they would be so treated for the purposes of section 10 of the Criminal Appeal Act 1968.

(4) No judge shall sit as a member of the Court of Appeal on the hearing of, or shall determine any application in proceedings incidental or preliminary to, a reference under this section of a sentence passed by himself.

(5) Where the Court of Appeal have concluded their review of a case referred to them under this section the Attorney General or the person to whose sentencing the reference relates may refer a point of law involved in any sentence passed on that person in the proceeding to the House of Lords for their opinion, and the House shall consider the point and give their opinion on it accordingly, and either remit the case to the Court of Appeal to be dealt with or deal with it themselves; and section 35(1) of the Criminal Appeal Act 1968 (composition of House for appeals) shall apply also in relation to any proceedings of the House under this section.

(6) A reference under subsection (5) above shall be made only with the leave of the Court of Appeal or the House of Lords; and leave shall not be granted unless it is certified by the Court of Appeal that the point of law is of general public importance and it appears to the Court of Appeal or the House or Lords (as the case may be) that the point is one which ought to be considered by that House.

(7) For the purpose of dealing with a case under this section the House of Lords may exercise any powers of the Court of Appeal.

(8), (9) *****

PART V
JURISDICTION, IMPRISONMENT, FINES, ETC
Jurisdiction

37. Certain either way offences relating to motor vehicles to be summary offences

(1) In section 12 of the Theft Act 1968 (taking motor vehicle or other conveyance without authority etc.)—

    (a) in subsection (2), for the words 'on conviction on indictment be liable to imprisonment for a term not exceeding three years.' there shall be substituted the words 'be liable on summary conviction to a fine not exceeding level 5 on the standard scale, to imprisonment for a term not exceeding six months, or to both.'; and

    (b) at the end of subsection (4) there shall be added the words 'and if he is found guilty of it, he shall be liable as he would have been liable under subsection (2) above on summary conviction.'.

(2) In Schedule 4 to the Road Traffic Act 1972 (prosecution and punishment of offences) as it applies in England and Wales, the following shall be substituted for columns 3 and 4 of the entry relating to offences under section 99(b) (driving while disqualified)—

'Summarily   6 months or level 5 on the standard scale or both.'.

38. Criminal damage etc. as summary offences

(1) In subsection (1) of section 22 of the Magistrates' Courts Act 1980 (under which, where an offence of or related to criminal damage is charged and it appears to a magistrates' court clear that the value involved does not exceed the relevant sum, the court is required to proceed as if the offence charged were triable only summarily) in the second paragraph (which states the relevant sum) for '£400' there shall be substituted '£2,000'.

(2) Subsection (1) above does not apply to an offence charged in respect of an act done before this section comes into force.

(3) *****

(4) Subsection (3) above does not apply where any of the offences are charged in respect of acts done before this section comes into force.

39. Common assault and battery to be summary offences

Common assault and battery shall be summary offences and a person guilty of either of them shall be liable to a fine not exceeding level 5 on the standard scale, to imprisonment for a term not exceeding six months, or to both.

40. Power to join in indictment count for common assault etc.

(1) A count charging a person with a summary offence to which this section applies may be included in an indictment if the charge—

    (a) is founded on the same facts or evidence as a count charging an indictable offence; or

    (b) is part of a series of offences of the same or similar character as an indictable offence which is also charged,

but only if (in either case) the facts or evidence relating to the offence were disclosed in an examination or deposition taken before a justice in the presence of the person charged.

(2) Where a count charging an offence to which this section applies is included in an indictment, the offence shall be tried in the same manner as if it were an indictable offence; but the Crown Court may only deal with the offender in respect of it in a manner in which a magistrates' court could have dealt with him.

(3) The offences to which this section applies are—

    (a) common assault;

(b) an offence under section 12(1) of the Theft Act 1968 (taking motor vehicle or other conveyance without authority etc.);

(c) an offence under [section 103(1)(b) of the Road Traffic Act 1988] (driving a motor vehicle while disqualified);

(d) an offence mentioned in the first column of Schedule 2 to the Magistrates' Courts Act 1980 (criminal damage etc.) which would otherwise be triable only summarily by virtue of section 22(2) of that Act; and

(e) any summary offence specified under subsection (4) below.

(4) The Secretary of State may by order made by statutory instrument specify for the purposes of this section any summary offence which is punishable with imprisonment or involves obligatory or discretionary disqualification from driving.

(5) A statutory instrument containing an order under this section shall be subject to annulment in pursuance of a resolution of either House of Parliament.

41. Power of Crown Court to deal with summary offence where person committed for either way offence

(1) Where a magistrates' court commits a person to the Crown Court for trial on indictment for an offence triable either way or a number of such offences, it may also commit him for trial for any summary offence with which he is charged and which—

(a) is punishable with imprisonment or involves obligatory or discretionary disqualification from driving; and

(b) arises out of circumstances which appear to the court to be the same as or connected with those giving rise to the offence, or one of the offences, triable either way,

whether or not evidence relating to that summary offence appears on the depositions or written statements in the case; and the trial of the information charging the summary offence shall then be treated as if the magistrates' court had adjourned it under section 10 of the Magistrates' Courts Act 1980 and had not fixed the time and place for its resumption.

(2) Where a magistrates' court commits a person to the Crown Court for trial on indictment for a number of offences triable either way and exercises the power conferred by subsection (1) above in respect of a summary offence, the magistrates' court shall give the Crown Court and the person who is committed for trial a notice stating which of the offences triable either way appears to the court to arise out of circumstances which are the same as or connected with those giving rise to the summary offence.

(3) A magistrates' court's decision to exercise the power conferred by subsection (1) above shall not be subject to appeal or liable to be questioned in any court.

(4) The committal of a person under this section in respect of an offence to which section 40 above applies shall not preclude the exercise in relation to the offence of the power conferred by that section; but where he is tried on indictment for such an offence, the functions of the Crown Court under this section in relation to the offence shall cease.

(5) If he is convicted on the indictment, the Crown Court shall consider whether the conditions specified in subsection (1) above were satisfied.

(6) If it considers that they were satisfied, it shall state to him the substance of the summary offence and ask him whether he pleads guilty or not guilty.

(7) If he pleads guilty, the Crown Court shall convict him, but may deal with him in respect of that offence only in a manner in which a magistrates' court could have dealt with him.

(8) If he does not plead guilty, the powers of the Crown Court shall cease in respect of the offence except as provided by subsection (9) below.

(9) If the prosecution inform the Court that they would not desire to submit evidence on the charge relating to the summary offence, the Court shall dismiss it.

(10) The Crown Court shall inform the clerk of the magistrates' court of the outcome of any proceedings under this section.

(11) Where the Court of Appeal allows an appeal against conviction of an offence triable either way which arose out of circumstances which were the same as or connected with those giving rise to a summary offence of which the appellant was convicted under this section—

    (a) it shall set aside his conviction of the summary offence and give the clerk of the magistrates' court notice that it has done so; and

    (b) it may direct that no further proceedings in relation to the offence are to be undertaken;

and the proceedings before the Crown Court in relation to the offence shall thereafter be disregarded for all purposes.

(12) A notice under subsection (11) above shall include particulars of any direction given under paragraph (b) of that subsection in relation to the offence.

(13) The references to the clerk of the magistrates' court in this section are to be construed in accordance with section 141 of the Magistrates' Courts Act 1980.

PART VIII
AMENDMENTS OF LAW RELATING TO JURIES

122. Autrefois acquit and autrefois convict

Where an accused pleads autrefois acquit or autrefois convict it shall be for the judge without the presence of a jury, to decide the issue.

PART XI
MISCELLANEOUS

Miscarriages of justice

133. Compensation for miscarriages of justices

(1) Subject to subsection (2) below, when a person has been convicted of a criminal offence and when subsequently his conviction has been reversed or he has been pardoned on the ground that a new or newly discovered fact shows beyond reasonable doubt that there has been a miscarriage of justice, the Secretary of State shall pay compensation for the miscarriage of justice to the person who has suffered punishment as a result of such conviction or, if he is dead, to his personal representatives, unless the non-disclosure of the unknown fact was wholly or partly attributable to the person convicted.

(2) No payment of compensation under this section shall be made unless an application for such compensation has been made to the Secretary of State.

(3) The question whether there is a right to compensation under this section shall be determined by the Secretary of State.

(4) If the Secretary of State determines that there is a right to such compensation, the amount of the compensation shall be assessed by an assessor appointed by the Secretary of State.

(5) In this section 'reversed' shall be construed as referring to a conviction having been quashed—

    (a) on an appeal out of time; or

    (b) on a reference—

        (i) under section 17 of the Criminal Appeal Act 1968;

        (ii) under section 263 of the Criminal Procedure (Scotland) Act 1975; or

        (iii) under section 14 of the Criminal Appeal (Northern Ireland) Act 1980.

(6) For the purposes of this section a person suffers punishment as a result of a conviction when sentence is passed on him for the offence of which he was convicted.

(7) Schedule 12 shall have effect.

LEGAL AID ACT 1988
(1988 c. 34)

An Act to make new provision for the administration of, and to revise the law relating to, legal aid, advice and assistance. (29th July 1988)

PART I
PRELIMINARY

1. Purpose of this Act

The purpose of this Act is to establish a framework for the provision under Parts II, III, IV V and VI of advice, assistance and representation which is publicly funded with a view to helping persons who might otherwise be unable to obtain advice, assistance or representation on account of their means.

2. Interpretation

(1) This section has effect for the interpretation of this Act.

(2) "Advice" means oral or written advice on the application of English law to any particular circumstances that have arisen in relation to the person seeking the advice and as to the step which that person might appropriately take having regard to the application of English law to those circumstances.

(3) "Assistance" means assistance in taking any of the steps which a person might take, including steps with respect to proceedings, having regard to the application of English law to any particular circumstances that have arisen in relation to him, whether by taking such steps on his behalf (including assistance by way of representation) or by assisting him in taking them on his own behalf.

(4) "Representation" means representation for the purposes of proceedings and it includes—

    (a) all such assistance as is usually given by a solicitor or counsel in the steps preliminary or incidental to any proceedings;

    (b) all such assistance as is usually so given in civil proceedings in arriving at or giving effect to a compromise to avoid or bring to an end any proceedings; and

    (c) in the case of criminal proceedings, advice and assistance as to any appeal; and related expressions have corresponding meanings.

(5) Regulations may specify what is, or is not, to be included in advice or assistance of any description, or representation for the purposes of proceedings of any description, to which any Part or provision of a Part of this Act applies and the regulations may provide for the inclusion, in prescribed circumstances, of advice or assistance given otherwise than under this Act.

(6) Advice, assistance and representation under this Act, except when made available under Part II, is only by persons who are solicitors or barristers, but in the case of Part II, may be by other persons.

(7) In any particular case, advice, assistance and representation under this Act, except when made available under Part II, shall be by solicitor and, so far as necessary counsel; but regulations may prescribe the circumstances in which representation is to be by counsel only or by solicitor only and regulate representation by more than one counsel.

(8) The Lord Chancellor may, if it appears to him to be necessary to do so for the purpose of fulfilling any obligation imposed on the United Kingdom or Her Majesty's Government in the United Kingdom by any international agreement, by order direct that such advice or assistance relating to the application of other laws than English law as is specified in the order shall be advice or assistance for any of the purposes of this Act.

(9) For the purposes of the application of subsection (8) above in the case of an

obligation to provide for the transmission to other countries of applications for legal aid under their laws, the reference to advice or assistance relating to the application of other laws includes a reference to advice or assistance for the purposes of making and transmitting such an application.

(10) In this Act "person" does not include a body of persons corporate or unincorporate which is not concerned in a representative, fiduciary or official capacity so as to authorise advice, assistance or representation to be granted to such a body.

(11) In this Act "legally assisted person" means any person who receives, under this Act, advice, assistance or representation and, in relation to proceedings, any reference to an assisted party or an unassisted party is to be construed accordingly.

PART II
LEGAL AID BOARD AND LEGAL AID

3. The Legal Aid Board

(1) There shall be established a body to be known as the Legal Aid Board (in this Act referred to as "the Board").

(2) Subject to subsection (3) and (4) below, the Board shall have the general function of securing that advice, assistance and representation are available in accordance with this Act and of administering this Act.

(3) Subsection (2) above does not confer on the Board any functions with respect to the grant of representation under Part VI for the purposes of proceedings for contempt.

(4) Subsection (2) above does not confer on the Board any of the following functions unless the Lord Chancellor so directs by order and then only to the extent specified in the order.

The functions referred to are—

 (a) determination of the costs of representation under Part IV;
 (b) functions as respects representation under Part V other than determination of the costs of representation for the purposes of proceedings in magistrates' courts;
 (c) functions as respects representation under Part VI for the purposes of care proceedings other than proceedings on an appeal from the decision of a juvenile court to the High Court;
 (d) determination of the financial resources of persons for the purposes of this Act.

(5) Subject to subsection (6) below, the Board shall consist of no fewer than 11 and more than 17 members appointed by the Lord Chancellor; and the Lord Chancellor shall appoint one of the members to be chairman.

(6) The Lord Chancellor may, by order, substitute, for the number for the time being specified in subsection (5) above as the maximum or minimum membership of the Board, such other number as he thinks appropriate.

(7) The Board shall include at least two solicitors appointed after consultation with the Law Society.

(8) The Lord Chancellor shall consult the General Council of the Bar with a view to the inclusion on the Board of at least two barristers.

(9) In appointing persons to be members of the Board the Lord Chancellor shall have regard to the desirability of securing that the Board includes persons having expertise in or knowledge of—

 (a) the provision of legal services;
 (b) the work of the courts and social conditions; and
 (c) management.

(10) Schedule 1 to this Act shall have effect with respect to the Board.

4. Powers of the Board

(1) Subject to the provisions of this Act, the Board may do anything—

(a) which it considers necessary or desirable to provide or secure the provision of advice, assistance and representation under this Act; or

(b) which is calculated to facilitate or is incidental or conducive to the discharge of its functions;

and advice, assistance and representation may be provided in different ways in different areas in England and Wales and in different ways in different fields of law.

(2) Without prejudice to the generality of subsection (1) above, the Board shall have power—

(a) to enter into any contract including, subject to subsection (7) below, any contract to acquire or dispose of land;

(b) to make grants (with or without conditions, including conditions as to repayment);

(c) to make loans;

(d) to invest money;

(e) to promote or assist in the promotion of publicity relating to the functions of the Board;

(f) to undertake any inquiry or investigation which the Board considers necessary or expedient in relation to the discharge of its functions; and

(g) to give the Lord Chancellor such advice as it may consider appropriate in relation to the provision of advice, assistance and representation under this Act.

(3) Subsection (1) above does not confer on the Board power to borrow money or to acquire and hold shares in bodies corporate or take part in forming bodies corporate.

(4) The powers to provide advice, assistance or representation under this Part and to secure its provision under this Part by means of contracts with, or grants or loans to, other persons or bodies—

(a) shall not be exercisable unless the Lord Chancellor so directs and then only to the extent specified in the direction; and

(b) if exercisable, shall be exercised in accordance with any directions given by him.

(5) The power to secure the provision of representation under Part IV by means of contracts with other persons shall only be exercisable in the classes of case prescribed in regulations.

(6) Advice, assistance and representation provided by the Board under this Part may be granted with or without limitations and may be amended, withdrawn or revoked.

(7) The power under subsection (2) above to enter into contracts to acquire or dispose of land shall not be exercised without the approval in writing of the Lord Chancellor.

(8) The Board may, from time to time, prepare and submit to the Lord Chancellor proposals for the assumption by it of any functions in relation to the provision of advice, assistance or representation under this Act.

5. Duties of the Board

(1) The Board shall, from time to time, publish information as to the discharge of its functions in relation to advice, assistance and representation including the forms and procedures and other matters connected therewith.

(2) The Board shall, from time to time, furnish to the Lord Chancellor such information as he may require relating to its property and to the discharge or proposed discharge of its functions.

(3) It shall be the duty of the Board to provide to the Lord Chancellor, as soon as possible after 31st March in each year, a report on the discharge of its functions during the preceding twelve months.

(4) The Board shall deal in any report under subsection (3) above with such matters as the Lord Chancellor may from time to time direct.

(5) The Board shall have regard, in discharging its functions, to such guidance as may from time to time be given by the Lord Chancellor.

(6) Guidance under subsection (5) above shall not relate to the consideration or disposal, in particular cases, of—
   (a) applications for advice, assistance or representation;
   (b) supplementary or incidental applications or requests to the Board in connection with any case where advice, assistance or representation has been made available.

(7) For the purposes of subsection (2) above the Board shall permit any person authorised by the Lord Chancellor for the purpose to inspect and make copies of any accounts or documents of the Board and shall furnish such explanations of them as that person or the Lord Chancellor may require.

6. Board to have separate legal aid fund

(1) The Board shall establish and maintain a separate legal aid fund.

(2) Subject to regulations, there shall be paid out of the fund—
   (a) such sums as are, by virtue of any provision of or made under this Act, due from the Board in respect of remuneration and expenses properly incurred in connection with the provision, under this Act, of advice, assistance or representation;
   (b) costs awarded to any unassisted party under section 13 or 18;
   (c) any part of a contribution repayable by the Board under section 16(4) or 23(7); and
   (d) such other payments for the purposes of this Act as the Lord Chancellor may, with the concurrence of the Treasury, determine.

(3) Subject to regulations, there shall be paid into the fund—
   (a) any contribution payable to the Board by any person in respect of advice, assistance or representation under this Act;
   (b) any sum awarded under an order of a court or agreement as to costs in any proceedings in favour of any legally assisted party which is payable to the Board;
   (c) any sum which is to be paid out of property recovered or preserved for any legally assisted party to any proceedings;
   (d) any sum in respect of the costs of an unassisted party awarded under section 13 or 18 which is repaid to the Board under that section;
   (e) the sums to be paid by the Lord Chancellor in pursuance of section 42(1)(a); and
   (f) such other receipts of the Board as the Lord Chancellor may, with the concurrence of the Treasury, determine.

7. Accounts and audit

(1) The Board shall keep separate accounts with respect to—
   (a) its legal aid fund; and
   (b) the receipts and expenditure of the Board which do not relate to that fund;
and shall prepare in respect of each financial year a statement of accounts.

(2)—(6) *****

(7) The Lord Chancellor shall lay before each House of Parliament a copy of every statement of accounts and report of the auditors sent to him under subsection (5) above.

(8) In this section "financial year" means the period beginning with the day on which the Board is established and ending with 31st March next following and each subsequent period of 12 months ending with 31st March in each year.

PART III
ADVICE AND ASSISTANCE

8. Scope of this part.

(1) Subject to the provisions of this section, this Part applies to any advice or assistance and advice and assistance under this Part shall be available to any person subject to and in accordance with the provisions of this section and sections 9, 10 and 11.

(2) This Part only applies to assistance by way of representation if, and to the extent that, regulations so provide; and regulations may make such provision in relation to representation for the purposes of any proceedings before a court or tribunal or at a statutory inquiry.

(2) Advice or assistance of all descriptions or advice or assistance of any prescribed description is excluded from this Part, or is so excluded as regards any area, if regulations so provide; and if regulations provide for all descriptions to be excluded as regards all areas then, so long as the regulations so provide, this Part (other than this subsection) shall not have effect.

(4) Advice or assistance of any prescribed description is restricted to its provision to prescribed descriptions of persons if regulations so provide.

(5) This Part does not apply to advice or assistance given to a person in connection with proceedings before a court or tribunal or at a statutory inquiry at a time when he is being represented in those proceedings under any other Part of this Act.

9. Availability of, and payment for, advice and assistance.

(1) Advice and assistance to which this Part applies shall be available to any person whose financial resources are such as, under regulations, make him eligible for advice or assistance under this Part.

(2) If regulations so provide, advice or assistance to which this Part applies shall be available to any person whose financial resources are such as, under regulations, make him eligible for advice or assistance under this Part.

(3) Subject to any prescribed exceptions, assistance by way of representation under this Part shall not be given without the approval of the Board.

(4) Approval under subsection (3) above may be given with or without limitations and may be amended, withdrawn or revoked.

(5) Except as provided by subsection (6) or (7) below, the legally assisted person shall not be required to pay to his solicitor any charge or fee.

(6) Except as provided by subsection (7) below, a legally assisted person shall, if his financial resources are such as, under regulations, make him liable to make a contribution, be liable to pay to his solicitor, in respect of the advice or assistance, charges or fees of such amount as is determined or fixed by or under the regulations.

(7) A legally assisted person to whom advice or assistance is made available by virtue of regulations under subsection (2) above shall, in circumstances prescribed by the regulations and, if the regulations apply only to persons of a prescribed description, he is a person of that description, be liable to pay his solicitor, in respect of the advice or assistance, a fee of such amount as is fixed by or under the regulations (in lieu of a contribution under subsection (6) above).

10. Financial limit on prospective cost of advice or assistance.

(1) Where at any time (whether before or after the advice or assistance has begun to be given) it appears to a solicitor that the cost of giving advice or assistance to a person under this Part is likely to exceed the prescribed limit—

    (a) the solicitor shall determine to what extent that advice or assistance can be given without exceeding that limit; and

    (b) shall not give it (nor, as the case may be, instruct counsel to give it) so as to exceed that limit except with the approval of the Board.

(2) Approval under subsection (1)(b) above may be given with or without limitations and may be amended, withdrawn or revoked.

(3) For the purposes of this section the cost of giving advice or assistance shall be taken to consist of such of the following as are applicable in the circumstances, namely—

(a) any disbursements, that is to say, expenses (including fees payable to counsel) which may be incurred by the solicitor or his firm in, or in connection with, the giving of the advice or assistance; and

(b) any charges or fees (other than charges for disbursements) which would be properly chargeable by the solicitor or his firm in respect of the advice or assistance.

11. Payment for advice or assistance otherwise than through legally assisted person's contribution.

(1) This section applies to any charges or fees which, apart from section 9, would be properly chargeable in respect of advice or assistance given under this Part, in so far as those charges or fees are not payable by the legally assisted person in accordance with that section.

(2) Except in so far as regulations otherwise provide, charges or fees to which this section applies shall constitute a first charge for the benefit of the solicitor—

(a) on any costs which are payable to the legally assisted person by any other person in respect of the matter in connection with which the advice or assistance is given, and

(b) on any property which is recovered or preserved for the legally assisted person in connection with that matter.

(3) In so far as the charge created by subsection (2) above in respect of any charges or fees to which this section applies is insufficient to meet them, the deficiency shall, subject to subsection (5) below, be payable to the solicitor by the Board.

(4) For the purposes of subsection (2) above, it is immaterial, in the case of costs, whether the costs are payable by virtue of a judgment, order of a court or otherwise and, in the case of property, what its nature is and where it is situated and the property within the charge includes the legally assisted person's rights under any compromise or settlement arrived at to avoid proceedings or bring them to an end.

(5) For the purpose of determining what charges or fees would be properly chargeable, and whether there is a deficiency to be paid by the Board, charges or fees in respect of advice or assistance under this Part shall, in prescribed circumstances, be determined in such manner as may be prescribed.

12. Limit on costs against person receiving assistance by way of representation.

(1) Where a person receives any assistance by way of representation in any proceedings before a court or tribunal or at a statutory inquiry, then, except in so far as regulations otherwise provide, his liability by virtue of an order for costs made against him with respect to the proceedings shall not exceed the amount (if any) which is a reasonable one for him to pay having regard to all the circumstances, including the financial resources of all the parties and their conduct in connection with the dispute.

(2) Regulations shall make provision as to the court, tribunal or person by whom that amount is to be determined and the extend to which any determination of that amount is to be final.

(3) None of the following, namely, a legally assisted person's dwelling house, clothes, household furniture and the tools and implements of his trade shall—

(a) be taken into account in assessing his financial resources for the purposes of this section, or

(b) be subject to execution or any corresponding process in any part of the United Kingdom to enforce the order,

except so far as regulations may prescribe.

13. Costs of successful unassisted parties.

(1) This section applies to proceedings in which a person who receives assistance by way of representation is a party and which are finally decided in favour of an unassisted party.

(2) In any proceedings to which this section applies the court by which the proceedings are so decided may, subject to subsection (3) and (4) below, make an order for the payment by the Board to the unassisted party of the whole or any part of the costs incurred by him in the proceedings.

(3) Before making an order under this section, the court shall consider what order for costs should be made against the assisted party and for determining his liability in respect of such costs.

(4) An order under this section in respect of any costs may only be made if—

    (a) an order for costs would be made in the proceedings apart from this Act;

    (b) as respects the costs incurred in a court of first instance, those proceedings were instituted by the assisted party and the court is satisfied that the unassisted party will suffer severe financial hardship unless the order is made; and

    (c) in any case, the court is satisfied that it is just and equitable in all the circumstances of the case that provision for the costs should be made out of public funds.

(5) Without prejudice to any other provision restricting appeals from any court, no appeal shall lie against an order under this section, or against a refusal to make such an order, except on a point of law.

(6) In this section "costs" means costs as between party and party, and includes the costs of applying for an order under this section; and where a party begins to receive the assistance after the proceedings have been instituted, or ceases to receive the assistance before they are finally decided or otherwise receives the assistance in connection with part only of the proceedings, the reference in subsection (2) above to the costs incurred by the unassisted party in the proceedings shall be construed as a reference to so much of those costs as is attributable to that part.

(7) For the purposes of this section proceedings shall be treated as finally decided in favour of the unassisted party—

    (a) if no appeal lies against the decision in his favour;

    (b) if an appeal lies against the decision with leave, and the time limited for applications for leave expires without leave being granted; or

    (c) if leave to appeal against the decision is granted or is not required, and no appeal is brought within the time limited for appeal;

and where an appeal against the decision is brought out of time the court by which the appeal (or any further appeal in those proceedings) is determined may make an order for the repayment by the unassisted party to the Board of the whole or any part of any sum previously paid to him under this section in respect of those proceedings.

(8) Where a court decides any proceedings in favour of the unassisted party and an appeal lies (with or without leave) against that decision, the court may, if it thinks fit, make or refuse to make an order under this section forthwith, but if an order is made forthwith it shall not take effect—

    (a) where leave to appeal is required, unless the time limited for applications for leave to appeal expires without leave being granted;

    (b) where leave to appeal is granted or is not required, unless the time limited for appeal expires without an appeal being brought.

(9) For the purposes of this section "court" includes a tribunal.

Part IV
Civil Legal Aid

14. Scope of this Part.

(1) This Part applies to such proceedings before courts or tribunals or at statutory inquiries in England and Wales as—

    (a) are proceedings of a description for the time being specified in Part I of Schedule 2 to this Act, except proceedings for the time being specified in Part II of that Schedule, and

    (b) are not proceedings for which representation may be granted under Part V,

and representation under this Part shall be available to any peson subject to and in accordance with sections 15 and 16.

(2) Subject to subsection (3) below, Schedule 2 may be varied by regulations so as to extend or restrict the categories of proceedings for the purposes of which representation is available under this Part, by reference to the court, tribunal or statutory inquiry, to the issues involved, to the capacity in which the person seeking representation is concerned or otherwise.

(3) Regulations under subsection (2) above may not have the effect of adding any proceedings before any court or tribunal or at any statutory inquiry before or at which persons have no right, and are not normally allowed, to be represented by counsel or a solicitor.

(4) Regulations under subsection (2) above which extend the categories of proceedings for the purposes of which representation is available under this Part shall not be made without the consent of the Treasury.

15. Availability of, and payment for, representation under this Part.

(1) Subject to subsections (2) and (3) below, representation under this Part for the purposes of proceedings to which this Part applies shall be available to any person whose financial resources are such as, under regulations, make him eligible for representation under this Part.

(2) A person shall not be granted representation for the purposes of any proceedings unless he satisfies the Board that he has reasonable grounds for taking, defending or being a party to the proceedings.

(3) A person may be refused representation for the purposes of any proceedings if, in the particular circumstances of the case is appears to the Board—

    (a) unreasonable that he should be granted representation under this Part, or

    (b) more appropriate that he should be given assistance by way of representation under Part III;

and regulations may prescribe the criteria for determining any questions arising under paragraph (b) above.

(4) Representation under this Part may be granted by the Board with or without limitations and may be amended, withdrawn or revoked.

(5) Where the case is one in which the Board has power to secure the provision of representation under this Part by means of contracts with other persons, the grant of representation under this Part may be limited under subsection (4) above as regards the persons who may represent the legally assisted person to representation only in pursuance of a contract made with the Board.

(6) Except in so far as he is required under section 16 to make a contribution, a legally assisted person shall not be required to make any payment in respect of representation under this Part and it shall be for the Board to pay his solicitor for acting for him and to pay any fees of counsel for so acting.

(7) The Board's obligation under subsection (6) above is—

    (a) in the case of representation provided by pursuance of a contract between

Legal Aid Act 1988

the Board and the legally assisted person's solicitor, to make such payments as are due under the contract; and

(b) in the case of representation provided otherwise than in pursuance of such a contract, to make such payments as are authorised by regulations.

(8) Nothing in subsection (6) above affects the duty of the solicitor to pay in the first instance expenses incurred in connection with the proceedings that would ordinarily be paid in the first instance by a person's solicitor.

16. Reimbursement of Board by contributions and out of costs or property recovered.

(1) A legally assisted person shall, if his financial resources are such as, under regulations, make him liable to make such a contribution, pay to the Board, a contribution in respect of the costs of his being represented under this Part.

(2) The contribution to be required of him by the Board shall be determined by the Board in accordance with the regulations and may take the form of periodical payments or one or more capital sums or both.

(3) The contribution required of a person may, in the case of periodical payments, be made payable by reference to the period during which he is represented under this Part or any shorter period and, in the case of a capital sum, be made payable by instalments.

(4) If the total contribution made by a person in respect of any proceedings exceeds the net liability of the Board on his account, the excess shall be repaid to him.

(5) Any sums recovered by virtue of an order or agreement for costs made in favour of a legally assisted person with respect to the proceedings shall be paid to the Board.

(6) Except so far as regulations otherwise provide—

(a) any sums remaining unpaid on account of a person's contribution in respect of the sums payable by the Board in respect of any proceedings, and

(b) a sum equal to any deficiency by reason of his total contribution being less than the net liability of the Board on his account,

shall be a first charge for the benefit of the Board on any property which is recovered or preserved for him in the proceedings.

(7) For the purposes of subsection (6) above it is immaterial what the nature of the property is and where it is situated and the property within the charge includes the right of a person under any compromise or settlement arrived at to avoid proceedings or bring them to an end and any sums recovered by virtue of an order for costs made in his favour in the proceedings (not being sums payable to the Board under subsection (5) above).

(8) The charge created by subsection (6) above on any damages or costs shall not prevent a court allowing them to be set off against other damages or costs in any case where a solicitor's lien for costs would not prevent it.

(9) In this section references to the net liability of the Board on a legally assisted person's account in relation to any proceedings are references to the aggregate amount of—

(a) the sums paid or payable by the Board on his account in respect of those proceedings to any solicitor or counsel, and

(b) any sums so paid or payable for any advice or assistance under Part III in connection with those proceedings or any matter to which those proceedings relate, being sums not recouped by the Board by sums which are recoverable by virtue of an order or agreement for costs made in his favour with respect to those proceedings or by virtue of any right of his to be indemnified against expenses incurred by him in connection with those proceedings.

(10) Where a legally assisted person has been represented in any proceedings in pursuance of a contract made with the Board on terms which do not differentiate between the remuneration for his and other cases, the reference in subsection (9)(a) above to

the sums paid or payable by the Board on his account in respect of the proceedings shall be contrued as a reference to such part of the remuneration payable under the contract as may be specified in writing by the Board.

17. Limit on costs against assisted party.

(1) The liability of a legally assisted party under an order for costs made against him with respect to any proceedings shall not exceed the amount (if any) which is a reasonable one for him to pay having regard to all the circumstances, including the financial resources of all the parties and their conduct in connection with the dispute.

(2) Regulations shall make provision as to the court, tribunal or person by whom that amount is to be determined and the extent to which any determination of that amount is to be final.

(3) None of the following, namely, a legally assisted person's dwelling house, clothes, household furniture and the tools and implements of his trade shall—

    (a)   be taken into account in assessing his financial resources for the purpose of this section, or

    (b)   be subject to execution or any corresponding process in any part of the United Kingdom to enforce the order,

except so far as regulations may prescribe.

18. Costs of successful unassisted parties.

(1) This section applies to proceedings to which a legally assisted person is a party and which are finally decided in favour of an unassisted party.

(2) In any proceedings to which this section applies the court by which the proceedings were so decided may, subject to subsection (3) and (4) below, make an order for the payment by the Board to the unassisted party of the whole or any part of the costs incurred by him in the proceedings.

(3) Before making an order under this section, the court shall consider what order for costs should be made against the assisted party and for determining his liability in respect of such costs.

(4) An order under this section in respect of any costs may only be made if—

    (a)   an order for costs would be made in the proceedings apart from this Act;

    (b)   as respects the costs incurred in a court of first instance, those proceedings were instituted by the assisted party and the court is satisfied that the unassisted party will suffer severe financial hardship unless the order is made; and

    (c)   in any case, the court is satisfied that it is just and equitable in all the circumstances of the case that provision for the costs should be made out of public funds.

(5) Without prejudice to any other provsion restricting appeals from any court, no appeal shall lie against an order under this section, or against a refusal to make such an order, except on a point of law.

(6) In this section "costs" means costs as between party and party, and includes the costs of applying for an order under this section; and where a party begins to receive representation after the proceedings have been instituted, or ceases to receive representation before they are finally decided or otherwise receives representation in connection with part only of the proceedings, the reference in subsection (2) above to the costs incurred by the unassisted party in the proceedings shall be construed as a reference to so much of those costs as is attributable to that part.

(7) For the purposes of this section proceedings shall be treated as finally decided in favour of the unassisted party—

    (a)   if no appeal lies against the decision in his favour;

    (b)   if an appeal lies against the decision with leave, and the time limited for applications for leave expires without leave being granted; or

(c) if leave to appeal against the decision is granted or is not required, and no appeal is brought within the time limited for appeal;
and where an appeal against the decision is brought out of time the court by which the appeal (or any further appeal in those proceedings) is determined may make an order for the repayment by the unassisted party to the Board of the whole or any part of any sum previously paid to him under this section in respect of those proceedings.

(8) Where a court decides any proceedings in favour of the unassisted party and an appeal lies (with or without leave) against that decision, the court may, if it thinks fit, make or refuse to make an order under this section forthwith, but if an order is made forthwith it shall not take effect—

(a) where leave to appeal is required, unless the time limited for applications for leave to appeal expires without leave being granted;

(b) where leave to appeal is granted or is not required, unless the time limited for appeal expires without an appeal being brought.

(9) For the purposes of this section "court" includes a tribunal.

PART V
CRIMINAL LEGAL AID

19. Scope of this Part.

(1) This Part applies to criminal proceedings before any of the following—

(a) a magistrates' court;

(b) the Crown Court;

(c) the criminal division of the Court of Appeal or the Courts-Martial Appeal Court; and

(d) the House of Lords in the exercise of its jurisdiction in relation to appeals from either of those courts;

and representation under this Part shall be available to any person subject to and in accordance with sections 21, 22, 23, 24 and 25.

(2) Representation under this Part for the purposes of the proceedings before any court extends to any proceedings preliminary or incidental to the proceedings, including bail proceedings, whether before that or another court.

(3) Representation under this Part for the purposes of the proceedings before a magistrates' court extends to any proceedings before a juvenile court or other magistrates' court to which the case is remitted.

(4) In subsection (2) above in its application to bail proceedings, "court" has the same meaning as in the Bail Act 1976, but that subsection does not extend representation to bail proceedings before a judge of the High Court exercising the jurisdiction of that Court.

(5) In this Part—

"competent authority" is to be construed in accordance with section 20;

"Court of Appeal" means the criminal division of that Court;

"criminal proceedings" includes proceedings for dealing with an offender for an offence or in respect of a sentence or as a fugitive offender and also includes proceedings instituted under section 115 of the Magistrates' Courts Act 1980 (binding over) in respect of an actual or apprehended breach of the peace or other misbehaviour and proceedings for dealing with a person for a failure to comply with a condition of a recognizance to keep the peace or be of good behaviour;

"proceedings for dealing with an offender as a fugitive offender" means proceedings before a metropolitan stipendiary magistrate under section 9 of the Extradition Act 1870, section 7 of the Fugitive Offenders Act 1967 or section 6 of the Criminal Justice Act 1988; and

"remitted", in relation to a juvenile court, means remitted under section 56(1) of the Children and Young Person Act 1933; and any reference, in relation to representation for the purposes of any proceedings, to the proceedings before a court includes a reference to any proceedings to which representation under this Part extends by virtue of subsection (2) or (3) above.

20. Competent authorities to grant representation under this Part.

(1) Subject to any provision made by virtue of subsection (10) below, the following courts are competent to grant representation under this Part for the purposes of the following proceedings, on an application made for the purpose.

(2) The court before which any proceedings take place, or are to take place, is always competent as respects those proceedings, except that this does not apply to the House of Lords; and, in the case of the Court of Appeal and the Courts-Martial Appeal Court, the reference to proceedings which are to take place includes proceedings which may take place if notice of appeal is given or an application for leave to appeal is made.

(3) The Court of Appeal or, as the case may be, the Courts-Martial Appeal Court is also competent as respects proceedings on appeal from decisions of theirs to the House of Lords.

(4) The magistrates' court—
   (a) which commits a person for trial or sentence or to be dealt with in respect of a sentence,
   (b) which has been given a notice of transfer under section 4 of the Criminal Justice Act 1987 (transfer of serious fraud cases), or
   (c) from which a person appeals against his conviction or sentence,
is also competent as respects the proceedings before the Crown Court.

(5) The magistrates' court inquiring into an offence as examining justices is also competent, before it decides whether or not to commit the person for trial, as respects any proceedings before the Crown Court on his trial.

(6) The Crown Court is also competent as respects applications for leave to appeal and proceedings on any appeal to the Court of Appeal under section 9(11) of the Criminal Justice Act 1987 (appeals against orders or rulings at preparatory hearings).

(7) On ordering a retrial under section 7 of the Criminal Appeal Act 1968 (new trials ordered by Court of Appeal or House of Lords on fresh evidence) the court ordering the retrial is also competent as respects the proceedings before the Crown Court.

(8) Any magistrates' court to which, in accordance with regulations, a person applies for representation when he has been arrested for an offence but has not appeared or been brought before a court is competent as respects the proceedings in relation to the offence in any magistrates' court.

(9) In the event of the Lord Chancellor making an order under section 3(4) as respects the function of granting representation under this Part for the purposes of proceedings before any court, the Board shall be competent as respects those proceedings, on an application made for the purpose.

(10) An order under section 3(4) may make provision restricting or excluding the competence of any court mentioned in any of subsections (2) to (8) above and may contain such transitional provisions as appear to the Lord Chancellor necessary or expedient.

21. Availability of representation under this Part.

(1) Representation under this Part for the purposes of any criminal proceedings shall be available in accordance with this section to the accused or convicted person but shall not be available to the prosecution except in the case of an appeal to the

Crown Court against conviction or sentence, for the purpose of enabling an individual who is not acting in an official capacity to resist the appeal.

(2) Subject to subsection (5) below, representation may be granted where it appears to the competent authority to be desirable to do so in the interests of justice; and section 22 applies for the interpretation of this subsection in relation to the proceedings to which that section applies.

(3) Subject to subsection (5) below, representation must be granted—
    (a) where a person is committed for trial on a charge of murder, for his trial;
    (b) where the prosecutor appeals or applies for leave to appeal to the House of Lords, for the proceedings on the appeal;
    (c) where a person charged with an offence before a magistrates' court—
        (i) is brought before the court in pursuance of a remand in custody when he may be again remanded or committed in custody, and
        (ii) is not, but wishes to be, legally represented before the court (not having been legally represented when he was so remanded),
for so much of the proceedings as relates to the grant of bail; and
    (d) where a person—
        (i) is to be sentenced or otherwise dealt with for an offence by a magistrates' court or the Crown Court, and
        (ii) is to be kept in custody to enable enquiries or a report to be made to assist the court,
for the proceedings on sentencing or otherwise dealing with him.

(4) Subject to any provision made under section 3(4) by virtue of section 20(10), in a case falling within subsection (3)(a) above, it shall be for the magistrates' court which commits the person for trial, and not for the Crown Court, to make the grant of representation for his trial.

(5) Representation shall not be granted to any person unless it appears to the competent authority that his financial resources are such as, under regulations, make him eligible for representation under this Part.

(6) Before making a determination for the purposes of subsection (5) above in the case of any person, the competent authority shall, except in prescribed cases, require a statement of his financial resources in the prescribed form to be furnished to the authority.

(7) Where a doubt arises whether representation under this Part should be granted to any person, the doubt shall be resolved in that person's favour.

(8) Where an application for representation for the purposes of an appeal to the Court of Appeal or the Courts-Martial Appeal Court is made to a competent authority before the giving of notice of appeal or the making of an application for leave to appeal, the authority may, in the first instance, exercise its power to grant representation by making a grant consisting of advice on the question whether there appear to be reasonable grounds of appeal and assistance in the preparation of an application for leave to appeal or in the giving of a notice of appeal.

(9) Representation granted by a competent authority may be amended or withdrawn, whether by that or another authority competent to grant representation under this Part.

(10) Regulations may provide for an appeal to lie to a specified court or body against any refusal by a magistrates' court to grant representation under this Part and for that other court or body to make any grant of representation that could have been made by the magistrates' court.

(11) Subsection (3) above shall have effect in its application to a person who has not attained the age of eighteen as if the references in paragraphs (c) and (d) to remand in custody and to being remanded or kept in custody included references to being committed under section 23 of the Children and Young Persons Act 1969 to the care of a local authority or a remand centre.

22. Criteria for grant of representation for trial proceedings.

(1) This section applies to proceedings by way of a trial by or before a magistrates' court or the Crown Court or on an appeal to the Crown Court against a person's conviction.

(2) The factors to be taken into account by a competent authority in determining whether it is in the interests of justice that representation be granted for the purposes of proceedings to which this section applies to an accused shall include the following—

    (a) the offence is such that if proved it is likely that the court would impose a sentence which would deprive the accused of his liberty or lead to loss of livelihood or serious damage to his reputation;

    (b) the determination of the case may involve consideration of a substantial question of law;

    (c) the accused may be unable to understand the proceedings or to state his own case because of his inadequate knowledge of English, mental illness or expert cross-examination of a witness for the prosecution;

    (e) it is in the interests of someone other than the accused that the accused be represented.

(3) The Lord Chancellor may, by order, vary the factors listed in subsection (2) above by amending factors in the list or by adding new factors to the list.

23. Reimbursement of public funds by contributions.

(1) Where representation under this Part is granted to any person whose financial resources are such as, under regulations, make him liable to make a contribution, the competent authority shall order him to pay a contribution in respect of the costs of his being represented under this Part.

(2) Where the legally assisted person has not attained the age of sixteen, the competent authority may, instead of or in addition to ordering him to make a contribution, order any person—

    (a) who is an appropriate contributor in relation to him, and

    (b) whose financial resources are such as, under regulations, make him liable to make a contribution,

to pay a contribution in respect of the costs of the representation granted to the legally assisted person.

(3) Regulations may authorise the making of a contribution order under subsection (1) or (2) above after the grant of representation in prescribed circumstances.

(4) The amount of the contribution to be required under subsection (1) or (2) above by the competent authority shall be such as is determined in accordance with the regulations.

(5) A legally assisted person or appropriate contributor may be required to make his contribution in one sum or by instalments as may be prescribed.

(6) Regulations may provide that no contribution order shall be made in connection with a grant of representation under this Part for the purposes of proceedings in the Crown Court, the Court of Appeal or the House of Lords in a case where a contribution order was made in connection with a grant of such representation to the person in question in respect of proceedings in a lower court.

(7) Subject to subsection (8) below, if the total contribution made in respect of the costs of representing any person under this Part exceed those costs, the excess shall be repaid—

    (a) where the contribution was made by one person only to him; and

    (b) where the contribution was made by two or more persons, to them in proportion to the amounts contributed by them.

(8) Where a contribution has been made in respect of the costs of representing any person under this Part in any proceedings and an order for costs is made in favour

Legal Aid Act 1988

of that person in respect of those proceedings, then, where sums due under the order for costs are paid to the Board or the Lord Chancellor under section 20(2) of the Prosecution of Offences Act 1985 (recovery regulations)—

    (a)   if the costs of the representation do not exceed the sums so paid, subsection (7) above shall not apply and the contribution shall be repaid;

    (b)   If the costs of the representation do exceed the sums so paid, subsection (7) above shall apply as if the costs of the representation were equal to the excess.

(9) References in subsection (8) above to the costs of representation include any charge or fee treated as part of those costs by section 26(2).

(10) In this Part—

"appropriate contributor", means a person of a description prescribed under section 34(2)(c); and

"contribution order" means an order under subsection (1) or (2) above.

24. Contributions orders: supplementary

(1) Where a competent authority grants representation under this Part and in connection with the grant makes a contribution order under which any sum is required to be paid on the making of the order, it may direct that the grant of representation shall not take effect until that sum is paid.

(2) Where a legally assisted person fails to pay any relevant contribution when it is due, the court in which the proceedings for the purposes of which he has been granted representation are being heard may, subject to subsection (3) below, revoke the grant.

(3) A court shall not exercise the power conferred by subsection (2) above unless, after affording the legally assisted person an opportunity of making representations in such manner as may be prescribed, it is satisfied—

    (a)   that he was able to pay the relevant contribution when it was due; and

    (b)   that he is able to pay the whole or part of it but has failed or refused to do so.

(4) In subsection (2) above "relevant contribution", in relation to a legally assisted person, means any sum—

    (a)   which he is required to pay by a contribution order made in connection with the grant to him of representation under this Part, and

    (b)   which falls due after the making of the order and before the conclusion of the proceedings for the purposes of which he has been granted such representation.

(5) Regulations with respect to contribution orders may—

    (a)   provide for their variation or revocation in prescribed circumstances;

    (b)   provide for their making in default of the prescribed evidence of a person's financial resources;

    (c)   regulate their making after the grant of representation;

    (d)   authorise the remission or authorise or require the repayment in prescribed circumstances of sums due or paid under such orders; and

    (e)   prescribe the court or body by which any function under the regulations is to be exercisable.

(6) Schedule 3 to this Act shall have effect with respect to the enforcement of contribution orders.

25. Payment of costs of representation under this Part.

(1) Where representation under this Part has been granted to any person the costs of representing him shall be paid—

    (a)   by the Lord Chancellor, or

    (b)   by the Board,

as the Lord Chancellor may direct.

(2) Subject to regulations, the costs of representing any person under this Part shall include sums on account of the fees payable to his counsel or solicitor and disbursements reasonably incurred by his solicitor for or in connection with his representation.

(3) The costs required by this section to be paid in respect of representing him shall not include any sum in respect of allowances to witnesses attending to give evidence in the proceedings for the purposes of which he is represented in any case where such allowances are payable under any other enactment.

26. Payment for advice or assistance where representation under this Part is subsequently granted.

(1) This section has effect where—

    (a) advice or assistance under Part III is given to a person in respect of any matter which is or becomes the subject of criminal proceedings against him; and

    (b) he is subsequently granted representation under this Part for the purposes of those proceedings.

(2) If the solicitor acting for the person under the grant of representation is the same as the solicitor who gave him the advice or assistance, any charge or fee in respect of the advice or assistance which, apart from this section, would fall to be secured, recovered or paid as provided by section 11 shall instead be paid under section 25 as if it were part of the costs of the representation.

(3) If a contribution order is made in connection with the grant of representation under this Part to him—

    (a) any sum which he is required by virtue of section 9(6) or (7) to pay in respect of the advice or assistance (whether or not already paid) shall be credited against the contribution order; and

    (b) section 25 shall have effect in a case to which subsection (2) above applies as if the charges and fees properly chargeable in respect of the advice or assistance were part of the costs of the representation under this Part and as if any such sum as is mentioned in paragraph (a) above which he has paid were part of the contribution made under the contribution order.

Parts VI.–VIII. *****

OTHER MATERIALS

STATUTORY INSTRUMENTS REGULATIONS 1947
SI 1948/1

Preliminary

1. **Interpretation, Citation and Commencement.**

(1) The Interpretation Act, [1978], shall apply to the interpretation of these Regulations as it applies to the interpretation of an Act of Parliament.

(2) In these Regulations:

    (a) "Principal Act" means the Statutory Instruments Act, 1946:

    (b) "responsible authority" means—

        (i) in relation to an Order in Council, the Minister responsible for the preparation of the draft of the Order submitted to His Majesty in Council, and

        (ii) in relation to any other instrument, the Minister by whom the instrument is made;

and in this definition references to a Minister include references to the Treasury, the Admiralty, the Board of Trade, and any other Government department, and to any other authority making a document which by virtue of Regulation 2 of these Regulations is such a statutory rule as is referred to in subsection (2) of Section 1 of the Principal Act:

    (c) "general instrument" and "local instrument" mean, respectively, an instrument classified as such under these Regulations: and

    (d) "Reference Committee" means the Statutory Instruments Reference Committee provided for by these Regulations.

(3) These Regulations may be cited as the Statutory Instruments Regulations 1947; and shall come into operation on the 1st day of January, 1948.

2. **Application to Statutory Rules within 56 & 57 Vict c 66.**

(1) Subject to the provisions of this Regulation, the following documents, namely—

    (a) every document being of a legislative and not an executive character made after the commencement of the Principal Act by a rule-making authority as defined in the Rules Publication Act, 1893, in the exercise of a statutory power conferred on that authority by or under any Act of Parliament passed before the commencement of the Principal Act, and

    (b) every other document which, by virtue of any enactment other than the said Act of 1893, would be subject to the provisions of Section 3 of that Act if that Section had not been repealed,

are hereby determined to constitute such a statutory rule as is referred to in subsection (2) of Section 1 of the Principal Act.

(2) Without prejudice to any Order in Council made under subsection (1) of Section 9 of the Principal Act, the confirmation or approval by a rule-making authority of any scheme, regulations or other subordinate legislation made by a person not being a rule-making authority shall not be deemed to constitute the making of such a statutory rule as aforesaid unless it is required by the enactment under which it is made to be effected by means of an Order in Council or Order made by that authority.

(3) Notwithstanding anything in this Regulation, subsection (2) of Section 1 of the Principal Act shall not apply to—

    (a) any document which, although of a legislative character, applies only to a named person or premises and is not required to be laid before or subject to confirmation or approval by Parliament or the House of Commons; or

    (b) any Order in Council which, being an Order for which the Lord President of the Council is the responsible authority, confirms or approves subordinate legislation in the nature of a local and personal or private Act; or

    (c)   any such document as is mentioned in the Schedule to these Regulations.

Numbering, Printing and Sale

3. Numbering.
All statutory instruments received by the King's printer of Acts of Parliament under subsection (1) of Section 2 of the Principal Act shall be allocated to the series of the calendar year in which they are made and shall be numbered in that series consecutively as nearly as may be in the order in which they are received:

Provided that where any such instrument—

    (a)   will not take effect unless it is confirmed or approved by Parliament or the House of Commons, or

    (b)   is subject to special parliamentary procedure, or will become subject thereto in certain events,

the instrument may be allocated and numbered as if it had been made and received on the date on which the responsible authority notified the King's printer that the instrument has become operative or will become operative: and

Provided also that any statutory instrument made before the commencement of the Principal Act shall be allocated to the series of the calendar year in which that Act commences.

4. Classification

(1) For the purposes of these Regulations, statutory instruments shall be classified as local or general according to their subject matter.

(2) Unless there are special reasons to the contrary in any particular case, a statutory instrument which is in the nature of a local and personal or private Act shall be classified as local, and a statutory instrument which is in the nature of a Public General Act shall be classified as general.

(3) The responsible authority shall, on sending a statutory instrument to the King's printer of Acts of Parliament, certify it as local or general as the case may be; and, unless the Reference Committee otherwise direct under these Regulations, the instrument shall be classified accordingly.

5. Exemption for local instruments and instruments otherwise regularly published.
The following statutory instruments shall, unless the Reference Committee in any particular case otherwise direct under these Regulations, be exempt from the requirements of subsection (1) of Section 2 of the Principal Act with respect to the printing and sale of copies, that is to say—

    (a)   any local instrument, and

    (b)   any general instrument certified by the responsible authority to be of a class of documents which is or will be otherwise regularly printed as a series and made available to persons affected thereby:

Provided that the responsible authority may, on sending to the King's printer of Acts of Parliament any statutory instrument certified by that authority as local, request him to comply with the requirements aforesaid.

6. Exemption for temporary instruments
If the responsible authority considers that the printing and sale of copies of a statutory instrument in accordance with the requirements of subsection (1) of Section 2 of the Principal Act is unnecessary having regard to the brevity of the period during which that instrument will remain in force and to any other steps taken or to be taken for bringing its substance to the notice of the public, he may, on sending it to the King's printer of Acts of Parliament, certify accordingly; and any instrument so certified shall,

unless the Reference Committee otherwise direct under these Regulations, be exempt from the requirements aforesaid.

7. Exemption for certain schedules, etc.

If the responsible authority considers that the printing and sale in accordance with the requirements of subsection (1) of Section 2 of the Principal Act of any schedule or other document which is identified by or referred to in a statutory instrument and would, but for the provisions of this Regulation, be required to be included in the instrument as so printed and sold, is unnecessary or undesirable having regard to the nature or bulk of the document and to any other steps taken or to be taken for bringing its substance to the notice of the public, he may, on sending it to the King's printer of Acts of Parliament, certify accordingly; and any instrument so certified shall, unless the Reference Committee otherwise direct under these Regulations, be exempt from the requirements aforesaid so far as concerns the document specified in the certificate.

8. Exemption for confidential instruments.

If the responsible authority considers that the printing and sale of copies of a statutory instrument in accordance with the requirements of subsection (1) of Section 2 of the Principal Act would, if effected before the coming into operation of that instrument, be contrary to the public interest, he may, on sending it to the King's printer of Acts of Parliament, certify accordingly; and any instrument so certified shall, so long as it has not come into operation, be exempt from the requirements aforesaid:

Provided that if at any time after the instrument has been so certified and before the instrument has come into operation it appears to the said authority that the printing and sale of copies of the instrument as aforesaid would no longer be contrary to the public interest, he shall notify the King's printer of Acts of Parliament to that effect, and thereupon the foregoing provisions of this Regulation shall cease to apply to that instrument.

9.–11. *****

THE COUNTY COURTS JURISDICTION ORDER 1981
SI 1981 No. 1123 (L.9)

2.
Subject to the transitional provisions set out in the Schedule to this Order, the enactments specified in column 1 of the following table shall be amended by substituting for the sum specified in column 2 opposite each such enactment, wherever such sum appears therein, the sum so specified in column 3:—

TABLE

Column 1	Column 2	Column 3
County Courts Act 1959:		
Section 39 (contract and tort)	£2,000	£5,000
Section 40 (money recoverable by statute)	£2,000	£5,000
Section 41 (abandonment of excess)	£2,000	£5,000
Section 45 (transfer from High Court to county court)	£2,000	£5,000
Section 47(1)(a) and (1A)(a) (county court costs in High Court)	£1,200	£3,000
Section 47(1)(b) and (1A)(b) (no costs in High Court)	£350	£600
Section 52 (equity)	£15,000	£30,000
Section 62 (probate)	£15,000	£30,000
Section 68 (transfer of interpleader from High Court to county court)	£2,000	£5,000
Section 80 (action by minor for wages)	£2,000	£5,000

Section 102(3)(c) (registrars' jurisdiction)	£200	£500[1]
Section 146 (attachment of debts)	£2,000	£5,000
First Schedule (miscellaneous jurisdiction)	£15,000	£30,000
	£2,000	£5,000
Settled Land Act 1925(a), section 113(3)	£15,000	£30,000
Solicitors Act 1974(b), section 69(3) (actions for solicitors' costs)	£2,000	£5,000
Consumer Credit Act 1974(c), section 139(5) (re-opening of extortionate credit agreements)	£2,000	£5,000
Charging Orders Act 1979(d), section 1(2)(c)	£2,000	£5,000

Note
[1]The registrars' jurisdiction was increased from £500 to £1,000 by the County Court (Amendment) Rules 1986 (SI 1986 No 636). County Courts Act 1984, s. 75(3)(d).

THE COUNTY COURTS APPEALS ORDER 1981
SI 1981 No. 1749

The Lord Chancellor, in exercise of the power conferred on him by section 108(2) of the County Courts Act 1959 and all other powers enabling him in that behalf, hereby makes the following Order:—

2. Leave to Appeal
There shall be no right of appeal under section 108 of the County Courts Act 1959 without the leave either of the judge of the county court or of the Court of Appeal in the following classes of proceedings:—

(a) where the claim (or counter claim, if larger) is for an amount not exceeding one half of the limit of the jurisdiction of a county court under one or other of the following provisions of the County Courts Act 1959:—
    section 39 (contract and tort),
    section 40 (money recoverable by statute),
    section 52 (equity),
    section 62 (probate),
    first schedule (miscellaneous jurisdiction);

(b) where the determination sought to be appealed from was made by the judge acting in an appellate capacity.

3. Savings for Injunctions and for Children
Article 2 shall not apply where the determination sought to be appealed from:—
    (a)   includes or preserves an injunction, or
    (b)   relates to the custody of or access to a child.

THE COURT OF APPEAL (CIVIL DIVISION) ORDER 1982
SI 1982 No. 543

The Lord Chancellor, in exercise of the power conferred on him by section 54(4)(e) of the Supreme Court Act 1981 and with the concurrence of the Master of the Rolls, hereby makes the following Order:—

2. Composition of court
A court of the civil division of the Court of Appeal shall, if it consists of two judges, be duly constituted for the purposes of hearing and determining—
    (a)   an appeal from a determination of a county court;
    (b)   an appeal from a judgment or order of the High Court, where the claim (or counter-claim, if larger) when made was for an amount not exceeding the limit

of the jurisdiction of a county court under one or other of the following provisions of the County Courts Act 1959:—
    section 39 (contract and tort),
    section 40 (money recoverable by statute),
    section 52 (equity),
    section 62 (probate),
    first schedule (miscellaneous jurisdiction);
  (c) an appeal in proceedings for summary judgment under Order 14 or Order 86 of the Rules of the Supreme Court 1965;
  (d) an appeal from a master or district registrar under Order 58, rule 2, 3 or 4 of the Rules of the Supreme Court 1965.

3. Saving
Article 2 shall not apply to an appeal which falls within section 54(4)(a),(b),(c) or (d) of the Supreme Court Act 1981.

MAGISTRATES' COURTS (ADVANCE INFORMATION) RULES 1985
SI 1985 No. 601

1. These Rules may be cited as the Magistrates' Courts (Advance Information) Rules 1985 and shall come into operation on 20th May 1985.

2. These Rules apply in respect of proceedings against any person ("the accused") for an offence triable either way other than proceedings where the accused was charged or an information was laid before the coming into operation of these Rules.

3. As soon as practicable after a person has been charged with an offence in proceedings in respect of which these Rules apply or a summons has been served on a person in connection with such an offence, the prosecutor shall provide him with a notice in writing explaining the effect of Rule 4 below and setting out the address at which a request under that Rule may be made.

4. (1) If, in any proceedings in respect of which these Rules apply, either before the magistrates' court considers whether the offence appears to be more suitable for summary trial or trial on indictment or, where the accused has not attained the age of 17 years when he appears or is brought before a magistrates' court, before he is asked whether he pleads guilty or not guilty, the accused or a person representing the accused requests the prosecutor to furnish him with advance information, the prosecutor shall, subject to Rule 5 below, furnish him as soon as practicable with either—
  (a) a copy of those parts of every written statement which contain information as to the facts and matters of which the prosecutor proposes to adduce evidence in the proceedings, or
  (b) a summary of the facts and matters of which the prosecutor proposes to adduce evidence in the proceedings.

(2) In paragraph (1) above, "written statement" means a statement made by a person on whose evidence the prosecutor proposes to rely in the proceedings and, where such a person has made more than one written statement one of which contains information as to all the facts and matters in relation to which the prosecutor proposes to rely on the evidence of that person, only that statement is a written statement for purposes of paragraph (1) above.

(3) Where in any part of a written statement or in a summary furnished under paragraph (1) above reference is made to a document on which the prosecutor proposes to rely, the prosecutor shall, subject to Rule 5 below, when furnishing the part of the written statement or the summary, also furnish either a copy of the document

or such information as may be necessary to enable the person making the request under paragraph (1) above to inspect the document or a copy thereof.

5. (1) If the prosecutor is of the opinion that the disclosure of any particular fact or matter in compliance with the requirements imposed by Rule 4 above might lead to any person on whose evidence he proposes to rely in the proceedings being intimidated, to an attempt to intimidate him being made or otherwise to the course of justice being interfered with he shall not be obliged to comply with those requirements in relation to that fact or matter.

(2) Where, in accordance with paragraph (1) above, the prosecutor considers that he is not obliged to comply with the requirements imposed by Rule 4 in relation to any particular fact or matter, he shall give notice in writing to the person who made the request under that Rule to the effect that certain advance information is being withheld by virtue of that paragraph.

6. (1) Subject to paragraph (2) below, where an accused appears or is brought before a magistrates' court in proceedings in respect of which these Rules apply, the court shall, before it considers whether the offence appears to be more suitable for summary trial or trial in indictment satisfy itself that the accused is aware of the requirements which may be imposed on the prosecutor under Rule 4 above.

(2) Where the accused has not attained the age of 17 years when he appears or is brought before a magistrates' court in proceedings in respect of which these Rules apply, the court shall, before the accused is asked whether he pleads guilty or not guilty, satisfy itself that the accused is aware of the requirements which may be imposed on the prosecutor under Rule 4 above.

7. (1) If, in any proceedings in respect of which these Rules apply the court is satisfied that, a request under Rule 4 of these Rules having been made to the prosecutor by or on behalf of the accused, a requirement imposed on the prosecutor by that Rule has not been complied with, the court shall adjourn the proceedings pending compliance with the requirement unless the court is satisfied that the conduct of the case for the accused will not be substantially prejudiced by non-compliance with the requirement.

(2) Where, in the circumstances set out in paragraph (1) above, the court decides not to adjourn the proceedings, a record of that decision and of the reasons why the court was satisfied that the conduct of the case for the accused would not be substantially prejudiced by non-compliance with the requirement shall be entered in the register kept under Rule 66 of the Magistrates' Courts Rules 1981.

PRACTICE STATEMENT [1966] 1 WLR 1234

LORD GARDINER L.C.: Their Lordships regard the use of precedent as an indispensable foundation upon which to decide what is the law and its application to individual cases. It provides at least some degree of certainty upon which individuals can rely in the conduct of their affairs, as well as a basis for orderly development of legal rules.

Their Lordships nevertheless recognise that too rigid adherence to precedent may lead to injustice in a particular case and also unduly restrict the proper development of the law. They propose, therefore, to modify their present practice and, while treating former decisions of this House as normally binding, to depart from a previous decision when it appears right to do so.

In this connection they will bear in mind the danger of disturbing retrospectively the basis on which contracts, settlements of property and fiscal arrangements have been entered into and also the especial need for certainty as to the criminal law.

This announcement is not intended to affect the use of precedent elsewhere than in this House.

PRACTICE DIRECTION (CRIME: MAJORITY VERDICTS) [1967] 1 WLR 1198

LORD PARKER C.J., at the sitting of the court said: The court would like to issue a practice direction. This practice direction is issued as a result of consultation between the judges of the Queen's Bench Divisioin and with the concurrence of those members of the Court of Appeal who sit in the Criminal Division of the Court of Appeal.

MAJORITY VERDICTS

The Criminal Justice Act, 1967, has now been passed and it is proposed to bring many of its provisions, including section 13 dealing with majority verdicts, into force on October 1, 1967. The section, however, does not apply to any person arraigned before that date (see paragraph 1 of Schedule 5).

Section 13 provides as follows:

"13. (1) Subject to the following provisions of this section, the verdict of a jury in criminal proceedings need not be unanimous if—

    (a)   in a case where there are not less than eleven jurors, ten of them agree on the verdict; and

    (b)   in a case where there are ten jurors, nine of them agree on the verdict;

and a verdict authorised by this subsection is hereafter in this section referred to as "a majority verdict."

"(2) A court shall not accept a majority verdict of guilty unless the foreman of the jury has stated in open court the number of jurors who respectively agreed to and dissented from the verdict.

"(3) A court shall not accept a majority verdict unless it appears to the court that the jury have had not less than two hours for deliberation or such longer period as the court thinks reasonable having regard to the nature and complexity of the case."

It is important that all those trying indictable offences should so far as possible adopt a uniform practice both in directing a jury in summing-up and also in receiving the verdict or giving further direction after retirement.

So far as the summing-up is concerned, it is inadvisable for the judge and indeed for counsel to attempt an explanation of the section for fear that the jury will be confused. Before the jury retire however the judge should direct the jury in some such words as the following:

"As you may know, the law permits me in certain circumstances to accept a verdict which is not the verdict of you all. Those circumstances have not as yet arisen so that when you retire I must ask you to reach a verdict upon which each one of you is agreed. Should, however, the time come when it is possible for me to accept a majority verdict, I will give you further direction."

Thereafter the practice should be as follows:

1. Should the jury return *before* the two hours (or such longer time as the judge thinks reasonable) has elapsed (see subsection (3)), they should be asked

    (i)   Have you reached a verdict upon which you are all agreed? Please answer "Yes" or "No."

    (ii) (a)   If *unanimous*—What is your verdict?

    (b)   If *not unanimous*—the jury should be sent out again for further deliberation with a further direction to arrive if possible at a unanimous verdict.

2. Should the jury return (whether for the first or second time) or be sent for *after* the two hours (or the longer period) has elapsed, questions (i) and (ii)(a) in the preceding paragraph should be put to them and if it appears that they are not unanimous they should be asked to retire once more and told that they should continue to endeavour to reach a unanimous verdict but that if they cannot the judge will accept a majority verdict as in subsection (1).

3. When the jury finally return they should be asked

(i) Have at least 10 (or 9 as the case may be) of you agreed upon your verdict? If "Yes,"
(ii) What is your verdict? Please only answer "Guilty" or "Not Guilty."
(iii) (a) If "Not Guilty"—accept the verdict without more ado.
(b) If "Guilty"—Is it the verdict of you all or by a majority?
(iv) If "Guilty" by a majority—How many of you agreed to the verdict and how many dissented?

The reason why subsection (2) is confined to a majority verdict of guilty and of the somewhat complicated procedure set out in paragraphs 2 and 3 above is to prevent it being known that a verdict of Not Guilty is a majority verdict. If the final direction in paragraph 2 continues to require the jury to arrive if possible at a unanimous verdict and the verdict is received as in paragraph 3 it will not be known for certain that the acquittal is not unanimous.

Where there are several counts (or alternative verdicts) left to the jury the above practice will of course need to be adapted to the circumstances. The procedure will have to be repeated in respect of each count (or alternative verdict) the verdict being accepted in those cases where the jury are unanimous and the further direction in paragraph 2 being given in cases in which they are not unanimous.

Should the jury in the end be unable to agree on a verdict by the required majority (i.e., if the answer to the question in paragraph 3(i) be in the negative) the judge in his discretion will either ask them to deliberate further or discharge them.

Section 13 will of course apply also to verdicts other than "guilty" or "not guilty," e.g., to special verdicts within the meaning of the Criminal Procedure (Insanity) Act, 1964, verdicts under that Act as to fitness to be tried, verdicts on pleas in bar, special verdicts on findings of fact, etc. Accordingly in such cases the questions to jurors will have to be suitably adjusted.

PRACTICE NOTE [1970] 1 WLR 916

LORD PARKER C.J. In the light of difficulties which, as disclosed by recent cases, are arising under section 13 of the Criminal Justice Act, 1967, the court desires to issue the following practice direction, supplementary to the *Practice Direction (Crime: Majority Verdicts)* [1967] 1 WLR 1198, dated July 31, 1967.

In future any verdict of a majority of a jury shall not be accepted until two hours and 10 minutes have elapsed between the time that the last member of the jury has left the jury box to go to the jury room and the time when there is put to the jury the first of the questions set out in paragraph 3 of the *Practice Direction (Crime: Majority Verdicts)* [1967] 1 WLR 1198, 1200. Moreover, before the first of those questions is put, the period that has elapsed since the last member of the jury left the jury box shall be stated in open court by the senior officer of the court present when the jury is about to be asked to return a verdict.

PRACTICE DIRECTION (DIVORCE TOWNS: DEFENDED CASES) [1971] 1 WLR 1762

Section 2(2) of the Courts Act 1971 (which comes into force on January 1, 1972) provides that, subject to rules of court, the places at which the High Court sits outside the Royal Courts of Justice are to be determined in accordance with directions given by or on behalf of the Lord Chancellor.

Subject to the approval of the Rule Committee it is proposed that as from January 1, 1972, there should be no distinction between "long" and 'short" defended matrimonial causes and that the list of divorce towns in Appendix 1 to the Matrimonial Causes Rules 1971 should be deleted. It is intended that prima facie all defended causes and

High Court ancillary applications for hearing by a judge should be tried or heard by judges of the High Court at such places as may be authorised for the particular proceedings, or proceedings of the class to which they belong.

*****

(*Note* – There then follows a list of towns.)
Issued with the concurrence of the Lord Chancellor.

PRACTICE NOTE
(COURT OF APPEAL: NEW PROCEDURE)
[1982] 1 WLR 1312

October 4. SIR JOHN DONALDSON M.R. at his first sitting as Master of the Rolls in the Court of Appeal handed down the following written explanation and informal commentary on the more important changes in the practice and procedure of the Court of Appeal following the amendments to R.S.C., Ord. 59 made by the Rules of the Supreme Court (Amendment No. 2) 1981 (S.I. 1981 No. 1734 (L. 21)).

References

Unless otherwise stated, references are to R.S.C., Ord. 59, as amended.

Leave to appeal

Applications for leave to appeal to the Court of Appeal will be heard by a single judge of the court sitting in chambers. No appeal will lie from his decision: Supreme Court Act 1981, section 54 (6).

Notice of appeal

Heretofore the time for serving notice of appeal has varied according to the nature of the appeal. In future there will be a single time limit of four weeks from the date on which the judgment or order of the court below was signed, entered or otherwise perfected, unless this limit is abridged or extended by order of the court below, the registrar, the single judge of the Court of Appeal or the Court of Appeal: rule 4(1). The only exception will be social security appeals with a six-week limit. Applications for leave to serve notice of appeal out of time will be heard by the registrar. In view of the importance of parties knowing whether a judgment is final or is still subject to possible appeal, it will only be in exceptional cases that such leave will be granted.

The content of the notice of appeal is much more important than is generally realised. A notice of appeal which complies fully with R.S.C., Ord. 59, r. 3 will both define and confine the area of controversy upon the hearing of the appeal, thus saving both time and expense to the parties. It is intended that wherever possible the members of the court will have read the notice of appeal and any respondent's notice and the reasons for the judgment under appeal before the appeal is called on and a properly drawn notice of appeal will enable counsel to come at once to the central issues without any or any prolonged opening. Failure to give the court this essential assistance by means of a carefully drawn notice of appeal may well lead to special orders being made in relation to time wasted and additional costs incurred.

The list of appeals

R.S.C., Ord. 59, r. 3(4) requires the notice of appeal to specify the list of appeals in which the appellant proposes that the appeal shall be set down. There are final and interlocutory lists of the following descriptions which are self-explanatory:

Chancery Division, Chancery Division (in Bankruptcy), Revenue Paper, Family Division, Queen's Bench Division, Queen's Bench Division (Admiralty), Queen's Bench Division (Commercial Court), Queen's Bench Division (Divisional Court),

County Courts, County Courts (Divorce), County Courts (Admiralty), Appeal Tribunals (Land), Appeal Tribunals (Patent), Appeal Tribunal (Employment), Appeal Tribunal (Social Security Commission), Restrictive Practices Court.

In the light of experience the number of lists may require alteration from time to time, but full notice will be given of any change. Meanwhile it is only necessary to mention that appeals from the Commercial Court and from the Queen's Bench Divisional Court, both of which were formerly submerged in the general Queen's Bench Division lists, now have their own final and interlocutory lists.

Setting down the appeal

R.S.C., Ord. 59, r. 5 requires the appellant to "set down" the appeal within seven days after the service of the notice of appeal on the parties. The time limit is important and will be strictly enforced. Any application for an extension of time must be made to the registrar. "Setting down" means filing the notice of appeal with the court, accompanied by the documents specified in rule 5(1). The registrar and his staff will have to be satisfied that the required documentation is complete and will not hesitate to reject any notice where this is not the case. When they are so satisfied, the appeal will be given a serial number identifying the list in which it will be included and its position in that list. This list is not to be confused with the "List of Forthcoming Appeals" in which appeals are included at a slightly later stage.

Respondent's notice

R.S.C., Ord. 59, r. 6 makes provision for the service of a respondent's notice within 21 days after the service of the notice of appeal. The content of any such notice is as important as that of the notice of appeal and for the same reason—it defines and confines the scope of the argument upon the appeal, enables the members of the court to inform themselves in advance of the hearing of what the appeal is about and so saves both time and expense. Again the time limit is important and will be strictly enforced, any application for an extension of time being made to the registrar unless the appeal is before the court itself at the time when the application is made.

Amendment of notice of appeal and respondent's notice

It is most desirable that both notices of appeal and respondents' notices should be full and accurate when first served. This should not be too difficult, since the judgment under appeal and the proceedings which led to it will be fresh in everyone's mind. Nevertheless it can happen that, on reflection, it is thought desirable to amend such notices. Rule 7 allows this to be done without leave at any time before the appeal first appears in the "List of Forthcoming Appeals." Thereafter leave will be required and application should be made to the registrar on notice to all other parties, unless the appeal is already before the court for some other purpose. The registrar will require good reasons to be shown why the amendment was not made before the appeal appeared in the "List of Forthcoming Appeals" and to be satisfied that the application has been made at the earliest possible moment.

Appearance of appeal in the List of Forthcoming Appeals

This is the second of the key stages in an appeal, the first being the service of the notice of appeal and the third the appearance of the appeal in the Warned List. Ultimately it will follow as soon after the appeal is set down as is reasonable, bearing in mind the steps which the appellant is then required to take. However, until the backlog of appeals has been reduced, there will be some cases in which there is a rather greater interval. The registrar is considering whether, and how, it will be possible to give solicitors advance notice that an appeal is to appear in the List of Forthcoming Appeals. However, it is the responsibility of the parties and their advisers to watch the Daily Cause List in which the List of Forthcoming Appeals will periodically be published.

Once an appeal appears in the List of Forthcoming Appeals, the appellant has seven days in which to lodge the various documents specified in rule 9.

Although the rules do not at present so require, it would greatly assist the efficient running of the court if at the same time as they are lodging documents pursuant to rule 9, appellants would provide an estimate of how much in-court time is likely to be needed for the hearing. In putting forward this estimate they should consult the respondents or their representatives and all concerned will no doubt wish to seek the views of counsel who will be appearing. It would also assist the court if appellants would indicate which counsel are being instructed by them and, where known, by the respondents. This will make it easier for the registrar when listing to take such account as is possible of counsel's other commitments, although it will be appreciated that this is only one factor amongst many which have to be considered if the current delays are to be eliminated and eliminated quickly.

It may be thought that seven days from the date when an appeal appears in the list of Forthcoming Appeals is rather a short time in which to do a lot of work, since the documentation required is substantially all that which will be needed for the hearing of the appeal. It is indeed a short time, but it must be remembered that parties and their advisers are free to file these documents as early as they like and the earlier that they in fact do so the better. As a matter of good practice they should start assembling the documents as soon as the appeal has been set down.

In the past much time has been wasted because appellants have failed to file all the appropriate documents, have filed an inadequate number of copies or have failed to ensure that bundles are properly paginated and are legible throughout. In the light of the contribution which this has made to the delay in hearing appeals, a serious view will be taken of any failure by appellants to comply with their obligations in this respect.

Directions by the registrar

R.S.C., Ord. 59, r. 9 has been amended so as to include a new sub-rule (3) in the following terms:

"After the documents have been lodged the registrar shall give such directions in relation to the documents to be produced at the appeal, and the manner in which they are to be presented, and as to other matters incidental to the conduct of the appeal, as appear adapted to secure the just, expeditious and economical disposal of the appeal."

This is perhaps the most important single change in the rules. The conduct of appeals by way of oral hearing lies at the heart of the English tradition and practice and neither the Scarman Committee [set up in February 1978 under the chairmanship of Lord Scarman to examine ways and means of relieving the pressure in hearing civil appeals] nor anyone else has suggested that it should be abandoned in favour of a system of written appeals supplemented by oral hearings which are subject to strict time limits, as is the practice in some other jurisdictions. Nevertheless, an oral hearing involving the presence of the members of the court, shorthandwriters, court staff, counsel, solicitors and, sometimes, the parties is extremely expensive in terms of time and therefore of money. Furthermore, time, and particularly judicial time, is a scarce commodity of which the best possible use should be made, if the current level of delay is to be reduced. The problem is how to achieve a proper balance between what can be done by way of pre-reading by the members of the court in their rooms, which involves only judicial time, and what must be left to oral presentation and argument in court which involves the time of many others.

There can never be any single universal answer. Every appeal is different, although patterns do emerge. The sub-rule therefore contemplates that once the documentation is complete the registrar, either at the request of the parties or of his own motion, shall consider whether any special directions can be given which will expedite the hearing and render it less costly. We have as yet little experience of how this will work, although in exceptional cases it has in the past been attempted with some success by the court itself. The Scarman Committee suggested the use of "perfected ground of appeal" on the lines of those used in the Criminal Divison of the Court of Appeal. These grounds of appeal often refer to the key authorities which will be relied upon and to the portions of the summing up and evidence which will be relied upon and to the portions of the summing up and evidence which are relevant to each ground of appeal. They permit members of the court to pre-read the relevant material, much of which is non-controversial, and, thus informed, to consider and adjudicate upon the basis of a much abbreviated oral argument and to do so in a fraction of the time which would be necessary if they took their places in court knowing nothing of the appeal. In the context of civil appeals, it may be possible to use "perfected grounds of appeal" but another possibility, which may be better, is for the parties to provide the court in advance with a skeleton outline of their respective arguments annotated by reference to the documents and authorities. The probability is that different approaches will be found appropriate to different types of appeal, but only time and experience will show which is the best method or methods.

What needs to be said now, and said with all possible emphasis, is that the better use of time is in the interests of everyone—the parties to the appeal, their advisers, parties to other appeals which will be delayed if time is not used to the best advantage and to the public at large which has an interest in the efficient administration of justice. Accordingly, the members of the court look forward with some confidence to all concerned giving serious thought to, and, where appropriate, discussing with the registrar, how each individual appeal can best be presented. The registrar will be ready and willing to assist at any stage, but the appropriate moment will probably be at or about the time when an appeal appears in the List of Forthcoming Appeals. The Bar Council and The Law Society will not be concerned with individual appeals, but there will be the fullest and most frequent consultation with them as to what experiments are worth trying and as to the success of those experiments. As experience is built up, and in the light of that experience, we have no doubt the rate of disposal of appeals can be increased without detriment to, and even with an improvement in, the quality of the justice which is administered.

The single judge of the Court of Appeal

In the past a court consisting of at least two judges has had to consider incidental applications, such as those for leave to appeal, for the imposition or removal of orders staying execution or for the grant, variation or discharge of injunctions pending appeal. This represented an extravagant use of judicial time and rule 10(9) will now enable all these matters to be considered and disposed of by a single judge sitting in chambers. All such applications will be made by motion: rule 14(1).

Internal appeals and referrals

The amended R.S.C., Ord. 59 gives the registrar power to refer matters to a single judge and the single judge power to refer matters to the Court of Appeal: rule 14(9) and (10). It also gives a right of appeal to the single judge from any determination of the registrar and from any determination of the single judge to the Court of Appeal. However, in respect of a determination by the registrar, there is no right of appeal to the Court of Appeal without the leave of that court if the registrar's determination has been reviewed by the single judge: rule 14(11) and (12). Nevertheless, the advantages of the new system would be substantially eroded if appeals became a matter of course and parties and their advisers should give serious consideration to where their best interests lie before launching such appeals.

Listing of appeals for hearing—"the Warned List"

The science, or more accurately the art, of a successful listing officer consists of an ability to quantify the unquantifiable and to predict the unpredictable. Factors of which he has to take account are the availability of judges, the availability of counsel, the speed with which the judges concerned will wish the argument to be presented, the inherent complexity of the appeal, the loquacity of counsel and the relative urgency of the appeal both objectively and in the eyes of the parties. If, against this background, a listing officer is instructed to give fixed dates for the hearing of all appeals and to specify far in advance by which court the appeal will be heard, the result is inevitable. Either he will over-estimate the hearing time needed for appeals and there will be gaps in the list which are too short to be filled by taking in other appeals or he will under-estimate and the fixed dates will not be met. Both have been happening, thereby causing delay and inconvenience to all concerned. Some new approach must be adopted, at least on an experimental basis.

The most obviously necessary change, and one recommended by the Scarman Committee, is to list for the Civil Division of the Court of Appeal as a whole and not for particular courts. This gives greater flexibility and will enable appeals orignally destined for Court A, whose cases are over-running, to be switched to Court B where an appeal has been withdrawn or for some other reason judges have become available. This recommendation is being implemented and the registrar will be the listing officer for the whole of the civil division.

The next aspect which needs to be looked at is the concept of all or the vast majority of appeals being given fixed dates and given them far in advance of the hearing of the appeal. Clearly parties to appeals, and more particularly those appearing for them, have to be able to plan their work and need to know with a greater or lesser degree of precision, according to circumstances, when an appeal will be heard. But giving fixed dates which, because they are fixed must be very far ahead and well spaced out if they are to be guaranteed, is no real service to the parties. On the other hand, failing to space the appeals out and instead giving fixed dates to a consecutive series of appeals will almost inevitably lead to a failure to meet some or all of these dates and that is worse than useless. Nevertheless, despite the difficulties inherent in a fixed date system, where appeals have already been given fixed dates, this commitment will be honoured if at all possible.

The reality is surely that only the most urgent appeals need to be heard with very short notice of the time of hearing and only a minority of appeals need to be allotted a fixed and guaranteed date far in advance. An obvious example of the latter category is the exceptionally heavy appeal upon which counsel, and to a lesser extent the court, will have to work for an extended period before the oral hearing begins. Listing is not unlike weather forecasting. The further away you are from the date for hearing, the more difficult it is to identify it precisely. But as you approach that day, it becomes more and more possible to do so and, in effect, to give a fixed date. Between the extremes of the very urgent appeal which must be heard almost at once, thus precluding substantial notice, and the exceptionally heavy case which requires long notice of a more or less fixed date, it may well be possible to meet the legitimate needs of the parties and of their advisers and also the public interest in reducing the number of appeals awaiting hearing by a system of long-range forecasting coupled slightly later with a more or less precise indication of the date for the hearing.

The maximum possible direct and continuing contact will be maintained between the court and the parties to appeals which are ready for hearing in order that they shall be heard as quickly as possible and with the minimum conflict with other commitments.

However, it is only fair to the registrar and his staff to point out that the task of establishing an entirely new office, creating a new administrative infra-structure for the court and also a new centralised system of listing will involve great problems for them in the initial stages and there are bound to be teething troubles. In future communications should be easier than heretofore, because telex is being installed in the Royal Courts of Justice. This will be the subject of a separate announcement.

Notwithstanding such communication, some form of published "Warned List" containing appeals to be heard in the immediate future will still be needed. The existing "Warned List" was designed to operate in connection with the unamended rules and is now inappropriate. Furthermore, cases appeared in it so long before they were likely to be heard that parties and their advisers, nor unreasonably, did not regard themselves as being warned of anything. A new "Warned List" will be published containing the appeals which are both ready for hearing and have already been given fixed dates, together with some other appeals of an urgent character. Meanwhile consideration will be given to what are the appropriate criteria for including appeals in a new style "Warned List."

In taking a fresh look at listing in the context of a new centralised system, the registrar and the court will be looking to both sides of the profession for constructive suggestions, advice and assistance, and experience shows that we shall not look in vain. This is supremely an area where it is necessary to try and to err before an effective system can be evolved.

Constitution of courts

Section 54 (4) of the Supreme Court Act 1981 and the Court of Appeal (Civil Division) Order 1982 (S.I. 1982, No. 543) have authorised the constitution of courts consisting of two judges instead of three in certain specified circumstances, mainly appeals from interlocutory decisions, which includes most family and divorce matters, and appeals from the county courts. If the very serious backlog of appeals is to be reduced, it is essential that the fullest use be made of this power. The main theoretical objection to an appellate court of two judges is that they might disagree. Should this be likely to occur, it would be possible to relist the appeal for argument before a differently constituted court of three, but experience in the Divisional Court of the Queen's Bench Division suggests that this is most unlikely to occur in other than an insignificant number of cases. Nevertheless it will sometimes happen that whilst an appeal is of such a nature that there is jurisdiction for a two-judge court to hear it, it is well recognised that despite the need to make the best possible use of the available judge power, there are some appeals falling within the jurisdiction of a two-judge court which raise issues of such complexity or general importance that a three-judge court is desirable. Should this appear to the registrar to be the case, he will list the appeal for hearing by a three-judge court. Should it appear to the parties that this is the case, they will be free to apply to the registrar for a special listing before a three-judge court, but it is hoped that they will only adopt this course if there are really good reasons for so doing.

Oral hearings

It is hoped and expected that early consideration by the parties of the extent to which judges can profitably read papers before the hearing and the assistance of the registrar at the stage at which an appeal appears in the Forthcoming List of Appeals will enable the length of the oral hearing to be considerably reduced and that all concerned will know in advance what is expected of them. However, the way in which the hearing is conducted will, as always, be a matter to be determined by the members of the court hearing the appeal and if it appears to them that the directions which have been given were mistaken or need to be supplemented, the court will take the appropriate action.

Written judgments

Where the court has prepared written judgments, consideration will be given by the judges concerned to the advantage of giving copies to counsel, the law reporters and the representatives of the press present in court instead of reading the judgements aloud. However where this is done, it must be understood that the purpose for which the copies are handed down is strictly limited, namely to save the parties the expense involved in prolonging the hearing, to allow the time saved to be devoted to deciding other appeals, to enable the representatives of the parties to make any necessary application following the announcement of the decision and to enable the law reporters and press to report the appeal in the same way as they would have done if the judgments had been read out in court. Copies so handed down must not be reproduced without the leave of the court and the only recognised record of the written judgments will be that contained in the official transcript which will be obtainable from the court shorthandwriters and will record not only the written judgments, but also the exchanges between the court and counsel which follow the judgments being handed down.

PRACTICE DIRECTION
(CROWN COURT BUSINESS: CLASSIFICATION)
[1987] 1 WLR 1671

With the concurrence of the Lord Chancellor and pursuant to sections 75(1) and (2) of the Supreme Court Act 1981 I direct that, with effect from 1 January 1988, the following directions shall supersede those given on 14 October 1971 in *Practice Direction (Crime: Crown Court Business)* [1971] 1 WLR 1535, as amended:

CLASSIFICATION

1. For the purposes of trial in the Crown Court, offences are to be classified as follows:

Class 1:
(1) Any offences for which a person may be sentenced to death.
(2) Misprison of treason and treason felony.
(3) Murder
(4) Genocide
(5) An offence under section 1 of the Official Secrets Act 1911
(6) Incitement, attempt or conspiracy to commit any of the above offences.

Class 2:
(1) Manslaughter.
(2) Infanticide.
(3) Child destruction.
(4) Abortion (section 58 of the Offences against the Person Act 1861).
(5) Rape.
(6) Sexual intercourse with a girl under 13.
(7) Incest with a girl under 13.
(8) Sedition.
(9) An offence under section 1 of the Geneva Conventions Act 1957.
(10) Mutiny.
(11) Piracy.
(12) Incitement, attempt or conspiracy to commit any of the above

Class 3:
All offences triable only on indictment other than those in Classes 1, 2, and 4.

Class 4:
   (1)   Wounding or causing grievous bodily harm with intent (section 18 of the Offences against the Person Act 1861).
   (2)   Robbery or assault with intent to rob (section 8 of the Theft Act 1968).
   (3)   Incitement or attempt to commit any of the above offences.
   (4)   Conspiracy at common law, or conspiracy to commit any offence other than those included in Classes 1 and 2.
   (5)   All offences which are triable either way.

Committals for trial

2. A magistrates' court on committing a person for trial under section 6 of the Magistrates' Courts Act 1980 shall, if the offence or any of the offences is included in Classes 1 to 3, specify the most convenient location of the Crown Court where a High Court judge regularly sits, and if the offence is in Class 4 shall specify the most convenient location of the Crown Court.

3. In selecting the most convenient location of the Crown Court, the justices shall have regard to the considerations referred to in section 7 of the Magistrates' Courts Act 1980, and to the location or locations of the Crown Court designated by a presiding judge as the location to which cases should normally be committed from their petty sessions area.

4. Where on one occasion a person is committed in respect of a number of offences, all the committals shall be to the same location of the Crown Court and that location shall be the one where a High Court judge regularly sits if such a location is appropriate for any of the offences.

Committals for sentence or to be dealt with

5. Where a probation order, order for conditional discharge or a community service order has been made, or suspended sentence passed, and the offender is committed to be dealt with for the original offence or in respect of the suspended sentence, he shall be committed in accordance with the paragraphs below.

6. If the order was made or the sentence was passed by the Crown Court, he shall be committed to the location of the Crown Court where the order was made or suspended sentence was passed, unless it is inconvenient or impracticable to do so.

7. If he is not so committed and the order was made by a High Court judge he shall be committed to the most convenient location of the Crown Court where a High Court judge regularly sits.

8. In all other cases where a person is committed for sentence or to be dealt with he shall be committed to the most convenient location of the Crown Court.

9. In selecting the most convenient location of the Crown Court the justices shall have regard to the location of the Crown Court designated by a presiding judge as the appropriate location for such proceedings originating in the area concerned.

Appeals and Proceedings under the Crown Court's original civil jurisdiction

10. The hearing of an appeal or of proceedings under the civil jurisdiction of the Crown Court shall take place at the location of the Crown Court designated by a presiding judge as the appropriate location for such proceedings originating in the area concerned.

Application for removal of a driving disqualification

11. Application should be made to the location of the Crown Court where the order of disqualification was made.

Transfer of proceedings between locations of Crown Court

12. Without prejudice to the provisions of section 76 of the Supreme Court Act 1981 (committal for trial: alteration of place of trial) directions may be given for the transfer from one location of the Crown Court to another of:
  (i)   appeals;
  (ii) proceedings on committal for sentence, or to be dealt with;
  (iii) proceedings under the original civil jurisdiction of the Crown Court where this appears desirable for expediting the hearing, or for the convenience of the parties.

13. Such directions may be given in a particular case by an officer of the Crown Court, or generally, in relation to a class or classes of case, by the presiding judge or a judge acting on his behalf.

14. If dissatisfied with such directions given by an officer of the Crown Court, any party to the proceedings may apply to a judge of the Crown Court who may hear the application in chambers.

ALLOCATION OF BUSINESS WITHIN THE CROWN COURT
General

1. Cases in Class 1 are to be tried by a High Court judge. A case of murder, or incitement, attempt or conspiracy to commit murder may be released, by or on the authority of a presiding judge, for trial by a circuit judge approved for the purpose by the Lord Chief Justice.

2. Cases in Class 2 are to be tried by a High Court judge unless a particular case is released by or on the authority of a presiding judge for trial by a circuit judge. A case of rape, or of a serious sexual offence against a child of any Class, may be released by a presiding judge for trial only by a circuit judge approved for the purpose by the Lord Chief Justice.

3. Cases in Class 3 may be tried by a High Court judge or, in accordance with general or particular directions given by a presiding judge, by a circuit judge or a recorder.

4. Cases in Class 4 may be tried by a High Court judge, a circuit judge, a recorder or an assistant recorder. A case in Class 4 shall not be listed for trial by a High Court judge except with the consent of that judge or of a presiding judge.

5. Appeals from decisions of magistrates and committals to the Crown Court for sentence shall be heard by:
  (i)   a resident or designated judge, or
  (ii) a circuit judge, nominated by the resident or designated judge, who regularly sits at the Crown Court centre, or
  (iii) an experienced recorder specifically approved by the presiding judges for the purpose, or
  (iv) where no circuit judge or recorder satisfying the requirements above is available and it is not practicable to obtain the approval of the presiding judges, by a circuit judge or recorder selected by the resident or designated judge to hear a specific case or cases.

6. Applications or matters arising before trial (including those relating to bail) should be listed where possible before the judge by whom the case is expected to be tried. Where a case is to be tried by a High Court judge who is not available, the application or matter should be listed before any other High Court judge then sitting at the Crown Court centre at which the matter has arisen; before a presiding judge;

before the resident or designated judge for the centre; or, with the consent of the presiding judge, before a circuit judge nominated for the purpose. In other cases, if the circuit judge, recorder or assistant recorder who is expected to try the case is not available, the matter shall be referred to the resident or designated judge or, if he is not available, to any judge or recorder then sitting at the centre.

7. Matters to be dealt with (e.g., in which a probation order has been made or suspended sentence passed) should, where possible, be listed before the judge who originally dealt with the matter, or, if not, before a judge of the same or higher status.

Allocation of proceedings to a court comprising lay judges

8. In addition to the classes of case specified in section 74 of the Supreme Court Act 1981 (appeals and proceedings on committals for sentence) any other proceedings apart from cases listed for pleas of not guilty which in accordance with these directions are listed for hearing by a circuit judge or recorder are suitable for allocation to a court comprising justices of the peace.

Transfer of cases between circuits

9. An application that a case be transferred from one circuit to another should not be granted unless the judge is satisfied that:—
    (i) the approval of the presiding judges and circuit administrator for each circuit has been obtained, or
    (ii) the case may be transferred under general arrangements approved by the presiding judges and circuit administrators.

10. When a resident or designated judge is absent from his centre, the presiding judges may authorise another judge who sits regularly at the same centre to exercise his responsibility.

Presiding judges' directions

11. For the just, speedy and economical disposal of the business of a circuit, presiding judges shall with the approval of the senior presiding judge issue directions as to the need where appropriate to reserve a case for trial by a High Court judge and as to the allocation of work between circuit judges, recorders and assistant recorders and where necessary the devolved responsibility of resident or designated judges for such allocation. In such directions specific provision should be made for cases in the following categories:—

    (a) Cases where death or serious risk to life, or the infliction of grave injury are involved, including motoring cases of this category arising from reckless driving and/or excess alcohol.
    (b) Cases where loaded firearms are alleged to have been used.
    (c) Cases of arson or criminal damage with intent to endanger life.
    (d) Cases of defrauding government departments or local authorities or other public bodies of amounts in excess of £25,000.
    (e) Offences under the Forgery and Counterfeiting Act 1981 where the amount of money or the value of goods exceeds £10,000.
    (f) Offences involving violence to a police officer which result in the officer being unfit for duty for more than 28 days.
    (g) Any offence involving loss to any person or body of a sum in excess of £100,000.
    (h) Cases where there is a risk of substantial political or racial feeling being excited by the offence or the trial.
    (i) Cases which have given rise to widespread public concern.
    (j) Cases of robbery or assault with intent to rob where gross violence was used, or serious injury was caused, or where the accused was armed with a dangerous

weapon for the purpose of the robbery, or where the theft was intended to be from a bank, a building society or a post office.

    (k) Cases involving the manufacture or distribution of substantial quantities of drugs.

    (l) Cases the trial of which is likely to last more than 10 days.

    (m) Cases involving the trial of more than five defendants.

    (n) Cases in which the accused holds a senior public office, or is a member of a profession or other person carrying a special duty or responsibility to the public, including a police officer when acting as such.

    (o) Cases where a difficult issue of law is likely to be involved, or a prosecution for the offence is rare or novel.

12. With the approval of the senior presiding judge, general directions may be given by the presiding judges of the South Eastern Circuit concerning the distribution and allocation of business of all Classes at the Central Criminal Court.

PRACTICE DIRECTION
(COUNTY COURT: TRANSFERS OUTSIDE LONDON)
[1988] 1 WLR 987

1. Section 40 of the County Courts Act 1984 provides for transfer of proceedings by the High Court of its own motion or on the application of any party to the proceedings (i) where the parties consent to the transfer, or (ii) where the amount in issue is or is likely to be within the monetary jurisdiction of the county court, or (iii) where the proceedings are not likely to raise any important question of law or fact and are suitable for determination by a county court.

2. Immediately after an action has been set down for trial at the trial centre, the district registry of the trial centre shall place before the district registrar of the trial centre the documents in the case. The district registrar will thereupon decide (a) whether or not the action appears to be suitable for transfer to a county court, and (b) which county court appears to him to be the appropriate court to try the action, if an order for transfer were made.

3. The following types of case will normally *not* be considered suitable for transfer to a county court. Cases involving:—(a) professional negligence; (b) fatal accidents (unless the damages are obviously modest); (c) allegations of fraud or undue influence; (d) jury trial; (e) claims against the police; (f) public rights or having special features of public interest; (g) novel or difficult point(s) of law; (h) complicated disputes of fact or of expert evidence; (i) more than about £25,000; (j) trials likely to last more than five days.

4. The district registrar of the trial centre shall serve a notice on all parties to an action in which he has decided that the action appears to be suitable for transfer to a county court ("a notice of proposed transfer").

5. Any party who objects to the proposed transfer or to transfer to the court specified in the notice of proposed transfer shall, within 14 days after service upon him of such notice, give notice stating briefly the grounds for objection, to the district registrar ("a notice of objection").

6. Where no notice of objection is received in the district registry within the time limited, the district registrar shall make an order transferring the action to the county court specified in the notice of proposed transfer.

7. Where notice of objection is received in the district registry from any party within the time limited, the district registrar shall fix an appointment for consideration of the question of transfer and shall serve notice thereof on all parties to the action.

8. At the appointment, the district registrar will consider all relevant matters and in particular those mentioned in paragraph 3. Where unliquidated damages are claimed

he will normally expect to receive an indication whether the award is likely to be more or less than £25,000; and in personal injury cases he will expect up-to-date medical reports to be available. After giving to all parties an opportunity to be heard, the district registrar will make an order transferring the action to a specified county court or will order that it remain in the High Court and will, in either case, make provision for the costs of the hearing.

9. Appeal from the order of the district registrar will lie to the presiding judge sitting on the circuit or to a High Court judge inivited to act on his behalf by one of the presiding judges of the circuit.

10. Cases transferred to county courts under section 40 shall be heard by a circuit judge and not by a recorder or assistant recorder without the prior approval of a presiding judge.

11. This direction will take effect on 3 October 1988.

Explanatory note. This practice direction lays down guidance for the transfer of Queen's Bench Division actions in district registries and establishes a system for enabling the court to consider whether cases should be transferred to a county court for trial. The system for the Royal Courts of Justice remains as set out in *Practice Direction (County Court: Transfer of Action)* [1984] 1 WLR 1023 and the *Practice Statement (Listings),* The Times, 13 January 1988.

PRACTICE DIRECTION (COURT OF APPEAL : PRESENTATION OF ARGUMENT)
[1989] 1 WLR 281

LORD DONALDSON OF LYMINGTON M.R., at the sitting of the court handed down the following introduction and practice direction.

IINTRODUCTION

The purpose of the practice direction which is being handed down this morning is to give advance notice of some important changes which the Civil Division of the Court of Appeal will be introducing with effect from 6 June 1989.

The principal changes relate to skeleton arguments, presentation of oral argument in court, and Court of Appeal listing.

Our objective is to reduce the amount of time spent in court whilst at the same time adhering to our long established tradition of oral argument in open court. Time spent in court is costly both to the nation and the parties. It is therefore vital that it is used economically and effectively.

The time lag between the date of lodging and the date of hearing of appeals is still far too long, particularly in the case of appeals against final orders made in the High Court. The average time lag in the case of such appeals (other than cases involving children and other urgent appeals) is still about 12 months. It is not right that a successful party to a High Court action, for instance a plaintiff who has been injured in a road or factory accident, should have to wait a year before knowing whether the award of damages in his or her favour is going to be upheld. This is particularly so bearing in mind the fact that the case is likely to have taken a considerable time to come to trial. Likewise, a defendant who has a decision against him or her which is erroneous, should not have to wait a year before having that judgment varied or set aside. Justice delayed is always unsatisfactory and it can amount to justice denied.

It is for those reasons that we have been giving thought to ways of reducing the amount of time spent in court and increasing the court's "productivity" without detracting from the quality of our appellate system.

A working party was set up under the chairmanship of Purchas L.J. A number of proposals were made as a result of the deliberations of that working party and there were very helpful discussions with the representatives of the solicitors' and barristers' professions. The proposals included the establishment of a team of lawyers to assist the Civil Division, along the lines of the system of office lawyers which has obtained in the Criminal Division for some time. The need for such a team has been accepted by the Lord Chancellor and it is in the course of being established.

A very important element in the working party's strategy, which has been endorsed by all the judges of the court, is that time spent in court will be shortened if the members of the court who are going to hear the appeal are able to do effective pre-reading. This can only be done if, well in advance of the hearing, the court has details of the points which are going to be argued and the authorities which are going to be cited. For that reason the keystone of the new system is that skeleton arguments will no longer be optional, but will be required for all civil appeals (other than appeals heard with exceptional urgency). So far as timing is concerned in all cases (other than those assigned to the Short Warned List, to which a different timetable will apply) skeleton arguments must be lodged not less than four weeks before the date on which the hearing is scheduled to begin.

Requiring the skeleton arguments to be lodged well before the appeal hearing has three main advantages. First and foremost, the judges can do really effective pre-reading and thus save a considerable amount of time which would otherwise be spent reading aloud in court. Second, they can consider whether the time estimate is realistic, and, if not, the court can direct the necessary adjustments to the listing to be made well in advance. Third, it brings forward the point of time at which the parties, particularly the appellant's side, have to make a firm decision whether or not to proceed to a hearing before the Court of Appeal, or whether to settle the case. Accelerating this point of decision should help to reduce the number of cases where the appeal is settled a matter of hours, or even minuts, before the hearing is due to commence or where an appeal is pursued simply because a true appreciation of the prospects of success was only reached so late that a settlement could save little or no expense. Settlements of appeals the night before or at the door of the court usually result in a court day being wasted, because it is then too late to call another appeal on from the Short Warned List. This is a hardship to the parties to appeals waiting to be heard.

There is an important point which I want to make clear at this stage. When the practice of inviting counsel to put in skeleton arguments for the use of the Court of Appeal was first introduced about five years ago, word filtered back to us that some lawyers took the view that this was a first step towards adopting the system which is operated by the appellate courts in the United States of having very full arguments submitted in writing and then limiting oral argument in court to a very short period. That is not the case. I cannot emphasise too strongly that the English Court of Appeal remains firmly wedded to its long established tradition of oral argument in open court. For that reason, as the practice direction makes clear, skeleton arguments should be confined to identifying the points, not arguing them.

The court recognises that calling for skeleton arguments to be lodged four weeks before the hearing date will involve counsel preparing the appeal well in advance of the hearing and then inevitably doing further work by way of recapitulation shortly before the hearing. For that reason and with a view to ensuring that counsel are entitled to appropriate remuneration for any *extra* work involved, the court is directing the taxing masters to tax the costs of preparing a skeleton argument separately from brief fees, but with due regard to the fact that more work may be involved in preparing the oral argument if the counsel presenting that argument has not been involved in the preparation of the skeleton.

The point was rightly made by the representatives of the two branches of the profession in our discussions about these new proposals that, if counsel are going to have to "get the case up" twice, that would make all concerned even more anxious to have counsel of their first choice to argue the appeal. We recognise that, and we are changing the arrangements relating to appeals which qualify for a fixture with a view to achieving greater certainty in relation to hearing dates. We are also giving directions designed to ensure that counsel's estimates of the length of hearing, which are a key factor in listing, are monitored and kept up to date.

I should make it clear, however, that it will still be necessary for the Court of Appeal to have a Short Warned List, I should perhaps say something about this. We do not maintain a Short Warned List on the basis of the notion, which may have obtained in earlier times, that the judge is such an important figure that not a moment of his time must be wasted and therefore there must always be cases on call to fill any gaps. In the modern Court of Appeal the Short Warned List is not based on the dignitas of the judiciary. It is there to ensure that we make full use of the courtrooms and judicial resources at our disposal. However there is reason to hope that improved listing and increased flexibility consequent upon judges devoting more of their time to pre-reading in their rooms may reduce, even if it is unlikely to eliminate, the need for appeals to be included in this list.

We recognise that in the case of appeals which are put into the Short Warned List a party's counsel of first choice may not be available on the day for which the appeal is called on and that in such circumstances the brief will have to change hands. This is an inevitable consequence of putting cases into a Short Warned List, but we have to maintain one for the reasons I have given. We also recognise that, in such a situation, equity requires that each counsel should be properly remunerated for the part which he or she has played in the whole process of preparing and presenting the appeal. We believe that our direction to the taxing masters will achieve that result.

The practice direction sets out changes in the way in which oral argument is to be presented in future in cases where skeleton arguments have been lodged in advance and pre-reading has been done by the judges with the aid of the skeleton. For the benefit of those appearing in the case, and particularly their clients, it is important that the documents and authorities which have been pre-read should be identified, and the presiding Lord Justice will do so at the commencement of the hearing. The rest of the directions dealing with oral argument are designed to achieve what we consider to be the proper and legitimate objective to ensuring that oral argument is devoted to making the relevant points, not working up to making them.

It is important that members of the legal profession should explain to their clients in advance of the appeal hearing what the Court of Appeal's practice is in relation to oral argument. Without such an explanation, the clients might jump to the mistaken conclusion that insufficient time has been allowed for their case to be put before the court. If it is explained to them that the appeal bundles and the cases which bear upon the branches of the law concerned have been studied by the members of the Court of Appeal, together with skeleton arguments, it will not come as a shock to the parties to find that the court then expects counsel to proceed to deal straightaway with the grounds of appeal.

These new arrangements represent the most fundamental change that has been made since October 1982, when the parts of the Supreme Court Act 1981 dealing with the Court of Appeal and the rules made in that connection came into force. When I introduced by practice statement in October 1982, *Practice Note (Court of Appeal: New Procedures)* [1982] 1 WLR 1312, explaining that new system, I said that we would need the co-operation of both branches of the profession. We have enjoyed that co-operation over the past six years, we have had it in the fullest measure in considering the changes which are now being introduced and I am sure that we shall continue to enjoy it in the future.

We recognised that so substantial a change in the practice of the court is bound to give rise to teething troubles, but are confident that, with assistance from both branches of the profession, they can quickly be overcome. We also recognise that as a result of lessons learned in what might be described as the "running-in period," it may be desirable to introduce modifications. In this context, as in all others, we shall welcome constructive criticisms from both branches of the profession and from users generally.

PRACTICE DIRECTION

1. The changes announced in this practice direction will apply to all appeals to the Civil Division of the Court of Appeal which have a hearing date commencing on or after 6 June 1989.

Skeleton arguments

2. With effect from that date skeleton arguments will be compulsory in the case of all appeals to the Civil Division of the Court of Appeal, except in the case of appeals which are heard as a matter of great urgency and any individual case where the court otherwise directs. If counsel consider that a skeleton argument is unnecessary, application should be made to the registrar for a special order.

Content of skeleton arguments

3. The purpose of a skeleton argument is to identify not to argue the points. A skeleton argument should therefore be as succinct as possible. In the case of points of law, it should state the point and cite the principal authority or authorities in support, with references to the particular page(s) where the principle concerned is enunciated. In the case of questions of fact, the skeleton argument should state briefly the basis on which it is contended that the Court of Appeal can interfere with finding of fact concerned, with cross-references to the passages in the transcript or notes of evidence which bear on the point. In the case of respondents whose arguments will be simply that the judgment of the court below is correct for the reasons given, counsel for the respondent can send in a letter to that effect in lieu of a skeleton argument. Where, however, the respondent is going to rely on any authority or refer to any evidence which is not dealt with in the judgment of the court below, a respondent's skeleton argument must be lodged. The respondent's side must always lodge a skeleton argument in any case where there is a respondent's notice. Skeleton arguments are *not* pleadings and, save in exceptional cases (see paragraph 8 below) need not answer the skeleton arguments of the other side.

Chronology of events

4. The appellant's skeleton argument must be accompanied by a written chonology of events relevant to the appeal. This must be a separate document in order that it can easily be consulted in conjunction with other papers.

Specialist law reports

5. There is no objection to counsel referring to specialist law reports, whether or not the decision is also reported in the official law reports, if doing so would assist the court. However it must be appreciated that such reports may not be readily available to the judges and photostat copies should be provided of any such authorities relied upon in the skeleton argument.

The official law reports are to be preferred both by reason of their nature and their general availability. Accordingly where a decision is reported in that series of reports, the need to refer to specialist reports should be explained.

Timetable for exchange and submission of skeleton arguments

6. *Appeal with fixed dates.* In the case of appeals which are given any form of fixture: i.e. all appeals, other than appeals assigned to the Short Warned List and appeals which are heard as a matter of urgency, the skeleton arguments must be sent or delivered to the other side and three copies lodged with the Civil Appeals Office not less than four weeks before the date on which the hearing is due to commence.

7. *Short Warned List Cases.* In the case of appeals assigned to the Short Warned List the skeleton arguments must be sent to the other side and three copies lodged with the Civil Appeals Office ten days before the date from which the Short Warned List appeal is "on call".

Supplementary skeleton arguments

8. Either side may lodge a supplementary skeleton argument if exceptional circumstances give rise to a need for one. This will only occur if (a) one side raised a point which could not have been anticipated upon a reading of the notice of appeal or any respondent's notice *and* (b) it called for an answer e.g. confession and avoidance. Wherever a supplementary skeleton argument is called for, a copy of it must be sent to the other side and three copies lodged with the Civil Appeals Office at the earliest possible moment.

Listing changes

9. Consequent upon the new arrangements for compulsory skeleton arguments, some changes will be made to the Court of Appeal listing arrangements.

10. *Fixtures.* The present system of giving fixtures to appeals estimated to last five days or more and a "flexible fixture" (i.e. a hearing date with a band) to appeals estimated at four days or less (see generally paragraph 59/1/10 of *The Supreme Court Practice 1988*) will be replaced by a single form of fixture. In the case of all appeals (other than those assigned to the Short Warned List) which have a hearing due to commence on or after 6 June 1989 (whenever fixed) the present system of "banded dates" will be replaced by a single form of flexible fixture which will apply to all such appeals, namely that the appeal will be booked to commence on a specified date, or on the next following sitting day. If it does not prove to be possible for the court concerned to take the appeal on the specified date or on the following sitting day, and the Listing Office are unable to transfer the appeal to another court, the hearing date will have to be rearranged.

The purpose of providing this new system is to assist both counsel and solicitors by providing greater certainty.

11. *Short Warned List.* Unless the court otherwise directs, three weeks' notice will be given of the entry of an appeal into the Short Warned List. This will allow time for the skeleton argument to be prepared, sent to the other side and lodged within the 10-day time limit prescribed above: see paragraph 7. The court appreciates that, in the case of appeals assigned to the Short Warned List, counsel who has prepared the skeleton argument may not always be available on the date on which the appeal is called on, with the result that the brief will have to change hands. In order to ensure that the original counsel who prepared the skeleton argument is appropriately remunerated for that work, and that the brief fee is suitably adjusted to take account of the fact that the skeleton has already been done, a general instruction is being given to taxing masters to tax the cost of preparing skeleton arguments separately from brief fees in all appeals.

Time estimates

12. The system to be adopted in relation to counsel's certified time estimates of

the length of the appeal hearing is that set out in the *Practice Direction (List of Forthcoming Appeals)* [1987] 1 WLR 1422: see also paragraph 59/1/9A in the current cumulative supplement to *The Supreme Court Practice 1988*. From 4 April 1989 it will be subject to this additional requirement, namely that a copy of the certified estimate must be placed and kept with counsel's papers. Each time counsel is asked to give any advice or to deal with anything in connection with the appeal he or she must look at the estimate and check whether it is still correct. It is particularly important that, when preparing the skeleton argument, counsel should check the certified time estimate to ensure that is is as realistic and accurate as possible. Efficient listing, which is in everyone's interests, is heavily dependent upon the accuracy of time estimates.

Oral hearing

13. The following procedure will be adopted in the case of all appeals to the Civil Division, unless the court announes in any individual case that some other course should be adopted: (a) The judges will already have read the notice of appeal, any respondent's notice, the judgment under appeal and the skeleton arguments. At the commencement of the hearing the presiding Lord Justice will state what other documents and authorities have also been read. (b) It will not normally be necessary to open the facts and, unless otherwise directed, counsel for the appellant will be expected to proceed immediately to the ground of appeal which is in the forefront of the appellant's case. Likewise, the respondent's counsel will be expected to proceed immediately with his or her submissions on the issues in the appeal without any preamble. In an exceptional case, such as where there is technical evidence which will need to be explained by counsel and to this extent some opening is necessary, the presiding Lord Justice will notify counsel in advance of the hearing. (c) When citing an authority which has been pre-read, counsel should not read the case at length, but go immediately to the passage in the judgment where the principle relied on in the skeleton argument is to be found. (d) When dealing with issues of fact, the passages in the transcripts or notes of evidence relied upon will have been listed in the skeleton argument, see paragraph 3 above, and accordingly counsel should so far as possible avoid reading from them in extenso.

14. It will be the duty of solicitors and counsel to ensure that their lay clients have had explained to them before the appeal hearing what the procedure will be and how the Court of Appeal now deals with oral argument. It is important that both appellants and respondents should be made aware of the new procedure, particularly the extent to which the court relies on pre-reading, so that the parties do not infer that, because the appeal hearing has been shorter than has hitherto been customary, their case has not been just as fully considered.

TREATY ESTABLISHING THE EUROPEAN ECONOMIC COMMUNITY AS AMENDED BY SUBSEQUENT TREATIES.
(Rome, 25 March 1957)

[*NOTE: Extracts printed relate to European community law and institutions as they form part of the institutions of the English legal system: and as a source of English law.*]

*****

PART ONE. PRINCIPLES

Article 1. By this Treaty, the High Contracting Parties establish among themselves an European Economic Community.

Article 2. The Community shall have as its task, by establishing a common market and progessively approximating the economic policies of Member states, to promote throughout the Community a harmonious development of economic activities, a continuous and balanced expansion, an increase in stability, an accelerated raising of the standard of living and closer relations between the States belonging to it.

Article 3. For the purposes set out in Art. 2, the activities of the Community shall include, as provided in this Treaty and in accordance with the timetable set out therein:

(a) the elimination, as between Member States, of customs duties and of quantitive restrictions on the import and export of goods, and of all other measures having equivalent effect;

(b) the establishment of a common customs tariff and of a common commercial policy towards third countries;

(c) the abolition, as between Member States, of obstacles to freedom of movement for persons, services and capital;

(d) the adoption of a common policy in the sphere of agriculture;

(e) the adoption of a common policy in the sphere of transport;

(f) the institution of a system ensuring that competition in the common market is not distorted;

(g) the application of procedures by which the economic policies of Member States can be coordinated and disequilibria in their balances of payments remedied;

(h) the approximation of the laws of Member States to the extent required for the proper functioning of the common market;

(i) the creation of a European Social Fund in order to improve employment opportunities for workers and to contribute to the raising of their standard of living;

(j) the establishment of a European Investment Bank to facilitate the economic expansion of the Community by opening up fresh resources;

(k) the association of the overseas countries and territories in order to increase trade and to promote jointly economic and social development.

Article 4. The tasks entrusted to the Community shall be carried out by the following institutions:
— an Assembly,
— a Council,
— a Commission,
— a Court of Justice.
Each institution shall act within the limits of the powers conferred upon it by this Treaty.

2. The Council and the Commission shall be assisted by an Economic and Social Committee acting in an advisory capacity.

3. The audit shall be carried out by a Court of Auditors acting within the limits of the powers conferred upon it by this Treaty.

Articles 5.-8. *****

[*Article 8A.* The Community shall adopt measures with the aim of progressively establishing the internal market over a period expiring on 31 December 1992, in accordance with the provisions of this Article and of Articles 8B, 8C, 28, 57(2), 59, 70(1), 84, 99, 100A and 100B and without prejudice to the other provisions of this Treaty.
The internal market shall comprise an area without internal frontiers in which the free movement of goods, persons, services and capital is ensured in accordance with the provisions of this Treaty.]

Articles 8B-99. *****

Article 100. The Council shall, acting unanimously on a proposal from the Commission, issue directives for the approximation of such provisions laid down by law, regulation or administrative action in Member States as directly affect the establishment or functioning of the common market.

The Assembly and the Economic and Social Committee shall be consulted in the case of directives whose implementation would, in one or more Member States, involve the amendment of legislation.

[*Article 100A*. By way of derogation from Article 100 and save where otherwise provided in this Treaty, the following provisions shall apply for the achievement of the objectives set out in Article 8A. The Council shall, acting by a qualified majority on a proposal from the Commission in cooperation with the European Parliament and after consulting the Economic and Social Committee, adopt the measures for the approximation of the provisions laid down by law, regulation or administrative action in Member States which have as their object the establishment and functioning of the internal market.

2. Paragraph 1 shall not apply to fiscal provisions, to those relating to the free movement of persons nor to those relating to the rights and interests of employed persons.

3. The Commission, in its proposals envisaged in paragraph 1 concerning health, safety, environmental protection and consumer protection, will take as a base a high level of protection.

4. If, after the adoption of a harmonisation measure by the Council acting by a qualified majority, a Member State deems it necessary to apply national provisions on grounds of major needs referred to in Article 36, or relating to protection of the environment or the working environment, it shall notify the Commission of these provisions.

The Commission shall confirm the provisions involved after having verified that they are not a means of arbitrary discrimination or a disguised restriction on trade between Member States.

By way of derogation from the procedure laid down in Articles 169 and 170, the Commission or any Member State may bring the matter directly before the Court of Justice if it considers that another Member State is making improper use of the powers provided for in this Article.

5. The harmonisation measures referred to above shall, in appropriate cases, include a safeguard clause authorising the Member States to take, for one or more of the non-economic reasons referred to in Article 36, provisional measures subject to a Community control procedure.]

Articles 100B.–154. ★★★★★

Article 155. In order to ensure the proper functioning and development of the common market, the Commission shall:
— ensure that the provisions of this Treaty and the measures taken by the institutions pursuant thereto are applied;
— formulate recommendations or deliver opinions on matters dealt with in this Treaty, if it expressly so provides or if the Commission considers it necessary;
— have its own power of decision and participate in the shaping of measures taken by the Council and by the Assembly in the manner provided for in this Treaty;
— exercise the powers conferred on it by the Council for the implementation of the rules laid down by the latter.

[Articles 156—63 were repealed by the merger Treaty.]

Article 164. The Court of Justice shall ensure that in the interpretation and application of this Treaty the law is observed.

Article 165. The Court of Justice shall consist of 13 Judges.

The Court of Justice shall sit in plenary session. It may, however, form chambers, each consisting of three or five Judges, either to undertake certain preparatory inquiries or to adjudicate on particular categories of cases in accordance with rules laid down for these purposes.

Whenever the Court of Justice hears cases brought before it by a Member State or by one of the institutions of the Community or, to the extent that the chambers of the court do not have the requisite jurisdiction under the Rules of Procedure, has to give preliminary rulings on questions submitted to it pursuant to Art. 177, it shall sit in plenary session.

Should the Court of Justice so request, the Council may, acting unanimously, increase the number of Judges and make the necessary adjustments to the second and third paragraphs of this Article and to the second paragraph of Art. 167.

Article 166. The Court of Justice shall be assisted by six Advocates-General.

It shall be the duty of the Advocate-General, acting with complete impartiality and independence, to make, in open court, reasoned submissions on cases brought before the Court of Justice, in order to assist the Court in the performance of the task assigned to it in Art. 164.

Should the Court of Justice so request, the Council may, acting unanimously, increase the number of Advocates-General and make the necessary adjustments to the third paragraph of Art. 167.

Article 167. The Judges and Advocates-General shall be chosen from persons whose independence is beyond doubt and who possess the qualifications required for appointment to the highest judicial offices in their respective countries or who are jurisconsults of recognised competence; they shall be appointed by common accord of the Government of the Member States for a term of six years.

Every three years there shall be a partial replacement of the Judges. Seven and six Judges shall be replaced alternately.

Every three years there shall be a partial replacement of the Advocates-General. Three Advocates-General shall be replaced on each occasion.

Retiring Judges and Advocates-General shall be eligible for re-appointment.

The Judges shall elect the President of the Court of Justice from among their number for a term of three years. He may be re-elected.

Article 168. The Court of Justice shall appoint its Registrar and lay down the rules governing his service.

[*Article 168A.*
1. At the request of the Court of Justice and after consulting the Commission and the European Parliament, the Council may, acting unanimously, attach to the Court of Justice a court with jurisdiction to hear and determine at first instance, subject to a right of appeal to the Court of Justice on points of law only and in accordance with the conditions laid down by the Statute, certain classes of action or proceeding brought by natural or legal persons. That court shall not be competent to hear and determine actions brought by Member States or by Community Institutions or questions referred for a preliminary ruling under Article 177.
2. The Council following the procedure laid down in paragraph 1, shall determine the composition of that court and adopt the necessary adjustments and additional provisions to the Statute of the Court of Justice. Unless the Council decide otherwise, the provisions of this Treaty relating to the Court of Justice, in particular the provisions of the Protocol on the Statute of the Court of Justice, shall apply to that court.
3. The members of that court shall be chosen from persons whose independence is beyond doubt and who possess the ability required for appointment to judicial office; they shall be appointed by common accord of the Governments of the Member States

for a term of six years. The membership shall be partially renewed every three years. Retiring members shall be eligible for reappointment.

4. That court shall establish its rules of procedure in agreement with the Court of Justice. Those rules shall require the unanimous approval of the Council.]

Article 169. If the Commission considers that a Member State has failed to fulfil an obligation under this Treaty, it shall deliver a reasoned opinion on the matter after giving the State concerned the opportunity to submit its observations.

If the State concerned does not comply with the opinion within the period laid down by the Commission the latter may bring the matter before the Court of Justice.

Article 170. A Member State which considers that another Member State has failed to fulfil an obligation under this Treaty may bring the matter before the Court of Justice.

Before a Member State brings an action against another Member State for an alleged infringement of an obligaiton under this Treaty, it shall bring the matter before the Commission.

The Commission shall deliver a reasoned opinion after each of the States concerned has been given the opportunity to submit its own case and its observations on the other party's case both orally and in writing.

If the Commission has not delivered an opinion within three months of the date on which the matter was brought before it, the absence of such opinion shall not prevent the matter from being brought before the Court of Justice.

Article 171. If the Court of Justice finds that a Member State has failed to fulfil an obligation under this Treaty, the State shall be required to take the necessary measures to comply with the judgment of the Court of Justice.

Article 172. Regulations made by the Council pursuant to the provisions of this Treaty may give the Court of Justice unlimited jurisdiction in regard to the penalties provided for in such regulations.

Article 173. The Court of Justice shall review the legality of acts of the Council and the Commission other than recommendations or opinions. It shall for this purpose have jurisdiction in actions brought by a Member State, the Council or the Commission on grounds of lack of competence, infringement of an essential procedural requirement, infringement of this Treaty or of any rule of law relating to its application, or misuse of powers.

Any natural or legal person may, under the same conditions, institute proceedings against a decision addressed to that person or against a decision which, although in the form of a regulation or a decision addressed to another person, is of direct and individual concern to the former.

The proceedings provided for in this Article shall be instituted within two months of the publication of the measure, or of its notification to the plaintiff, or, in the absence thereof, of the day on which it came to the knowledge of the latter, as the case may be.

Article 174. If the action is well founded, the Court of Justice shall declare the act concerned to be void.

In the case of a regulation, however, the Court of Justice shall, if it considers this necessary, state which of the effects of the regulation which it has declared void shall be considered as definitive.

Articles 175. and 176. *****

Article 177. The Court of Justice shall have jurisdiction to give preliminary rulings concerning:

(a) the interpretation of this Treaty;
(b) the validity and interpretation of acts of the institutions of the Community;
(c) the interpretation of the statutes of bodies established by an act of the Council, where those statutes so provide.

Where such a question is raised before any court or tribunal of a Member State, that court or tribunal may, if it considers that a decision on the question is necessary to enable it to give judgment, request the Court of Justice to give a ruling thereon.

Where any such question is raised in a case pending before a court or tribunal of a Member State, against whose decision there is no judicial remedy under national law, that court or tribunal shall bring the matter before the Court of Justice.

Article 178. The Court of Justice shall have jurisdiction in disputes relating to the compensation for damage provided for in the second paragraph of Art. 215.

Articles 179.-182. *****

Article 183. Save where jurisdiction is conferred on the Court by this Treaty, disputes to which the Community is a party shall not on that ground be excluded from the jurisdiction of the courts or tribunals of the Member States.

Article 184. Notwithstanding the expiry of the period laid down in the third paragraph of Art. 173, any party may, in proceedings in which a regulation of the Council or of the Commission is in issue, plead the grounds specified in the first paragraph of Art. 173, in order to invoke before the Court of Justice the inapplicability of that regulation.

Article 185. Actions brought before the Court of Justice shall not have suspensory effect. The Court of Justice may, however, if is considers that circumstances so require, order that application of the contested act be suspended.

Article 186. The Court of Justice may in any cases before it prescribe any necessary interim measures.

Article 187. The judgments of the Court of Justice shall be enforceable under the conditions laid down in Art. 192.

Article 188. The Statute of the Court of Justice is laid down in a separate Protocol.

[The Council may, acting unanimously at the request of the Court of Justice and after consulting the Commission and the European Parliament, amend the provisions of Title III of the Statute.]

The Court of Justice shall adopt its rules of procedure. These shall require the unanimous approval of the Council.

Article 189. In order to carry out their task the Council and the Commission shall, in accordance with the provisions of this Treaty, make regulations, issue directives, take decisions, make recommendations or deliver opinions.

A regulation shall have general application. It shall be binding in its entirety and directly applicable in all Member States.

A directive shall be binding, as to the result to be achieved, upon each Member State to which it is addressed, but shall leave to the national authorities the choice of form and methods.

Recommendations and opinions shall have no binding force.

Article 190. Regulations, directives and decisions of the Council and of the Commission shall state the reasons on which they are based and shall refer to any proposals or opinions which were required to be obtained pursuant to this Treaty.

Article 191. Regulations shall be published in the Official Journal of the community.

They shall enter into force on the date specified in them or, in the absence thereof, on the twentieth day following their publication.

Directives and decisions shall be notified to those to whom they are addressed and shall take effect upon such notification.

Article 192. Decisions of the Council or of the Commission which impose a pecuniary obligation on persons other than States shall be enforceable.

Enforcement shall be governed by the rules of civil procedure in force in the State in the territory of which it is carried out. The order for its enforcement shall be appended to the decision, without other formality than verification of the authenticity of the decision, by the national authority which the Government of each Member State shall designate for this purpose and shall make known to the Commission and to the Court of Justice.

When these formalities have been completed on application by the party concerned, the latter may proceed to enforcement in accordance with the national law, by bringing the matter directly before the competent authority.

Enforcement may be suspended only by a decision of the Court of Justice. However, the courts of the country concerned shall have jurisdiction over complaints that enforcement is being carried out in an irregular manner.

Articles 193.–209. *****

PART SIX. GENERAL AND FINAL PROVISIONS

Article 210. The Community shall have legal personality.

Article 211. In each of the Member States, the Community shall enjoy the most extensive legal capacity accorded to legal persons under their laws; it may, in particular, acquire or dispose of movable and immovable property and may be a party to legal proceedings. To this end, the Community shalll be represented by the Commission.

Article 212. . . .

Articles 213. and 214. *****

Article 215. The contractual liability of the Community shall be governed by the law applicable to the contract in question.

In the case of non-contractual liability, the Community shall, in accordance with the general principles common to the laws of the Member States, make good any damage caused by its institutions or by its servants in the performance of their duties.

The personal liability of its servants towards the Community shall be governed by the provisions laid down in their Staff Regulations or in the Conditions of Employment applicable to them.

Articles 216.–219. *****

Article 220. Member States shall, so far as is necessary, enter into negotiations with each other with a view to securing for the benefit of their nationals:
— the protection of persons and the enjoyment and protection of rights under the same conditions as those accorded by each State to its own nationals;
— the abolition of double taxation within the Community;
— the mutual recognition of companies or firms within the meaning of the second paragraph of Art. 58, the retention of legal personality in the event of transfer of their seat from one country to another, and the possibility of mergers between companies or firms governed by the laws of different countries;
— the simplification of formalities governing the reciprocal recognition and enforcement of judgments of courts or tribunals and of arbitration awards.

Article 221. *****

Article 222. This Treaty shall in no way prejudice the rules in Member States governing the system of property ownership.

Articles 223.–234. *****

Articles 235. If action by the Community should prove necessary to attain, in the course of the operation of the common market, one of the objectives of the Community and this Treaty has not provided the necessary powers, the Council shall, acting unanimously on a proposal from the Commission and after consulting the Assembly, take the appropriate measures.

Articles 236. The Government of any Member State or the Commission may submit to the Council proposals for the amendment of this Treaty.
If the Council, after consulting the Assembly and, where appropriate, the Commission, delivers an opinion in favour of calling a conference of representatives of the Governments of the Member States, the conference shall be convened by the President of the Council for the purpose of determining by common accord the amendments to be made to this Treaty.
The amendments shall enter into force after being ratified by all the Member States in accordance with their respective constitutional requirements.

*****

EC COUNCIL DECISION
PUBLISHED IN [1988] OJ L 319/1 (25 November 1988)

COURT OF FIRST INSTANCE
Council Decision of 24 October 1988 establishing a Court of First Instance of the European Communities
(88/591/ECSC, EEC, Euratom)

Having regard—
to *****
to the Treaty establishing the European Economic Community, and in particular Article 168a thereof,
to *****
to the request of the Court of Justice,
to the opinion of the Commission,
to the opinion of the European Parliament;
Whereas—

(1) Article 32d of the ECSC Treaty, Article 168a of the EEC Treaty and Article 140a of the Euratom Treaty empower the Council to attach to the Court of Justice a Court of First instance called upon to exercise important judicial functions and whose members are independent beyond doubt and possess the ability required for performing such functions.

(2) The aforesaid provisions empower the Council to give the Court of First Instance jurisdiction to hear and determine at first instance, in accordance with the proceedings brought by natural or legal persons, subject to the right of appeal to the Court of Justice on questions of law alone.

(3) The Council is to determine, pursuant to the aforesaid provisions, the composition of that court and adopt the necessary adjustments and additional provisions to the Statutes of the Court of Justice.

(4) In respect of actions requiring close examination of complex facts, the establishment of a second court will improve the judicial protection of individual interests.

(5) It is necessary, in order to maintain the quality and effectivness of judicial

review in the Community legal order, to enable the Court to concentrate its activities on its fundamental task of ensuring uniform interpretation of Community law

(6) It is therefore necessary to make use of the powers granted by Article 32d of the ECSC Treaty, Article 168a of the EEC Treaty and Article 140a of the Euratom Treaty and to transfer to the Court of First Instance jurisdiction to hear and determine at first instance certain classes of action or preceeding which frequently require an examination of complex facts, that is to say actions or proceedings brought by servants of the Communities and also, in so far as the ECSC Treaty is concerned, by undertakings and associations in matters concerning levies, production, prices, restrictive agreements, decisions or practices and concentrations, and so far as the EEC Treaty is concerned, by natural or legal persons in competition matters.

THE COUNCIL, for these reasons, HAS DECIDED AS FOLLOWS:

Article 1

A Court, to be called the Court of First Instance of the European Communities, shall be attached to the Court of Justice of the European Communities. Its seat shall be at the Court of Justice.

Article 2

1. The Court of First Instance shall consist of 12 members.
2. The members shall elect the President of the Court of First Instance from among their number for a term of three years. He may be re-elected.
3. The members of the Court of First Instance may be called upon to perform the task of an Advocate General.
It shall be the duty of the Advocate General, acting with complete impartiality and independence, to make, in open court, reasoned submissions on certain cases brought before the Court of First Instance in order to assist the Court of First Instance in the performance of its task.
The criteria for selecting such cases, as well as the procedures for designating the Advocates General, shall be laid down in the Rules of Procedure of the Court of First Instance.
A member called upon to perform the task of Advocate General in a case may not take part in the judgment of the case.
4. The Court of First Instance shall sit in chambers of three or five judges. The composition of the chambers and the assignement of cases to them shall be governed by the Rules of Procedure. In certain cases governed by the Rules of Procedure the Court of First Instance may sit in plenary session.
5. Article 21 of the Protocol on Privileges and Immunities of the European Communities and Article 6 of the Treaty establishing a Single Council and a Single Commission of the European Communities shall apply to the members of the Court of First Instance and to its Registrar.

Article 3

(4) The Court of First Instance shall exercise at first instance the jurisdiction conferred on the Court of Justice by the Treaties establishing the Communities and by the acts adopted in implementation thereof:

(a) in disputes between the Communities and their servants referred to in Article 179 of the EEC Treaty and in Article 152 of the Euratom Treaty;

(b) in actions brought against the Commission pursuant to the second paragraph of Article 33 and Article 35 of the ECSC Treaty by undertakings or by associations of undertakings referred to in Article 48 of that Treaty, and which concern individual acts relating to the application of Article 50 and Articles 57 to 66 of the said Treaty;

(c) in actions brought against an institution of the Communities by natural or legal persons pursuant to the second paragraph of Article 173 and the third paragraph of Article 175 of the EEC Treaty relating to the implementation of the competition rules applicable to undertakings.

2. Where the same natural or legal person brings an action which the Court of First Instance has jurisdiction to hear by virtue of paragraph 1 of this Article and an action referred to in the first and second paragraphs of Article 40 of the ECSC Treaty, Article 178 of the EEC Treaty, or Article 151 of the Euratom Treaty, for compensation for damage caused by a Community institution through the act or failure to act which is the subject of the first action, the Court of First Instance shall also have jurisdiction to hear and determine the action for compensation for that damage.

3. The Council will, in the light of experience, including the development of jurisprudence, and after two years of operation of the Court of First Instance, re-examine the proposal by the Court of Justice to give the Court of First Instance competence to exercise jurisdiction in actions brought against the Commission pursuant to the second paragraph of Article 33 and Article 35 of the ECSC Treaty by undertakings or by associations of undertakings referred to in Article 48 of that Treaty, and which concern acts relating to the application of Article 74 of the said Treaty as well as in actions brought against an institution of the Communities by natural or legal persons pursuant to the second paragraph of Article 173 and the third paragraph of Article 175 of the EEC Treaty and relating to measures to protect trade within the meaning of Article 113 of that Treaty in the case of dumping and subsidies.

*****

INDEX

Administration of Justice Act 1960
    ss 1–6, 13, 17 *26–9*
Administration of Justice Act 1968
    s 1 *44–5*
Administration of Justice Act 1969
    ss 12–15 *62–4*
Administration of Justice Act 1985
    ss 11, 12, 20 *270–1*
Administration of Justice (Appeals) Act 1934
    s 1 *9*
Appellate Jurisdiction Act 1876
    ss 3–6, 12, 25 *3–5*
Appellate Jurisdiction Act 1887
    ss 3, 5 *5–6*
Arbitration Act 1950
    ss 1, 4, 6–10, 12, 22, 23, 25, 26, 32 *21–25*
Arbitration Act 1979
    ss 1–3 *139–42*
Bail Act 1976
    ss 1–9, sch 1 *114–25*
Children and Young Persons Act 1933
    ss 44–50, 53, 55, sch 2 *9–14*
Children and Young Persons Act 1969
    ss 4, 5, 7 *60–2*
Consolidation of Enactments (Procedure) Act 1949
    ss 1, 2 *17–18*
Contempt of Court Act 1981
    ss 1–12, 14, 16, 17, 19, 20, sch 1 *188–94*
Coroners Act 1988
    ss 1–3, 5, 8–12 *274–8*
County Courts Act 1984
    ss 1, 5, 6, 9–11, 15–23, 25, 32–45, 51, 60–62, 64, 66–72, 74–77, 79–84, 118, 142, 147 *238–57*
County County Courts Appeals Order 1981, The (SI 1981 No 1749)
    ord 2, 3 *302*
County Courts Jurisdiction Order 1981, The (SI 1981 No 1123)
    ord 2 *301–2*
Court of Appeal (Civil Division) Order 1982, The (SI 1982 No 543)
    ord 2, 3 *302–3*
Courts Act 1971
    ss 16, 17, 21, 24 *64–6*
Criminal Appeal Act 1968
    ss 1–23, 29–35, 38, 42–44, 48–51 *45–60*
Criminal Evidence Act 1898
    ss 1–4, 6 *6–7*
Criminal Justice Act 1967
    ss 7–11, 17, 22, 56 *40–4*
Criminal Justice Act 1972
    s 36 *71*
Criminal Justice Act 1982
    ss 1–3, 8, 9, 35–38 *231–7*
Criminal Justice Act 1987
    ss 4, 6–8 *272–4*
Criminal Justice Act 1988
    ss 35–41, 122, 133 *278–83*
Criminal Procedure (Insanity) Act 1964
    ss 1, 4–6, 8 *29–31*
EC Council Decision, 1988 [1988] OJ L 319/1 *330–2*
Employment Protection (Consolidation) Act 1978
    ss 128, 130, 131, 135, 136, sch 9, sch 11 *132–9*
European Communities Act 1972
    ss 1–3, sch 2 *72–4*
European Communities (Amendment) Act 1986
    s 3 *271–2*
Insolvency Act 1986
    s 375 *271*
Interpretation Act 1978
    ss 1–21, sch 1 *125–32*
Judicial Committee Act 1833
    ss 1, 3–6 *1–2*
Judicial Committee Act 1844
    s 1 *2–3*
Judicial Committee Act 1881
    s 1 *5*
Juries Act 1974
    ss 9–13, 16–18, sch 1 *96–101*
Justices of the Peace Act 1361 *1*
Justices of the Peace Act 1979
    ss 1, 4–8, 13, 14, 18, 25, 26, 28, 31, 33, 44–48, 50–54, 63, 64 *142–51*
Lands Tribunal Act 1949
    ss 1, 2, 8 *19–21*
Law Commissions Act 1965
    ss 1, 3, 4, 6 *31–2*
Legal Aid Act 1988
    ss 1–26 *283–98*
Magistrates' Courts Act 1980
    ss 1, 2, 4–33, 35, 36, 38–40, 42–43A, 51, 52, 58, 60, 63–67, 69, 71, 73, 74, 97, 98, 101, 102, 104, 106–113, 115, 117, 120–122, 127–129, 132, 133, 148, sch 1, sch 2 *152–87*
Magistrates' Courts (Advance Information) Rules 1985 (SI 1985 No 601)
    r 1–7 *303–4*
Matrimonial and Family Proceedings Act 1984
    ss 32–39 *257–9*
Parliament Act 1911
    ss 1–7 *7–9*

Parliamentary Commissioner Act 1967
　ss 1, 3-12, sch 3　*32-9*
Police and Criminal Evidence Act 1984
　s 81　*259*
Powers of Criminal Courts Act 1973
　ss 1, 2, 6-8, 11, 14, 16, 18, 20, 20A, 21-28, 30-32, 34-38, 42-43A, 57　*74-95*
Prosecution of Offences Act 1985
　ss 1-10, 15-19, 21, 23　*260-9*
Practice Direction (Court of Appeal: Presentation of Argument) [1989] 1 WLR 281　*318-23*
Practice Direction (County Court: Transfers Outside London) [1988] 1 WLR 987　*317-18*
Practice Direction (Crime: Majority Verdicts) [1967] 1 WLR 1198　*305-6*
Practice Direction (Crown Court Business: Classification) [1987] 1 WLR 1671　*313-17*
Practice Direction (Divorce Towns: Defended Cases) [1971] 1 WLR 1762　*306-7*
Practice Note [1970] 1 WLR 916　*306*
Practice Note (Court of Appeal: New Procedure) [1982] 1 WLR 1312　*307-13*

Practice Statement [1966] 1 WLR 1234　*304*
Restrictive Practices Court Act 1976
　ss 1-3, 6-10　*112-14*
Solicitors Act 1974
　ss 1, 19-23, 25, 31, 35-37, 41-47A, 49, 50, 81　*102-12*
Statutory Instruments Act 1946
　ss 1-7　*15-17*
Statutory Instruments Regulations 1947 (SI 1948/1)
　reg 1-8　*299-301*
Summary Jurisdiction Act 1857
　ss 6, 7, 10, 12　*3*
Supreme Court Act 1981
　ss 1-12, 15-19, 25, 26, 28-43, 45-71, 73-81, 83, 84, 138, 140, 151, sch 1, sch 2　*195-231*
Treaty of Rome 1957
　arts 1-4, 8A, 100, 100A, 155, 164-174, 177, 178, 183-192, 211, 215, 220, 222, 235, 236　*323-30*
Tribunals and Inquiries Act 1971
　ss 1-3, 5, 7, 8, 10, 12-14　*66-70*

BLACKSTONE'S STATUTES

TITLES IN THE SERIES

Contract & Tort Statutes
Public Law Statutes
Employment Law Statutes
Criminal Law Statutes
Criminal Procedure: Evidence and Sentencing Statutes
Family Law Statutes
Property Law Statutes
Commercial Law Statutes
Company Law Statutes
English Legal System Statutes